Using
QuickBooks Pro®
FOR ACCOUNTING
2006

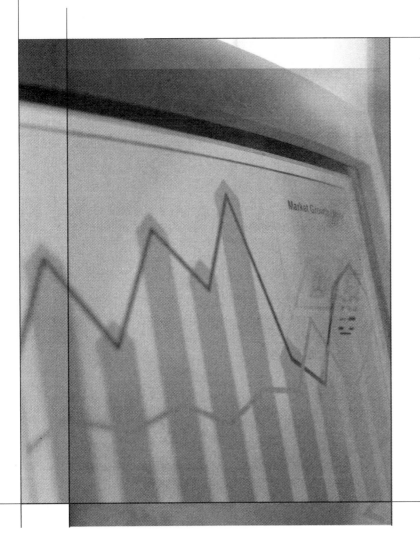

Glenn Owen

Allan Hancock College

*University of California
at Santa Barbara*

THOMSON

SOUTH-WESTERN

Australia · Brazil · Canada · Mexico · Singapore · Spain · United Kingdom · United States

THOMSON

SOUTH-WESTERN

Using QuickBooks Pro® 2006 for Accounting
Glenn Owen

VP/Editorial Director:
Jack W. Calhoun

Publisher:
Rob Dewey

Acquisitions Editor:
Matt Filimonov

Associate Developmental Editor:
Allison Rolfes

Marketing Manager:
Chris McNamee

Sr. Content Project Manager:
Amy McGuire

Manager of Technology, Editorial:
Vicky True

Technology Project Editor:
Robin Browning

Sr. Manufacturing Coordinator:
Doug Wilke

Production House:
LEAP Publishing Services, Inc.

Compositor:
International Typesetting and Composition

Printer:
Edwards Brothers, Inc.
Ann Arbor, MI

Art Director:
Linda Helcher

Internal & Cover Designer:
Chris Miller

Cover Images:
Getty Images

Thomson Higher Education
5191 Natorp Boulevard
Mason, OH 45040
USA

For more information about our products,
contact us at:
Thomson Learning Academic
Resource Center
1-800-423-0563

For permission to use material from this
text or product, submit a request online
at **http://www.thomsonrights.com**.

Brief Contents

Contents

Preface

What if you could integrate a popular computerized accounting program into your classroom without using confusing and complicated manuals? What if your students could use this program and reinforce basic accounting concepts in an online and interactive case setting? What if you could accomplish both without spending a fortune and a vast amount of time preparing examples, cases, and illustrations? In fact, *Using QuickBooks® Pro 2006 for Accounting* by Owen is a textbook that fulfills and expands upon all three of these "what ifs."

Why Is This Textbook Needed?

The first course in accounting has evolved significantly over the last several years. Educators are responding to the demand of accounting and nonaccounting faculty who rely on this course to lay a foundation for other courses. Moreover, the accounting profession relies on this course to attract the "best and the brightest" to become accounting majors. The evolution of this course has also put pressure on instructors to integrate computers into the classroom and, in doing so, develop students' skills in intelligently using and interpreting accounting information.

Faculty often want to incorporate computerized accounting into the first course, but are reluctant to invest the time and effort necessary to accomplish this laudable goal. Existing materials are often "preparer" driven in that they focus on the creation of financial reports only. Students are often discouraged in their use of computers in the first accounting course because of the complicated and confusing accounting software manuals that concentrate on accounting mechanics.

This text responds to all of these needs. It provides a self-paced, step-by-step environment in which students use *QuickBooks® Pro 2006* or *QuickBooks® Basic 2006* to create financial statements and other financial reports, to reinforce the concepts they learn in their first course, and to see how computer software can be used to make business decisions.

What Are the New Features in This Version of QuickBooks?

Use the new home page to start your key tasks with just one click. The home page gives you one-click access to all of your most important QuickBooks activities, all in one place—from invoicing and writing checks to making deposits and reconciling bank accounts. It presents a big picture view of how everything fits together, with arrows to guide you from one task to the next. QuickBooks previously showed these activities in multiple navigators, but the new home page consolidates key activities in one place. The home page also lets you see account balances that are updated automatically as you work. If you want to hide these balances for privacy, just click the minus button next to the Account Balances list.

The Customer Center, Vendor Center, and Employee Center let you access your lists, contact information, notes, and transactions all on one simple screen. The QuickBooks Centers consolidate all the key information about your customers, vendors, and employees.

From the Centers, you can:

- Click on a name to get immediate access to contact information for customers, vendors, or employees.

- View and edit transaction information in the same window, such as open invoices, unpaid bills, or paychecks.

- See a summary list of customers, vendors, or employees, or click the maximize button to see more columns.

- View and edit notes about the customer, vendor, or employee while you are viewing other relevant information.

Do all this and more in a single location, rather than having to run separate reports to get the information.

If you need help managing your inventory and its associated costs, you'll find a number of new and improved features to help you manage your product-based business more effectively. You can:

- Store an unlimited number of ship-to addresses per customer.

- Include the manufacturer's part number as part of your item definition, making reordering faster and easier.

- Set prices that end in .99, .49, or whatever you choose with QuickBooks's improved price rounding options.

What Is New with This Version of the Textbook?

In *Using QuickBooks Pro 2005 for Accounting* we introduced a new case (Century Kitchens) to introduce the student to the "use" of the QuickBooks software in one chapter with five sessions. In this edition, we've placed the "use" of QuickBooks software into Part 1 containing five chapters. Part 2 now contains Chapters 6 through 11, which explain how QuickBooks is used to record business transactions for later reporting.

Part 2 also contains a new case, Wild Water Sports, instead of the previous Phoenix Systems which is used throughout Chapters 6 through 11. This new case will help students create a new company using the Easy-Step Interview, record cash and noncash transactions, make adjustments for accrual accounting, create and manage budgets, and generate useful reports for decision making. This case also utilizes the job cost features of QuickBooks to transfer materials and labor incurred on a job to invoice billing the customer for work performed. It also starts off with beginning balances which students include in their creation of the original file.

A new service only company, Aloha Property Management, has been added as a comprehensive case at the end of Chapters 8 and 11. This case contains no product-related transactions, instead focusing on service-based accounting issues.

A payroll appendix has been added to help students understand where payroll deductions originate. Throughout this text you will be provided information for employee payroll tax withholding and employer payroll tax expenses. QuickBooks has the ability to calculate each of these for you: however, they charge you an annual fee to do so. Some businesses will find this service very valuable and worth the cost, and some will not. Payroll tax computations are not straightforward. They are, in fact, quite convoluted and dependent on all sorts of exceptions and rules. For example, federal income tax withholding is dependent on an employee's income, whether they are being paid weekly, biweekly, semimonthly, monthly, etc., the number of exemptions they claim, and their filing status: married, single, head of household, etc.

This appendix is designed to provide you a basic overview of the payroll tax conundrum and is focused on federal taxes only, as each state has their own rules for income tax withholding, unemployment, etc.

What Are the Goals of This Textbook?

This textbook takes a user perspective by illustrating how accounting information is both used and created. QuickBooks is extremely user friendly and provides point and click simplicity with excellent and sophisticated accounting reporting and analysis tools. The textbook uses a proven and successful pedagogy to demonstrate the software's features and elicit student interaction.

The text's first and foremost goal is to help students learn or review fundamental accounting concepts and principles through the use of QuickBooks and the analysis of business events. The content complements the first course in accounting and, therefore, should be used in conjunction with a core text on accounting.

A second goal is to enable students to view financial statements from a user perspective. After an initial tour of QuickBooks, students learn how to use QuickBooks to understand and interpret financial statements.

A third goal of the text is to provide students a means to investigate the underlying source documents that generate most financial accounting information, such as purchase orders, sales invoices, and so on. Students will experience this process by entering a few business events for later inclusion in financial reports.

A fourth goal is to provide students a means of exploring some managerial aspects of accounting by performing financial analysis and comparisons. Budgets are created and compared to actual operating results, and receivables and payables are aged for analysis of cash management and cash flow projections.

A fifth goal of this text is to reduce the administrative burdens of accounting faculty by providing a self-paced environment, data sets, cases, and a correlation table describing how this text might be used with a variety of popular accounting texts.

What Are the Key Features of This Textbook?

The key features of this book are outlined below.

- This book will work with either *QuickBooks® Pro 2006* or *QuickBooks® Basic 2006*. However, only QuickBooks Pro includes the export to Excel feature covered briefly in Chapter 11. The basic version of QuickBooks does not include that feature.

- The chapters incorporate a continuing, interesting, realistic case—WILD WATER SPORTS—that helps students apply QuickBooks's features and key accounting concepts.

- A tested, proven, step-by-step methodology keeps students on track. Students enter data, analyze information, and make decisions all within the context of the case. The text constantly guides students, letting them know where they are in the course of completing their accounting tasks.

- Numerous screen shots include callouts that direct students' attention to what they should look at on the screen. On almost every page in the book, you will find examples of how steps, screen shots, and callouts work together.

- *Trouble?* paragraphs anticipate the mistakes that students are likely to make or problems they are likely to encounter, and then help students recover and continue with the chapter. This feature facilitates independent learning and frees you to focus on accounting concepts rather than on computer skills.

- With very few exceptions, QuickBooks does not require the user to record journal entries to record business events. An appendix on traditional accounting records gives you the flexibility to teach journal entries at your discretion. It provides the information necessary for students to make journal entries to record the events described in Chapters 6 through 11.

- Questions begin the end-of-chapter material. They are intended to test students' recall of what they learned in the chapter.

- Chapter Assignments follow the Questions and provide students additional hands-on practice with QuickBooks skills. Some Chapter Assignments are designated as Internet Assignments. These are optional.

- A continuing Case Problem—Ocean View Flowers, a wholesale flower distributor—is included in Chapters 6 through 11. This is a series case which needs to be completed for each chapter before the following chapter's case can be performed. Unlike the Jennings & Associates Case (to follow), there are no data files for this case. This initial file, created in Chapter 6, is used in each successive chapter. The Case Problems ask the students to apply the same QuickBooks skills they learned in the chapter to this entirely new case.

- A continuing assignment—Central Coast Cellular, a retail cellular phone sales and consulting service—is included in Chapters 6 through 11. Like Ocean View, there are no data files in this case. The original QuickBooks file created in Chapter 2 is used in each successive chapter, once again asking the students to apply the same skills they learned in the chapter to this new case.

- A continuing Case Problem—Jennings & Associates, an advertising firm—concludes each chapter. This case has approximately the same scope as the Wild Water Sports chapter case.

- Comprehensive problems appear at the end of Chapters 7 and 11. These problems provide an opportunity for students to demonstrate their comprehensive understanding of QuickBooks procedures.

- The Instructor's Package contains an *Instructor's Manual,* which includes solutions to end-of-chapter materials and troubleshooting tips.

Dates

QuickBooks, as all accounting programs, is extremely date sensitive. This follows from the accounting periodicity concept, which requires accounting information to be organized by accounting periods such as months, quarters, or years. It is very important that while using this text you be aware of entering the proper dates to record business transactions or to view business reports. For example, if you are using this book in 2006 (and thus your computer has a system date of 10/1/06, for example), you will need to adjust the date references. In the Employee Center, for example, the concept of "The Calendar Year" means 2006, and thus to view Century Kitchens data, you need to change the date reference to "Next Calender Year" since all of Century Kitchens's transactions are recorded in 2007. However, if you are using this book in 2007 (and thus your computer has a system date of 2/1/07, for example), the reference to "The Calender Year" now refers to 2007 and you wouldn't need to change the date reference.

About the Author

Glenn Owen is a tenured member of Allan Hancock College's Accounting and Business faculty, where he has lectured on accounting and information systems since 1995. In addition, he is a lecturer at the University of California at Santa Barbara, where he has been teaching accounting and information systems courses since 1980 and a lecturer at the Orfala College of Business at Cal Poly San Luis Obispo teaching financial and managerial accounting courses. His professional experience includes five years at Deloitte & Touche, vice-president of finance positions at Westpac Resources, Inc., and Expertelligence, Inc. He has authored many Internet-related books and accounting course supplements and is currently developing online accounting instruction modules for his Internet-based financial accounting courses. Mr. Owen has recently published another text, *Excel and Access in Accounting,* which gives accounting students specific, self-paced instruction on the use of spreadsheets (Excel) and database applications (Access) in accounting. His innovative teaching style emphasizes the decision maker's perspective and encourages students to think creatively. His graduate studies in educational psychology and his 31 years of business experience combine for a balanced blend of theory and practice.

Note to Student and Instructor

QuickBooks Version and Payroll Tax Tables

The text and related data files created for this text were constructed using *QuickBooks® Pro 2006* release R_3. To check your release number, open *QuickBooks® Pro 2006* and type **Ctrl 1.** If your release is less than number R_3, use the QuickBooks Update Service under the Online menu to update your version. This is a free service to version 2006 Pro users and requires an Internet connection. The files accompanying this text can be used in any *QuickBooks® Pro 2006* release R_3 or higher.

In this version of QuickBooks, Intuit continues its use of a basic payroll service. This is a requirement in order to use the QuickBooks payroll features that automatically calculate taxes due to federal or state agencies. Initially, QuickBooks comes with the current tax tables; however, they become out of date, which can occur within a month of purchase, and the payroll feature is disabled unless the user subscribes to the payroll service.

Some previous versions of this text utilized whatever tax tables were in effect at the time of publication. Users who had different tax tables often noted differences in solutions as a result. This new requirement solves that problem. The author decided to utilize the manual payroll tax feature, which requires that students manually enter the tax deductions. This alleviates the discrepancies between the solutions manual and the students' data entry and lifts the burden of having to purchase the tax table service for each copy of QuickBooks installed in a lab environment. Instructions on how to set up payroll for manual calculation of payroll taxes are provided in the text. For more information, see your QuickBooks documentation.

All reports have a default feature which identifies the basis in which the report was created, such as accrual or cash, and the date and time the report was printed. The date and time shown on your report will, of course, be different from that shown in this text.

Getting Started with QuickBooks

In this part, you will:

- **Take an interactive tour of QuickBooks**
- **Create a balance sheet and modify its presentation**
- **Create an income statement and modify its presentation**
- **Create a statement of cash flows and modify its presentation**
- **Create supporting reports and modify their presentation**

Part 1 is designed to help you navigate through QuickBooks. It provides a foundation for Part 2, which will show you how to create a new QuickBooks file and record a variety of operating, investing, and financing transactions.

This part is divided into five chapters—each with its own set of questions, assignments, and case problems. Chapter 1 gives you a quick interactive tour of QuickBooks, in which you will create your Working Disk and become familiar with QuickBooks's essential features. Chapters 2, 3, 4, and 5 introduce you to creating and preparing the balance sheet, the income statement, the statement of cash flows, and supporting reports.

An Interactive Tour of QuickBooks

Learning Objectives

In this chapter, you will:

- Make your QuickBooks Working Disk
- Launch and exit QuickBooks in Windows
- Identify the major components of the QuickBooks window and the major menu commands
- Open and close a QuickBooks file
- Use QuickBooks Help
- View and print a set of financial statements

Case: **Century Kitchens**

You've been working in a part-time job at a restaurant, and today you decide that you've served your last hamburger. You want a new part-time job—one that's more directly related to your future career in business. As you skim the want ads, you see an ad for an administrative assistant at Century Kitchens, a remodeling contractor. Century specializes in remodeling existing homes and is well known in town for its quality construction and timely completion of projects. The ad says that job candidates must have earned or be earning a business degree, have some computer skills, and be willing to learn on the job. This looks promising. And then you see the line "Send a résumé to Scott Montalvo." You know Scott! He was in one of your marketing classes two years ago; he graduated last year with a degree in business. You decide to send your résumé to Scott right away.

A few days later you're delighted to hear Scott's voice on the phone. He remembers you well. He explains that he wants to hire someone to help him with clerical and other administrative tasks in support of his new company, Century Kitchens. He asks if you could start right away. When you say yes, he offers you the job on the spot! You start next Monday.

When you arrive Monday morning, Scott explains that the first thing he needs you to learn is how to use a software package called QuickBooks. You quickly remind Scott that you're not an accounting major. Scott laughs as he assures you you'll have no problem with QuickBooks because it is so user oriented. He chose QuickBooks exactly for that reason and has been using it for about three months.

Scott wants accurate, useful, and timely financial information to help him make sound business decisions, and he's not an accountant.

Scott explains that the company incorporated on January 1, 2007, and he's been using QuickBooks since then. Since 1/1/07 he's been entering each transaction, but he's become so busy at Century that he needs someone else in the office who can enter transactions, generate reports for the managers, and so on. So he says that today he will give you a tour of QuickBooks and teach you some of the basic features and functions of this package. You tell him that you're familiar with Windows and you're ready to start.

Using this Text Effectively

Before you begin the tour of QuickBooks, note that this textbook assumes you are familiar with the basics of Windows: how to control windows, how to choose menu commands, how to complete dialog boxes, and how to select directories, drives, and files. If you do not understand these concepts, please consult your instructor. Also note that this book is designed to be used with your instructor's and/or another textbook's discussion of essential accounting concepts.

The best way to work through this textbook is to carefully read the text and complete the numbered steps, which appear on a shaded background, as you work at your computer. Read each step carefully and completely before you try it.

As you work, compare your screen with the figures in the chapter to verify your results. You can use QuickBooks with any Windows operating system. The screen shots you will see in this book were captured in a Windows XP Professional environment. So if you are using Windows 98, 2000, ME, or XP you may see some minor differences between your screens and the screens in this book. Any significant differences that result from using the different operating systems with QuickBooks will be explained.

Don't worry about making mistakes—that's part of the learning process. The **Trouble?** paragraphs identify common problems and explain how to correct them or get back on track. Follow the suggestions *only* if you are having the specific problem described.

After you complete a chapter, you can do the questions, assignments, and case problems found at the end of each chapter. They are carefully structured so that you will review what you have learned and then apply your knowledge to new situations.

Data Files CD

To complete the chapters and exercises in this book, you must have access to data files. The CD located inside the back cover of this book contains backups of all the practice files you need for the chapters, the assignments, and the case problems.

You will need to restore the backup files to their original format. The files on your Data Files CD are named to correspond to chapters and sessions in this book.

To restore a backup file (file with a .qbb extension) to its original format (file with a .qbw extension):

1 Insert your Data Files CD into your CD drive.

2 Launch QuickBooks.

3 Click **File,** and then click **Restore.**

4 Click the **Browse** button in the Get Company Backup From: section of the Restore Company Backup window, and then locate the backup file you want to restore on your Data Files CD. Select a file, Century Kitchens, for example, and then click **Open.**

5 Next, click the **Browse** button in the Restore Company Backup To: section of the Restore Company Backup window to change the location of where you want the file to be restored on your computer's hard drive. Be sure to note its location for future use. See the example in Figure 1.1. Then click **Save.**

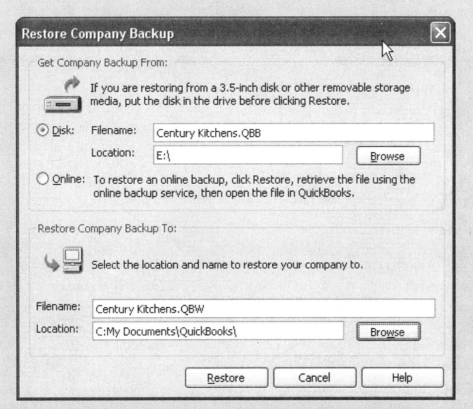

Figure 1.1

Restore Company
Backup Window

6 Click **Restore** in the Restore Company Backup window.

7 Click **OK** in the QuickBooks Information window, which should indicate that your data was restored successfully.

8 Continue this process for all the backup files on your Data Files CD as you need them.

Working from your computer's hard drive is the most efficient way to use the QuickBooks program. However, if you are in a lab environment and want to take your file with you when you leave, you'll need to make a backup copy of the file and save it to a removable disk (ideally a portable USB drive).

To create a backup file (file labeled with a .qbb extension) from one in an original format (file labeled with a .qbw extension):

1 Attach your portable USB drive (in this case labeled F:\).

2 Launch QuickBooks (if not already running).

3 Open the file you want to back up (once again, only if it is not already open).

4 Click **File,** and then click **Back Up.**

5 Change the backup location to your disk. See the example in Figure 1.2.

Figure 1.2

QuickBooks Backup Window

6 Click **OK** to begin the backup process.

7 Click **OK** once again in the QuickBooks information window, which should indicate that your data was backed up successfully.

To restore the .qbb file you just created to a different computer:

1 Attach your USB drive.

2 Launch QuickBooks.

3 Click **File,** and then click **Restore.**

4 Change the location of the Get Company Backup From: section of the Restore Company Backup window to F:\ (assuming you want to restore the file from the disk located in drive F:)

5 Change the location of the Restore Company Backup To: section of the Restore Company Backup window to a location on your computer's hard drive, being sure to note its location for future use.

6 Click **Restore.**

7 Click **OK** in the QuickBooks Information window, which should indicate that your data was restored correctly.

What Is QuickBooks?

Scott is excited about using QuickBooks since it is the best selling small business accounting software on the market today. He explains that **QuickBooks** is an automated accounting information system that describes an entity's financial position and operating results and that helps managers make more effective business decisions. He also likes QuickBooks's reports and graphs, which quickly and easily organize and summarize all the data he enters.

Scott says he especially likes QuickBooks because it can handle all of Century Kitchens' needs to invoice customers and maintain receivables, as well as pay bills and maintain payables. It can track inventory and create purchase orders using Century Kitchens' on-screen forms—all without calculating, posting, or closing. Scott can correct all transactions he's recorded at any time, while an audit trail feature automatically keeps a record of any changes he makes.

Scott explains further that QuickBooks has four basic features that, when combined, help manage the financial activity of a company. The four features—lists, forms, registers, and reports and graphs—work together to create an accounting information system. Let's take a closer look at each of these four features.

Lists

Lists are groups of names, such as customers, vendors, employees, inventory items, and accounts, and information about those names. Lists are created and edited either from a list window or while completing a form, such as an invoice, bill, or time sheet. Figure 1.3 (on the following page) shows a list of Century

Figure 1.3

A Customer List from
Century Kitchens

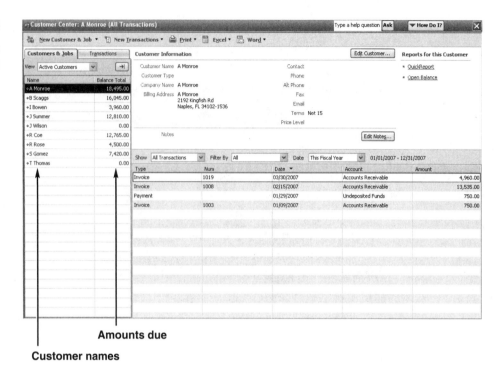

Amounts due

Customer names

Kitchens' customer names with jobs for each of these customers, balances owed
for each job, and any explanatory notes.

Forms

Forms are QuickBooks's electronic representations of the paper documents used
to record business activities, such as customer invoices, a vendor's bill for goods
purchased, or a check written to a vendor. The customer invoice form in Figure 1.4
contains many **fields,** or areas on the form that you can fill in.

If you fill in a field, such as the Customer:Job field, QuickBooks often automatically fills in several other fields with relevant information to speed up data
entry. In Figure 1.4, for example, the BILL TO, TERMS, and Tax fields are filled
in as soon as the Customer:Job field is entered.

Also, filling in a field is made easier through the use of drop-down lists.
Whenever you see an arrow next to or in a field, that field is a drop-down list.

Registers

A QuickBooks **register** contains all financial activity for a specified balance sheet
account. Examples of registers include checking (cash), accounts receivable,
inventory, and accounts payable. The checking register in Figure 1.5 shows some
of Century Kitchens' cash payments and cash receipts, and provides cash balances
after each transaction.

The financial effects of business transactions may be entered directly into the
register or into the forms that automatically record the effects of these transactions
in the relevant register. For example, if an owner's cash contribution is recorded
on a Deposit form, the increases in both the checking account and relevant owner's
equity account are simultaneously recorded in the Checking register and
Contributed Capital register.

Your screen may show the words Print, Send, Ship, and Find if your Create Invoice window is expanded. QuickBooks automatically removes words to save space when the window size is reduced.

Figure 1.4

An Invoice Form for Century Kitchens

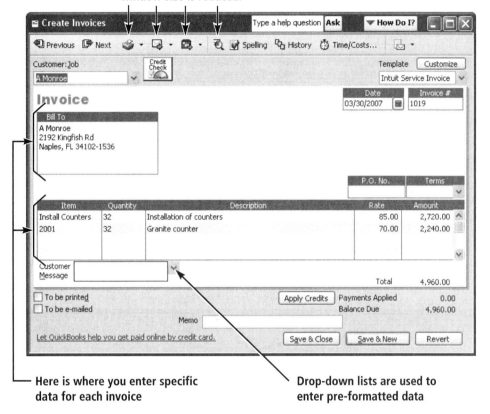

Here is where you enter specific data for each invoice

Drop-down lists are used to enter pre-formatted data

Note the four-digit year   Cash payments   Cash receipts

Figure 1.5

A Section of the Checking Register from Century Kitchens

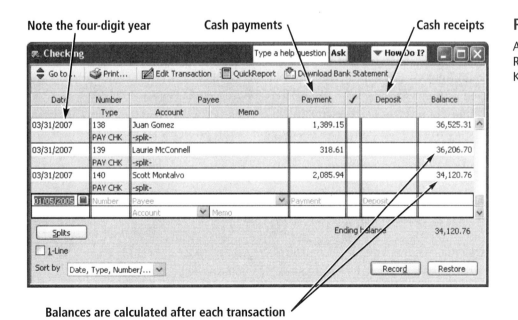

Balances are calculated after each transaction

Figure 1.6

A Profit and Loss Report (Income Statement) from Century Kitchens

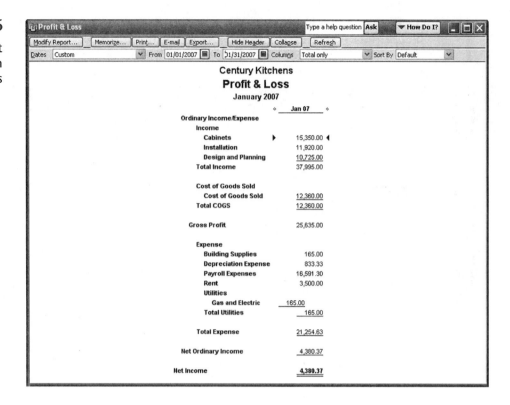

Reports and Graphs

QuickBooks **reports** and **graphs** present the financial position and the operating results of a company in a way that makes business decision making easier. The Profit and Loss report in Figure 1.6 shows the revenues and expenses of Century Kitchens for a specific period of time. Note that QuickBooks uses the title "Profit and Loss," but the generally accepted accounting title for this report is "Income Statement." Titles for this and other reports are all changeable using QuickBooks's Header/Footer tab. You can modify reports in many other ways, such as by comparing monthly periods, comparing this year with prior years, or examining year-to-date activity.

QuickBooks can also graph data to illustrate a company's financial position and operating results. For example, the bar chart in Figure 1.7 illustrates sales by month and the pie chart illustrates sales by construction category.

Launching QuickBooks

Now that you know about lists, forms, registers, and reports and graphs, you are ready to launch QuickBooks. Scott invites you to join him in his office and use his large-screen monitor to start your tour. You open Windows, and Scott tells you how to launch QuickBooks.

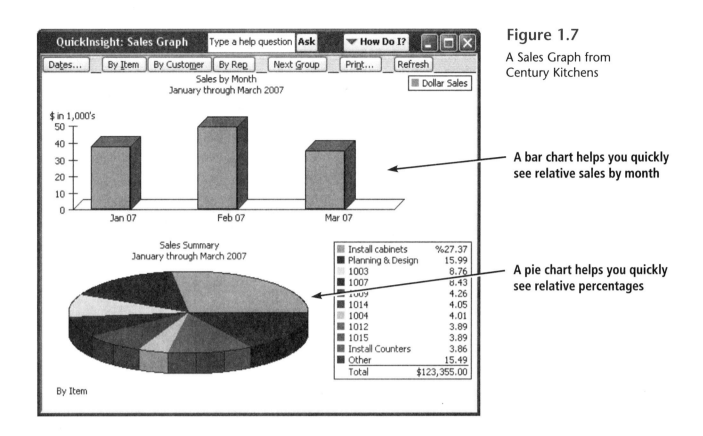

Figure 1.7

A Sales Graph from Century Kitchens

A bar chart helps you quickly see relative sales by month

A pie chart helps you quickly see relative percentages

To launch QuickBooks in Windows:

1 Click the **Start** button.

2 Select the **Programs** menu and look down the list for QuickBooks.

3 Once you've located the QuickBooks program, click and release the QuickBooks icon or name.

Trouble? If, when QuickBooks was last used, the file being worked on was closed, you will see a No Company Open window. If, however, a QuickBooks file is open, click **File,** and then click **Close Company.** Be sure to close any open files before you proceed to the next set of steps.

Now that you have launched QuickBooks, you can begin to learn how to use it.

Restoring and Opening a QuickBooks File

Scott hands you a disk and tells you to open a file called Century Kitchens.qbw. (You will find a backup of this file included on your Data Files CD.)

To restore and open the Century Kitchens Company file:

1 Insert your Data Files CD into your CD ROM drive.

2 Launch QuickBooks.

3 Click **File,** then click **Restore.** You should see a window like Figure 1.8.

Figure 1.8

Restore Company
Backup Window

4 Change the location of the Get Company Backup From section of the Restore Company Backup window to E:\ (assuming drive E is your CD ROM drive), as shown in Figure 1.9.

5 Change the location of the Restore Company Backup To section of the Restore Company Backup window to a location on your computer's hard drive, being sure to note its location for future use, perhaps as shown in Figure 1.10.

6 Click **Restore.**

7 Click **OK** in the QuickBooks Information window, which should indicate that your data was restored correctly.

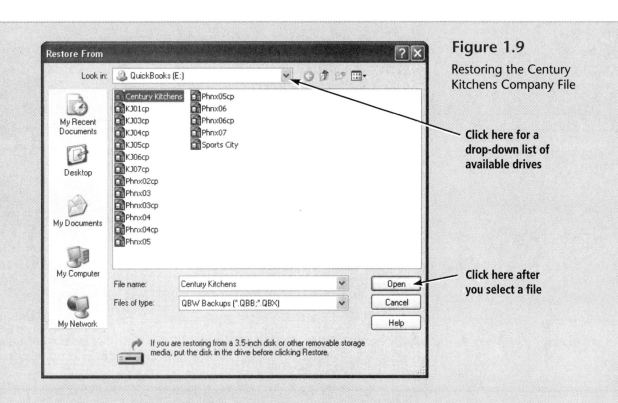

Figure 1.9

Restoring the Century Kitchens Company File

Click here for a drop-down list of available drives

Click here after you select a file

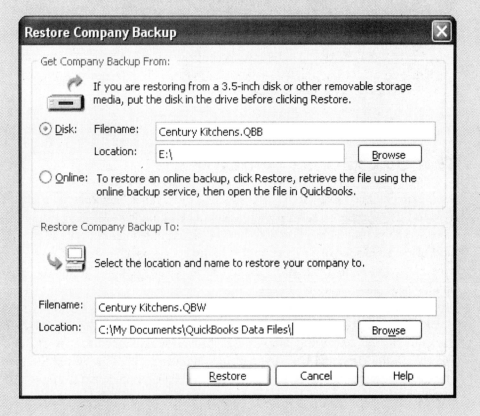

Figure 1.10

Restore Company Backup

Trouble? If a reminder window appears, click **Mark as Done** to close the window.

8   Click the **OK** button. The QuickBooks Learning Center window may appear. Let's skip this for now and click **Close box.** The QuickBooks home page should appear. See Figure 1.11. QuickBooks automatically opens this window every time you open a file. You will learn more about this later. If it does not appear, click the **Home** icon on the toolbar.

Figure 1.11

QuickBook Home Page

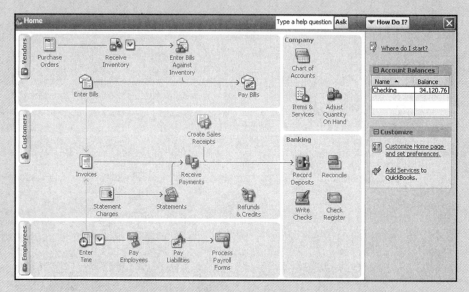

Trouble? If your QuickBooks Application window does not already fill the desktop, click the Application window **Maximize** button, located next to the **Close** button.

The QuickBooks Window

Scott explains that QuickBooks operates like most other Windows programs, so most of the QuickBooks window controls will be familiar to you if you have used other Windows programs. He reaches for the mouse and quickly clicks a few times until his screen looks like Figure 1.12. The main components of the QuickBooks window are shown in this figure. Let's take a look at these components so you are familiar with their location and use.

The **title bar** at the top of the window tells you that you are in the QuickBooks program and identifies the company file currently open. The **menu bar** contains the **command menus,** which open windows within QuickBooks. The File, Edit, View, and Help menus are similar to other Windows programs in that they allow you to perform such common tasks as open, save, copy, paste, find, and get help.

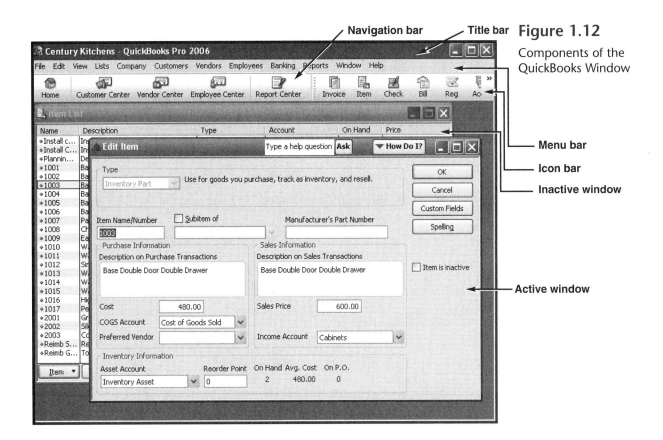

Navigation bar   Title bar **Figure 1.12**
Components of the
QuickBooks Window

Menu bar

Icon bar

Inactive window

Active window

The Lists menu gives you access to all lists, including the chart of accounts, customers, vendors, employees, and inventory items, to name a few. The Company, Customers, Vendors, Employees, and Banking menus provide easy access to the previously mentioned Centers as well as common tasks unique to that menu. For instance, in the Customers menu you can create invoices, enter cash sales, create credit memos, receive payments, etc. The Reports menu will give you quick access to common reports and graphs for easy creation. The Window menu allows you to choose the format for window displays, such as cascade or tile vertically. Finally, the Help menu will give you immediate access to an index of help topics.

The **navigation bar** gives you one-click access to the QuickBook Centers and Home page. From time to time, you may want to hide the navigation bar so you can have more horizontal space for the customizable icon bar.

The **icon bar** includes icons representing tasks you do on a daily basis, such as entering and paying bills, creating invoices, and receiving payments. If you use QuickBooks payroll system, you might consider adding icons for your payroll forms. Icons can be added, removed, or reordered to fit your needs. Use the View menu to hide or display the icon bar and make any changes.

The **active window** is the window in which you can enter or edit data, and it is identified by a solid window title bar. Only one window may be active at a time. Other windows may be open, but they are inactive. If the active window is closed, or if a window behind it is selected, it becomes **inactive,** and the window selected becomes active.

Saving and Closing a QuickBooks File

Now that you have seen the components of the QuickBooks screen, Scott wants to show you how to close a file, so that you will always be able to save your work and exit QuickBooks. He explains that to close a QuickBooks file, you can do one of three things:

- Exit QuickBooks using the Exit command on the File menu.
- Open another company file using the Open Company command.
- Close the file using the Close Company command on the File menu.

To close the Century Kitchens Company's file:

1 Click **File.**

2 Click **Exit.** The Century Kitchens Company file is automatically saved and closed. A dialog box might display the message "Intuit highly recommends backing up your data to avoid any accidental loss. Would you like to back up now?" Another message about QuickBooks Update Service might also appear. Close this message window for now. See Figure 1.13.

Figure 1.13

Closing Files

3 Click **No** to exit QuickBooks and return to Windows.

Then Scott tells you something very unusual. He says that unlike other Windows programs, QuickBooks *does not have a Save command*. In other words, in QuickBooks you cannot save a file whenever you want. You stare at Scott in disbelief and ask how that can be possible. Scott explains that *QuickBooks automatically saves all of the data you input and the changes you make as soon as you make them and click OK*. Scott admits that when he first used QuickBooks, he was uneasy about exiting the program until he could find a way to save his work. But he discovered that there are no Save or Save As commands on the QuickBooks File menu as there are on most other Windows programs. He reassures you that as unsettling as this is, you'll get used to it when you become more familiar with QuickBooks.

QuickBooks's Menus and Shortcut List

Scott explains that to enter sales receipts, create invoices, pay bills, receive payments, and so on, you use QuickBooks menu commands. Some of these functions are also available from buttons on the QuickBooks icon bar.

Some QuickBooks menus are dynamic; in other words, the options on the menu change depending upon what form, list, register, or report with which you are working. For instance, when you enter sales receipts information, the File and Edit menus change to include menu commands to print the sales receipts, or to edit, delete, memorize, or void the sales receipts, as shown in Figure 1.14.

Because this is all new to you, Scott suggests that first you become familiar with how managers at Century Kitchens use QuickBooks to make business decisions.

Using QuickBooks to Make Business Decisions: An Example at Century Kitchens

Once transactions are entered into the QuickBooks accounting information system, they can be accessed, revised, organized, and reported in many ways to aid business decision making. This ability is what makes a computerized accounting information system so valuable to managers.

Figure 1.14

Dynamic Menu Example

While you're sitting with Scott, he receives a phone call from Laurie McConnell. Laurie needs some information on whether any accounts are past due. You know from your accounting course that Laurie is really asking for information about Century Kitchens' **accounts receivable,** or amounts due from customers from previously recorded sales. Laurie wants to know how much is due from customers and how current those receivables are; specifically, which customers owe Century Kitchens and when their payments were due. Scott tells Laurie he'll look into this immediately and call her right back.

Be aware that dates are critical to retrieving relevant information in QuickBooks. In most cases when you ask for a report, QuickBooks will give you that report as of the system date (today's date, whatever that might be). For example, if you are working on this assignment on January 5, 2007, and you request a report on receivables, QuickBooks will give you a report of receivables as of January 5, 2007. If you want a report as of March 31, 2007, you will need to change the date on the report and then refresh the report to see that information.

To identify the customers who owe Century Kitchens money and the total amount of receivables due from these customers:

1 Click **Reports,** click **Customers & Receivables,** and then click **A/R Aging Detail.** Change the report date to **3/31/2007;** then click the **Refresh** button. The report in Figure 1.15 appears below.

Change the report date here

Click here to refresh the report for the change you make in the report date

Figure 1.15
Accounts Receivable Detail

Purchase order column; resized to view the entire width of the report

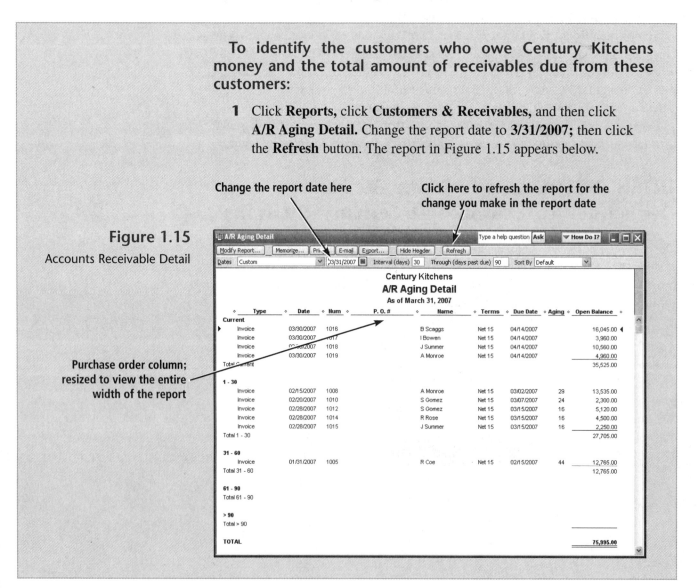

Trouble? The report you see might be slightly different from the one shown in Figure 1.15. Some column widths have been altered. Use the scroll bars to view this report both vertically and horizontally.

2 Note that customers owe Century Kitchens a total of $75,995.00.

3 Scott wants to see a graphic illustration of this information. From the Menu bar, click **Reports,** click **Customers & Receivables,** then click **Accounts Receivable Graph.** Change the report date to 3/31/2007. The graphic in Figure 1.16 appears below.

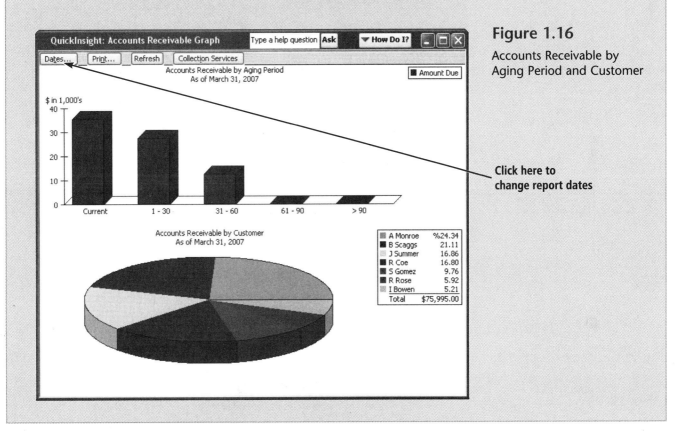

Figure 1.16

Accounts Receivable by Aging Period and Customer

Scott calls Laurie back and tells her that $75,995.00 is due from customers. He explains that only the R Coe account is past due. Laurie would like to know specifically what invoices were sent to R Coe, when payments were made, and in what amounts. Scott knows he can easily get this information by accessing the Customer Balance Detail report for R Coe.

To access the Customer Balance Detail for R Coe:

1 From the Menu bar, click **Reports,** click **Customers & Receivables,** then click **Customer Balance Detail.**

2 Scroll down the report to **R Coe's** detailed information shown in Figure 1.17. This report describes the two invoices that billed R Coe for services rendered. It also shows the cash payment received to date from R Coe.

Figure 1.17

Customer Balance Detail

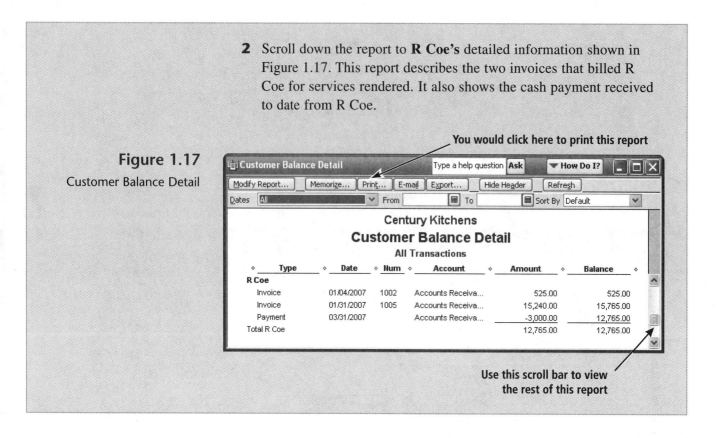

Scott calls Laurie back and tells her that the invoice dates are 1/04/2007 and 1/31/2007, and that a payment was made on 3/31/2007. He has quickly and easily accessed financial information from the company's QuickBooks data file, and Laurie thanks him. She is grateful for his quick response so she can make her decision. She asks if, before the end of the day, he would print out a copy of this information and leave it on her desk. Scott is happy to oblige.

Printing in QuickBooks

Scott suddenly remembers a meeting he must attend. But before exiting QuickBooks, you remind him that he promised to print a Customer Balance Detail report for Laurie.

To print a Customer Balance Detail report:

1 If you have closed the Customer Balance Detail report, click **Reports,** click **Customers & Receivables,** and then click **Customer Balance Detail.**

2 Click the **Print** button located on the button bar. See Figure 1.17.

3 Click **Print** in the Print Reports dialog box. The report prints out.

> ***Trouble?*** You might have to set up a printer before printing. If necessary, click **Cancel** in the Print Report dialog box. Then select Printer Setup from the File menu. QuickBooks allows you to set up different printers for different functions. Click the Settings tab and select the printer you would like to use from the printer name drop-down list.
>
> **4** You've opened several windows and not closed them. Click **Window** in the menu bar, and then click **Close All** to close all open windows and return to the QuickBooks opening window.
>
> Since you may have modified the settings for one or more reports, a Memorized Reports window may appear. Since we don't plan to use this report again, click **No.**

Scott asks you to drop off this report at Laurie's desk sometime after lunch.

Using QuickBooks Help

Scott suggests you explore QuickBooks's Help features while he is at his meeting. He tells you that QuickBooks Help has the standard features and functions of Windows Help, and, in addition, has other help features specific to QuickBooks. These other features are listed in the main Help menu shown in Figure 1.18.

As with other Windows programs, you can access Help by clicking on the Help menu or pressing F1. QuickBooks Help is context sensitive—that is, different help screens appear depending on where you are in the program. You can get help for a specific topic by choosing the Help Index menu item.

You decide to follow up on Scott's suggestion to look at a help feature he finds very useful, the Help Index. You are specifically interested in how QuickBooks uses accounts.

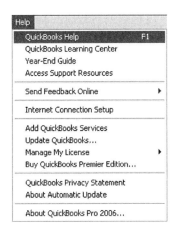

Figure 1.18

The Help Menu

To use the Help Index:

1 Click **Help** from the menu bar. Then click **QuickBooks Help** on the menu. Click the **Index** tab.

2 Type the word **accounts** as a keyword.

3 Double-click **adding** under the caption accounts (managing) to view the QuickBooks Help window shown in Figure 1.19.

4 Click the **Print** button, then click **Print** to print this screen.

5 Close this window.

Figure 1.19

Help Index

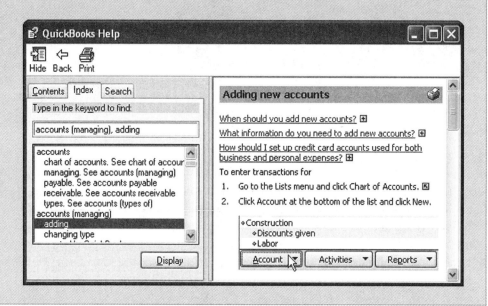

You will have an opportunity to use most of these options in this and later chapters.

Ask Button

Scott returns from his meeting. He asks if you've tried the Ask button as he's found this an effective way to quickly access the QuickBooks Help feature. The Ask button appears on the title bar of most windows in QuickBooks.

To see how the Ask button can help you use QuickBooks:

1 Click the **Check** icon in the icon bar.

2 Type **How do I pay a bill** (as shown in Figure 1.20) in the Ask edit box, then click **Ask.**

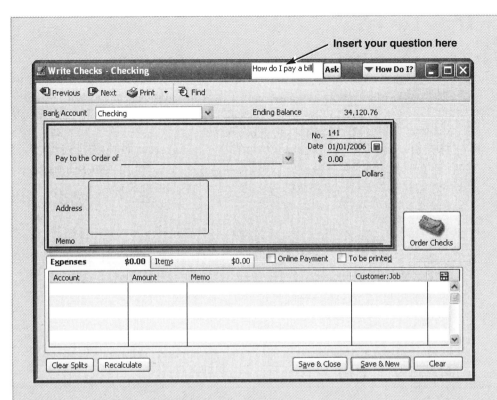

Figure 1.20

Ask Button

3 Click once on the topic shown in the QuickBooks Help window to reveal the window shown in Figure 1.21. How does paying bills work?

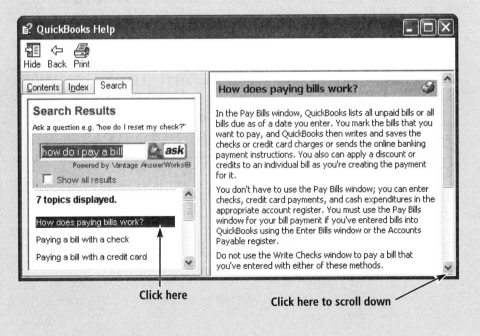

Figure 1.21

QuickBooks Help

4 Close all windows.

How Do I Buttons

Scott then asks if you've discovered the "How Do I" button. He finds all of QuickBooks's features very useful, but he particularly recommends that you use the "How Do I" feature as you begin to work with QuickBooks. The "How Do I" button provides a drop-down menu for context sensitive help. Scott offers to demonstrate this unique feature of QuickBooks.

The "How Do I" button appears on the title bar of every window in QuickBooks. The drop-down menus provide access to various sections of QuickBooks Help including step-by-step procedures and other context-sensitive help.

To see how the "How Do I" button can help you use QuickBooks:

1 Click **Customers,** and then click **Create invoices.**

2 Click on the **How Do I** button to reveal a drop-down menu.

3 Move the cursor over the words **Use invoices,** then move the cursor over the words **Fill out an invoice.** Your screen should look similar to Figure 1.22.

Figure 1.22

"How Do I" as a Help Feature

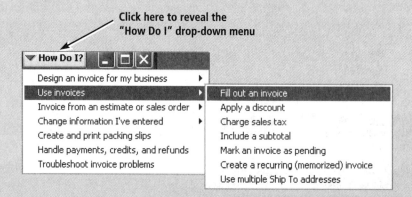

4 Click on the words **Fill out an invoice** and then click **Use step-by-step instructions** to reveal the instructions for completing an invoice. See Figure 1.23.

5 Close all windows.

QuickBooks Learning Center

The tutorials in the QuickBooks Learning Center will help you get started right away. You will get a "big picture" overview of important concepts in QuickBooks, as well as step-by-step instructions for key tasks.

Scott offers to demonstrate these tutorials by examining one on creating invoices.

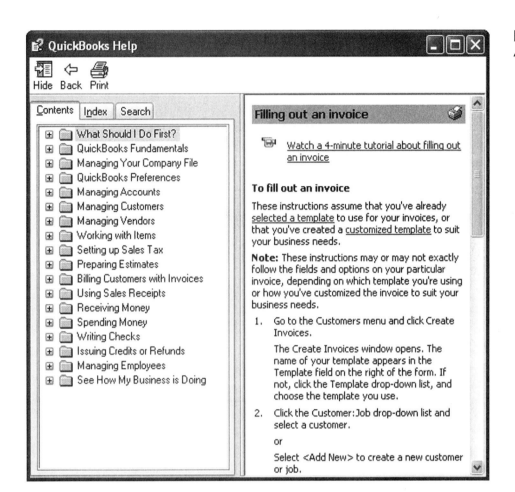

Figure 1.23
"How Do I" Results

To access QuickBooks Learning Center and understand how to create invoices in QuickBooks:

1 Click **Help,** and then click **QuickBooks Learning Center.**

2 Click the **Customers and Sales** button, and then click the text **"How to create an invoice."** To hear the audio portion, you will need some headphones or speakers attached to your computer. If you do not have either, then click the **Audio Transcript** button in the lower right corner of the QuickBooks Tutorial window.

3 Close all windows when you are done watching the tutorial.

"Wow!" you exclaim, "That was pretty easy."

Scott explains that all of these help features are yours for the taking as you explore how to use QuickBooks.

The QuickBooks Home Page

Scott reminds you that another feature he previously mentioned was the QuickBooks home page shown again in Figure 1.24 below. The QuickBooks home page provides a big picture of how your essential business tasks fit together. Tasks are organized into logical groups (Customers, Vendors, Employees, Company, and Banking) with workflow arrows to help you learn how tasks relate to each other and to help you decide what to do next.

Figure 1.24

QuickBooks Home Page

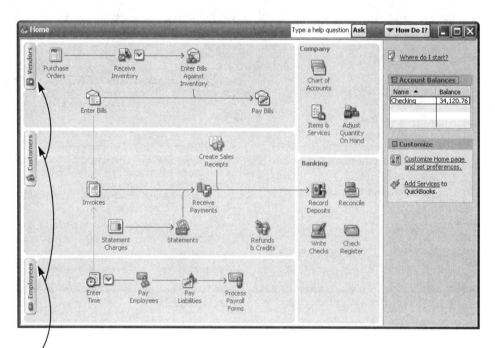

Click here to access the Vendor, Customer, or Employee Center

The workflow arrows indicate a logical progression of business tasks in QuickBooks. However, these arrows do not restrict you from doing tasks in a different order or an order that works better for your business needs.

The Customer portion of the home page includes two main activities: invoicing and receiving payments. Note, however, that invoices may receive input from the vendor section (when we're billing customers for parts purchased from a vendor) as well as the employee section (when we're billing customers for employee time).

The Vendor portion of the home page includes four main activities: creating purchase orders, receiving items, establishing a liability, and paying that liability. QuickBooks provides you the means of managing all of these tasks with the click of an icon.

The Employee portion of the home page includes two main activities: recording employee time and paying employees and tax authorities. The work flow here does require sequential input in that employee time must be entered first before employees and tax authorities can be paid.

The Banking and Company portions of the home page are generic to the whole company and aren't necessarily business processes requiring work flow steps. The Company section allows you to update your chart of accounts, items, services, and physical quantities of items on hand. The Banking section allows you to record deposits write checks and reconcile your bank accounts.

The home page also provides you access to lists of customers, vendors, employees, etc., via the Customer, Vendor, and Employee Centers, respectively. In these Centers, QuickBooks provides easy access to managing customers, vendors, and employees and entering transactions for each. For example, in the Employee Center you can view an employee's recent paychecks, edit that employee's information, enter new employee, enter time, and enter a new paycheck.

Scott reminds you that the home page is one of many ways to access the core features of any accounting information system like QuickBooks. There are menus, icons, centers, and work flow diagrams, all of which eventually take you to the same place to edit, enter, or process business events.

To view and explore the Home page:

1 Click **home** from the icon bar.

2 Click the **Enter Bills** icon in the Vendor section to view the Enter Bills window where later you'll enter bills received from vendors as shown in Figure 1.25.

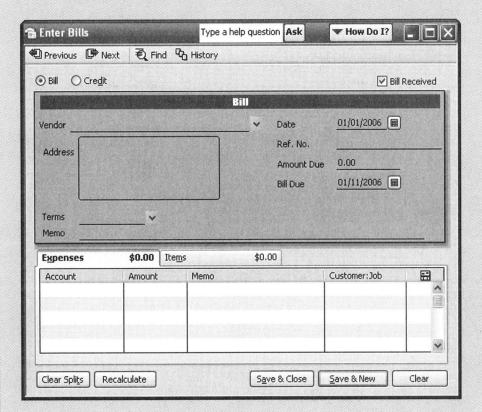

Figure 1.25

Entering Bills

3 Close the Enter Bills window.

4 Click the **Receive Payments** icon in the Customer section to view the Receive Payments window where later you'll enter amounts received from customers as shown below in Figure 1.26.

Figure 1.26

Receive Payments

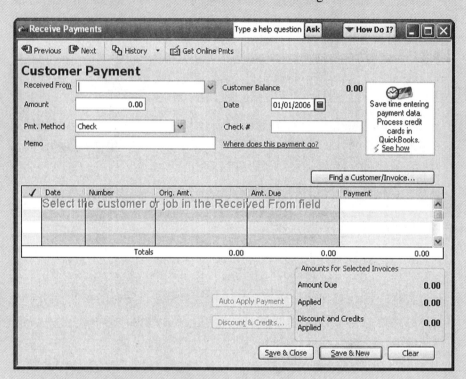

5 Close the Receive Payments window.

6 Click **Employees** to view the Employee Center as shown in Figure 1.27.

Figure 1.27

Employee Center

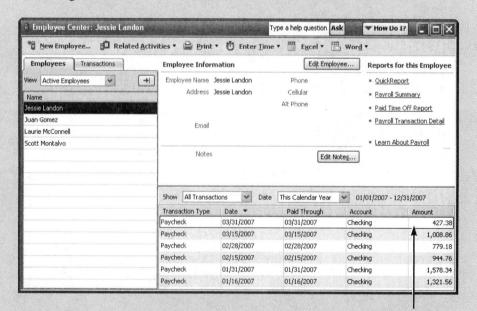

7 Double-click Jessie Landon's paycheck dated 3/31/2007 to examine the specific check used to pay this employee as shown in Figure 1.28.

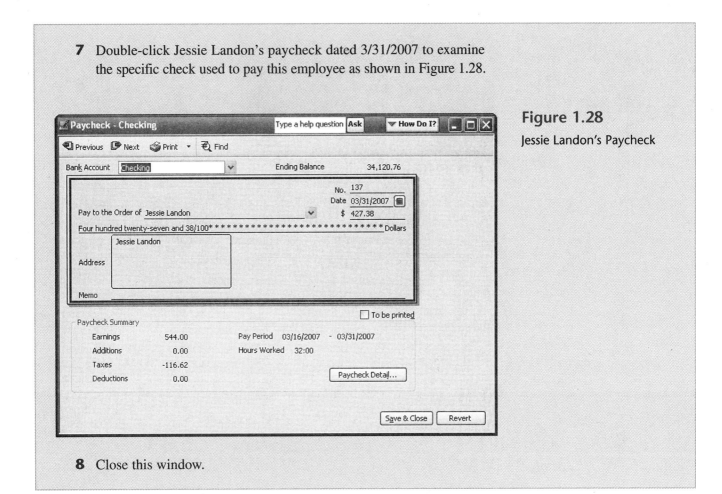

Figure 1.28

Jessie Landon's Paycheck

8 Close this window.

After you have learned the basics about QuickBooks in this course, you might decide to use QuickBooks Centers and workflow diagrams more often. But for now, follow the steps as they are written in this text.

Exiting QuickBooks

You thank Scott for taking the time to introduce you to QuickBooks as he rushes off to yet another meeting. You know you can probably exit QuickBooks on your own, using standard Windows commands. You choose to use the Exit command on the File menu.

To exit QuickBooks:

1 Click **File** on the QuickBooks menu bar to display the File menu.

2 Click **Exit.** Once again, a dialog box might display the message "Intuit highly recommends backing up your data to avoid any accidental data loss. Would you like to back up now?"

3 Click **No** to exit QuickBooks and return to Windows. Good accounting practice encourages backing up data files, but backup is not necessary now with these sample files.

End Note

Scott has shown you some of the features of QuickBooks, how to navigate these features, and how business decisions can be aided by the reporting and analysis of accounting information afforded by QuickBooks. You are impressed by the speed at which information is made available and are anxious to learn more.

Chapter 1 Questions

1 Describe, in your own words, the various uses of QuickBooks.

2 List the four basic features of QuickBooks.

3 Describe how lists are used in QuickBooks.

4 Describe how forms are used in QuickBooks.

5 Name three forms used in QuickBooks.

6 Describe how registers are used in QuickBooks.

7 Describe how reports and graphs are used in QuickBooks.

8 Describe the function of the navigators in QuickBooks.

9 Describe how to print a report in QuickBooks.

10 Describe two of the Help features available in QuickBooks.

Chapter 1 Assignments

1 *Working with Files*

Use the Century Kitchens file to practice opening, closing, and printing. Create a report of Open Invoices as of 3/31/2007 from the Customers & Receivables menu item on the Reports menu. Print the resulting Open Invoices report.

2 *Practice Using the QuickBooks Help Menu*

Use the QuickBooks Help menu to learn more about QuickBooks's features.

    a. From the Help menu, select **QuickBooks Help.** Find the index section on reports. View the section for changing the date range in the "dates in" section in a report, and print this topic.

    b. Find the index section on adding a customer. Print this topic.

    c. Find the index section on calculating payroll taxes manually. Print this topic.

    d. Click **Chart of Accounts** from the Company menu. Press **F1,** and then print the topic.

3 *Using the QuickBooks Learning Center*

From the Help menu, select **QuickBooks Learning Center.** Click **Inventory,** and then watch the tutorial on using reports to manage inventory. Explain what information is provided on the Inventory Valuation Summary report.

4 *Using the South-Western Home Page for More Assignments or Cases*

Go to the home page for this textbook at **www.thomsonedu.com/accounting/ owen.** Click **Additional Problem Sets,** and then select the **Chapter 1** section, and complete the problem(s) your instructor assigns.

Chapter 1 Case Problem:
CENTURY KITCHENS

merchandising

1 *Accessing Inventory Data*

Scott Montalvo wants to know the amount and nature of inventory on hand as of January 31, 2007. Use Century Kitchens.qbw to obtain this inventory information. Open Century Kitchens.qbw. Open an Inventory Valuation Summary report as of January 31, 2007. Write your responses to questions below and print the Inventory Valuation Summary report.

    a. What is Item 3?

    b. How many of this item were on hand on that date?

    c. What was the average cost of this item on that date?

    d. Print the Inventory Valuation Summary report in landscape orientation.

2 *Accessing Sales Data*

Scott also wants to know the company's sales for the period January 1 through January 31, 2007. Use Century Kitchens.qbw to obtain this sales information. Open Century Kitchens.qbw. Open the Sales by Customer Detail report for the period January 1 through January 31, 2007. Write your responses to questions below and print the Sales by Customer Detail report.

    a. How much was J Wilson billed this period?

    b. What was S Gomez billed for this period?

    c. What was the total amount billed during this period?

    d. Print the Sales by Customer Detail report.

Preparing a Balance Sheet Using QuickBooks

2

Learning Objectives

In this chapter, you will:

- Create a comparative balance sheet and a summary balance sheet
- Investigate detail supporting balance sheet items
- Use the Balance Sheet Report button bar
- Create a balance sheet as of a specific date other than the system date
- Print a balance sheet

Case: Century Kitchens

It's your second day at your new job, and you arrive early. Scott is already hard at work at the computer. He tells you he is preparing for Century Kitchens' quarter year end on March 31, 2007. Since this is the first time he will prepare financial statements using QuickBooks, he's a little nervous.

You recall from your accounting course that a balance sheet reports the assets, liabilities, and owners' equity of a company at a specific point in time. As part of your continued training on QuickBooks, Scott asks you to watch what he does as he prepares the balance sheet. He explains that his immediate goals are to familiarize himself with how to prepare a balance sheet using QuickBooks, and to examine some of the valuable features QuickBooks provides to help managers analyze and interpret financial information.

Creating a Balance Sheet

You know from your business courses that the information on a balance sheet can be presented in many ways. Scott tells you that QuickBooks provides four preset ways to present a balance sheet; QuickBooks also allows him to customize the way he presents the information. He decides to examine one of the preset balance sheets first. He chooses what QuickBooks calls the Standard balance sheet report.

To create a Standard Balance Sheet report:

1 Open Century Kitchens.qbw.

2 Click **Reports, Center** from the navigation bar. Click **Company & Financial** on the left, scroll down the window, and then click **Balance Sheet Standard** under the heading **Balance Sheet & Net Worth.** Change the As of date to **3/31/2007.** Then click **Refresh.** QuickBooks's Standard balance sheet appears. See Figure 2.1.

Change As of date here

Figure 2.1

Century Kitchens' Balance Sheet as of March 31, 2007, in QuickBooks's Standard Preset Report

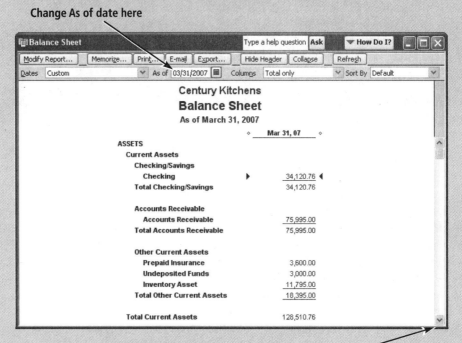

Scroll down to see the rest of the Balance Sheet

3 Scroll down the Balance Sheet. Notice that this report shows the balance in each account, with subtotals for assets, liabilities, and owners' equity. Unlike standard accounting practice, QuickBooks displays net income for the year to date as part of owners' equity. In particular, take note of the current assets, fixed assets, current liabilities, long-term liabilities, and owners' equity. Note that QuickBooks refers to "owners' equity" as simply "equity."

4 Do not close this window.

Trouble? On many of these reports, when you change the size of a column, then close the window, a "Memorized Report" window pops up asking if you want to memorize these new settings ("Would you like to memorize this report?") I suggest at this point that you just click **No.**

Scott is amazed at how rapidly QuickBooks created this balance sheet compared to how long it's taken him to create one manually in the past. As you both look over this balance sheet, Scott comments that because he generated this information so quickly with so little effort, he might now be able to add information to balance sheets that he didn't have time to include before. For example, he has always wanted to include comparative information on balance sheets to help him make better business decisions.

Creating a Comparative Balance Sheet

By using the help function of QuickBooks, Scott discovered how easy it is to create a comparative balance sheet. He learns that by modifying the existing standard balance sheet he just created, he can create one which compares each month of the quarter just ended. When he sees how easily he can create a comparative balance sheet, he decides to create one comparing the balance sheet of January, February, and March of 2007.

To create a comparative balance sheet report for January, February, and March 2007:

1 Modify the standard balance sheet you just created by clicking the **Modify Report** button. (*Note:* If you closed the standard balance sheet window, follow the previous steps to recreate it.)

2 Change the From date to **1/1/2007.** (*Note:* The To date should already be 3/31/2007.)

3 Change the Columns text box from Total Only to **Month,** and then click **OK.**

4 Click the **Refresh** button to view the comparative balance sheet shown below in Figure 2.2.

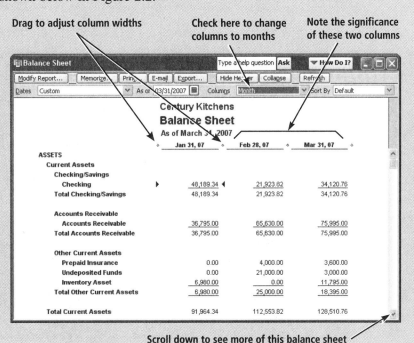

Figure 2.2

QuickBooks's Comparison Balance Sheet Report for Century Kitchens for January, February, and March 2007

5 Scroll down and across this balance sheet. Note that this report is similar to the Standard report, except that the columns compare the amounts for this year to date and last year to date, and show the change in dollar amount and percent.

Trouble? The balance sheet on your screen might not be the same as Figure 2.1 because the column widths are different. To change the column widths on any QuickBooks report, click and hold the mouse over the small diamond-shaped symbols to the right or left of any column. Drag to the right or left to increase or decrease each column's width. A dialog box might appear asking if you want to make all columns the same width. You may answer yes or no.

6 Close this window.

Creating a Summary Balance Sheet

Scott wonders if QuickBooks has a preset report that summarizes balance sheet information—in other words, one that provides no detail, only totals. In annual reports, such a summary is useful to external financial statement users, who usually do not have much interest in detailed balance sheet information. Scott again consults Help and learns that QuickBooks has a Summary balance sheet preset report.

To create a Summary Balance Sheet report:

1 From the Reports Center, click **Company & Financial,** and then click **Balance Sheet Summary.** (*Note:* This is not clicking the Reports menu item, it's clicking Company & Financial from the Reports Center.) Change the As of date to **3/31/2007,** and then click **Refresh.** See Figure 2.3.

2 Scroll down the summary balance sheet. Note that it is a brief version of the Standard balance sheet; it shows amounts for each account type, such as Other Current Assets, but not for individual accounts within each account type.

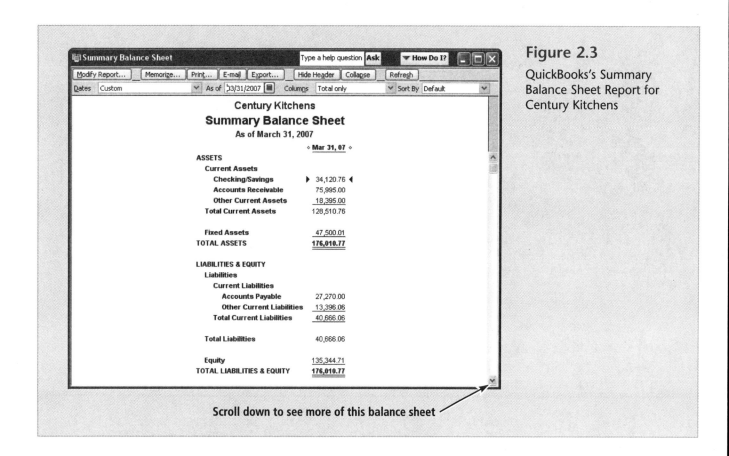

Figure 2.3

QuickBooks's Summary Balance Sheet Report for Century Kitchens

Investigating the Balance Sheet Using QuickZoom

Now that Scott knows he can generate the type of reports he wants, he decides to investigate QuickZoom—a feature he has heard QuickBooks provides for most reports. He tells you that QuickZoom shows you what transaction or transactions underlie any amount found in a report. You know that this is a helpful feature because managers often need to be able to quickly explain report balances; thus, knowledge of the underlying detailed transactions is essential.

Scott decides to practice using QuickZoom by analyzing the transactions that make up the Accounts Receivable balance.

To use QuickZoom:

1 Place the cursor over the Accounts Receivable balance of **75,995.00.** A cursor shaped like a magnifying glass and containing a "Z" appears. This cursor indicates that a QuickZoom report is available for this amount. See Figure 2.4.

Figure 2.4

Using QuickZoom

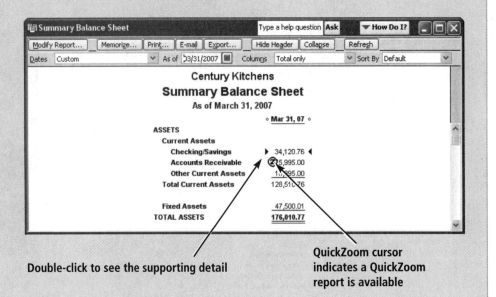

Double-click to see the supporting detail

QuickZoom cursor indicates a QuickZoom report is available

2 Double-click the amount **75,995.00.** The Transactions by Account report appears but lists only one item. That's because this report is showing only the events that took place on 3/31/2007.

3 Change the From date to **3/1/2007** and leave the To date at 3/31/2007, and then click **Refresh.** The resulting Transactions by Account report now appears with all changes to Accounts Receivable occurring during the month of March as shown in Figure 2.5.

Transactions are listed for 3/1/07 to 3/31/07

Figure 2.5

Viewing Transactions by Account

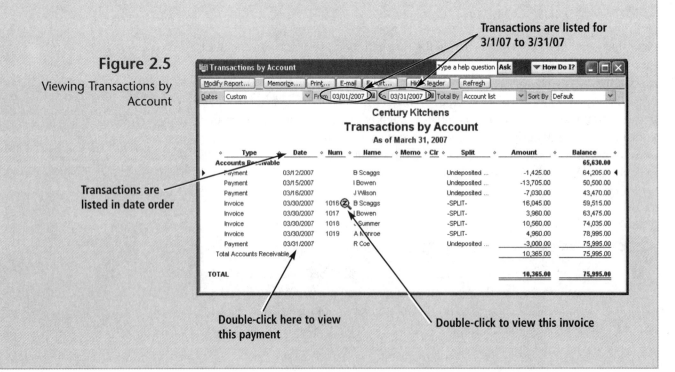

Transactions are listed in date order

Double-click here to view this payment

Double-click to view this invoice

4 Double-click **invoice 1016** in the Num column to examine one of the actual invoices which increased accounts receivable during March. See Figure 2.6 below.

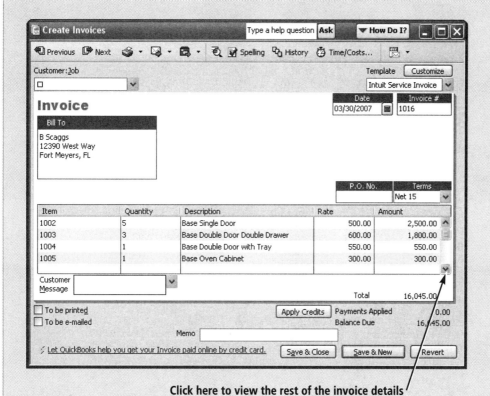

Figure 2.6

Examining Invoice Number 1016 for B Scaggs

Click here to view the rest of the invoice details

5 Close the Create Invoices window. The Transactions by Account report, which was hidden while you examined Invoice number 1016, reappears.

Trouble? If the transactions report does not reappear, activate the Transactions by Account report by clicking Transactions by Account on the Window menu; or, if you closed the window, repeat Steps 1 through 4 above as necessary.

6 Double-click anywhere on the row containing the payment made by R Coe posted 3/31/2007. A Receive Payments window appears. See Figure 2.7. Note that this payment was a payment on account and was applied to invoices 1002 and 1005.

7 Close the Receive Payments window.

8 Close the Transactions by Account window.

Figure 2.7

Customer Payment Received
from R Coe on 3/31/2007

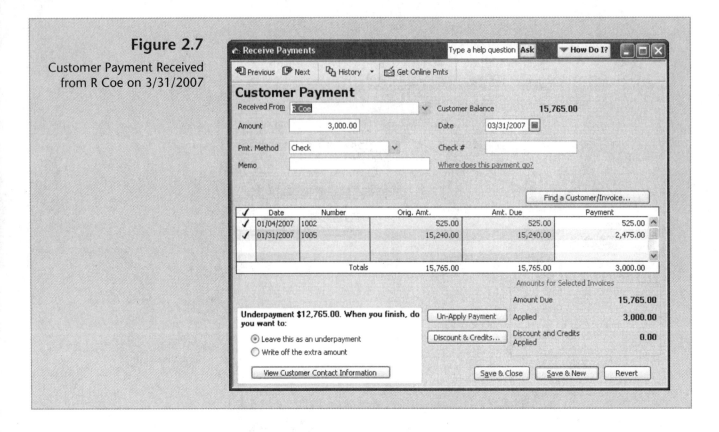

Scott is pleased with the QuickZoom feature of QuickBooks because it allows him to quickly and easily investigate any of the balances reported.

Modifying Balance Sheet Reports

The balance sheet report, like all other reports created in QuickBooks, can be modified using the report button bar, located on the menu bar. Scott decides that since this summary balance sheet is for internal use, he wants to change the heading, include the previous month's balances, report the numbers in thousands, and make a few other appropriate cosmetic changes.

To modify the Summary Balance Sheet report:

1 Click the **Modify Report** button on the report button bar. (*Note:* The summary balance sheet should still be open. If not, recreate it.)

2 Click the **Display** tab if it is not already active; then change the From date to **2/1/2007,** change Display columns by setting to **Month,** and check the **% of Column** checkbox, as shown in Figure 2.8.

3 Click the **Fonts & Numbers** tab as shown in Figure 2.8.

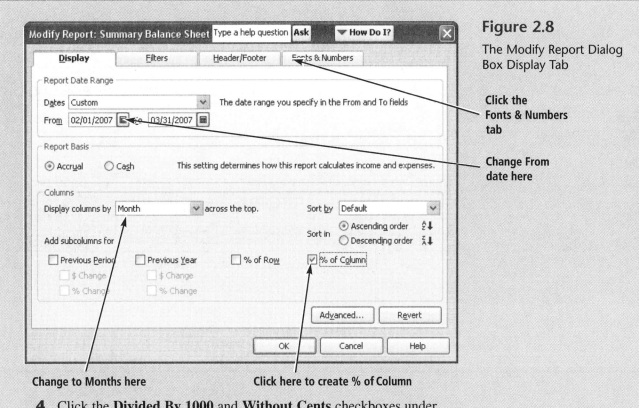

Figure 2.8

The Modify Report Dialog Box Display Tab

Click the Fonts & Numbers tab

Change From date here

Change to Months here

Click here to create % of Column

4 Click the **Divided By 1000** and **Without Cents** checkboxes under the Show All Numbers section of the Modify Report dialog box. See Figure 2.9.

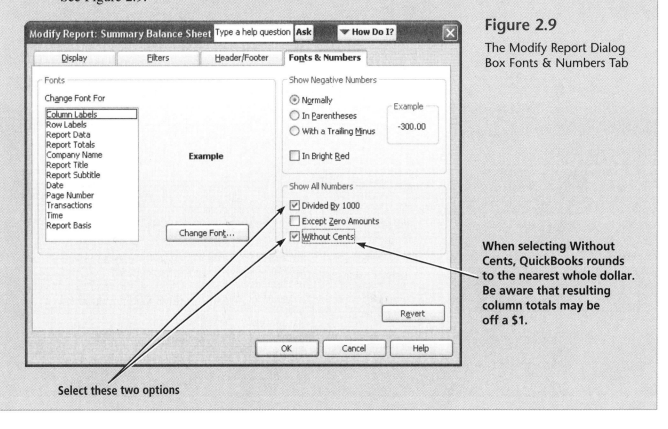

Figure 2.9

The Modify Report Dialog Box Fonts & Numbers Tab

When selecting Without Cents, QuickBooks rounds to the nearest whole dollar. Be aware that resulting column totals may be off a $1.

Select these two options

5 Click the **Header/Footer** tab.

6 Click inside the Report Title edit box. Change the name of the report from Summary Balance Sheet to Comparative Summary Balance Sheet by typing the word **Comparative** as shown in Figure 2.10. (*Note:* To properly identify this report as yours, you may want to type your name in the Extra Footer Line of the Header/Footer tab.)

Figure 2.10

The Header/Footer Tab

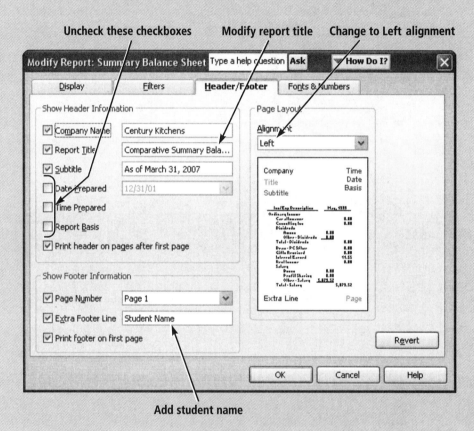

Uncheck these checkboxes   Modify report title   Change to Left alignment

Add student name

7 Change the alignment by clicking the **Down Arrow** in the Page Layout section and clicking **Left.** This changes the alignment of the title text to a left alignment. Uncheck the Date Prepared, Time Prepared, and Report Basis checkboxes.

8 Click **OK** to close the Modify Report window. The resulting report is shown in Figure 2.11 on the next page.

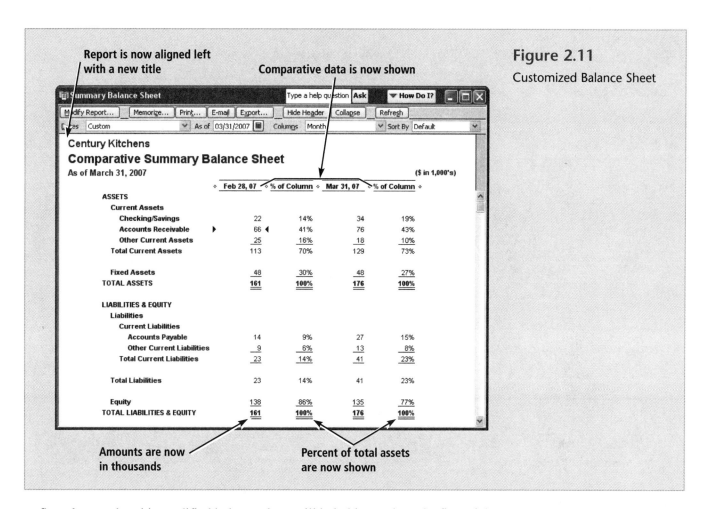

Figure 2.11

Customized Balance Sheet

Scott knows that this modified balance sheet will help him analyze the financial information more easily and quickly. You will have an opportunity to explore other report modification features available in QuickBooks in the chapter assignments.

Memorizing a Report in QuickBooks

Scott, knowing that he wants you to be efficient in your use of QuickBooks, suggests that you learn how to memorize the report just created so it can be produced again. He explains that, while standard reports are always available, unique reports like the one you just created should be memorized. Later they can be accessed, dates changed if necessary, and then recreated.

"How will I know where they are when I need them?" you ask.

Scott explains that he will create a memorized report group for you using your name. That way when you need them again, they will be easy to find.

To memorize the comparative balance sheet just prepared:

1 Open the Report Center.

2 Click the **Memorized text** at the top of the Report Center.

3 Click the **Memorized Report** button at the bottom of the Memorized Report List window, and then click **New Group.**

4 Type your name as the new group, and then click **OK.** (For illustration purposes, the list will show "Student Name" as your name below.)

5 Go to the Summary Balance Sheet still open in QuickBooks by clicking its name from the Open Windows List.

6 Click the **Memorize . . .** button at the top of the report.

7 Check the **Saved in Memorized Report Group** checkbox, and select your name from the drop-down list.

8 Click **OK** to memorize the report accepting the default report title provided.

9 Activate the Memorized Report List window, which should look similar to that shown in Figure 2.12. Then close the Memorize Report List.

Figure 2.12

Memorized Report List

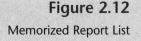
Your name will appear instead of "Student Name"

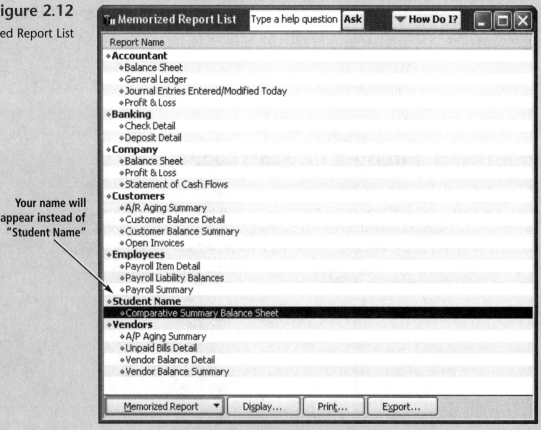

Printing the Balance Sheet

Scott receives a phone call from Frances Wu, an accountant with Century's CPA firm of Stoddard & Wong. Frances says she needs a printed copy of the company's balance sheet as of 3/31/2007 to analyze the need for an allowance for uncollectible accounts. Scott knows that printing the balance sheet he just created will provide her with the information she needs. He knows that printing a balance sheet is the same as printing any report in QuickBooks.

To print the Comparative Summary Balance Sheet report:

1 Click **Print** on the report button bar.

2 Click **Preview** in the Print Reports dialog box to preview the report. See Figure 2.13.

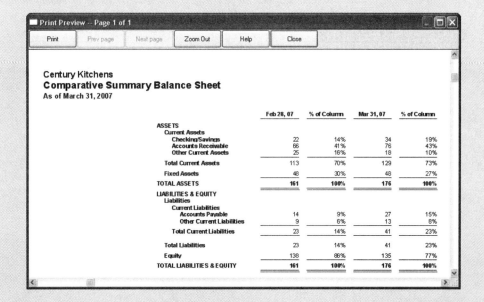

Figure 2.13

Preview the Balance Sheet

3 Click the **Zoom In** button to see what the report will look like when printed. (Alternatively, you could have clicked anywhere on the screen to zoom in on the report.)

4 Click the **Print** button if you would like to print the report.

5 Close all windows and, if you are not proceeding to Chapter 3, exit QuickBooks. If a Memorized Report window appears, click in the checkbox next to Do not display this message in the future, and then click **No.**

Scott feels much more confident about using QuickBooks. You are quickly becoming more comfortable with QuickBooks as well.

In the next chapter, you will expand your QuickBooks knowledge to include the creation, modification, and printing of another useful financial statement—the income statement.

Chapter 2 Questions

1 List the preset ways in which QuickBooks can present a balance sheet.

2 What time period alternatives does QuickBooks provide for a balance sheet?

3 List the steps you would take to create a balance sheet for a date other than the current system date.

4 Describe the steps to generate a balance sheet in QuickBooks.

5 Describe the steps to resize the columns of a comparative balance sheet.

6 Describe the different types of transactions you might find in a transactions by account report on accounts receivable.

7 Describe how QuickZoom gives you more information about a balance sheet.

8 How might a manager use QuickZoom to analyze a business's financial position as reported in a balance sheet?

9 List five ways you can customize a QuickBooks report.

10 Suppose you wanted to include a column in a balance sheet that described what percentage each asset, liability, and owners' equity account was of the total assets amount. How would you do this in QuickBooks?

Chapter 2 Assignments

1 *Creating a Balance Sheet for Century Kitchens*

Scott asks you to help him prepare a balance sheet. (Be sure to type your name in the Extra Footer line of this report.)

merchandising

a. He asks you to prepare and print a summary balance sheet as of January 31, 2007. He wants the amounts represented in thousands without cents, with no date prepared, time prepared, or report basis shown. Memorize this report, and save it in your report group.

b. Scott also asks you to prepare and print a standard balance sheet as of January 31, 2007. He wants amounts to be displayed in thousands, without cents and the page layout left-aligned with no date prepared, time prepared, or report basis shown. Memorize this report, and save it in your report group.

2 *Investigating the Balance Sheet Using QuickZoom*

Scott asks you to help him investigate the Accounts Receivable balance as of January 31, 2007. Create a summary balance sheet as of January 31, 2007, and then investigate the Accounts Receivable balance.

a. Print the resulting Transactions by Account report.

b. Examine and print a copy of invoice 1005.

3 *Using the South-Western Home Page for More Assignments or Cases*

Go to the home page for this textbook at **www.thomsonedu.com/accounting/ owen.** Click **Additional Problem Sets,** and then select the **Chapter 2** section, and complete the problem(s) your instructor assigns.

4 *Customizing a Balance Sheet*

Modify the balance sheet you created in Assignment 1a (remember, you memorized it, so it is easy to recall) to include January and February amounts with a percent of column. Change the report title and format the page as shown in Figure 2.14. (*Hint:* Use the Modify Reports button.) Print the report with your name in the Extra Footer line in portrait orientation.

Figure 2.14

Customized Balance Sheet

Century Kitchens
Comparative Balance Sheet
As of February 28, 2007

($ in 1,000's)

	Jan 31, 07	% of Column	Feb 28, 07	% of Column
ASSETS				
Current Assets				
Checking/Savings	48	34%	22	14%
Accounts Receivable	37	26%	66	41%
Other Current Assets	7	5%	25	16%
Total Current Assets	92	65%	113	70%
Fixed Assets	49	35%	48	30%
TOTAL ASSETS	141	100%	161	100%
LIABILITIES & EQUITY				
Liabilities				
Current Liabilities				
Accounts Payable	7	5%	14	9%
Other Current Liabilities	5	3%	9	6%
Total Current Liabilities	12	8%	23	14%
Total Liabilities	12	8%	23	14%
Equity	129	92%	138	86%
TOTAL LIABILITIES & EQUITY	141	100%	161	100%

Chapter 2 Case Problem:
JENNINGS & ASSOCIATES

service

Kelly Jennings has just started working full-time in her new business—an advertising agency named Jennings & Associates located in San Martin, California. Like many eager entrepreneurs, she started her business while working full-time for another firm. At first, her billings were quite small. But as her client base and her billings grew, she decided to leave her job and set out on her own. Two of her colleagues and friends—Cheryl Boudreau and Diane Murphy—see Kelly's eagerness and dedication, and decide the time is right for them too. They ask Kelly if they can join her sole proprietorship as employees, and so together they leave the traditional corporate agency environment.

Kelly knows that one of the first tasks she must accomplish is to set up an accounting system for Jennings & Associates. Also, she has just received a request from her banker to submit a balance sheet as documentation for a business loan. As a close, personal friend, you recommend she use QuickBooks, and you volunteer to help her get started.

Kelly tells you that in 2007 she borrowed $5,000 to start the business. Now she is applying for a loan to help expand the business. She also reminds you that although she did conduct some business in 2007, her first full-time month was January 2008.

Prepare and print the following reports using Kelly Jennings.qbw (include your name in the Extra Footer line of each report where possible). (Remember, you'll need to restore this file from your Data Files CD.)

1 A standard balance sheet as of December 31, 2007.

2 A standard balance sheet as of January 31, 2008.

3 A Transactions List by Date report for the month of January 2008 in landscape orientation. (***Hint:*** This report is listed in the Report menu section labeled Accountant & Taxes.)

4 A summary balance sheet as of January 31, 2008, formatted in thousands and without cents, without the date prepared, time prepared, or report basis included.

5 A report of those transactions recorded in January 2008 that affected accounts payable. (***Hint:*** Create a summary balance sheet and double-click accounts payable.)

Preparing an Income Statement Using QuickBooks

3

- Change the way dates are formatted in QuickBooks
- Create income statements for different time periods
- Create an income statement with year-to-date comparative information
- Investigate the detail underlying income statement items
- Use the Income Statement Report button bars
- Print an income statement

Case: Century Kitchens

Now that Scott has created a balance sheet, he is ready to create an income statement for the period January 1, 2007, through March 31, 2007. You recall from your accounting course that the income statement reports revenues and expenses for a specific period.

Again, as part of your training with QuickBooks, Scott asks you to watch how he prepares the income statement. He expects to use many of the same functions and features to prepare an income statement that he used to prepare the balance sheet.

Date Formats

You mention to Scott that the default four-digit year format in QuickBooks (12/15/2007) seems a bit excessive, and perhaps they should return to the more standard date format (12/15/07).

Scott agrees and decides to show you the steps necessary to change the date preferences.

> **To change date preferences, open the Century Kitchens.qbw file, and then:**
>
> 1 Click **Edit,** then click **Preferences.**
>
> 2 Click the **General** icon on the left of the Preferences window, and then click the **Company Preferences** tab.

3 Uncheck the **Always show years as 4 digits (1999)** checkbox.

4 Click **OK** to save the changes, and close the Preferences window.

5 To restore the Company Navigator, click **Company** in the Open Windows list.

Scott explains that now dates in QuickBooks registers, report windows, etc., will be in the standard format of a two-digit year (12/15/07).

Creating an Income Statement

As with the Balance Sheet and other reports available in QuickBooks, the income statement can be presented in preset ways and can be customized. Scott decides to examine one of the preset income statement formats first—the format called Standard.

Before he does, he calls your attention to the fact that QuickBooks does not use the traditional name for this report. Instead of calling it the income statement, QuickBooks refers to this report as the "Profit and Loss" report. Scott prefers the name "income statement" because it is really the most accurate name for this report. And he says that although he cannot change the report title on the menu, he'll show you later how you can change the title on the report itself.

To create a standard income statement:

1 Open Century Kitchens.qbw.

2 Open the Reports Center, then click **Company & Financial** and then click Profit and Loss **Standard.** Change the From date to **3/1/07** and the To date to **3/31/07.** Then click **Refresh.** The report shown in Figure 3.1 should appear.

3 Scroll down the Century Kitchens income statement. This report summarizes revenues and expenses for this month-to-date. Notice that QuickBooks does not use the standard accounting term "revenue," but instead uses the term "income." Note that subtotals are included for revenues and expenses. Note also the period specified for this particular report is March 1–31, 2007, the period for this report period.

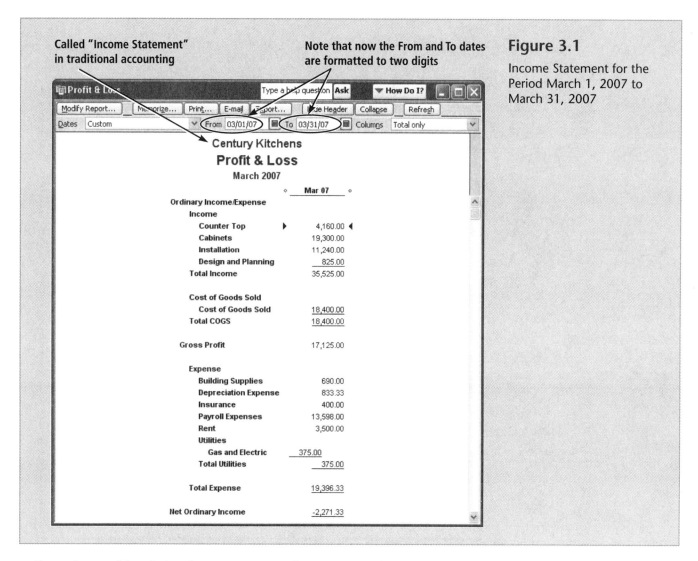

Called "Income Statement" in traditional accounting

Note that now the From and To dates are formatted to two digits

Figure 3.1

Income Statement for the Period March 1, 2007 to March 31, 2007

Scott changes his mind and wants a year-to-date statement for his preliminary income statement.

Modifying an Income Statement

Scott decides to revise the previously created income statement to make it a year-to-date income statement for the period January 1, 2007, through March 31, 2007. He also wants to show you how to change the report title from "Profit and Loss" to the more accurate "Income Statement." For this title change you will modify the header, a function you already learned how to perform with the balance sheet.

To revise the period of time and the report title:

1 Change the From date on the previously created income statement to **1/1/07.** Click **Refresh.** The revised report appears. See Figure 3.2.

Figure 3.2

The Revised Income Statement for the Period January 1 to March 31, 2007

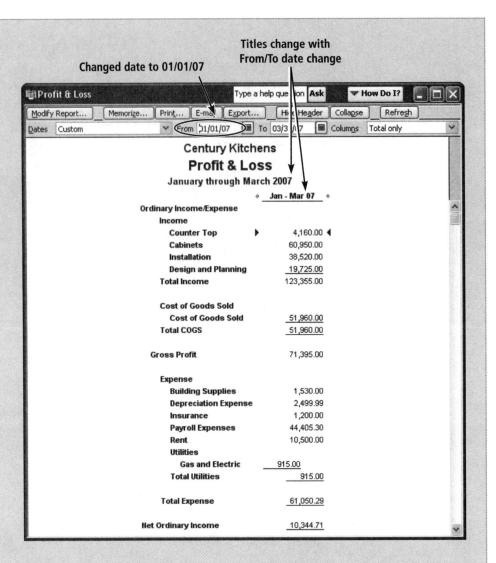

Changed date to 01/01/07

Titles change with From/To date change

2 To change the report title, click **Modify Report,** and then click **Header/Footer.** The Header/Footer tab appears. See Figure 3.3.

3 Move the cursor to the Report Title edit box and delete Profit and Loss. Type **Income Statement.** Also uncheck the **Date Prepared, Time Prepared,** and **Report Basis** checkboxes. (*Note:* To properly identify this report as yours, you may want to type your name in the Extra Footer Line of the Header/Footer tab.)

4 Click **OK** to view the revised report. See Figure 3.4.

5 When you have finished viewing the revised report, close this window.

6 This time, when the Memorize Report window appears, click **Yes** to memorize this report.

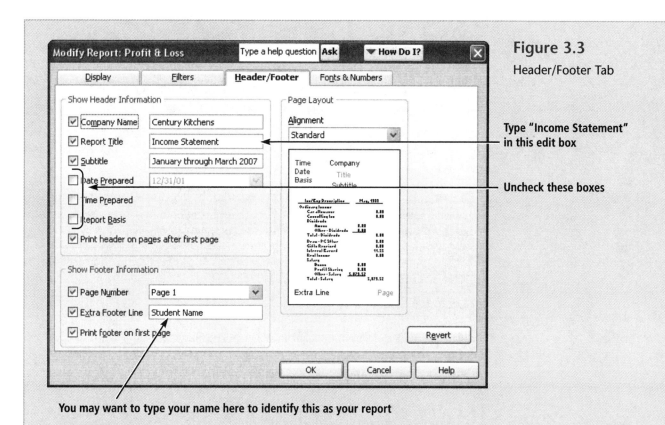

Figure 3.3

Header/Footer Tab

Type "Income Statement" in this edit box

Uncheck these boxes

You may want to type your name here to identify this as your report

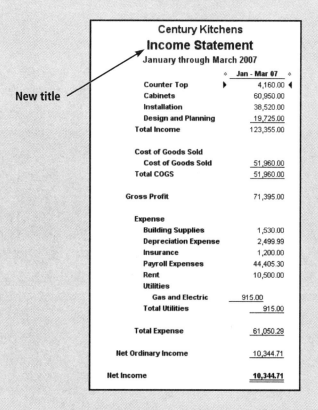

New title

Figure 3.4

Revised Income Statement with Corrected Title

7 Click **New** when asked if you want to replace the old standard income statement.

8 Save this report as Income Statement in the Memorized Report Group you created last chapter (Your Name!), and then click **OK.**

Once again Scott comments on how remarkably fast this process is compared to creating income statements manually. As with the balance sheet, he decides to create a comparison report—this time with the income statement.

Creating a Comparative Income Statement

QuickBooks has several features which allow you to create comparative reports as you saw with the balance sheet. Scott suggests that you help him create a comparative income statement illustrating the performance of Century Kitchens in March and February. You guess that the process will be very similar to how you prepared the comparative balance sheet. He also suggests changing the name and look of the statement as you've done previously.

To create a comparative income statement for March and February:

1 From the Reports Center, click **Company & Financial,** and then click **Standard** located under the title Profit & Loss (income statement).

2 Set the From date to **3/1/07** and the To date to **3/31/07,** and then click **Refresh.**

3 Click the **Modify Report. . .** button, and then check the **Previous Period, $ Change,** and **% Change** checkboxes located under the caption Add subcolumns for as shown in Figure 3.5.

4 Click the **Header/Footer** tab, and uncheck the **Date Prepared, Time Prepared,** and **Report Basis** checkboxes.

5 Change the name of the statement from Profit & Loss to **Comparative Income Statements,** align the statement **Right,** put your name in the Footer, and then click **OK** to see the revised report. See Figure 3.6.

6 Do not close this report, as it will be used in the next section.

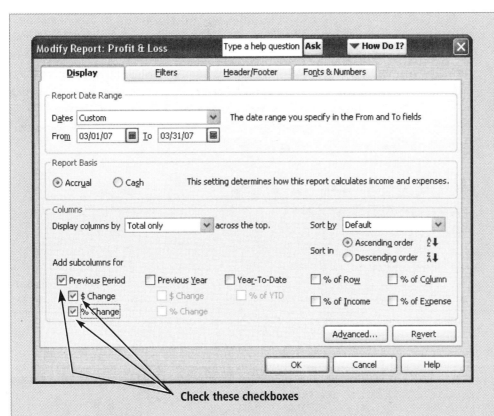

Figure 3.5

Creating a Previous Period for a Comparative Income Statement

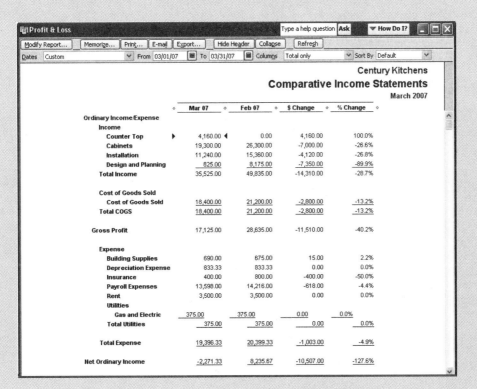

Figure 3.6

Comparative Income Statements for March and February 2007

Scott had been concerned about the company's performance in March and now he can see how things differed between March and February. His most immediate concern is the dropoff in design and planning revenues since he knows that will correlate to future reductions in revenues for cabinet and counter purchases and installations. Further, he sees that his expenses seem fairly consistent between periods, making his biggest concern the decrease in revenues. He is, however, a bit curious about payroll expenses and decides to use QuickBooks QuickZoom feature to investigate.

Using QuickZoom with the Income Statement

To investigate payroll expenses for March, Scott uses the QuickZoom feature of QuickBooks to examine the underlying source of various business events. He knows that he can "drill down" behind the income statement to view Transactions Detail By Account reports and further to a paycheck and then paycheck details. He explains that the paycheck in this example is referred to as a source document and will prove helpful in his analysis.

To use QuickZoom with an income statement:

1 Place the QuickZoom cursor over the March Payroll Expenses amount of 13,598.00, and then double-click that amount to reveal a Transactions Detail By Account report for March payroll expenses as shown in Figure 3.7.

Figure 3.7

Transactions Detail By Account Report for March Payroll Expenses

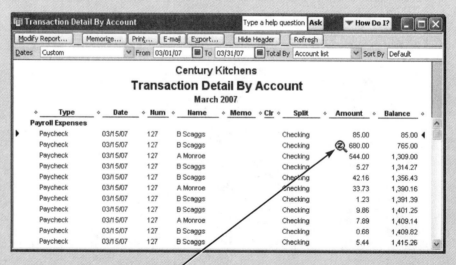

Double-click here to view detail

2 Double-click the **680.00** as shown in Figure 3.7 to reveal the paycheck that caused this particular payroll expense to be incurred. The resulting paycheck source document is shown in Figure 3.8.

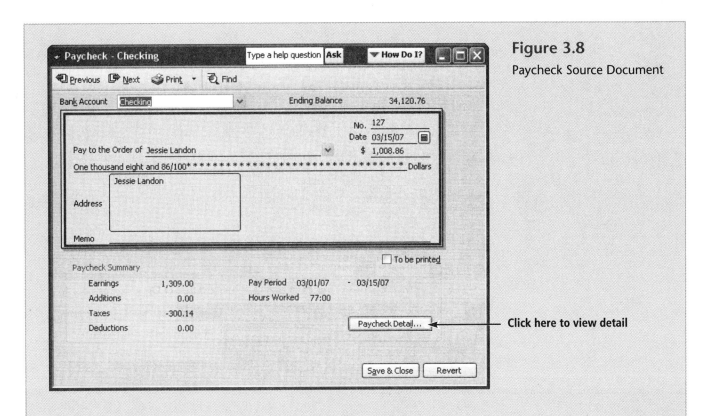

Figure 3.8
Paycheck Source Document

Click here to view detail

3 Click the **Paycheck Detail** button to reveal a Review Paycheck window as shown in Figure 3.9.

This transaction supports the $680 found on the detail report

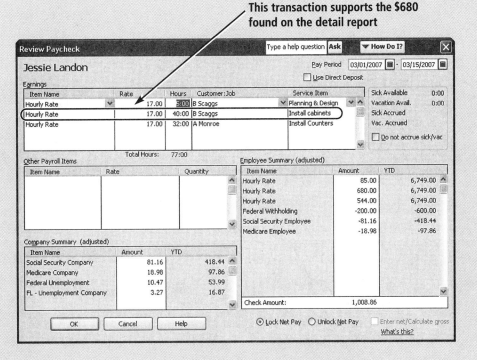

Figure 3.9
Review Paycheck Window

4   Note the second line of the earnings section, which shows that Jessie Landon worked 40 hours (at $17 per hour) for a total of $680.00 installing cabinets for our customer B Scaggs.

5   Close the Review Paycheck, Paycheck, and Transactions By Account windows. Do not memorize the Transactions By Account report.

6   Close your newly created Comparative Income Statements report, and memorize it in your Report Group.

You have now seen that the QuickZoom feature of QuickBooks is available with the income statement as well as with the balance sheet and that it provides background detail relating to revenues and expenses.

Modifying the Income Statement Report

The Income Statement report, like all other reports created in QuickBooks, can be modified using the Report button bar. Scott knows from experience that when he works with income statements in the future he will definitely need to add columns, change report dates, use different number formats, modify headings, and so on. So he decides to explore additional ways he can modify an income statement. He decides first to create a first-quarter income statement and add a percentage of net income column.

To add percentage of net income columns and to change the dates on an Income Statement report:

1   From the Reports Center, click **Company & Financial,** and then click **Standard** from the list of Profit and Loss Reports.

2   Click the **Modify Report** button on the Report button bar, and then select the **Display** tab if it is not already selected.

3   Click the **% of Income** checkbox in the Columns section to report monthly amounts as a percent of total income—actually a percent of total revenue. See Figure 3.10.

4   Click the **From** edit box, and change the date from your current system date to **1/1/07.**

5   Click the **To** edit box, and change the date from your current system date to **3/31/07.** See Figure 3.10. These two changes customize the report so it reports on the months of January through March only. (Alternatively, you can select the calendar icons and click the arrows and specific dates.)

6   Select the **Header/Footer** tab, and uncheck the **Date Prepared, Time Prepared,** and **Report Basis** checkboxes.

Change to these dates

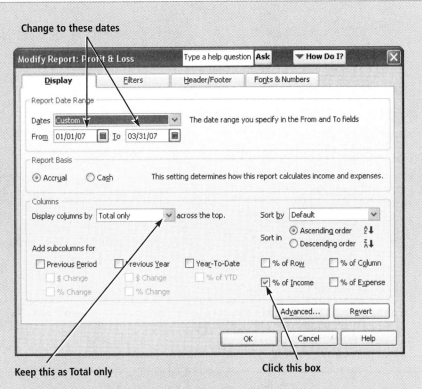

Figure 3.10

The Modify Report Window

Keep this as Total only

Click this box

7 Click **OK** to accept these changes. A revised report appears. See Figure 3.11. Do not close this report window.

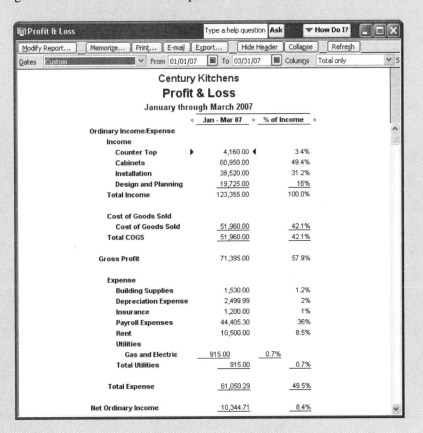

Figure 3.11

Quarterly Income Statement

Scott decides that he wants to report the numbers without cents and to collapse expenses.

To report the amounts without cents:

1 Click **Modify Report** on the Report button bar, and then click the **Font & Numbers** tab.

2 Click the **Without Cents** checkbox under the Show All Numbers section of the Format Report window. A check mark appears in the box.

3 Click **OK** to accept these changes.

4 Click the **Collapse** button or the **Report Button Bar** to view the revised quarterly Income Statement. See Figure 3.12.

Figure 3.12

Income Statement with Numbers Reported without Cents

Click on Collapse button which then changes to an Expand button

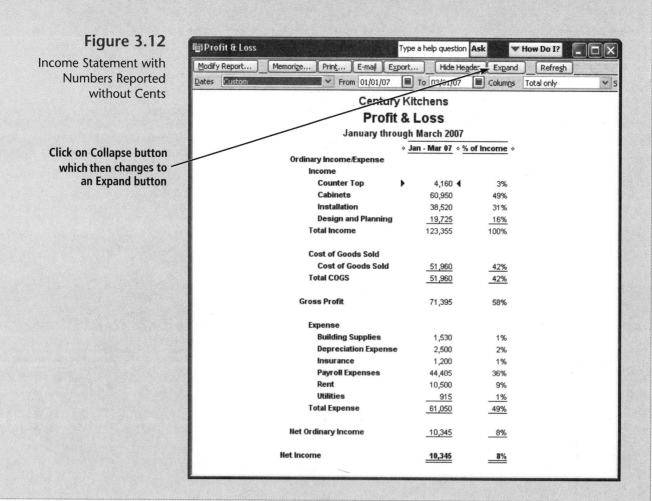

As Scott looks over the latest version of the income statement, he sees that again he must correct the report title. Also, he decides the title would look better if it appeared in the center of the report and if it included each separate month.

To modify the title and its layout:

1 Click **Modify Report,** on the Report button bar, and then click the **Header/Footer** tab.

2 Click inside the **Report Title** edit box, and change the name of the report from Profit and Loss to **Income Statement** as you have done before.

3 Change the title alignment by clicking the **Down Arrow** in the Page Layout section and changing the selection from Standard to **Center.**

4 Before you accept these changes, look at the Subtitle edit box. Notice that QuickBooks had changed the subtitle of this report. QuickBooks does this automatically for you whenever you change the dates in the To and From edit boxes. (***Note:*** Once again, you may want to type your name in the Extra Footer Line.)

5 Click **OK** to accept the changes. Change the Columns text box from Total Only to **Month.** The modified income statement appears. See Figure 3.13.

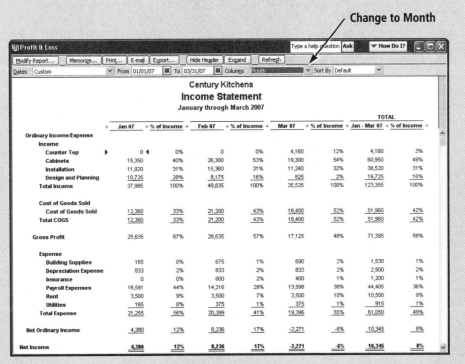

Change to Month

Figure 3.13

The Modified Income Statement

6 Do not close this report window.

QuickBooks provides many other ways to modify a report—-grouping and subtotaling data, sorting transactions, and specifying which columns appear in a report, to name just a few. Scott encourages you to explore these additional options when you generate reports in the future.

Printing the Income Statement

Scott would like to print this modified report so he can show some of the managers at Century Kitchens an example of the type of reports he can generate for them. He'd like this example to fit on one piece of 8 1/2" × 11" paper—both to save paper and to make analysis of the report easier. He decides to use QuickBooks's preview option to preview the report and see if it will fit onto one piece of paper.

To preview the modified income statement:

1 Click **Print** on the Report button bar.

2 Click **Preview** in the Print Reports window. A miniature reproduction of the report appears. See Figure 3.14. (Do not resize the columns.) The heading "Page 1 of 2" may appear at the top of the window. This indicates how many pages the report contains and which page you are previewing.

Figure 3.14

The Print Preview Window

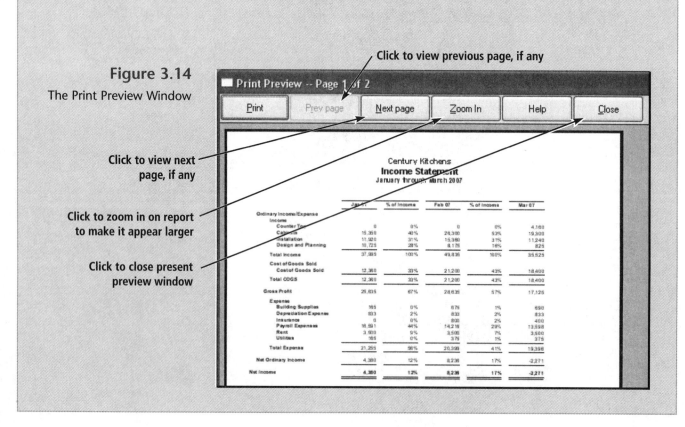

Click to view previous page, if any

Click to view next page, if any

Click to zoom in on report to make it appear larger

Click to close present preview window

Trouble? Your screen may indicate Page 1 of 1 depending on your computer and printer settings. If so, skip to Step 4, but continue reading so that you are familiar with the options that can help fit a long report on one page.

3 Notice the Next page and Prev page buttons below the window heading. The Prev page button is grayed out, which indicates that there is no previous page. But the Next page button is not grayed out. Click **Next page** to preview Page 2 of the report.

4 After previewing the statement, click the **Close** button on the button bar, and then click **Cancel** in the Print Reports window. The report reappears.

Scott has seen that the report is not much more than one page and so it might fit onto one page if he reduces the size of the type font.

To reduce the font size of the type in a report:

1 Click **Modify Report** on the Report button bar, then click the **Fonts & Numbers** tab. See Figure 3.15.

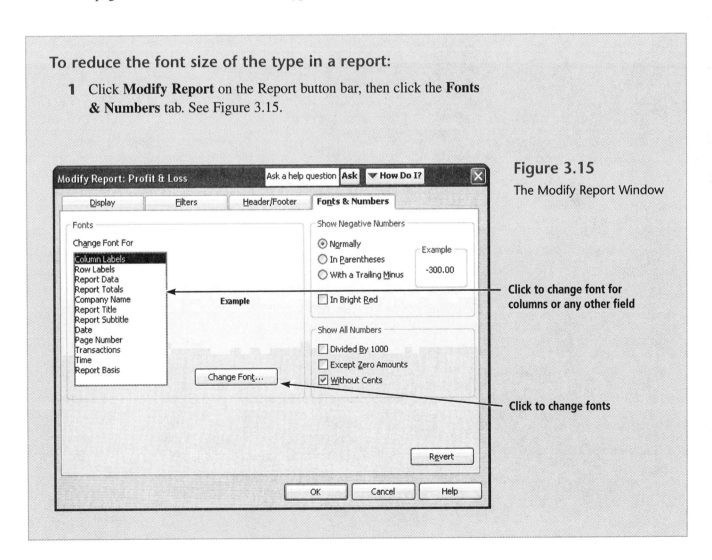

Figure 3.15
The Modify Report Window

Click to change font for columns or any other field

Click to change fonts

2 Click the **Change Font** button located in the bottom center of the window. The Column Labels window appears. See Figure 3.16.

3 Click the **Size** edit box. Delete 9 and type (or click on) **8** to reduce the font size by one. Then click the **Font** edit box, and choose **Arial Narrow**, if available, or choose another font that is small enough to accomplish your goal.

4 Click **OK** to accept this new size. A Changing Font window will appear asking if you want to make the change to all related fonts. Click **Yes**. Then click **OK** again. The revised report appears—now in Size 8 font.

Figure 3.16

The Column Labels Window

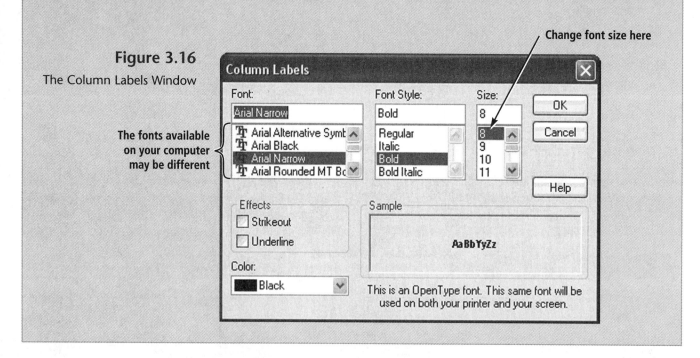

Scott hopes that this change will make the example report now fit on one page. To see if it worked, he again previews the report. If it fits on one page, he'll print it.

To preview the modified income statement again:

1 Click **Print** on the Report button bar.

2 Click **Preview.** The Print Preview window appears. Notice that the heading for this window may still include the words "Page 1 of 2." The change of font size has reduced the report size but not adequately to fit the report on one page.

3 Click **Close,** and then click **Cancel** in the Print Reports window.

Suddenly Scott realizes there might be another way to fit the report on one page. He decides to change the orientation of the page from portrait—a vertical orientation—which is the default setting, to landscape—a horizontal orientation.

To change a document from portrait to landscape orientation:

1 Click **Print** on the Report button bar to view the Print Reports window. See Figure 3.17.

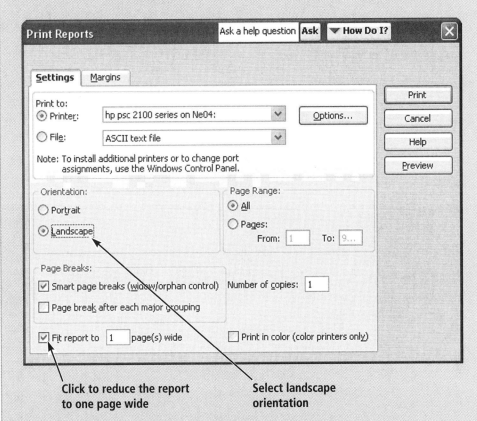

Figure 3.17
The Print Reports Window

Click to reduce the report to one page wide

Select landscape orientation

2 Click the **Landscape** button in the Orientation box.

3 Click **Fit report to 1 page(s) wide.**

4 Click **Preview** once again. The report should now fit on one page.

5 Click **Print** from the Print Preview window. Your completed report should look like Figure 3.18, as shown on the next page.

> ***Trouble?*** If your printer still prints this document on two pages consult with your lab personnel. Different printers may result in different output.

6 Close all windows, and exit QuickBooks as you have done before. Do not memorize this report.

Figure 3.18 Modified Income Statement on One Page

Century Kitchens
Income Statement
January through March 2007

	Jan 07	% of Income	Feb 07	% of Income	Mar 07	% of Income	TOTAL Jan - Mar 07	% of Income
Ordinary Income/Expense								
Income								
Counter Top	0	0%	0	0%	4,160	12%	4,160	3%
Cabinets	15,350	40%	26,300	53%	19,300	54%	60,950	49%
Installation	11,920	31%	15,360	31%	11,240	32%	38,520	31%
Design and Planning	10,725	28%	8,175	16%	825	2%	19,725	16%
Total Income	37,995	100%	49,835	100%	35,525	100%	123,355	100%
Cost of Goods Sold								
Cost of Goods Sold	12,360	33%	21,200	43%	18,400	52%	51,960	42%
Total COGS	12,360	33%	21,200	43%	18,400	52%	51,960	42%
Gross Profit	25,635	67%	28,635	57%	17,125	48%	71,395	58%
Expense								
Building Supplies	165	0%	675	1%	690	2%	1,530	1%
Depreciation Expense	833	2%	833	2%	833	2%	2,500	2%
Insurance	0	0%	800	2%	400	1%	1,200	1%
Payroll Expenses	16,591	44%	14,216	29%	13,598	38%	44,405	36%
Rent	3,500	9%	3,500	7%	3,500	10%	10,500	9%
Utilities	165	0%	375	1%	375	1%	915	1%
Total Expense	21,255	56%	20,399	41%	19,396	55%	61,050	49%
Net Ordinary Income	4,380	12%	8,236	17%	-2,271	-6%	10,345	8%
Net Income	**4,380**	**12%**	**8,236**	**17%**	**-2,271**	**-6%**	**10,345**	**8%**

Now that you have completed Chapters 2 and 3, you see how easily QuickBooks creates the two financial reports most commonly used to communicate accounting information to external users—the balance sheet and the income statement. In Chapter 4, you will continue your quick overview of QuickBooks by creating a statement of cash flows.

Chapter 3 Questions

1 List at least three of the preset formats QuickBooks provides for an income statement.

2 Identify the different periods of time that QuickBooks provides for an income statement.

3 Describe the steps necessary to create an income statement for a period other than one ending with the current system date of the computer.

4 Describe the steps necessary to generate an income statement in QuickBooks.

5 Describe the steps necessary to reformat the columns of a comparative income statement.

6 Describe the steps necessary to modify an income statement to include comparative information.

7 How does QuickZoom help you further investigate an income statement?

8 How could a manager use QuickZoom to access underlying information as reported in an income statement?

9 List five report modification features that QuickBooks provides with an income statement.

10 How would you modify an income statement to include a column describing the percentage relationship between expenses and total revenues?

Chapter 3 Assignments

merchandising

1 *Preparing an Income Statement for Century Kitchens*

Scott has asked you to help him prepare a new income statement. Include your name in the Extra Footer Line of all reports printed.

a. First he asks you to prepare and print a modified income statement that includes operating information for February 2007. He wants the income statement to include amounts (without cents) and columns reflecting the dollar change and percentage change between periods. (**Hint:** Set the dates to reflect February only, and be sure the Previous Period box, $ Change, and % Change boxes are also checked in the Modify Report window.) He asks you to change the title to "Comparative Income Statements." Finally, he wants you to format the page layout to the left, collapsed, without a reference to the date prepared, time prepared, or report basis, and printed in a portrait orientation.

b. Next, Scott asks you to prepare and print a standard income statement for Century Kitchens for the month of January 2007 in a format different from what you used in *a* above.

2 *Investigating the Century Kitchens Income Statement Using QuickZoom*

Scott asks you to help him investigate the $675.00 Building Supplies Expense balance shown on a standard income statement created for the month of February 2007. Investigate the $675 of Building Supplies expense. ***Trouble?*** Remember to change the From/To dates on the income statement to reflect the fiscal year-to-date amounts. Examine the check used to pay this expense.

a. Which vendor provided the building supplies?

b. What check number was used to pay this expense?

3 *Using the South-Western Home Page for More Assignments or Cases*

Go to the home page for this textbook at **www.thomsonedu.com/accounting/ owen.** Click **Additional Problem Sets,** and then select the **Chapter 3** section, and complete the problem(s) that your instructor assigns.

4 *Modifying an Income Statement*

Modify the income statement created in Chapter Assignment 1 as follows. Include your name in the Extra Footer Line of all reports printed. Change the To/From dates to include amounts from just March 2007. Change the columns to no longer reflect comparative information. Change the columns to include year-to-date amounts and year-to-date percentages. *Hint:* Customize the report by checking the Year-to-Date and % of YTD boxes found in the Display section of the Modify Reports window. Print this customized income statement.

Chapter 3 Case Problem:
JENNINGS & ASSOCIATES

service

As you learned in Chapter 2, Kelly Jennings prepared a balance sheet to submit to her banker with her application for a business loan. When she delivered the balance sheet to the banker, he told her that he also needed information about her operations. In other words, her banker needed an income statement.

Kelly asks you to help her prepare and print three versions of the income statement, one of which she will include with her application. She gives you a QuickBooks file named Kelly Jennings.qbw. Include your name in the Extra Footer Line of all reports printed.

1   Prepare a standard income statement for the month of January 2008.

2   Prepare a standard income statement for the month of January 2008 without cents, formatted with a left layout, and with the title "Income Statement."

3   Modify the income statement you prepared for 2 above by adding a % of Income column.

Preparing a Statement of Cash Flows Using QuickBooks

4 chapter

Learning Objectives

In this chapter, you will:

- Create and customize a statement of cash flows for a specified period
- Investigate the detail underlying statement of cash flow items
- Format and print a statement of cash flows

Case: Century Kitchens

One of the main financial statements used by businesses is the statement of cash flows. Your previous experience with this statement has not always been good so the thought of the computer preparing this one for you is quite enticing. You recall that this statement reports cash flow from operating, investing, and financing activities for a specific period.

Once again, as a part of your training with QuickBooks, Scott asks you to work with him as he prepares a statement of cash flows for the period January 1, 2007, through March 31, 2007.

Creating a Statement of Cash Flows

Unlike both the balance sheet and income statement, the statement of cash flows in QuickBooks is presented in only one format, although it can be modified after it is created. There is another report for cash flows, called Forecast, which creates a forecast of future cash flows based on the current period's cash flow and is not addressed in this text. Scott decides to create the statement of cash flows and modify it later.

To create a statement of cash flows:

1   Open Century Kitchens.qbw.

2   From the Reports Center, click **Company & Financial,** and then click **Statement of Cash Flows.** *Remember,* this is not clicking the

Reports menu item, it's clicking Company & Financial from the Reports Center.

3 Scroll down this report as shown in Figure 4.1 and notice the three sections: operating activities, investing activities, and financing activities. Notice at the bottom of the statement the net cash increase for the period is reported. It is then added to the cash at the beginning of the period to yield cash at the end of the period.

Make sure you've changed the From and To dates

Click here to modify the layout of the statement of cash flows

Figure 4.1

Statement of Cash Flows for the Period January 1, 2007, through March 31, 2007

| Statement of Cash Flows | Type a help question | Ask | How Do I? |

| Modify Report... | Memorize... | Print... | E-mail | Export... | Hide Header | Refresh | Classify Cash... |

Dates Custom   From 01/01/07 To 03/31/07

Century Kitchens
Statement of Cash Flows
January through March 2007

	Jan - Mar 07
OPERATING ACTIVITIES	
Net Income	10,344.71
Adjustments to reconcile Net Income	
to net cash provided by operations:	
Accounts Receivable	-75,995.00
Prepaid Insurance	-3,600.00
Inventory Asset	-11,795.00
Accounts Payable	27,270.00
Payroll Liabilities	13,396.06
Net cash provided by Operating Activities	-40,379.23
INVESTING ACTIVITIES	
Equipment:Original Cost	-50,000.00
Equipment:Depreciation	2,499.99
Net cash provided by Investing Activities	-47,500.01
FINANCING ACTIVITIES	
Capital Stock	125,000.00
Net cash provided by Financing Activities	125,000.00
Net cash increase for period	37,120.76
Cash at end of period	37,120.76

Note current location of changes in accumulated depreciation

In your examination of the Statement of Cash Flows, you notice in the operating activities section that several adjustments are made to reconcile net income to net cash provided by operations. Scott points out that one of the more common adjustments should be depreciation expense, since it reduces income but does not use cash. However, depreciation is not shown in this reconciliation. Instead, Scott finds that changes in accumulated depreciation (which, of course, usually result from depreciation expense) are shown in the investing activities section of the statement.

"We need to modify this statement's layout to properly reflect changes in accumulated depreciation as adjustments to net income in the operating activities section, not as line items in the investing activities section," he says. To do this, he uses the Classify Cash button on the Statement of Cash Flows window.

To modify the layout of the statement of cash flows:

1 Click **Classify Cash** to open the Preferences window with the Reports and Graphs icon selected and the **Company Preferences** tab selected as shown in Figure 4.2.

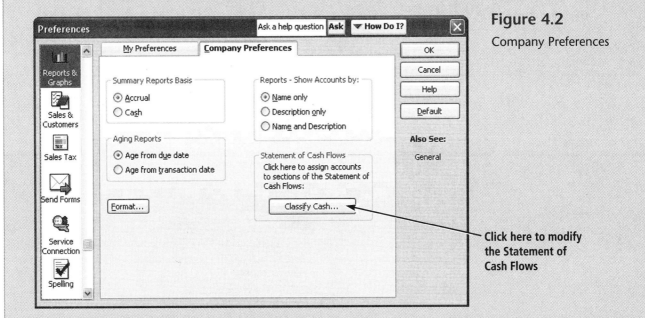

Figure 4.2
Company Preferences

Click here to modify the Statement of Cash Flows

2 Click **Classify Cash** in the Preferences window to view the Classify Cash window as shown in Figure 4.3.

3 Click in the Operating column next to **Equipment: Depreciation** to move the change in depreciation from an investing activity to an operating activity as shown in Figure 4.3.

Trouble? If you accidentally click in the wrong column, simply click the correct column for the item you accidentally reclassified.

4 Click **OK** in the Preferences window to close it. A Report needs to be refreshed window may appear indicating that the changes you made require refreshing of the report. Click **Yes** to refresh the report. Note how the report has been adjusted to reflect changes in depreciation (depreciation expense) as an adjustment to operating activities and not an investing activity. See Figure 4.4.

Figure 4.3

Classify Cash Window for Modifying the Statement of Cash Flows Layout

Click here to reclassify changes in accumulated depreciation to Operating Activities

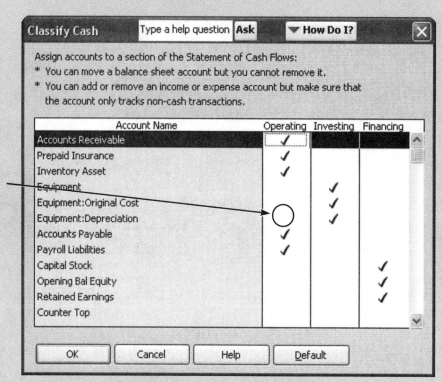

Figure 4.4

Statement of Cash Flows after Changes in Types of Accounts

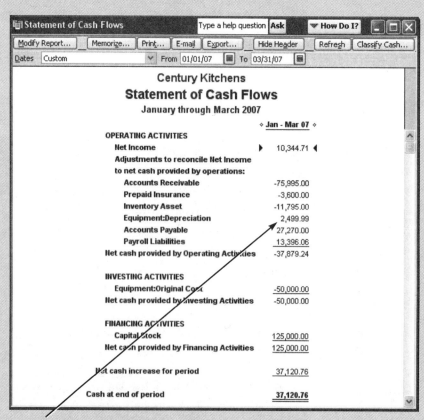

Note change in location of Depreciation

"How about modifying the Statement of Cash Flows to reflect comparative amounts like prior years? Isn't there a previous year comparative report available like we saw for the income statement?" you ask.

"Well, no." Scott explains. "Not only is there no present comparative report in QuickBooks, but there is no way to modify the report to show percentage changes or year-to-date amounts like we can do for the income statement. Maybe in the next version."

Using QuickZoom with the Statement of Cash Flows

You then ask about the QuickZoom feature you found so helpful in examining information on the income statement. Scott responds with a big smile. "Let's check it out!"

To use QuickZoom with the statement of cash flows:

1 Double-click the **27,270.00** amount on the report reflecting changes in Accounts Payable to open a Transactions Detail by Account window as shown in Figure 4.5.

Figure 4.5

Transaction Detail for Accounts Payable in the Statement of Cash Flows

2 Double-click the **Kraft Maid** bill dated 1/16/07 as shown in Figure 4.5.

3 Close both the bill and the Transaction Detail by Account window. Do not memorize the Transaction Detail by Account window.

4 Do not close the revised Statement of Cash Flows.

You have now seen that the QuickZoom feature works for the balance sheet, income statement, and statement of cash flows. However, the QuickZoom feature in the statement of cash flows does not necessarily provide much help. In the case above, the accounts payable amount in the statement of cash flows reflects the changes in accounts payable, an increase in this case, which needs to be added to net income to reconcile to cash provided by operating activities. Thus, it is the change, in this case an increase, which is being analyzed, not the underlying transactions.

Formatting and Printing the Statement of Cash Flows

Scott would like to print this statement of cash flows in a format without cents.

To modify and print the statement of cash flows:

1 Click **Modify Report** on the report button bar, and then click the **Fonts & Numbers** tab.

2 Click in the **Without Cents** checkbox, and then click **OK** to close the window.

3 Click **Print** on the report button bar to reveal the Print Reports window.

4 Click **Print** in the Print Reports window to print the report.

5 Close all remaining windows. Memorize the revised Statement of Cash Flows Report in your report group.

You've now seen how all three of the key financial statements, the balance sheet, income statement, and statement of cash flows, can be easily created, modified, and printed from within QuickBooks. In Chapter 5, you will complete your overview of QuickBooks by creating supporting reports for accounts receivable, inventory, and accounts payable.

Chapter 4 Questions

1 List the reports available for reporting cash flows.

2 Describe the steps necessary to create a statement of cash flows.

3 What additional steps are necessary to create a statement of cash flows for a period other than one ending with the current system date of the computer?

4 Identify three different periods of time that QuickBooks provides for a statement of cash flows.

5 List the three sections of the statement of cash flows.

6 Describe the statement of cash flow operating section created by QuickBooks.

7 Describe the one adjustment necessary to reconcile net income to cash provided by operations that was not initially a part of the Century Kitchens statement of cash flows until you made some changes in the reports layout.

8 Describe the steps necessary to make changes in the statement of cash flows report layout to properly reflect the adjustments necessary to reconcile net income to cash provided by operations.

9 Describe how the QuickZoom feature of QuickBooks does or does not provide the same help in the statement of cash flows as it does in the income statement.

10 Describe the steps necessary to format and print a statement of cash flows different from the software provided Statement of Cash Flows header.

Chapter 4 Assignments

1 *Preparing a Statement of Cash Flows for Century Kitchens*

Scott has asked you to prepare and print a customized statement of cash flows for the month of January 2007. He wants the statement to include amounts (without cents), with a left page layout. *Hint:* Be sure accumulated depreciation is classified correctly. Include your name in the Extra Footer Line of all reports printed.

merchandising

2 *Using the South-Western Home Page for More Assignments or Cases*

Go to the home page for this textbook at **www.thomsonedu.com/accounting/ owen.** Click **Additional Problem Sets,** and then select the **Chapter 4** section, and complete the problem(s) your instructor assigns.

service

Chapter 4 Case Problem:
JENNINGS & ASSOCIATES

Continuing your work from Chapter 3, Kelly has asked you to prepare two versions of the statement of cash flows, one of which she will include with her application. Open the Kelly Jennings.qbw file. Include your name in the Extra Footer Line of all reports printed.

1 Prepare a statement of cash flows for the period 1/1/08 to 1/31/08. ***Hint:*** Be sure accumulated depreciation accounts are properly classified.

2 Prepare a statement of cash flows for the same period, 1/1/08 to 1/31/08, but without cents and with a right page layout.

Creating Supporting Reports to Help Make Business Decisions

Learning Objectives

In this chapter, you will:

- Create, print, and analyze an Accounts Receivable Aging report
- Create and print a Customer Account Balance Summary
- Create, print, and analyze an Inventory Valuation Summary
- Create, print, and analyze an Accounts Payable Aging report
- Create and print a Vendor Balance Summary

Case: **Century Kitchens**

You arrive at work, and two phones are ringing. As Scott hangs up from one call and is about to answer another, he quickly explains what's happening—he's thinking about expanding the business and needs to borrow from the bank, and they are requesting up-to-the-minute information. You quickly answer a phone and write down the banker's request for some information on inventory. As you hang up from the call, Scott asks you to come into his office. You compare notes—he has requests for information on accounts receivable and accounts payable. You show him your note requesting information on Century Kitchen's inventory.

Scott has shown you that QuickBooks can easily generate transaction reports, but you can see that the banker's requests require more detailed information. You remember from your accounting course that accountants frequently use what are called supporting schedules—reports that provide the underlying details of an account. You ask Scott if QuickBooks can help. He smiles and says, "You bet. QuickBooks calls these schedules 'reports,' but they are the same thing. Let's get to work."

Creating and Printing an Accounts Receivable Aging Report

You know from your accounting course that accounts receivable represent amounts due from customers for goods or services they have received but for which they have not yet paid. QuickBooks provides several preset accounts receivable reports that anticipate the information managers most often need.

The banker wants information on a particular customer's past due account balance, and she wants to know the total amount due from customers as of today.

Scott tells you that the best way to get information on past due accounts is to create a schedule that QuickBooks calls an "Accounts Receivable Aging report"—but what you learned in your accounting course is usually called an "accounts receivable aging schedule." You remember that an aging schedule is a listing of how long each receivable has been uncollected.

To create an Accounts Receivable Aging report:

1 Open Century Kitchens.qbw.

2 From the Reports Center, click **Customers & Receivables,** and then click **Summary** under the title A/R Aging.

3 Change the report date to **3/31/07,** and click **Refresh** to see the company A/R Aging summary, as shown in Figure 5.1.

Figure 5.1

A/R Aging Summary
as of 3/31/07

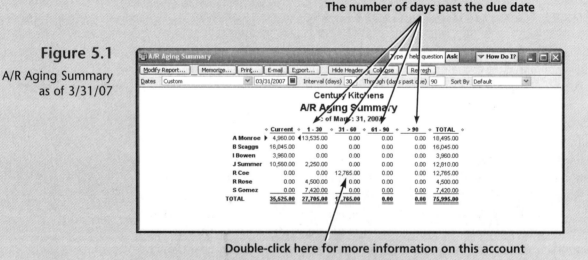

You can see that this report gives Scott an up-to-date listing of customers and their balances. It tells him how long each receivable has been uncollected so he can take appropriate action.

You ask Scott the name of the customer about whom the banker requested information. He says the customer's name is R Coe and that the banker wants to know the status of his account and his payment history. He says that, as you have done with other reports, you can use QuickZoom to gather this information.

To investigate a particular receivable on an Accounts Receivable Aging report:

1 Double-click the **12,765.00** balance owed by R Coe.

2 An A/R Aging QuickZoom report appears. See Figure 5.2. This report indicates that Invoice 1005, dated 1/31/07, was due 2/15/07 and is presently 44 days late.

QuickZoom report title

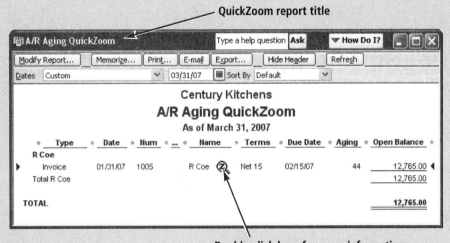

Double-click here for more information
on this invoice

Figure 5.2

A/R Aging
QuickZoom Report

3 Double-click this invoice to investigate further. Invoice 1005 appears. See Figure 5.3. Invoice 1005 describes the items purchased and installation fees charged.

4 Click the **Down Arrow** in the invoice's scroll box to view more of the invoice. Notice that the balance due—12,765.00—matches the receivable balance you are investigating. But notice also that Invoice 1005 totals 15,240.00. How can that be?

5 Click the **History** button on the top of the window to help you investigate this difference. The transaction history of this invoice appears. See Figure 5.4. Notice that a payment of 2,475.00 was applied to this invoice on 3/31/07. Let's investigate further.

6 Be sure that the 2,475 payment is highlighted. Then click **Go To** to examine the payment in more detail. The Receive Payments window appears. See Figure 5.5. Notice that a $3,000.00 check was received from R Coe on 3/31/07. Of this payment, $525.00 was applied to pay off Invoice 1002. The balance of the $3,000.00—2,475.00—was applied to Invoice 1005. This explains why the balance due and the invoice amount were different.

7 Close all open windows without memorizing any reports.

Figure 5.3

Invoice 1005

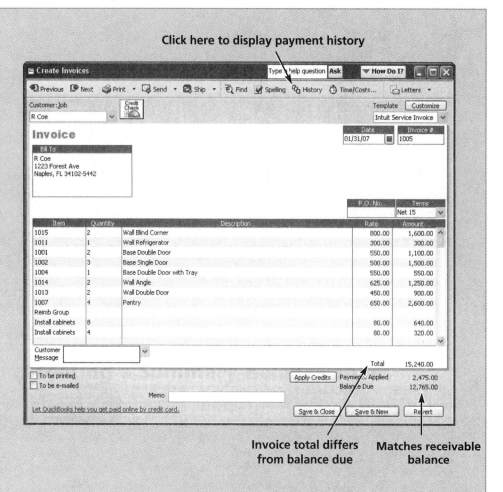

Click here to display payment history

Invoice total differs from balance due

Matches receivable balance

Figure 5.4

Invoice 1005
Transaction History

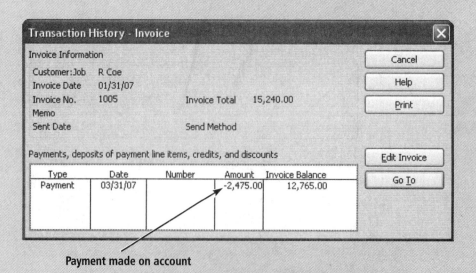

Payment made on account

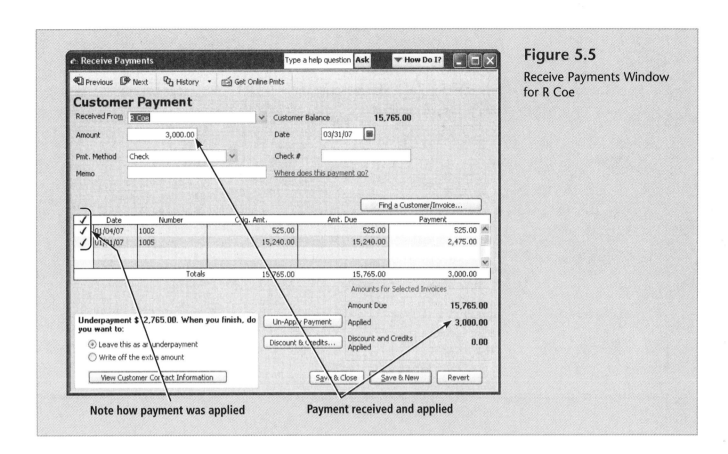

Figure 5.5

Receive Payments Window for R Coe

Note how payment was applied

Payment received and applied

Scott has copied down the information the banker requested—R Coe is 44 days past due on Invoice 1005, he owes $12,765.00 on that invoice, and Invoice 1002 was paid off on 3/31/07. He is now ready to fulfill the banker's other request.

Creating and Printing a Customer Balance Summary

Scott says that the banker's request for the total amount due from customers as of today is easy to fulfill because QuickBooks has a built-in feature that prepares a customer balance summary. He can provide the banker this information with only a few clicks of the mouse.

To create a Customer Balance Summary:

1 From the Reports Center, click **Customers & Receivables** and then click **Summary** located under the Customer Balance title. See Figure 5.6.

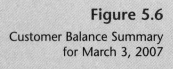

Figure 5.6

Customer Balance Summary
for March 3, 2007

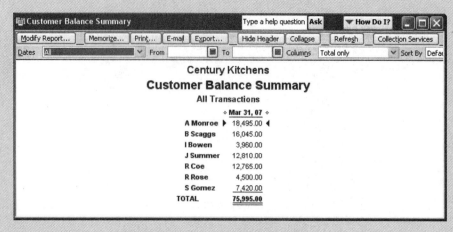

2 Notice that this is exactly the information the banker has requested—
a list of the total amounts each customer owes Century Kitchens as
of March 31, 2007. When you have finished viewing this report,
close this window.

Scott prints this report for the banker and asks you to fax it. He's ready to handle
the second request.

Creating and Printing an Inventory Valuation Summary Report

Scott asks you about the request you took over the phone. You show him your
notes; you spoke to Kim Hui, one of the company's investors. He stopped by the
other day and noticed a lot of cabinet inventory in the shop and wondered why we
had so much.

Scott explains that in his business he never places a purchase order to a cabinet
or counter top manufacturer unless it's been signed off by a customer. "We hold
the inventory until we can schedule it for installation. Once installed, we then bill
the customer and the inventory becomes cost of goods sold."

He suggests that you use QuickBooks to show, via an Inventory Valuation
Summary report, just exactly what inventory you have and which customer it is to
be billed to.

To create an Inventory Valuation Summary:

1 From the Reports Center, click **Inventory,** and then click **Summary**
located under the Inventory Valuation title. Set the report date to
3/31/07. The Inventory Valuation Summary appears. See Figure 5.7.
Resize the columns as necessary to view this report.

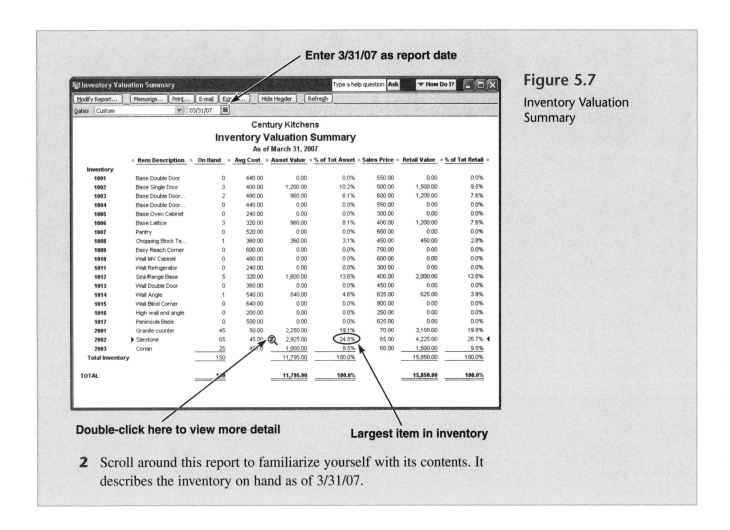

Figure 5.7

Inventory Valuation Summary

2 Scroll around this report to familiarize yourself with its contents. It describes the inventory on hand as of 3/31/07.

Scott decides to investigate the largest dollar value cost item in inventory to see which customer it belongs to.

To view the underlying documentation of the Inventory Valuation Summary:

1 Double-click on item **#2002 Silestone** representing 24.8% of the cost of inventory on hand. An Inventory Valuation Detail appears. By default, this report shows activity for just 3/31/07. But Scott wants to know the *total* inventory on hand and to see activity for the quarter. To find this information, you need to change the From date to 1/1/07.

2 Type **1/1/07** in the box, then click **Refresh.** A new report appears. See Figure 5.8.

Figure 5.8

Inventory Valuation Detail from January 1 through March 31, 2007

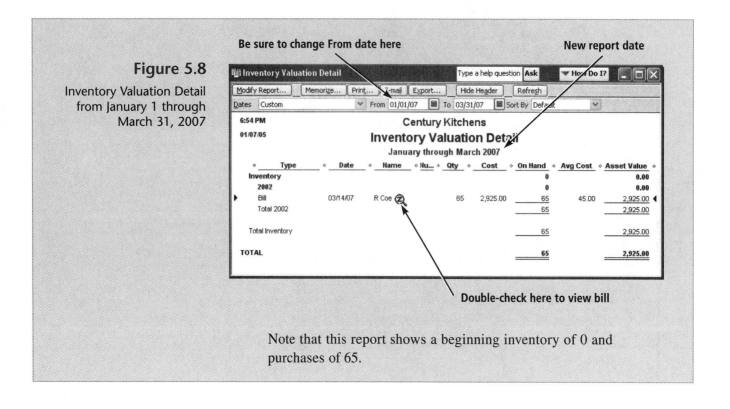

Be sure to change From date here

New report date

Double-check here to view bill

Note that this report shows a beginning inventory of 0 and purchases of 65.

You ask Scott if QuickZoom lets you view the actual invoices. "Sure does," he says. "Let's look at one."

To view an actual bill:

1 Double-click anywhere in the row containing information on the bill for this item. The bill appears as shown in Figure 5.9 on the following page. Adjust your window size or scroll as necessary to view the entire invoice.

2 After you examine this bill, close all open windows. Do not memorize any reports.

Scott retrieves the Inventory Valuation Summary and prints it for Kim. He notes that this item was purchased for customer R Coe, who has a fairly large past due account. He makes a note to contact Mr. Coe and find out what is going on. He asks you to mail this report to Kim when you have a chance. He's now ready to fulfill the last request.

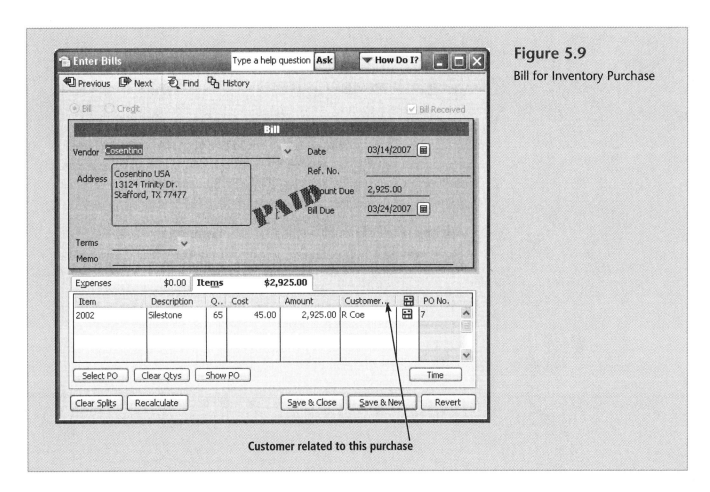

Figure 5.9

Bill for Inventory Purchase

Customer related to this purchase

Creating, Printing, and Analyzing an Accounts Payable Aging Report

The last request to which you and Scott need to respond is from Juan Gomez, who handles all inventory purchase orders, pays bills, and monitors accounts payable. He wants two reports so he can plan next month's cash flow.

You quickly ask if QuickBooks handles accounts payable aging the same way it handles accounts receivable aging. Scott smiles. "You catch on fast," he says. "Let's start with an Accounts Payable Aging report. It provides the detail Juan needs. Then we'll print him a Vendor Balance Summary."

To create an Accounts Payable Aging report:

1 From the Reports Center, click **Vendors & Payables,** and then click **Summary** under the title A/P Aging. Change the report date to **3/31/07.** The A/P Aging Summary report appears. See Figure 5.10.

2 Scroll through the A/P Aging Summary. If necessary, change the column widths so the entire report displays on your screen.

Figure 5.10

Accounts Payable
Aging Summary

As of 3/31/07

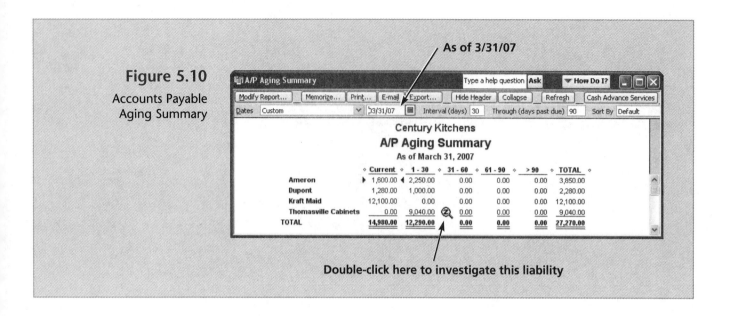

Double-click here to investigate this liability

After Scott prints this report for Juan, you look it over. You notice a large outstanding balance 1–30 days past due to Thomasville Cabinets, and you suggest using QuickZoom to investigate it further. Scott and you both decide to investigate this liability to whom Century Kitchens owes $9,040.00.

To analyze the Thomasville Cabinets liability:

1 Double-click the Thomasville Cabinets liability balance of **9,040.00.** An A/P Aging report appears. See Figure 5.11.

Figure 5.11

A/P Aging QuickZoom
Report for Thomasville
Cabinets

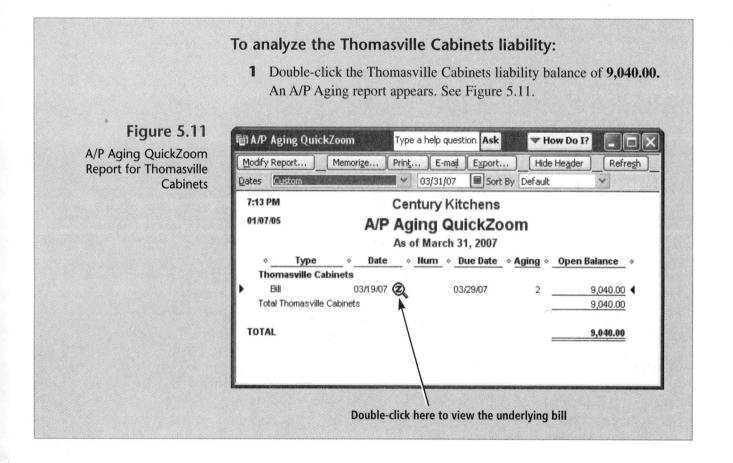

Double-click here to view the underlying bill

2 Double-click anywhere in the entry for the bill dated **3/19/07.** The details of this bill appear. See Figure 5.12. Notice that this bill documents cabinet costs incurred in the B Scaggs kitchen remodeling job.

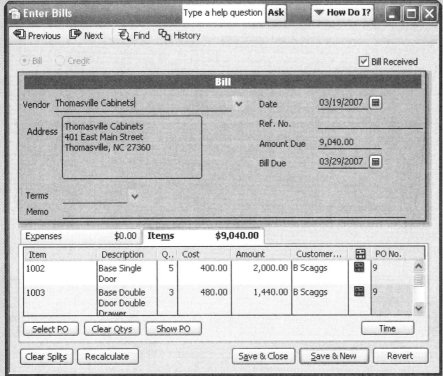

Figure 5.12

Thomasville Cabinets Bill

3 When you have finished viewing this bill, close all open windows. Do not memorize any reports.

Creating and Printing a Vendor Balance Summary

The final supporting report for Juan is a Vendor Balance Summary. This report is also a preset report available from the QuickBooks Reports menu. It will summarize for Juan all of the unpaid balances due to vendors and will be valuable information for his cash planning.

To create and print a Vendor Balance Summary:

1 From the Reports Center, click **Vendors & Payables,** and then **Vendor Balance Summary.** Change the report To date to **3/31/07** and the From date to **1/1/07.** The Vendor Balance Summary appears. See Figure 5.13. Notice that the vendors are listed alphabetically.

Figure 5.13

Vendor Balance Summary
as of 3/31/07

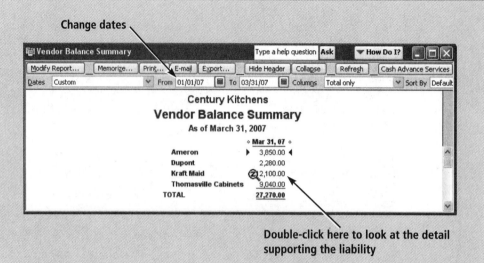

2 To investigate, Scott suggests you look further into the Kraft Maid balance. Double-click the **12,100.00** balance to reveal a Vendor Balance Detail report shown in Figure 5.14.

Figure 5.14

Vendor Balance
Detail Report

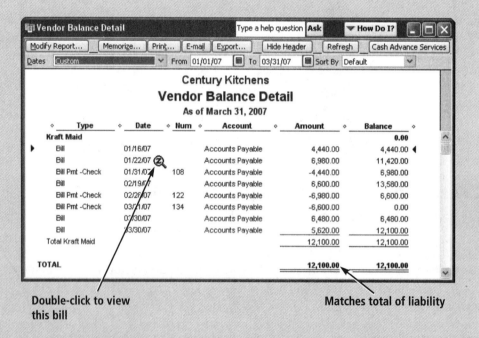

3 Double-click the **1/22/07** bill for 6,980.00 to reveal the paid bill as shown in Figure 5.15.

4 Click the **Show PO** button to view the purchase order Century Kitchens generated to order these cabinets. See Figure 5.16.

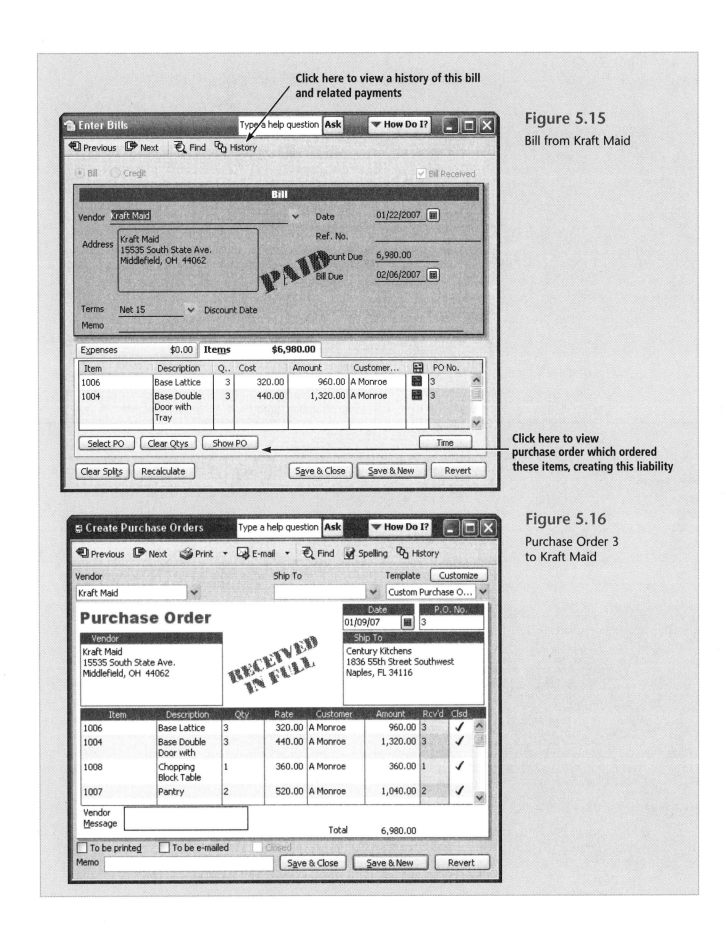

Click here to view a history of this bill and related payments

Figure 5.15

Bill from Kraft Maid

Click here to view purchase order which ordered these items, creating this liability

Figure 5.16

Purchase Order 3 to Kraft Maid

5 Close the purchase order, and then click the **History** button to reveal the bill's history. See Figure 5.17.

Figure 5.17

Transaction History of
Kraft Maid Bill

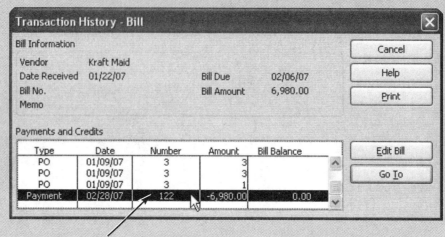

Double-click here to view the check

6 Scroll down the history listing, and then double-click the payment reference to view the related check used to pay this bill. See Figure 5.18, Bill Payment (Check #122).

7 When you finish viewing this report, close all windows, and do not memorize any reports.

Figure 5.18

Bill Payment (Check #122)

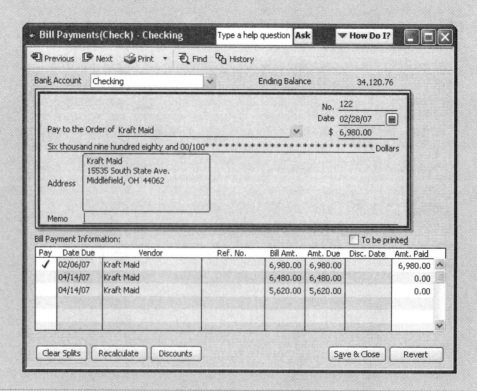

Scott prints the Vendor Balance Summary for Juan, and looks at you. "Yes, I'll deliver this one too," you volunteer good naturedly.

End Note

As you gather the reports and set out to deliver them, you are struck by how easily and quickly Scott has been able to respond to the managers' requests. Within a short time, QuickBooks has generated accurate, up-to-the-minute financial information to help Scott and his staff make important business decisions. The many preset reports—summaries, details, and supporting documentation—anticipate the information that owners often need to make sound business decisions.

Chapter 5 Questions

1 Which menu in QuickBooks provides you access to supporting reports?

2 What information does an Accounts Receivable Aging report provide?

3 What types of transactions might appear in a QuickZoom report created from an Accounts Receivable Aging report? Give two examples.

4 How might the payment history of an account receivable help you analyze the Accounts Receivable Aging report?

5 What information does an Inventory Valuation Summary provide?

6 What types of transactions might appear in a QuickZoom report created from an Inventory Summary? Give two examples.

7 What information does an Accounts Payable Aging report provide?

8 What types of transactions might appear in a QuickZoom report created from an Accounts Payable Aging report?

9 What options can you choose from the Print Reports dialog box to help you print a report?

10 How can you create a supporting report for a date other than the system date? Describe a situation for which you would want to do this.

Chapter 5 Assignments

1 *Creating Supporting Reports for Century Kitchens*

Remember to include your name in the Extra Footer Line of all reports printed.

Scott wants you to help him provide supporting reports. Use Century Kitchens.qbw on your Working Disk for this assignment. Create the reports Scott has requested, and write down the answers to the following questions:

a. Create and print a Customer Balance Summary as of 1/31/07. Other than the $15,765 receivable from R Coe, what is the amount of the largest customer receivable and what is the customer's name? What invoices support that receivable? What is the nature of each invoice?

b. Create and print an Aging Accounts Receivable report as of 1/31/07. List all past due invoices. When is each due? What is the nature of each invoice?

c. Create and print an Aging Accounts Payable report as of 2/28/07. What is the largest vendor liability? What bill makes up this liability? What is the nature of this bill? When was it due?

d. Create and print an Inventory Valuation Summary as of 1/31/07. What is the item with the largest asset cost? What was its cost and retail value?

2 *Creating More Supporting Reports for Century Kitchens*

Scott wants you to help him provide more supporting reports. Create the reports he has requested, and write down the answers to the following questions:

a. Create and print a Customer Balance Summary as of 2/28/07 and examine the QuickZoom reports for A Monroe. What invoice created this receivable? What was A Monroe invoiced for on 2/15/07? What are the terms of this invoice?

b. Create and print an Aging Accounts Receivable report as of 2/28/07 and examine the QuickZoom reports for J Summer. What invoice is represented by this receivable? What was J Summer invoiced for? What are the terms of this invoice?

c. Create and print an Aging Accounts Payable report as of 1/31/07 and examine the QuickZoom reports for Kraft Maid. What bill is represented by this payable? What was Century Kitchens billed for? What are the terms of this invoice?

d. Create and print an Inventory Valuation Summary as of 2/28/07. Describe the nature of items on hand as of this date.

   Trouble? Don't forget to change the Dates field to "This Fiscal Year-to-Date."

3 *Using the South-Western Home Page for More Assignments or Cases*

Go to the home page for this textbook at **www.thomsonedu.com/accounting/ owen.** Click **Additional Problem Sets,** and then select the **Chapter 5** section, and complete the problem(s) your instructor assigns.

Chapter 5 Case Problem:
JENNINGS & ASSOCIATES

service

Kelly Jennings created financial reports and submitted them to her banker to secure a loan. Today Kelly received a phone call from her banker. He told her that the balance sheet she submitted requires further explanation. He'd like to see some documentation to support her company's receivables, inventory, and payables balances.

Kelly asks you to prepare and print three supporting reports using her QuickBooks file Kelly Jenning.qbw.

1 Prepare an Accounts Receivable Aging Summary report for January 31, 2008. Print this report. Write a brief paragraph in which you explain the status of the two largest balances—that is, how old they are, what was sold, and so on.

2 Prepare an Accounts Payable Aging report for January 31, 2008. Print this report. Write a brief paragraph in which you explain the status of the two largest balances—that is, how old they are, what was purchased, and so on.

3 Prepare an Inventory Valuation Summary for January 31, 2008. Print this summary. Write a brief paragraph in which you describe the most recent purchase of film. Be sure to include the date, vendor, amount, and cost per unit.

Creating a QuickBooks File to Record and Analyze Business Events

part

2

Q

In this part, you will:

- **Set Up Your Business's Accounting System**
- **Enter Cash-Oriented Business Activities**
- **Enter Additional Business Activities**
- **Enter Adjusting Entries**
- **Perform Budgeting Activities**
- **Generate Reports of Business Activities**

Part 2 is designed to teach you how to use QuickBooks and the accounting methods and concepts you've learned in your introductory accounting course. This part is divided into six chapters, each with its own set of questions, assignments, and case problems. You'll follow the adventures of Donna and Karen at Wild Water Sports who have hired you to help them set up their business in QuickBooks, capture various business transactions, make adjusting entries, set up and use budgets, and generate key business reports. You'll utilize QuickBooks EasyStep Interview to establish accounts, customers, vendors, items, and employees and then record business transactions using key source documents like sales receipts, invoices, bills, deposits forms, and checks. You will learn how to create journal entries in QuickBooks to accrue revenues and expenses, adjust deferred assets and liabilities, and record depreciation of long-lived assets. Finally, you'll learn how QuickBooks's budgeting and reporting process can help Wild Water Sports plan and control their business activities.

Setting Up Your Business's Accounting System

Learning Objectives

In this chapter, you will:

- Create a new company file using the EasyStep Interview
- Set up company preferences
- Set up company items
- Set up customers, vendors, and accounts
- Set up payroll and employees
- Create a backup file

Case: **Wild Water Sports, Inc.**

Donna Chandler and her best friend Karen Wilson have been water sports enthusiasts since they were six years old. They would spend a good portion of each summer vacation wake boarding and skiing the lakes and reservoirs of Central Florida. After high school, both went their separate ways. Donna went off to a four-year college and then a career in real estate, while Karen attended a local community college and began a career in small business accounting.

They became reacquainted at their 10-year high school reunion reminiscing about their fun-filled weekends and summers with boats and boys. They pondered how they could mix their careers and their fun and love of boating into a business. Both vowed to keep in touch. Later that year, Donna called with a plan. She had run into a business investor, Ernesto Martinez, who had opened a retail boat dealership in Orlando, Florida, but didn't have the time to mind the details. Donna figured she could handle the marketing and sales if Karen could handle the day-to-day business operations. Wild Water Sports was born. The company has some existing cash, receivables, inventory, equipment, and liabilities. The plan is for Karen and Donna to make an investment by purchasing common stock in the existing company resulting in each having a one-third interest in the corporation, the remaining one-third belonging to Ernesto.

Karen knew she would need some help with the daily accounting records and chose QuickBooks as her accounting program to replace the manual accounting system which currently exists. She contacted an employment agency to find a part-time accountant. You answered her call as a student who could use some spending money and had completed a basic accounting course. You were hired the same day.

Your job will be to work with Karen to establish and maintain accounting records for Wild Water Sports using QuickBooks. The company will open its doors for business under new ownership in January but needs to set up accounts, items, customers, vendors, and employees before it gets started. The company rents its showroom and service bays from a former auto dealership. It plans to sell top-of-the-line ski-boats from Malibu, Tige, and MB Sports. It also plans to service boats providing engine repair, engine service, and boat cleaning.

You agree to meet with Karen the next day to get started.

Creating a New Company File Using the EasyStep Interview

When you return to Karen's office, she's already purchased a new computer, the QuickBooks software, Microsoft's Office suite, and supplies. The software is loaded and ready to go. Karen explains that you have two choices to begin setting up the company. QuickBooks has a built-in EasyStep Interview that can guide you through the company setup process, or you can skip the interview and set up the company yourself. Given this is your first time setting up a company in QuickBooks, you opt for the interview. The EasyStep Interview process provides a step-by-step guided series of questions that you can answer to help you choose various QuickBooks features. The alternative process requires you to enter basic company information, establish a set of accounts, provide sales tax information, and determine a file name.

"Starting with the interview is probably a good idea," Karen says. "Besides, no matter which method you start with, you can always change the decisions you make during setup later."

To create a new company file:

1   Start QuickBooks. Close any previously created company file if one appears.

2   Click **Create a new company.** The EasyStep Interview window appears.

3   Input the information from Figure 6.1.

4   Click **Next,** and do not enter an administrator password.

5   Click **Next** to choose a file name.

6   Accept the default file name Wild Water Sports, and then click the drop-down arrow in the Save in: text box to specify where

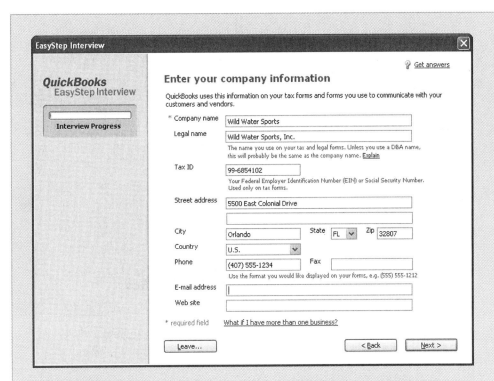

Figure 6.1

EasyStep Interview

you want your data file saved. Note that in this example the file was saved in a QuickBooks folder as shown in Figure 6.2. Then click **Save.**

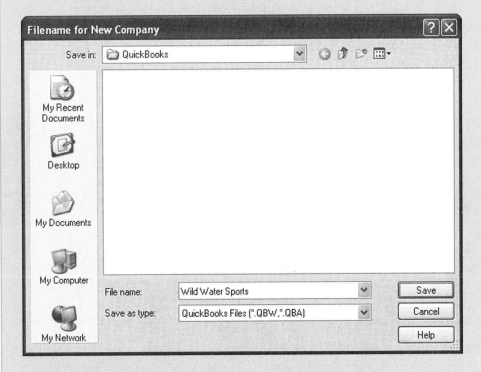

Figure 6.2

Saving Your Data File

7 Click **Next** to continue.

8 Scroll down the listing of industries, and select **Retail Establishments** under the Retail industry as shown in Figure 6.3.

Select Retail
Establishments here

9 Select **Both services and products,** and then click **Next.**

10 Select **Record each sale individually,** and then click **Next.**

11 Select **I don't sell online and I am not interested in doing so,** and then click **Next.**

12 Select **Yes** in answer to the question about charging sales tax, and then click **Next.**

13 Select **No** in answer to the question about creating estimates, and then click **Next.**

14 Select **Yes** in answer to the question about using sales receipts, and then click **Next.**

15 Select **Yes** in answer to the question about using statements, and then click **Next.**

16 Select **Yes** in answer to the question about using invoices, and then click **Next.**

17 Select **No** in answer to the question about using progress invoicing, and then click **Next.**

18 Select **Yes** in answer to the question about keeping track of bills you owe, and then click **Next.**

19 Select **Yes** in answer to the question about keeping track of inventory, and then click **Next.**

20 Select **I accept credit cards and debit cards,** and then click **Next.**

21 Select **Yes** in answer to the question about keeping track of time, and then click **Next.**

22 Select **Yes** in answer to the question about having employees, check **We have W-2 employees,** and then click **Next.**

23 Click **Next** to set up your chart of accounts.

24 Choose **12/31/06** as your start date as shown in Figure 6.4.

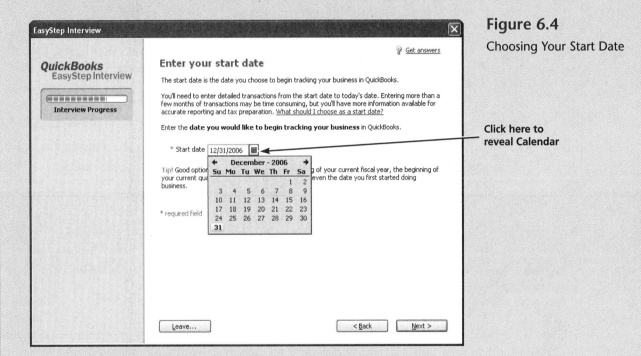

Figure 6.4

Choosing Your Start Date

Click here to reveal Calendar

25 Click **Yes** to add an existing bank account, and then click **Next.**

26 Type **Bank of Florida** as your Bank account name, select **Before** to answer the question about when your account was open, and then click **Next.**

27 Type **12/30/06** as the statement ending date and **25000** as the ending balance as shown in Figure 6.5.

28 Click **Next** to continue, and then select **No** when asked if you want to add another bank account.

29 Click **Next** to continue, and then select **Yes** to accept the given expense accounts.

30 Click **Next** to continue, and then select **Yes** to accept the given income accounts.

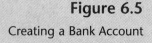

Figure 6.5

Creating a Bank Account

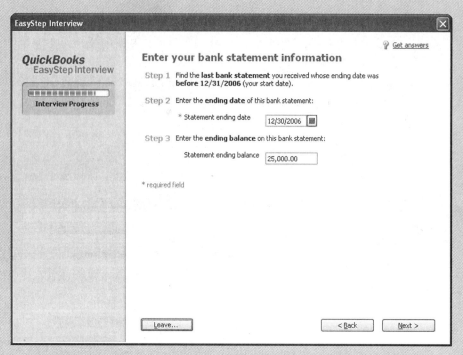

31 Click **Finish.** Feel free to watch any or all of the videos to get a better understanding of how to use QuickBooks. When you're done, uncheck the box **Show this window at startup,** and then click **Begin Using QuickBooks.**

"That wasn't too bad," you comment. "QuickBooks seems pretty thorough in getting you started. Plus I like the videos."

"That they are," Karen replies. "But we still have a long way to go before we can start entering transactions for January. We need to set up preferences, customers, vendors, employees, etc."

Set Up Company Preferences

"In QuickBooks," Karen explains, "preferences provide a way for turning certain features on or off, changing the look of the QuickBooks desktop, and customizing how QuickBooks performs."

To set up preferences:

1 Close any Alert windows which may have popped up indicating they've been done.

2 Click the **Edit** menu, and then click **Preferences.**

3 Scroll to the top of the preferences list, and click **Accounting.**

4 Click the **Company Preferences** tab, and then check **Use account numbers.**

5 Click **Checking** from the preferences list, and click **Yes** when asked if you want to save your changes.

6 Click the **My Preferences** tab, and then check all the boxes specifying default accounts to be used for different processes. Select **Bank of Florida** as the default account as shown in Figure 6.6.

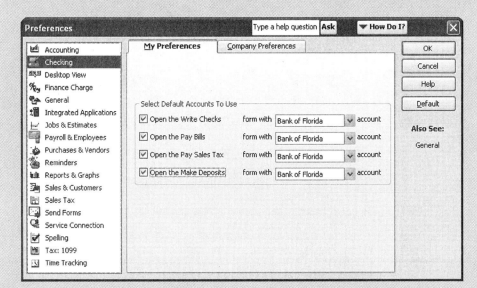

Figure 6.6

Checking Account Preferences

7 Click **Desktop View** from the preferences list, and click **Yes** when asked if you want to save your changes.

8 Select the **Multiple Windows** option, and make sure the **Show Home page** checkbox is checked.

9 Click **General** from the preferences list, and click **Yes** when asked if you want to save your changes.

10 Check all the items shown in Figure 6.7.

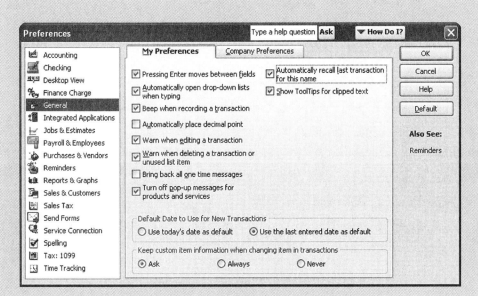

Figure 6.7

General Preferences

11 Click the **Company Preferences** tab, and uncheck the **Always show years as 4 digits** box.

12 Click **Reminders** from the preferences list, and click **Yes** when asked if you want to save your changes.

13 Click **OK** if you see a warning message.

14 Click the **Company Preferences** tab, and choose the **Don't Remind Me** option button for all the reminders as shown in Figure 6.8.

Figure 6.8

Reminders

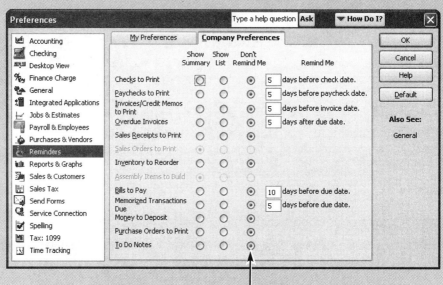

Make sure all of these Don't Remind Me option buttons are selected

15 Click **Reports & Graphs** from the preferences list, and click **Yes** when asked if you want to save your changes.

16 Click the **My Preferences** tab, and choose the option to **Refresh Automatically.**

17 Click **Sales Tax** from the preferences list, and click **Yes** when asked if you want to save your changes.

18 Select **Add New** from the list of Most common sales tax.

19 Select **Sales Tax Item** from the Type list.

20 Type **Florida Sales Tax** as the Tax Name.

21 Type **Sales Tax** as the Description.

22 Type **6.5%** as the Tax Rate (%).

23 Select **Florida Department of Revenue** as the Tax Agency, and then click **OK.**

24 Click the **Set Up** button in the Vendor Not Found window that appears (since this vendor had not previously been established).

25 Type **1379 Blountstown Hwy** in the Name and Address text box of the New Vendor window just below the vendor's name.

26 Then type **Tallahassee FL 32304-2716** below the highway address you just typed.

27 Click **OK** to accept this new vendor.

28 Click **OK** to close the New Item window.

29 Click **OK** to exit the Preferences window, and click **Yes** when asked if you want to save your changes.

"Why did we choose to use account numbers," you ask. "Why not just use account names?"

Karen explains that most businesses use account numbers to help manage their accounting systems. Certain account sequences are followed. For example assets are commonly assigned numbers beginning with a 1, liabilities with a 2, equities with a 3, revenues with a 4, and expenses with a 5. QuickBooks will assign all assets a 1000–1999 account number depending on the asset type. Liabilities will be assigned a 2000–2999 number, etc. While there is no requirement in QuickBooks for account numbers, Karen has decided to use them.

You've accomplished quite a bit having told QuickBooks that you collect sales tax, use the payroll features, account numbers, accrual-based reports, etc. In addition, you've set certain look and feel features of QuickBooks to help you navigate around. Now it's time to specifically address income and expense accounts and items.

Set Up Company Items

Karen explains that it's now time to set up items. In QuickBooks, an *item* is anything that your company buys, sells, or resells in the course of business, such as products, shipping and handling charges, discounts, and sales tax (if applicable). You can think of an item as something that shows up as a line on an invoice or other sales form. For example, you just set up a sales tax item which defined how much sales tax you need to collect from customers when you sell a product or provide a service.

Items help you fill out the line item area of a sales or purchase form quickly. When you choose an item from your Item List, QuickBooks fills in a description of the line item and calculates its amount for you. QuickBooks provides 11 different types of items. Some—such as the service item or the inventory part item—help you record the services and products your business sells. Others—such as the subtotal item or discount item—are used to perform calculations on the amounts in a sale.

She suggests that you now set up some new service items and inventory part items. For Wild Water Sports, service items would be things like changing engine oil and filter, engine tune ups, and 20-hour service checks for example. Inventory part items would include boats and parts for repairs.

To set up items Karen and Donna had to agree on prices for common service items, hourly service rates for nonstandard repairs, and pricing for products to be sold. They also had to set up item names and descriptions. One item they both notice is used for consignment sales, which they don't plan on doing. They both agree to remove that item from the item list.

To set up and modify items:

1 Click **Items & Services** from the Company section of the home page. This opens the Item List window. Note the Florida Sales Tax item you recently created. Also note the existing generic service item set up and the generic inventory item 1 and inventory item 2. Karen has decided you will set up specific service items and specific inventory items for Wild Water.

2 Select the **Consignment Item** from the Item List.

3 Click the **Item** button in the lower left corner of the Item List window, and then select **Delete Item.**

4 Click **Yes** to confirm.

5 Click the **Item** button again, and then select **New.**

6 Select **Service** from the Type drop-down list.

7 Type **Engine Service** in the Item Name text box.

8 Type **Labor for changing engine oil and filter** in the Sales Description text box.

9 Type **125** in the Rate text box.

10 Select **Tax** as the Tax Code.

11 Select **4020 – Service** as the Account from the drop-down list. Your screen should look like Figure 6.9.

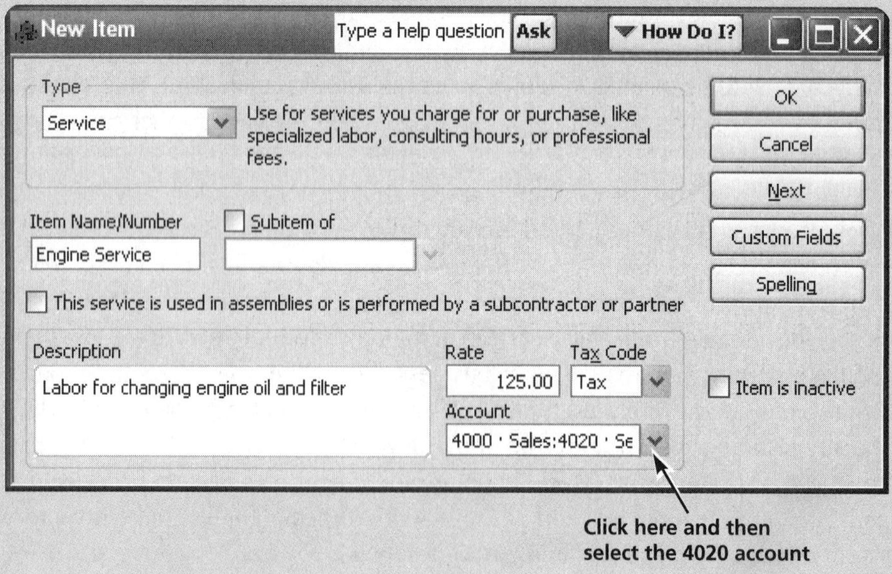

Figure 6.9

Adding a New Service Item

Click here and then select the 4020 account

12 Click **Next** to set up another service item.

13 Continue this process for the remaining service items listed below.

Item Name	Sales Description	Rate	Taxable	Income A/C
Engine Tune Up	Labor for engine tune up	$250.00	Yes	4020 – Service
20 Hour Service	Labor for 20 hour service check	$175.00	Yes	4020 – Service
Check Service	Hourly service rate	$ 85.00	Yes	4020 – Service

14 Once you've entered all the service items above, it is time to enter new inventory parts.

15 Select **Inventory Part** from the Type drop-down list.

16 Type **Malibu Sunsetter LXi** in the Item Name text box.

17 Type **Malibu Sunsetter LXi** in the Purchase Description text box since our purchase description is the same as our item name.

18 Type **48000** in the Cost text box. (*Note:* All merchandise is marked up 25% of cost, thus all merchandise cost is 80% of the sales price.)

19 Type **5000 – Cost of Goods Sold** as the COGS account.

20 Type **60000** in the Sales Price text box.

21 Select **Tax** as the Tax Code.

22 Select **4010 – Merchandise** as the Account from the drop-down list.

23 Select **1300 – Inventory Asset** from the Asset Account drop-down list. (*Note:* Karen mentions that 1300 was the account assigned by QuickBooks. She would prefer to use a different account number, and she'll change it later on.)

24 Type **0** as the reorder point, and then type **1** in the Qty on Hand text box indicating that as of the beginning of the year the firm had a quantity of one unit on hand for sale.

25 Type **12/31/06** in the As of text box. Your screen should look like Figure 6.10.

26 Click **Next** to set up another inventory part item. Click **Add** whenever the Check Spelling on Form window appears as long as you've correctly typed the part name.

27 Continue this process for the remaining inventory part items listed on the next page. Be sure to specify 12/31/06 in the As of text box for all items added.

Figure 6.10

Adding a New
Inventory Item

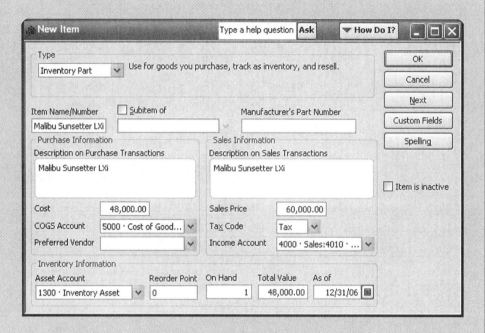

Item Name	Sales Price	Taxable	Income A/C	Cost	Qty
Malibu Sportster LX	$52,000	Yes	4010 – Merchandise	$41,600	1
Malibu Sunscape LSV	$65,000	Yes	4010 – Merchandise	$52,000	2
Malibu Vride	$48,000	Yes	4010 – Merchandise	$38,400	2
Malibu WakeSetter VLX	$57,000	Yes	4010 – Merchandise	$45,600	1
Malibu WakeSetter XTI	$70,000	Yes	4010 – Merchandise	$56,000	1

28 Choose **OK** after you've entered all six inventory part items.

29 Prepare this window for printing by clicking the **Reports** button at the bottom of the window and then selecting **Item Listing.**

30 Click the **Modify Report** button.

31 Click the **Display** tab, and then uncheck **Sales Tax Code, Quantity on Purchase Order, Reorder Point** and **Preferred Vendor.**

32 Click the **Header/Footer** tab, and then uncheck **Subtitle, Date Prepared,** and **Time Prepared.**

33 Click **OK**.

34 Click the **Print** button on the top of the reports window, choose **Landscape** orientation, and then click **Print.**

35 Close both the Item Listing report and the Chart of Accounts window. Do not memorize these reports.

36 Close the Item List window.

"We are well on our way to getting this company set up," Karen explains.

"Should we save our work?" you ask.

"Funny you should mention that," Karen responds. "QuickBooks automatically saves every event you record. In fact, QuickBooks doesn't even have a save or save as feature like most other software."

"Shouldn't we at least make a copy of the file in case something happens to this one?" you inquire.

"Good point," Karen says. "Once we're set up we can use the QuickBooks backup procedure to save a copy."

Karen explains that it's now time to enter our existing customers and vendors into QuickBooks and establish beginning balances.

Set Up Customers, Vendors, and Accounts

Donna has met with Ernesto and determined he did have some outstanding balances from a few customers and owed some vendors for purchases made in the previous months. He has an existing bank account and a MasterCard credit card account for the business. He also owned some equipment and a related note payable.

Karen has also decided to use QuickBooks's job tracking feature to follow service-related efforts for customers. The firm plans to market its service program to existing customers and will need to track costs for each job as well as bill based on hours worked and materials used for each job.

job costing

Karen has gathered the information she needs and is ready for you to input it into the system.

To set up existing customers:

1. Click **Customers** from the Customer section of the home page. This opens the Customer Center window.

2. Click **New Customer & Job,** and then click **New Customer** from the short-cut menu.

3. Type **Orlando Water Sports** in the Customer Name text box and the Company Name text box, and then click **OK.**

4. Click **New Customer & Job,** and then click **Add Job** from the short-cut menu.

5. Type **Boat Sales** in the Job Name text box.

6. Type **43000** in the Opening Balance text box.

7. Type **12/31/06** in the As of text box. Your screen should look like Figure 6.11.

8. Click **Next** to enter another job for Orlando Water Sports.

9. Type **Malibu #21390** as the Job Name.

Figure 6.11

Adding a New Job

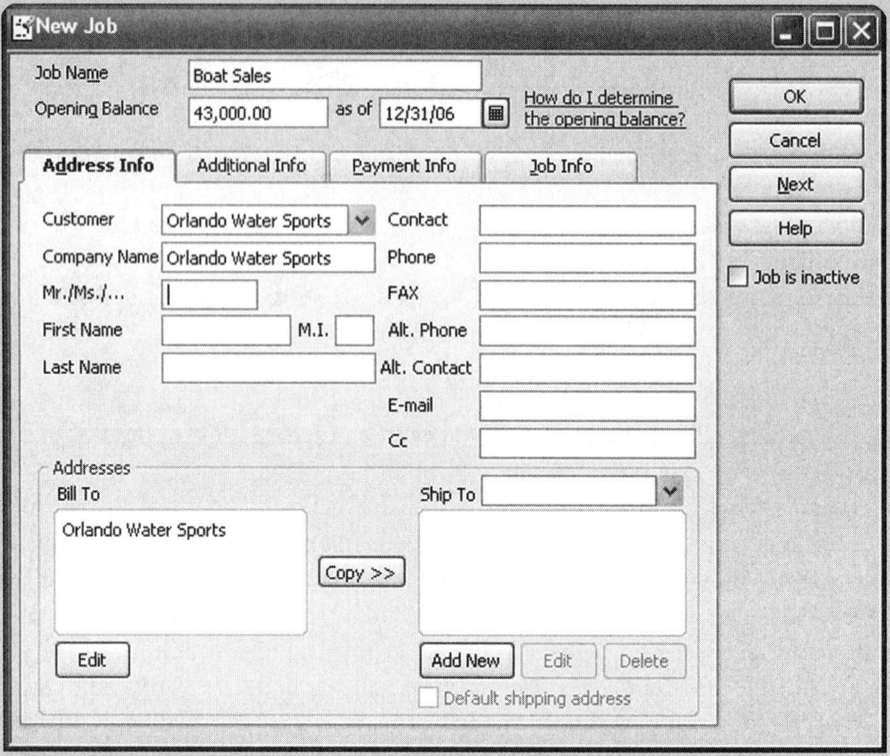

10 Type **5300** in the Opening Balance text box.

11 Type **12/31/06** in the As of text box, and then click **OK** to end entering new jobs for this customer.

12 The Customer Center window should now look like Figure 6.12.

Figure 6.12

Customer Details

◇Orlando Water Sports	48,300.00
◇Boat Sales	43,000.00
◇Malibu #21390	5,300.00

13 Continue this process for the remaining customers and jobs listed below. Once again, be sure to type the date 12/31/06 in the As of text box for all jobs and customers.

Customer Name	Job Name	Balance Due
Buena Vista Water Sports	Boat Sales	$30,000
Buena Vista Water Sports	Malibu #21228	$3,000
Walking on Water		$15,000

14 Your Customer Center should now look like Figure 6.13.

15 Click the **Reports** menu, click **Customers & Receivables,** and then click **Customer Balance Summary.**

Figure 6.13

Completed Customer Center

16 Type **1/1/07** as the From and To dates.

17 Click the **Modify Report** button.

18 Click the **Header/Footer** tab and then uncheck **Date Prepared** and **Time Prepared.**

19 Click the **Display** tab, click the **Advanced** button, and then choose **All** in the Display Rows section.

20 Click **OK** to close the Advanced Options window.

21 Click **OK** to close the Modify Report window.

22 Click the **Print** button on the top of the Reports window.

23 Choose the printer you want to print to, choose **Portrait** Orientation, and click **Print.**

24 Close the Customer Balance Summary window.

25 Click in the checkbox "**Do not display this message in the future,**" and then click **OK.**

26 To print a customer contact list click the **Reports** menu, click **List,** and then click **Customer Contact List.**

27 Resize the columns of the report to fit it on to one page by clicking on the column handles and moving them left or right.

28 Click the **Print** button on the top of the Reports window.

29 Choose the printer you want to print to, choose **Landscape** orientation, and then click **Print.**

30 Close the Customer Contact List window.

31 To print a customer and job list, click the **Print** located at the top of the Customer Center window and then select **Customer & Job List.**

32 Click **OK** if a List Reports window appears.

33 Select **Portrait** orientation in the Print Reports window, and then click **Print.**

34 Close the Customer Center window.

"That will be fine for now, and as we add new customers, we'll follow the same process," Karen explains. "As you can see, we have several options for printing a list of customers. The Customer Balance Summary only prints those customers who have outstanding balances at the dates we specified. The Customer & Job List prints all customers regardless of their balances. The Customer Contact List prints all customers with the addresses and phone numbers we provided. Now let's set up Malibu Boats as our only current vendor."

To set up existing vendor:

1 Click **Vendors** from the Vendor section of the home page. This opens the Vendor Center window.

2 Click **New Vendor.**

3 Type **Malibu Boats** in the Vendor Name text box and Company Name text box.

4 Type **76000** in the Opening Balance text box.

5 Type **12/31/06** in the As of text box. Your screen should look like Figure 6.14.

Figure 6.14

New Vendor

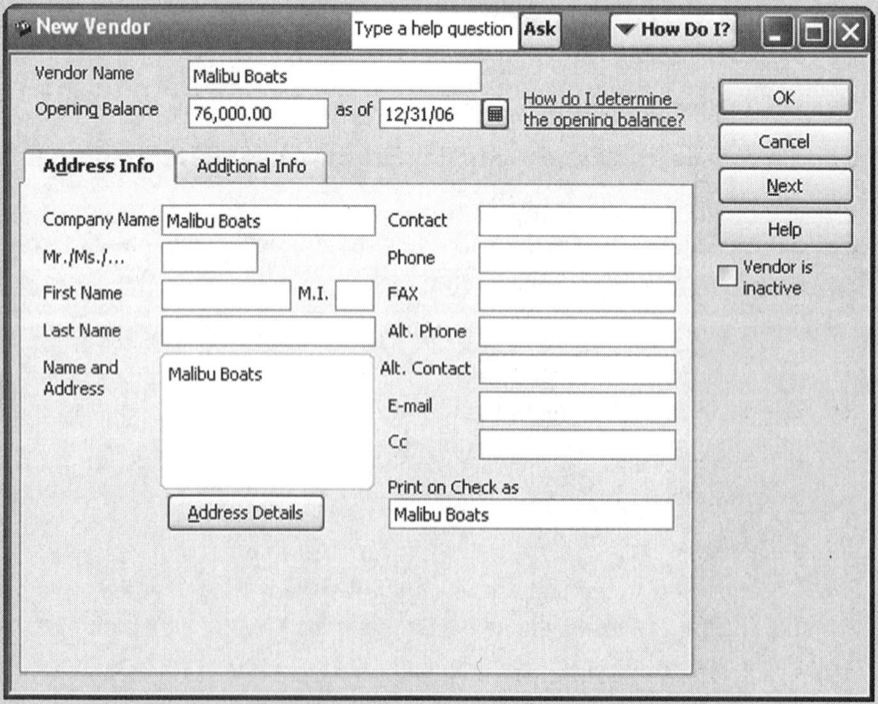

6   Click **OK** to finish adding existing vendors.

7   Click the **Reports** menu, click **Vendors & Payables,** and then click **Vendor Balance Summary.**

8   Type **1/1/07** as the From and To dates.

9   Click the **Modify Report** button.

10 Click the **Header/Footer** tab, and then uncheck **Date Prepared** and **Time Prepared.**

11 Click the **Display** tab, click the **Advanced** button, and then choose **All** in the Display Rows section.

12 Click **OK** to close the Advanced Options window.

13 Click **OK** to close the Modify Report window.

14 Click the **Print** button on the top of the Reports window.

15 Choose the printer you want to print to, choose **Portrait** orientation, and then click **Print.**

16 Close the Vendor Balance Summary window.

17 To print a vendor contact list click the **Reports** menu, click **List,** and then click **Vendor Contact List.**

18 Resize the columns of the report to fit it on one page.

19 Click the **Print** button on the top of the Reports window.

20 Choose the printer you want to print to, choose **Landscape** orientation, and then click **Print.**

21 Close the Vendor Contact List window.

22 To print a vendor list click the **Print** located at the top of the Vendor Center window and then select **Vendor List.**

23 Click **OK** if a List Reports window appears.

24 Select **Portrait** orientation in the Print Reports window, and then click **Print.**

25 Close the Vendor Center window.

Karen explains that while Malibu Boats is the only vendor she needed to add currently, she'll be adding more "on the fly" as she enters transactions for January later on. Now she suggests you complete the setup process by adding some new accounts to establish the company's credit card and long-term liability as well as their fixed asset balances on 12/31/06.

"This is also a good time to fix our account number issue I mentioned before," Karen comments. "I want to use 1120 as the account number for inventory, and I don't need an Inventory Consignment account."

To set up create and modify accounts:

1 Click **Chart of Accounts** from the Company section of the home page.

2 The first thing you should notice is that all accounts listed have an account number specified except the Bank of Florida bank account. That's because you didn't specify that account numbers were required until after you set up the bank account during the EasyStep Interview. Click the **Bank of Florida** account name once to select it.

Trouble? If you accidentally double-click the account, its register will open. Just close this window and click the account name once.

3 With the Bank of Florida account name selected, click the **Account** button located in the lower left corner of the window and select **Edit Account.**

4 Type **1010** in the Number text box, and then click **OK.**

5 You also remember that Karen wanted to change some account numbers. With the **Inventory** account name selected, click the **Account** button located in the lower left corner of the window and select **Edit Account.**

6 Type **1120** in the Number text box in place of the existing account number 1300 and then click **OK.**

7 With the **1350 – Inventory on Consignment** account name selected, click the **Account** button located in the lower left corner of the window and select **Delete Account.**

8 Click **Yes** to confirm.

9 Click the **Account** button, and select **New.**

10 Select **Credit Card** from the Type drop-down list.

11 Type **2050** in the Number text box.

12 Type **MasterCard** in the Name text box.

13 Type **1000** in the Opening Balance text box.

14 Type **12/31/06** in the As of text box. Your screen should look like Figure 6.15.

15 Click **Next** to enter another account.

16 Select **Long-Term Liability** from the Type drop-down list.

17 Type **2500** in the Number text box.

18 Type **Loan Payable** in the Name text box.

19 Type **383800** in the Opening Balance text box.

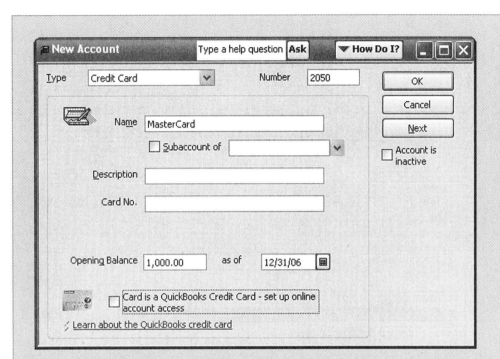

Figure 6.15

Establishing a Credit Card Account

20 Type **12/31/06** in the As of text box.

21 Click **Next** to enter another account.

22 Select **Fixed Asset** from the Type drop-down list.

23 Type **1300** in the Number text box.

24 Type **Equipment** in the Name text box.

25 Click **Next** to enter another account.

26 Select **Fixed Asset** from the Type drop-down list.

27 Type **1310** in the Number text box.

28 Type **Cost** in the Name text box.

29 Place a check in the **Subaccount of** checkbox.

30 Select **1300 – Equipment** from the drop-down list of subaccounts.

31 Type **75000** in the Opening Balance text box.

32 Type **12/31/06** in the As of text box. Your screen should look like Figure 6.16.

33 Click **Next** to enter another account.

34 Select **Fixed Asset** from the Type drop-down list.

35 Type **1390** in the Number text box.

36 Type **Accumulated Depreciation** in the Name text box.

37 Place a check in the **Subaccount of** checkbox.

38 Select **1300 – Equipment** from the drop-down list of subaccounts.

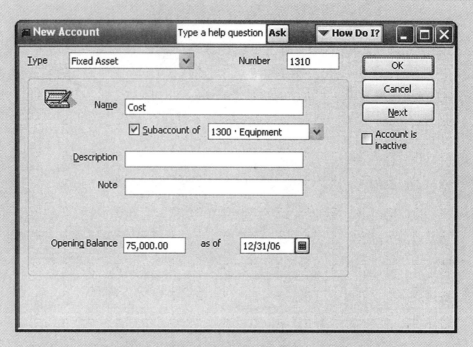

Figure 6.16

Adding an Equipment Cost Account

39 Type **–7500** in the Opening Balance text box. (Be sure to type the minus sign in front of this amount!)

40 Type **12/31/06** in the As of text box.

41 Click **OK** to accept this account, and then close the Chart of Accounts window.

Karen explains that it is important to set up a main fixed asset account, followed by two subaccounts like Cost and Accumulated Depreciation to track each category. Financial accounting requires disclosure of both asset cost and related accumulated depreciation so with this account set up you have all the information you need. You have now completed basic setup accounts, but you're not done setting up your QuickBooks file. You still need to set up payroll and employees, which will be done next.

You are curious whether, after entering all of these opening balances, the accounts are in balance. Karen explains that QuickBooks establishes an opening equity balances account that is used as a figure to balance all the assets and liabilities established with this opening balances effort except for accounts receivable and accounts payable. The beginning accounts receivable balances were assigned to an account called Uncategorized Income on 12/31/06, and all beginning accounts payable balances were assigned to an account called Uncategorized Expenses as of the same date.

"But aren't we mostly concerned with balances beginning 1/1/07?" you question.

Karen points out that QuickBooks will automatically close these accounts to retained earnings as of 1/1/07. She does suggest, however, that you recategorize the retained earnings balance as of 1/1/07 to the opening equity balances account. She also suggests it might make sense to transfer the resulting balance in the opening equity balance account to the common stock account since that's the basis the company will use for Karen and Donna's new investment in the company.

She enlightens you by explaining the arrangement they have with Ernesto. The three agreed that the opening balance equity (assets – liabilities) was $100,000. Donna and Karen will each be purchasing stock in the company on January 1 for $100,000, thus giving the company a value of $300,000. Each stockholder—Ernesto, Donna, and Karen—will have a one-third interest in the company.

"Are we sure that our opening balance effort yielded an opening balance equity of $100,000?" you ask.

"We'll check while we make the adjustments for an opening equity we just spoke of," Karen responds. "First let's look at a trial balance as of 1/1/07, which will give us the account balances as of that date."

To view opening balances and recategorize the opening balance equity and uncategorized account balances:

1 Click **Reports** from the menu, select **Accountant & Taxes,** and then select **Trial Balance.**

2 Change the To and From dates to **1/1/07** to view the trial balance shown below in Figure 6.17.

Figure 6.17

Trial Balance

Wild Water Sports
Trial Balance
As of January 1, 2007

	Jan 1, 07	
	Debit	Credit
1010 · Bank of Florida	25,000.00	
1200 · Accounts Receivable	96,300.00	
1120 · Inventory Asset	372,000.00	
1300 · Equipment:1310 · Cost	75,000.00	
1300 · Equipment:1390 · Accumulated Depreciation		7,500.00
2000 · Accounts Payable		76,000.00
2050 · MasterCard		1,000.00
2500 · Loan Payable		383,800.00
3000 · Opening Bal Equity		79,700.00
3900 · Retained Earnings		20,300.00
TOTAL	568,300.00	568,300.00

3 Close the Trial Balance window, clicking **No** when asked if you want to memorize this report.

4 Select **Chart of Accounts** from the Company section of the Home page.

5   Double-click the **Opening Bal Equity** account to use the register.

6   Scroll down the account until an empty row can be seen.

7   Type **1/1/07** in the date column in the first open row available.

8   Type **20300** in the increase column of that same row.

9   Select **3900 – Retained Earnings** from the account drop-down list.

10 Click **Yes** when asked if you really want to make an adjustment to this account.

11 Click **Record.**

12 Type **1/1/07** in the date column in the next open row available.

13 Type **100000** in the decrease column of that same row.

14 Select **Add New** from the account drop down list.

15 Select **Equity** from the Type drop-down list.

16 Type **3100** in the Number text box.

17 Type **Common Stock** in the Name text box, and then click **OK.**

18 Click **Record.** Your screen should now look like Figure 6.18.

Figure 6.18

Opening Bal Equity
Account Register

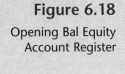
Double-click here to
reveal journal entry

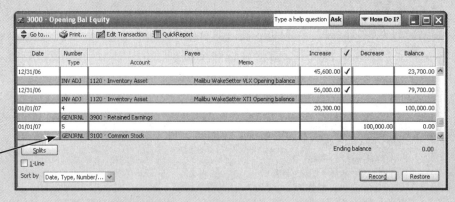

19 Double-click **GENJRNL** under the number 5 to reveal the general journal entry that was created when you adjusted the opening balance equity account as shown in Figure 6.19.

20 Close the Opening Bal Equity and the Make General Journal Entries windows.

21 The Opening Bal Equity and Retained Earnings accounts should now be zero, and the common stock account should be $100,000. Your chart of accounts should now look like Figure 6.20.

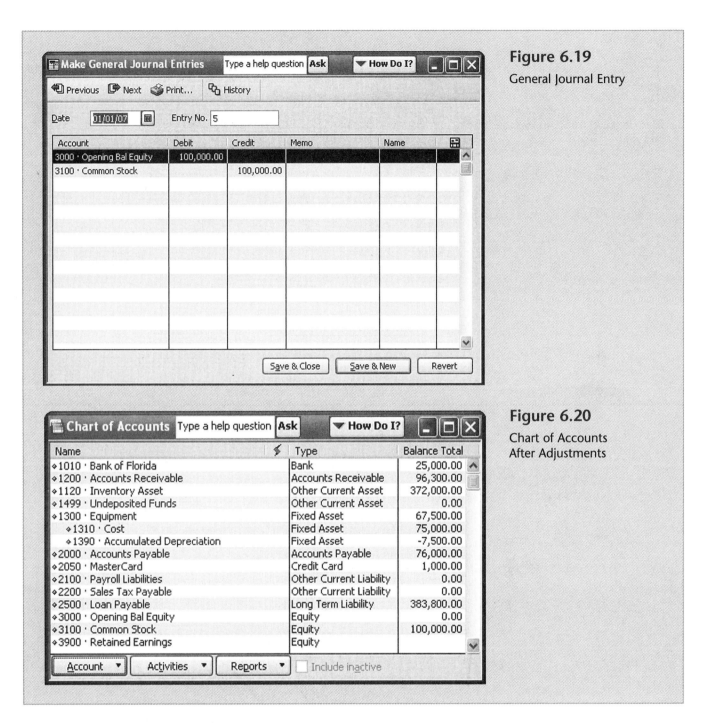

Figure 6.19
General Journal Entry

Figure 6.20
Chart of Accounts
After Adjustments

"Much better," you proclaim.

Karen suggests you print this chart of accounts for later reference.

To print the chart of accounts:

1 Prepare this window for printing by clicking the **Reports** button at the bottom of the window and then selecting **Account Listing.**

2 Click the **Modify Report** button.

3 Click the **Header/Footer** tab, and then uncheck **Subtitle, Date Prepared,** and **Time Prepared.**

4 Click the **Display** tab, and then uncheck **Tax Line.**

5 Click **OK.**

6 Click the **Print** button on the top of the reports window, choose **Landscape** orientation, and then click **Print.** Alternatively, you can access this list by clicking the **Reports** menu, then **List,** and then **Account Listing.**

7 Close both the Account Listing report and the Chart of Accounts window. Do not memorize these reports.

Karen points out the opening equity balance in the accounts listing is in fact the $100,000 they expected. Her stock purchase and Donna's stock purchase will occur in the first few days of January. All that's left in the company creation process is setting up payroll and adding employees.

Set Up Payroll and Employees

"Now it's time to establish information about our employees in QuickBooks," Karen says. "QuickBooks has some very nice payroll features that will help us track employee information, prepare payroll tax reports, and account for our employee cost."

"Will it calculate payroll withholding for federal and state taxes?" you ask.

"It will if we purchase a payroll tax table service from Intuit," Karen answers, "but we decided not to do that."

First, we have to set up QuickBooks to recognize that we want to compute payroll manually. That, as you'll see, is not a straightforward proposition. QuickBooks makes you do some fairly strange things to get started doing payroll manually and none are very intuitive or easy to discover. In fact, one way to get started is through the Help menu. The other requires an Internet connection. Since you have an Internet connection, you decide to use that method, but Karen agrees to show you an alternative method of setting up payroll manually if you don't have an Internet connection.

To set up payroll (if you have an Internet connection):

1 First, note that the home page only lists two icons (Enter Time and Learn about Payroll Options) in the Employee section. Now click **Learn about Payroll Options** from the home page.

2 Click **OK** in the Launch Web Browser window.

3 Scroll down the page and click on the **Learn More** text located at the end of a sentence as shown in Figure 6.21.

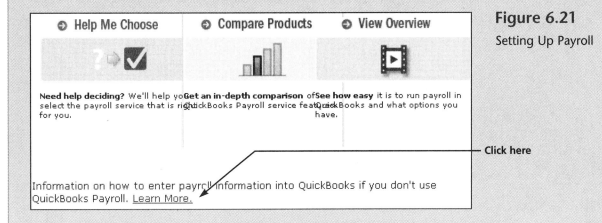

Figure 6.21
Setting Up Payroll

4 Click the bright orange button in the middle of the window that appears and looks like Figure 6.22.

Figure 6.22
Enabling Manual Paycheck Entry

5 Click **OK** two times. Notice that the home page now contains new icons that will allow you to process payroll and no longer contains the icon Learn about Payroll Options.

"What if you don't have an Internet connection?" you ask.

"In that case, you would use the Help menu approach," Karen answers. "Here's the process you would go through."

To set up payroll (if you do not have an Internet connection):

1 First, note that the home page lists only two icons (Enter Time and Learn about Payroll Options) in the Employee section. Now press the **F1** key to start QuickBooks Help.

2 Click the **Contents** Tab.

3 Double-click **Managing Employees.**

4 Click **Learn about payroll options** as shown in Figure 6.23.

5 Click the text **Calculate your payroll taxes manually.**

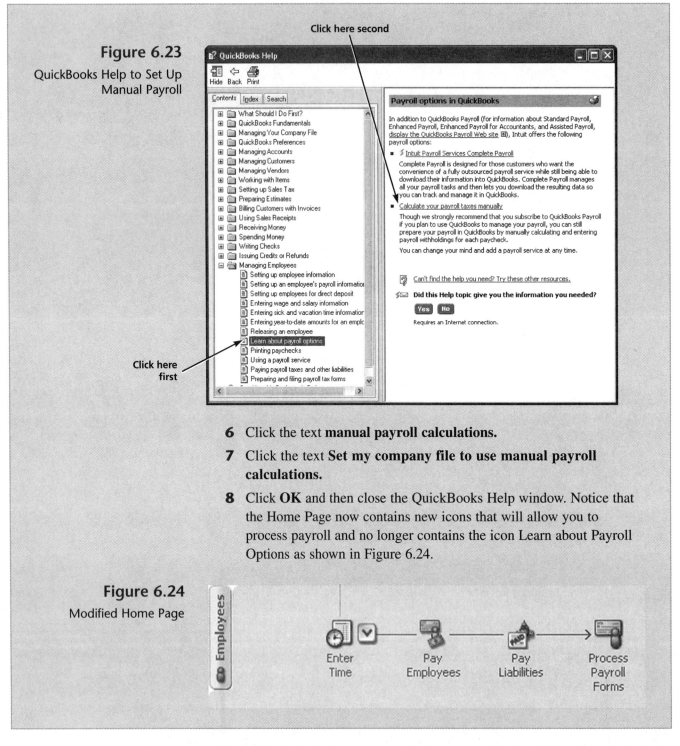

Figure 6.23

QuickBooks Help to Set Up
Manual Payroll

6 Click the text **manual payroll calculations.**

7 Click the text **Set my company file to use manual payroll calculations.**

8 Click **OK** and then close the QuickBooks Help window. Notice that the Home Page now contains new icons that will allow you to process payroll and no longer contains the icon Learn about Payroll Options as shown in Figure 6.24.

Figure 6.24

Modified Home Page

Regardless of whether you use the Internet method or Help menu method, the process of managing payroll manually is the same once you have established your plan to complete payroll manually. Now it's time to enter payroll details for January. Karen explains that during the month of January, she and Donna will work full time as salaried employees. Ryder and Pat, sales staff and service technicians, will work occasional days until the end of the month when the business is more established. For the first few weeks, most of their work will be setting up the business, passing out marketing flyers, and trying to sell boats. Later in the month, they will begin servicing some boats.

For each employee, you'll need to add personal, address and contact, and tax information. In doing so, Karen points out, you'll also be setting up payroll tax items like salary and hourly as well as identifying how often your employees are paid (monthly in this case). You'll also be identifying each employee's salary or hourly rate, taxes to be withheld, state worked, filing status, tax rates (like unemployment), and tax payees (like the Florida Department of Revenue) to whom state taxes are paid. Karen then explains the actual process of entering employees into QuickBooks for Wild Water Sports by using Donna as an example.

To enter Donna as an employee into QuickBooks:

1 Click **Employees** from the Employee section of the home page.

2 Click **New Employee.** A New Employee window appears.

3 Be certain that the Personal tab is selected. Then, fill in the blank spaces on this tab using the information in Figure 6.25.

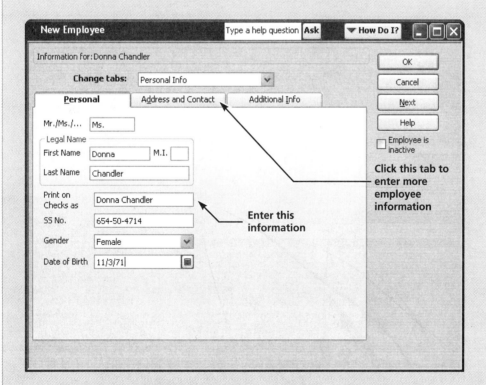

Figure 6.25

Adding Address Information for a New Employee

4 Click the **Address and Contact** tab, and then enter Ms. Chandler's address as **12 Ridgeway Lane, Orlando, FL 32807.**

5 Select the **Payroll and Compensation Info** from the drop-down text box labeled Change tabs.

6 Type **Salary** in the Earnings Item Name section, and then press the **[Tab]** key.

7 Click **Set Up** in the Payroll Item Not Found window.

8 Be sure the **Annual Salary** option button is selected, and then click **Next** in the Add new payroll item window.

9 Be sure the **Regular Pay** option button is selected, and then click **Next.**

10 Click **Next** again, and then click **Finish** to complete the payroll item set up process and accept account 6560 – Payroll Expenses as the account for tracking this expense.

11 Type **50000** as the Annual Rate of earnings for Donna.

12 Select **Monthly** as the Pay Period. Your screen should look like Figure 6.26.

Figure 6.26

Payroll and compensation Information for Donna Chandler

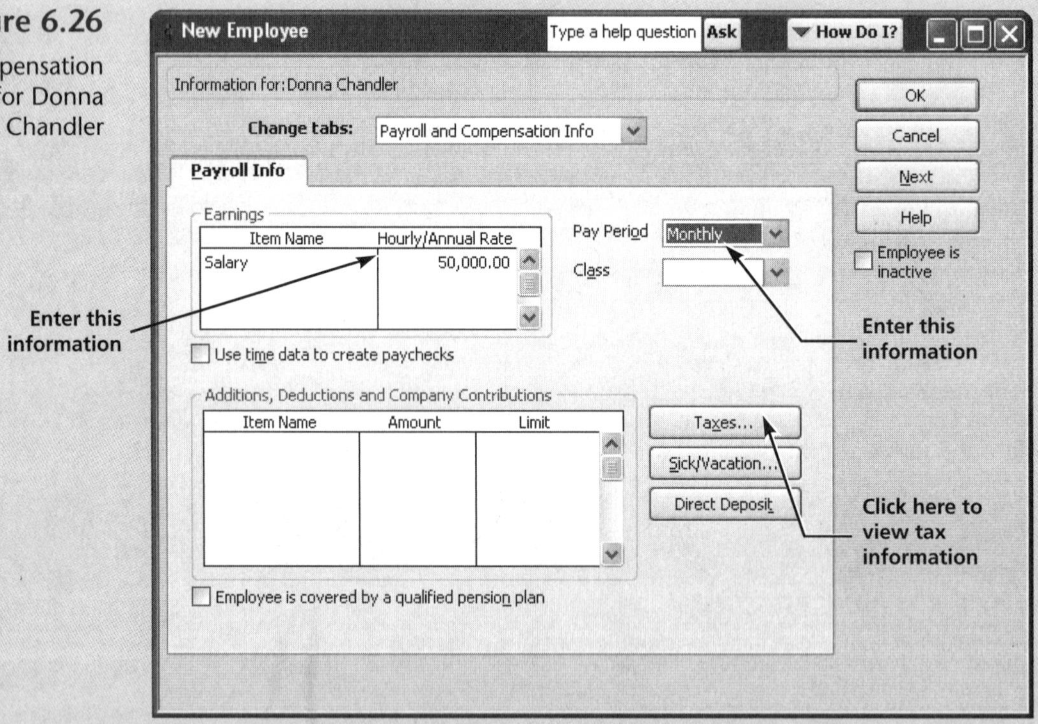

13 Click **Taxes.** The Tax window appears.

14 Complete the federal taxes for Donna Chandler using the information in Figure 6.27. Click **OK** to accept this information and return to the Payroll Info tab.

Trouble? Be sure all tax checkboxes are checked and set filing status to Married.

Setting Up Your Business's Accounting System

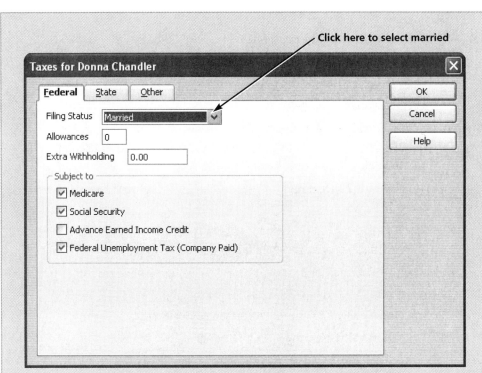

Figure 6.27

Adding Federal Tax Information for Donna Chandler

15 Select the **Taxes** button again, and then click the **State** tab. The State Tax window should appear as shown in Figure 6.28.

16 Select **FL** as the State Worked. QuickBooks then provides one checkbox option for state unemployment insurance (SUI).

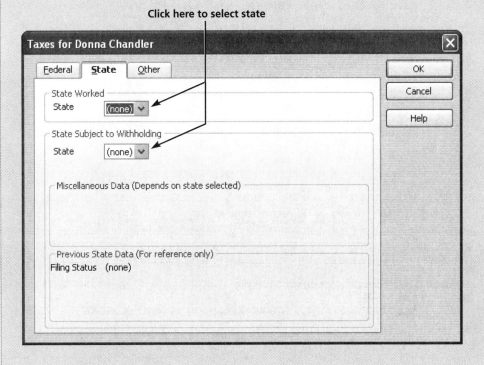

Figure 6.28

Adding State Tax Information for Donna Chandler

17 Now select **FL** as the State Subject to Withholding.

18 Click **OK.** A Payroll Item Not Found window should appear.

19 Click the **Setup** button, and then click **Next** to accept FL – Unemployment Company as the new payroll item.

20 Select **Florida Department of Revenue** as the agency to which the liability is paid (since this is Florida's revenue collection agency), and then click in the text box below.

21 Type **6854102** as the number that identifies you to that agency, and then click **Next.**

22 Accept the tax rates provided by clicking **Next.** (They should be 2.7% for each period presented. If not, change them all to 2.7%)

23 Click **Finish** to complete the process of adding a new payroll item.

24 Click **OK** in the New Employee window, and then click **Leave As Is** in the New Employee: Payroll Info (other) window.

25 Do not close the Employee List window.

You note that Donna Chandler is now set up as an employee for the company, but you still have more employees to go. Karen suggests you add one employee for now, perhaps Ryder Zacovic, an hourly employee. You respond that you're up to the task.

To enter Ryder as an employee into QuickBooks:

1 Click **New Employee.** A New Employee window appears.

2 Be certain that the Personal tab is selected. Then, fill in the form with the following information:

Name: Mr. Ryder Zacovic
Social security number: 556-74-6585
Gender: Male
Date of Birth: 2/19/85
Address: 1554 Rose Avenue Apt. #4, Orlando, FL 32804

3 Change to the Payroll and Compensation Info tab, and select **Add New** from the Item Name drop-down list.

4 Select **Hourly Wages** as the new payroll item, and then click **Next.**

5 Select **Regular Pay** in the next window, and then click **Next.**

6 Type **Hourly** as the name for this payroll item, and then click **Next.**

7 Click **Finish** to accept the payroll expense account provided.

8 Type **15** as the hourly rate to be paid to Ryder, and select **Monthly** as the pay period.

9 Click the **Taxes** button as before. Ryder is single and subject to Medicare, Social Security, and Federal Unemployment Tax.

10 Click the **State** tab, and identify Ryder as working in Florida (FL) and subject to Florida withholding.

11 Click **OK** two times to finish entering Ryder as a new employee.

12 Once again, click **Leave As Is** when asked if you want to set up other payroll information.

13 A partial view of the revised Employee Center is shown in Figure 6.29.

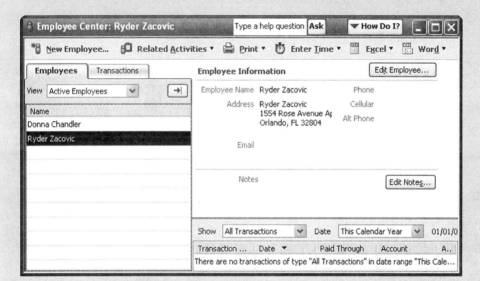

Figure 6.29

Partial View of the Revised Employee Center

14 Click the **Reports** menu, click **List,** and then click **Employee Contact List.**

15 Click the **Modify Report** button.

16 Click the **Header/Footer** tab, and then uncheck **Date Prepared** and **Time Prepared.**

17 Click the **Display** tab, and then uncheck **Phone** from the list of Columns.

18 Click **OK** to close the Modify Report window.

19 Resize the remaining columns of the report to fit it on to one page.

20 Click the **Print** button on the top of the Reports window.

21 Choose the printer you want to print to, choose **Portrait** Orientation, and then click **Print.**

22 Close the Employee Contact List window.

23 Close the Employee Center window.

You have now completed the essential effort of setting up new company file, establishing company preferences, setting up company items, customers, vendors, accounts, and employees.

Your final task is to back up your data file for safe keeping.

Backing Up Your Company File

"It is very important to keep a backup of your company file just in case your computer hard drive crashes or your data file gets corrupted or destroyed," Karen explains. She goes on to explain that some business users save their files to USB drives, CD ROMs, Zip disks, or floppy disks. Floppy disks do not have enough room to hold the typical data file and are too slow to work from. Zip drives are also too slow to work from, and CD ROMs are often read-only and thus can't be used to work from but can be used to store a backup.

"USB drives are ideal if you can afford one," you point out. "Plus, they hold so much information that it's easier just to copy your current file from your hard drive to your USB drive and not even worry about the typical backup process, which shrinks the file size."

Karen suggests that the two of you try both methods of creating backups and see which you prefer.

To back up and restore a file using QuickBooks Backup procedures to an external disk:

1 Open the Wild Water Sports file, if by chance you closed it after the last lesson.

2 Click **Back Up** from the File menu. If a portable Company File Feature window appears choose the Do not display check box then click OK.

3 Choose a location you'd like to back up your file to. In Figure 6.30 we chose to back up the file to an external disk located in Drive F in a folder we called QuickBooks. Click **Browse** to locate the drive and location you would like to back up your file to.

4 Click **OK** to begin the backup process.

5 Click **OK** again when QuickBooks informs you that your file has been backed up successfully.

6 To restore that same file from the external drive to your hard drive, choose **Restore** from the QuickBooks File menu.

7 Identify the location of your backup file and the location and name to restore your file as shown in Figure 6.31. (Once again, your location will be different than shown.)

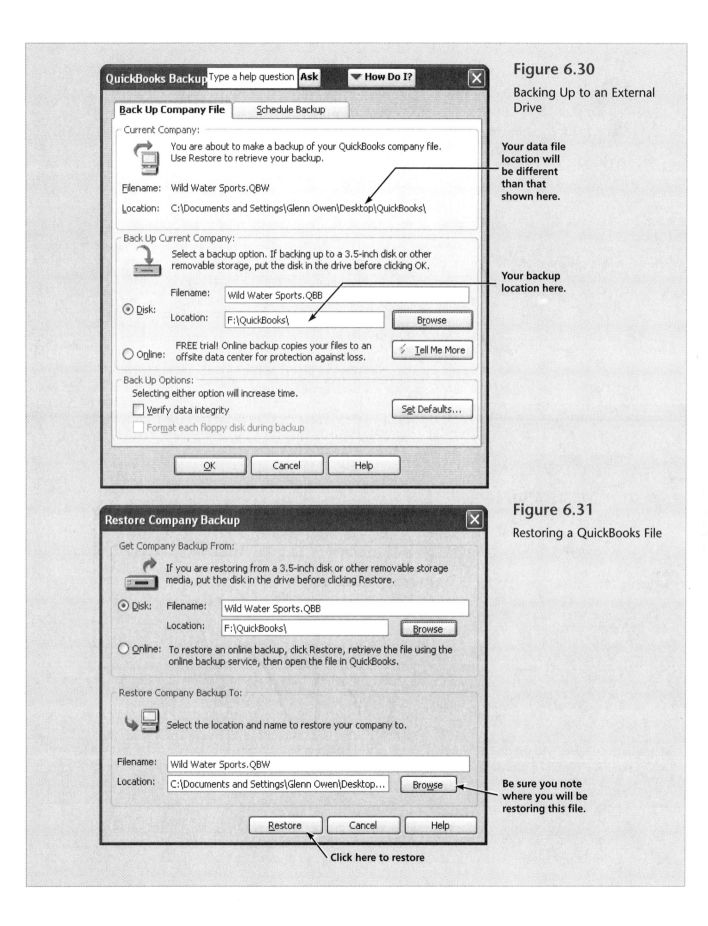

Figure 6.30

Backing Up to an External Drive

Your data file location will be different than that shown here.

Your backup location here.

Figure 6.31

Restoring a QuickBooks File

Be sure you note where you will be restoring this file.

Click here to restore

8 Click **Restore.** Be careful not to overwrite a file you want to save.

9 Click **OK** when QuickBooks informs you that your file has been restored successfully.

Alternatively, you can use Windows Explorer to copy files to an external drive.

To copy a file to an external disk using Windows Explorer:

1 Be sure QuickBooks is closed and the Wild Water Sports file is no longer open.

2 Using Windows Explorer, open the folder containing the Wild Water Sports file.

3 Open another folder in the location you want to copy to.

4 Click your existing data file and, holding down the left mouse key, drag the file from the computer's hard drive to the location you want to copy to. In this case, the original file is in the My Documents folder and the backup location is a folder on my USB drive (labeled F:\QuickBooks Backup Files). See Figure 6.32.

Figure 6.32

Making a Copy of a QuickBooks File Using Windows Explorer

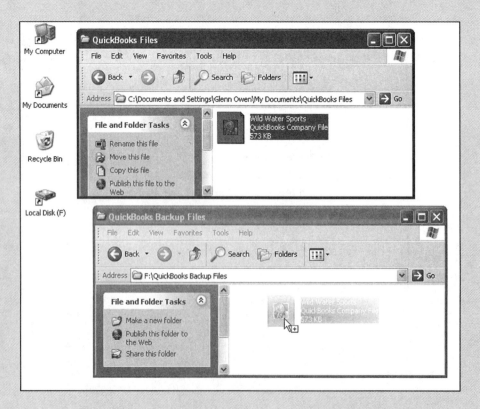

5 Rename the new file backed up on your external drive. Right-click the backed up file on your external drive and select **Rename.**

6 Type a new name for your file with the current date to identify it as a backup file created on that date. See Figure 6.33.

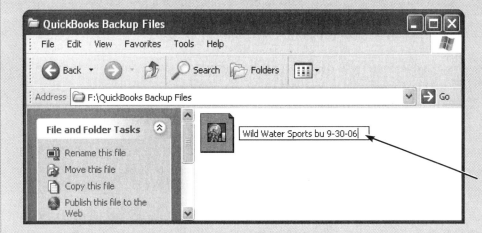

Figure 6.33

Renaming Your Backup File with a Date

Your data will be different

7 Your file is now backed up. If the original file gets lost or corrupted, simply open the two windows up again in Windows Explorer and copy the latest backup file from your external drive to your local hard drive.

8 Be sure to rename the newly copied file Wild Water Sports without the backup reference and date so you know that's the file currently in use.

End Note

Karen thanks you for your patience in helping create a QuickBooks file for Wild Water Sports. You've created a new company, set up company preferences, company items, customers, vendors, accounts, and employees. Next up, you'll begin recording business transactions.

Chapter 6 Questions

1 Describe the two setup approaches that you can use to create a new QuickBooks company file (i.e., with the EasyStep Interview and without the EasyStep Interview).

2 What is the purpose of setting preferences in QuickBooks?

3 Why do businesses often use account numbers?

4 Give examples of service items and inventory part items used by Wild Water Sports.

5 Why would a company use QuickBooks's job tracking feature?

6 Explain the process of establishing new accounts for fixed assets that will be depreciated like equipment.

7 What happens when you first establish beginning balances for accounts receivable and accounts payable?

8 Describe the process for telling QuickBooks you want to manage payroll manually if you don't have an Internet connection.

9 Why is it important to back up your QuickBooks file?

10 What are the two alternative methods for backing up a QuickBooks file?

Chapter 6 Assignments

merchandising

1 *Adding More Information to Wild Water Sports*

Restore the file Wild Water Sports Ch 6A.qbb found on the text CD or download it from the text website. Add a new income type account titled "Parts" and a subaccount of Sales with a number 4030. Add a new other current asset account titled "Inventory Parts" with a number 1130.

Add the following service items:

Item Name	Sales Description	Sales Price	Tax Code	Income a/c #
Cleaning	Labor for cleaning boat	$75.00	Tax	4020
Painting & body repairs	Hourly rate for painting and repairs	$80.00	Tax	4020

Add the following inventory parts:

Item Name & Description	Sales Price	Tax Code	Income a/c #	Inventory a/c #	Cost	Qty
Engine oil (quart)	5.00	Tax	4030	1130	4.00	0
Oil filter	15.00	Tax	4030	1130	12.00	0
Tune up parts	250.00	Tax	4030	1130	200.00	0
Air filter	35.00	Tax	4030	1130	28.00	0

Add the following customers:

Customer Name	Balance Due
Freebirds	$0
Florida Sports Camp	$0

Add the following vendors:

Vendor Name	Address	Phone	Balance Owed
MB Sports	280 Air Park Road Atwater, CA 95301	209-357-4153	$0
Tige Boats	6803 US Hwy 83 N., Abilene, TX 79601	325-676-7777	$0

Add the following employees:

Employee Name	Karen Wilson	Pat Ng
Address	16 Ocean Dr. Orlando, FL 32807	432 West Hwy 33 Orlando, FL 32807
Social Security number	654-85-7844	125-95-4123
Gender	Female	Male
Salary	$50,000 per year	n/a
Hourly wage	n/a	$18 per hour
Filing status	Single	Single
Taxes	Subject to Medicare, Social Security FUT, and all applicable State taxes	Subject to Medicare, Social Security FUT, and all applicable State taxes
Filing state	Florida	Florida
Pay period	Monthly	Monthly

Print the following as of 1/1/07 (Similar to what you did in the chapter):

a. Customer Balance Summary

b. Customer Contact List

c. Vendor Balance Summary

d. Vendor Contact List

e. Employee Contact list

f. Account Listing (account, type, and balance total only)

g. Item Listing (List only item, description, type, cost, quantity on hand, and price.)

h. Trial balance

merchandising

2 *Creating a New Company: Central Coast Cellular*

Van Morrison would like to use QuickBooks for his new company, Central Coast Cellular. The company resides at 950 Higuera St., San Luis Obispo, CA 93401. The company's phone number is 805-555-9874, and its fiscal and tax year begins in January 2003. The company's main business is cellular phone sales and rentals, but it also earns revenue by consulting with customers on alternative cellular phone plans. Choose Other/None as the Industry for this case. The company's federal tax ID is 77-9418745. The company does not use account numbers.

Change the preferences in QuickBooks as follows: Set QuickBooks to move between fields after pressing the [Enter] key. Set dates to a two-digit year format. Set up sales tax at 8% payable to the State Board of Equalization. Make inventory and purchase orders active. Enable manual payroll features. Enable reports and graphs to refresh automatically. Do not use account numbers.

Set up the following customers:

- Tribune, 3825 S. Higuera St., San Luis Obispo, CA 93401, 805-781-7800, Terms: Net 30, Contact: Sara Miles

- City of San Luis Obispo, 990 Palm Street, San Luis Obispo, CA 93401, 805-781-7100, Terms: Net 30, Contact: Robert Preston

- Sterling Hotels Corporation, 4115 Broad Street, Suite B-1, San Luis Obispo, CA 93401, 805-546-9388, Terms: Net 30, Contact: Monica Flowers.

Set up the following vendors:

- Verizon Communications, 1255 Corporate Drive, Irving, TX 75038, 972-507-5000, Terms: Net 30, Contact: Francisco Rojas

- Nokia Mobile Phones, 23621 Park Sorrento Road, Suite 101, Calabasas, CA 91302, 818-876-6000, Terms: Net 30, Contact: Brandy Parker

- Ericsson, Inc., 740 East Campbell Road, Richardson, TX 75081, 972-583-0000, Terms: Net 30, Contact: Monty Python.

Set up the following employees using the company's federal tax ID # 77-9418745. All employees are paid semi-monthly and subject to Social Security, FUTA (at 3%), Medicare, SUI, SDI, and California's Employment Training Taxes payable to the Employment Development Department (EDD).

- Name: Mr. Jay Bruner, Address: 552 Olive St., San Luis Obispo, CA 93401, Phone: 805-555-7894, SS#: 578-94-3154, Start date: 1/1/03, Salary: $3,000 per month, Filing Status: Single.

- Name: Mr. Alex Rodriguez, Address: 1480 Monterey St., San Luis Obispo, CA 93401, Phone: 805-555-1579, SS#: 487-98-1374, Start date: 1/1/03, Salary: $4,000 per month, Filing Status: Married with one income.

- Name: Ms. Megan Paulson, Address: 400 Beach St., San Luis Obispo, CA 93401, Phone: 805-555-4489, SS#: 547-31-5974, Start date: 1/1/03, Hourly: $12 per hour, Filing Status: Married with two incomes.

Modify the existing chart of accounts to include the following:

- Checking, Type: Bank.

- Accounts Receivable, Type: Accounts Receivable

- Phone Sales, Type: Income

- Phone Rentals, Type: Income

- Consulting, Type: Income

Set up the following items:

- Consulting Services: Type: Service, Rate: $95, Taxable, and using income account: Consulting.

- Inventory Part: Item name/description: Nokia 8290, Cost: $150, Preferred vendor: Nokia, Sales price: $225, Taxable, and using income account: Phone Sales.

- Inventory Part: Item name/description: Nokia 8890, Cost: $175, Preferred vendor: Nokia, Sales price: $250, Taxable, and using income account: Phone Sales.

- Inventory Part: Item name/description: Nokia 3285, Cost: $200, Preferred vendor: Nokia, Sales price: $300, Taxable, and using income account: Phone Sales.

- Inventory Part: Item name/description: Ericsson LX588, Cost: $50, Preferred vendor: Ericsson, Sales price: $85, Taxable, and using income account: Phone Sales.

- Inventory Part: Item name/description: Ericsson T19LX, Cost: $75, Preferred vendor: Ericsson, Sales price: $100, Taxable, and using income account: Phone Sales.

Print the following as of 1/1/03 (Be sure to keep this QuickBooks file in a safe place as it is used as a starting file for this case in the next chapter.)

a. Customer Contact List

b. Vendor Contact List

c. Employee Contact list

d. Account Listing (Account, type, and balance total only)

e. Item Listing (List only item, description, type, cost, quantity on hand, and price.)

3   *Using the South-Western Home Page for More Assignments or Cases*

Go to the home page for this textbook at **www.thomsonedu.com/accounting/ owen.** Click **Additional Problem Sets,** and then select the **Chapter 6** section, and complete the problem(s) that your instructor assigns.

Chapter 6 Case Problem 1:
ALOHA PROPERTY MANAGEMENT

service   easy step

Aloha Property Management, Inc., a property manager, is located at 4-356 Kuhio Highway, Suite A-1, Kapaa Kauai, Hawaii 96746 808-823-8375. The company specializes in Hawaii Vacation Rentals. Their federal tax ID number is 72-6914707, and they plan to start using QuickBooks as their accounting program January 1, 2008. They have been in business for two years using a manual accounting system but wish to have you help them migrate to QuickBooks. They are a property management corporation filing form 1120 each year and collecting a 4% general excise tax (Tax name: HI Sales Tax, description: Sales Tax) on all rental income which must be paid to the State of Hawaii Department of Taxation located at P.O. Box 1425 Honolulu, HI 96806-1425. Choose Other/None as the Industry for this case.

They plan to use QuickBooks's service invoice format and use sales receipts to record cash sales. They also plan to use QuickBooks payroll features but plan to calculate payroll manually as they currently have two W-2 employees. They don't prepare estimates or track employee time or segments. They do, however, plan to enter bills as received and then enter payments later. Reports are to be accrual based and they plan to use the income and expense accounts created in QuickBooks for a property management company and they will be providing services only, no products. Most of their revenue comes from renting their properties located on the island of Kauai to individual and corporate accounts. It's the company's policy to usually collect a 50% deposit upon reservation with the balance upon arrival. Some customers (those that have prior credit approval) are invoiced upon arrival, and the remaining payment is due 30 days thereafter. Deposits are recorded as payments on account even though revenue is not recorded until they arrive. Other customers (those that don't have prior credit approval) must pay upon arrival, at which time a sales receipt is generated and the remaining payment is collected. The company doesn't use QuickBooks's statement feature. Service items are used, but no inventory is maintained. Existing service items, customers, vendors, and employee information is provided below. *Note:* Deposits for rentals not yet provided are shown as negative numbers.

Service Item Name	Description	Income a/c	Rate
Moana Unit #1	Weekly rent for Moana Unit #1	4130	$2,000
Moana Unit #2	Weekly rent for Moana Unit #2	4130	$2,500
Moana Unit #3	Weekly rent for Moana Unit #3	4130	$4,000
Moana Unit #4	Weekly rent for Moana Unit #4	4130	$12.000
Villa Kailani Unit #1	Weekly rent for Villa Unit #1	4130	$3,000
Villa Kailani Unit #2	Weekly rent for Villa Unit #2	4130	$4,500
Villa Kailani Unit #3	Weekly rent for Villa Unit #3	4130	$4,200
Villa Kailani Unit #4	Weekly rent for Villa Unit #4	4130	$6,000

Customer Name	Balance Due (Deposits)
Boeing	$10,000
General Motors	$75,000
Brice Montoya	($3,000)
Sara Rice	($6,000)
Apple Computer	$25,000

Vendor Name	Balance Owed
Reilly Custodial	$4,500
Blue Sky Pools	$1,800

Employee Name	Fran Aki	Danièle Castillo
Social Security number	128-85-7413	984-74-1235
Salary	$75,000 per year	n/a
Hourly wage	n/a	$20 per hour
Filing status	Married	Single
Taxes	Subject to Medicare, Social Security, FUT, and all applicable state taxes	Subject to Medicare, Social Security, FUT, and all applicable state taxes
Filing state	Hawaii	Hawaii

The company owns two properties: Moana Lani Kai located in Princeville and Villa Kailani located in Poipu. They owed $3,875,000 (a 25-year mortgage) on the two properties for which they paid $2,000,000 and $3,000,000, respectively, several years ago. Both of these are to be treated as fixed assets using Moana and Villa as fixed asset account names. Accumulated depreciation on the two assets as of 12/31/07 was $500,000 and $700,000, respectively.

The company has one checking account, which had a balance of $15,000 as of 12/31/07 with the Bank of Hawaii. Their Hawaii withholding, unemployment, and disability identification number is 84325184. Their unemployment rate is 2.4%, and disability rate is 0.01%. Only two payroll items are used: Salary and Hourly. Federal taxes are paid to the U.S. Treasury and state taxes are paid to the Hawaii State Tax Collector. All employees are paid monthly.

You've been asked to reclassify the uncategorized income and expenses to the opening balance equity account. After that, you are to reclassify the new balance in the opening balance equity account to capital stock ($10,000) and retained earnings ($24,700). You've also been asked to use account numbers for all accounts. Use the following for specific new account names and numbers:

Account Name	Account Number	Balance as of 12/31/07
Bank of Hawaii (checking a/c)	1000	15,000
Moana	1600	
Cost	1610	2,000,000
Accumulated Depreciation	1620	-500,000
Villa	1700	
Cost	1710	3,000,000
Accumulated Depreciation	1720	-700,000
Loan Payable (long-term liability)	2600	3,875,000
Capital Stock (create a/c)	3100	
Retained Earnings (change a/c #)	3200	

Use the information provided above to create a new QuickBooks file for Aloha. (**Hint:** Read the entire case before you begin, establish the new company file accepting the default name provided, and modify preferences like you did in the main chapter. Enter all beginning asset, liability, and equity account balances as of 12/31/07. Use journal entry adjustments to close the uncategorized income and expense amounts to the Opening Bal Equity account and then close the Opening Bal Equity account so that there is $10,000 in the Capital Stock account and $24,700 in the Retained Earnings account. Change account numbers so they match up with the trial balance below.) After adjustments, your trial balance at 12/31/07 should look like this:

Aloha Property Management, Inc.
Trial Balance
As of December 31, 2007

	Dec 31, 07 Debit	Dec 31, 07 Credit
1000 · Bank of Hawaii	15,000.00	
1200 · Accounts Receivable	101,000.00	
1600 · Moana:1610 · Cost	2,000,000.00	
1600 · Moana:1620 · Accumulated Depreciation		500,000.00
1700 · Villa:1710 · Cost	3,000,000.00	
1700 · Villa:1720 · Accumulated Depreciation		700,000.00
2000 · Accounts Payable		6,300.00
2600 · Loan Payable		3,875,000.00
3000 · Opening Bal Equity	0.00	
3100 · Capital Stock		10,000.00
3200 · Retained Earnings		24,700.00
4999 · Uncategorized Income	0.00	
6999 · Uncategorized Expenses	0.00	
TOTAL	**5,116,000.00**	**5,116,000.00**

Once you've entered all the beginning information, print the following reports as of 1/1/08. (Be sure to keep this QuickBooks file in a safe place as it is used as a starting file for this case in the next chapter.)

a. Customer Balance Summary

b. Customer Contact List

c. Vendor Balance Summary

d. Vendor Contact List

e. Employee Contact List

f. Account Listing (account, type, and balance total only)

g. Item Listing (list only item, description, type, and price.)

h. Trial Balance

Chapter 6 Case Problem 2:
OCEAN VIEW FLOWERS

merchandising

easy step

Ocean View Flowers, a wholesale flower distributor, is located at 100 Ocean Ave. in Lompoc, California, 93436. Ocean View started business January 1, 2008, and the owners would like you to use QuickBooks to keep track of their business transactions. Ocean View is a calendar year company (for both fiscal and tax purposes) and will need to use the inventory, purchase order, and manual payroll features of QuickBooks. The company established a bank account, titled Union Checking, at the beginning of the year. In addition, the company filed for federal (91–3492370) and state (23–432) tax ID numbers. All employees are paid semi-monthly but do not earn sick or vacation pay. All state taxes are paid to the Employment Development Department. The state unemployment tax (SUTA) rate is 1%. The company's expected customers and vendors are shown below.

Customer	Address	Terms	Contact
Valley Florists	101 Main St. Los Angeles, CA 90113	2/10 net 30	Sam Davies
FTD	2033 Lakewood Dr. Chicago, IL 60601	net 30	Beverly Rose
California Beauties	239 Hyde Street San Francisco, CA 95114	2/10 net 30	Farrah Faucet
Eastern Scents	938 42nd Street New York, NY 10054	2/10 net 30	Nick Giovanni
Latin Ladies	209 Zona Rosa Mexico City, Mexico	2/10 net 30	Juan Valdez

Vendor	Address	Terms	Contact
Hawaiian Farms	2893 1st Street Honolulu, HI 05412	Net 30	Mahalo Baise
Brophy Bros. Farms	90 East Hwy 246 Santa Barbara, CA 93101	Net 30	Tim Beach
Princess Flowers	92 West Way Medford, OR 39282	Net 30	Bonnie Sobieski
Keenan's Pride	10 East Betteravia Santa Maria, CA 93454	2/10 net 30	Kelly Keenan
Vordale Farms	62383 Lido Isle Newport, CA 90247	Net 30	Donna Vordale

Ocean View Flowers employees (all of whom are considered regular-type employees) were hired on 1/4/08 and are subject to federal and state taxes and withholdings, state unemployment, state disability, and state employee training taxes. A list of employees is shown on the next page.

Employee	Address	Social Security #	Compensation	Filing Status
Margie Coe	2322 Courtney Buellton, CA 93246	654-85-1254	$12/hour	Head of Household
Kelly Gusland	203 B St. Lompoc, CA 93436	567-78-1334	$15/hour	Single
Stan Comstock	383 Lemon St. Lompoc, CA 93436	126-85-7843	Annual Salary of $50,000	Married, one income
Marie McAninch	1299 College Ave. Santa Maria, CA 93454	668-41-9578	Annual Salary of $60,000	Married, two incomes
Edward Thomas	1234 St. Andrews Way Lompoc, CA 93436	556-98-4125	Annual Salary of $70,000	Single

Assignment

Create a new company file for Ocean View Flowers using the EasyStep Interview. Then add the customers, vendors, employees, accounts, items, and other information above. (Be sure to keep this QuickBooks file in a safe place as it is used as a starting file for this case in the next chapter.) Print the following as of 1/1/08:

a.   Customer Contact List

b.   Vendor Contact List

c.   Employee Contact List

Cash-Oriented Business Activities

7

Case: Wild Water Sports, Inc.

You and Karen completed the initial setup of the QuickBooks program at the beginning of January and are ready to begin recording business transactions for the month. The new company has completed its first month of business and Ernesto is pleased with the new business relationship he established with Karen and Donna. However, no one knows the extent of their profitability or financial position since none of the accounting events have yet been recorded into QuickBooks. You had to start the spring semester, and Karen has been busy just keeping the business going.

"I'm brand new to QuickBooks" you explain. "I know a little about financial accounting and I'm taking a managerial class right now, but I haven't had a course in QuickBooks or any other computerized accounting program for that matter."

"No problem," Karen says, trying to reassure you. "QuickBooks is very easy for first-time users to learn, and you'll be pleased with how much it will help the company understand its performance and financial position."

The two of you agree to meet today to review the business transactions which took place in January. Karen agrees to explain the nature of each transaction and how it should be recorded in QuickBooks. She suggests that the best way to accomplish this is to view each transaction by the three fundamental business activities: financing, investing, and operating.

"I remember studying those concepts in my first accounting course," you comment. "If I remember correctly, financing activities are initiated when money or other resources are obtained from short-term nontrade creditors, long-term creditors, and/or owners. Financing activities are completed when amounts owed are repaid to or otherwise settled with these same creditors and/or owners. Investing activities are initiated when the money obtained from financing activities is applied to nonoperating uses, such as buying investment securities and/or productive assets like equipment, buildings, land, or furniture and fixtures. Investing activities are completed when the investment securities and/or productive assets are sold. Finally, operating activities occur when the money obtained from financing activities and the productive assets obtained from investing activities are applied to either purchase or produce goods and services for sale. These operating activities are substantially completed when goods are delivered or when services are performed."

"Wow, they taught you well!" Karen exclaims. "Let's begin with a few cash-oriented financing activities."

Recording Cash-Oriented Financing Activities

You begin with two financing activities. The first occurred on January 3 when the company received $200,000 from Karen and Donna ($100,000 each) as their purchase of stock in the company.

To record the deposit received from Karen and Donna:

1 Start the QuickBooks program.

2 Restore the Wild Water Sports Ch 7.qbb file from your Data Files CD or downloaded from the Internet. See "Data Files CD" in Chapter 1 if you need more information.

3 The newly restored Wild Water Sports Ch 7.qbw file should now be open.

4 Click the **Record Deposits** icon from the Banking section of the home page. The Make Deposits window appears. Note that QuickBooks has automatically inserted today's date.

5 Enter the information for Karen and Donna's stock purchase as shown in Figure 7.1. Be sure to enter the correct date.

6 Click **Save & New** to record the deposit. Do not close the Make Deposits window.

The second deposit was made on January 4 when the company borrowed $250,000 from their bank (Bank of Florida) at 5% payable in 5 years.

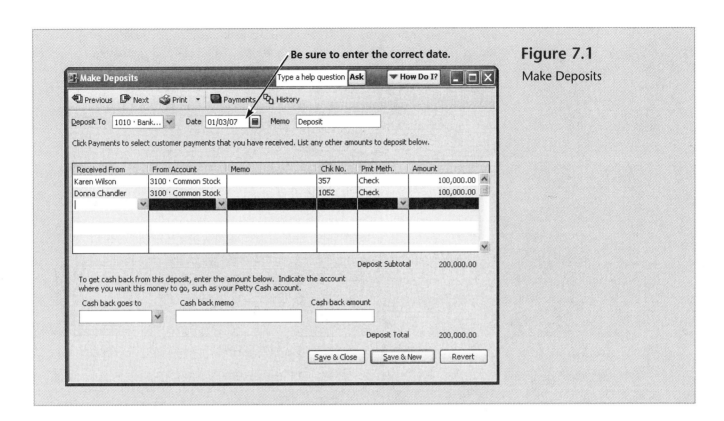

Figure 7.1
Make Deposits

To record the long-term loan from the Bank of Florida:

1 Select account **1010 – Bank of Florida** as the Deposit To account.

2 Type **01/04/07** as the deposit date.

3 Type **Bank of Florida** in the received from text box then press **[Tab]**.

4 Click **Quick Add** in the Name Not Found window.

5 Click **Other** in the Select Name Type window and then click **OK**.

6 Select account **2500 – Loan Payable** as the From Account.

7 Type **250000** as the amount and then click **Save & Close.**

You have now recorded two different cash-oriented financing activities: the sale of stock to investors and the borrowing of funds on a long-term basis. Now it's time to look at recording cash-oriented investing activities.

Recording Cash-Oriented Investing Activities

After making the deposits from investors and creditors, the company decided to temporarily invest those funds into a money-market account with its bank. By transferring those funds from its checking to a money market account, the company expected to generate some interest revenue until the funds were needed.

To accomplish this transfer, Karen wrote check number 1001 on January 8 from the company's checking account with Bank of Florida and deposited the check into their new money market account with ETrade.

"Do we have a general ledger account for this?" you ask.

"No, but we can create one while we record this transaction," Karen answers.

To create new general ledger account and record the purchase of money market funds:

1 Click the **Write Checks** icon from the Banking section of the home page. The Write Checks window appears.

2 Uncheck the To be printed checkbox if it is checked.

3 Type **1001** as the check number.

4 Type **01/08/07** as the date.

5 Type **ETrade** in the Pay to the Order section of the check, and then press **[Tab]**.

6 Click **Quick Add** in the Name Not Found window.

7 Select **Other** in the Select Name Type window and then click **OK.**

8 Type **300000** as the check amount, and then press **[Tab]** five times or until the cursor is in the account section of the check.

Trouble? Near the bottom of the Write Checks window are two tabs—one labeled Expenses and one labeled Items. The Expenses tab is somewhat misleading because you can type or select any account to appear here, including assets. On the other hand, you use the Items tab to enter inventory acquisitions only. The main difference between them is that the items tab has a column for quantities purchased and the expenses tab has a column for an account.

9 In the Expenses tab select **Add New** from the drop-down arrow list of accounts. (*Note:* You may have to scroll up the list to the top to find Add New.) A New Account window should appear.

10 Select **Bank** as the account Type.

11 Type **1050** as the account Number.

12 Type **Short-Term Investments** as the Name of the account. Your screen should look like Figure 7.2.

13 Click **OK** to record this new general ledger account.

14 Press **[Tab]** two times. Your Write Checks window should look like Figure 7.3.

15 Click **Save & New** to record this transaction. Do not close this window.

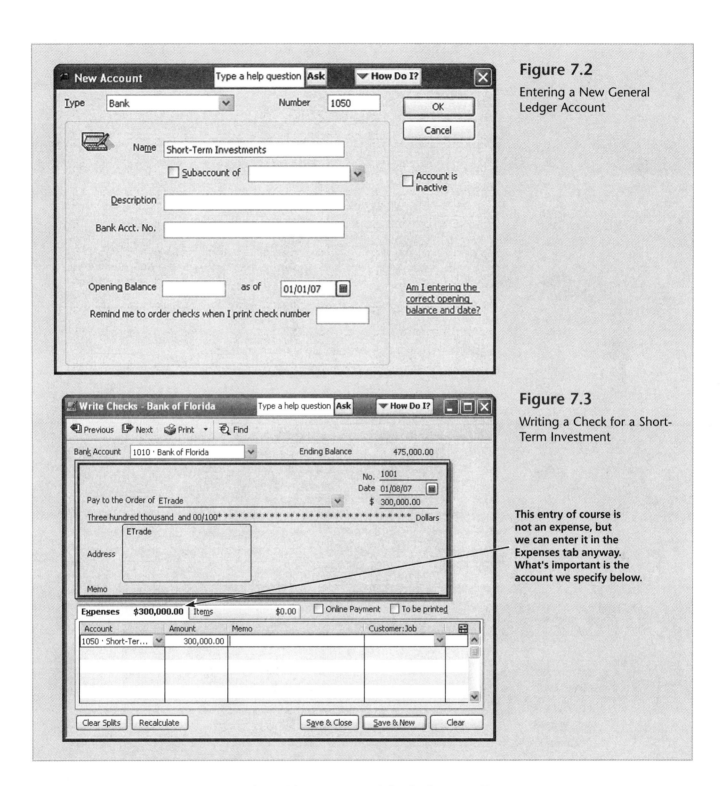

Figure 7.2

Entering a New General Ledger Account

Figure 7.3

Writing a Check for a Short-Term Investment

This entry of course is not an expense, but we can enter it in the Expenses tab anyway. What's important is the account we specify below.

Wild Water also had other cash-oriented investment activity in January. On January 10 they purchased new office furniture for the sales, marketing, and service staff from the local Staples store and new equipment for the service bays from AJ Marine Equipment.

"How should we classify the purchase of furniture and fixtures since the only fixed asset account we have is Equipment?" you ask.

"We'll have to create a few new accounts," Karen responds. "QuickBooks now has a tracking system we could use to monitor the location of our various fixed assets but, since we won't have that many individual assets, we won't worry about tracking them at this point."

To record the purchase of furniture and equipment:

1 Click the **Chart of Accounts** icon from the Company section of the home page to open the Chart of Accounts window.

   Trouble? If the Write Checks window prevents you from seeing the Chart of Accounts icon, move the Write Checks window down slightly.

2 Click the **Account** button at the bottom of the Chart of Accounts window and then click **New.**

3 Select **Fixed Assets** as the account type.

4 Type **1400** as the account number.

5 Type **Furniture & Fixtures** as the account name. Your window should look like Figure 7.4.

Figure 7.4

Adding a New Account

This will be the main account, but all of our input will go to the subaccounts Cost and Accumulated Depreciation that you're about to create

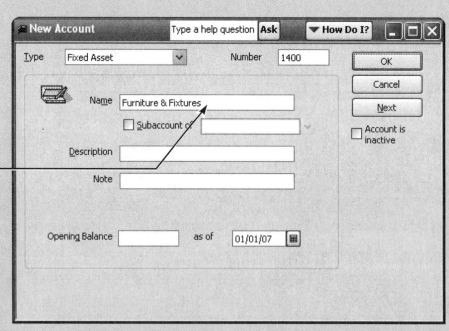

6 Click **Next** to add another account.

7 Type **1410** as the account number and type **Cost** as the account name.

8 Click in the check box **Subaccount of** and select **1400 – Furniture & Fixtures** from the drop-down arrow list.

9 Click **Next** to add another account.

10 Type **1490** as the account number and type **Accumulated Depreciation** as the account name.

11 Click in the checkbox **Subaccount of** and select **1400 – Furniture & Fixtures** from the drop-down arrow list.

12 Click **OK** to finish adding new accounts. Note the new account you just created in the Chart of Accounts window.

13 Close the Chart of Accounts window. The Write Checks window is probably hidden from view. It's actually just under the home page. Click the **Window** menu and select **Write Checks – Bank of Florida** to make that window active.

14 Type **1002** as the check number (if it is not already there).

  Trouble? If you previously closed the Write Checks window, open it again by clicking the Write Checks icon on the home Page.

15 Type **01/10/07** as the date of purchase in the Write Checks window.

16 Type **Staples** in the Pay to the Order section of the check, and then press **[Tab]**.

17 Click **Quick Add** in the Name Not Found window.

18 Select **Vendor** in the Select Name Type window and then click **OK.**

19 Type **70000** as the check amount, and then press **[Tab]** five times or until the cursor is in the account section of the check.

20 In the Expenses tab type **1410** from the drop-down arrow list of accounts.

21 Click **No** from the Tracking Fixed Asset window and click in the checkbox **Do not display this message in the future.** (Karen explains that while this is a nice feature for a company with many fixed assets, it is an add-on cost to QuickBooks and not worth it given their amount of fixed assets.)

22 Click **Save & New** to enter another purchase.

23 Type **1003** as the check number.

24 Type **01/10/07** as the date of purchase in the Write Checks window.

25 Type **AJ Marine Equipment** in the Pay to the Order section of the check, and then press **[Tab]**.

26 Click **Quick Add** in the Name Not Found window.

27 Select **Vendor** in the Select Name Type window and then click **OK.**

28 Type **100000** as the check amount, and then press **[Tab]** five times or until the cursor is in the account section of the check.

29 In the Expenses tab, type **1310** from the drop-down arrow list of accounts and then press **[Tab]** twice. Your check should look like

Figure 7.5. Note that even though you typed 1310 as the account, your screen will display only part of the account number. The full account number for this transaction is 1300 · Equipment:1310 · Cost.

Figure 7.5

Writing a Check to
Purchase Equipment

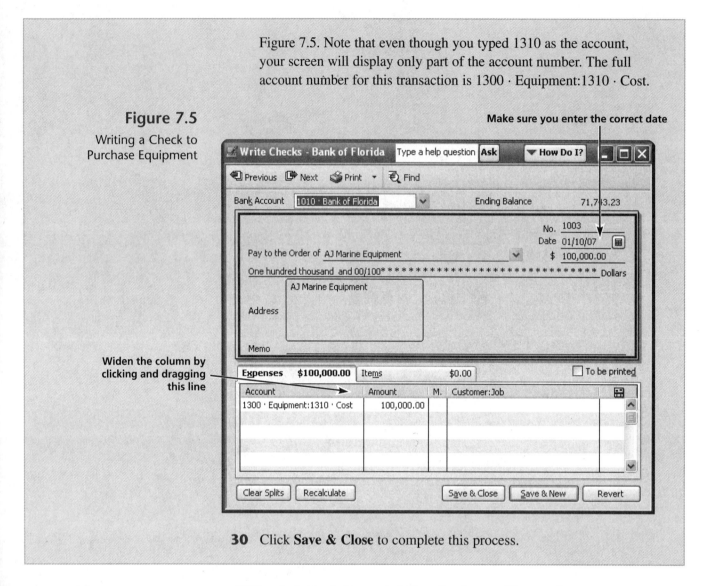

30 Click **Save & Close** to complete this process.

"When is depreciation recorded on fixed assets?" you ask.

"Not until the end of the accounting period, before we create financial statements," Karen responds. "But we have lots to do before that."

Recording Cash-Oriented Operating Activities

Karen explains that Wild Water uses purchase orders to help manage its business activities. She remarks that, typically, purchase orders don't have an impact on financial statements, but they do play an important role as a control feature in QuickBooks. So she plans on using them.

"For example," she says, "we ordered two custom boats for two customers in January using purchase orders 4001 and 4002. Let me show you how purchase orders are used in QuickBooks."

"Are all purchase orders related to customers?" you ask.

"Not necessarily," Karen responds. "Sometimes we order for inventory to have in our showroom, but in these two we were ordering boats for specific customers."

The first boat was an existing inventory item (Malibu WakeSetter XTI sold for $70,000) and was ordered for an existing customer from an existing vendor. The second boat was for a new item (Tige 22v sold for $78,750) and was ordered from an existing vendor but for a new customer. In both transactions, the customer was required to pay a 25% deposit upon order ($17,500.00 and $19,687.50, respectively).

"How do you account for the amounts received?" you ask.

"We treat them just like payments received from customers, but since there is no invoice to allocate them to, we just leave them as credit balances in customers' accounts," Karen answers. "Accounting would normally require you to treat these as unearned revenue and record them as liabilities; however, we only make adjustments for credit balances in accounts if, prior to preparing financial statements, we still have remaining credits in customer accounts."

Karen decides first to show you the purchase orders generated to place the order with the vendors and second how the two deposits on sales were accounted for.

To create a purchase order:

1 Click the **Purchase Orders** icon from the Vendors section of the home page to open the Create Purchase Orders window.

2 Select **Malibu Boats** from the Vendor drop-down list.

3 Type **1/11/07** as the date.

4 Type **4001** as the purchase order number.

5 Select **Malibu Wakesetter XTI** as the item, type **1** as the Qty (quantity), and select **Florida Sports Camp** as the customer for which we are ordering the boat. Your purchase order should now look like Figure 7.6.

6 Click **Save & New.** Note that QuickBooks may identify a word it doesn't know and, before processing this purchase order, a Check Spelling on Form window may appear to verify the spelling of WakeSetter, as shown in Figure 7.7.

7 Click **Add** to add the word WakeSetter to QuickBooks dictionary.

8 Also click **Add** to add the XTI to QuickBooks dictionary. (***Note:*** This dictionary is unique to the program, not to the data file. Later, if you work on a different computer with a different copy of QuickBooks, this message may reappear.)

9 Select **Tige Boats** from the Vendor drop-down list.

10 Type **1/11/07** as the date (if it's not already there).

11 Type **4002** as the purchase order number (if it's not already there).

Figure 7.6

Purchase Order 4001

Be sure to specify the customer name here so that later you will properly bill them for this boat

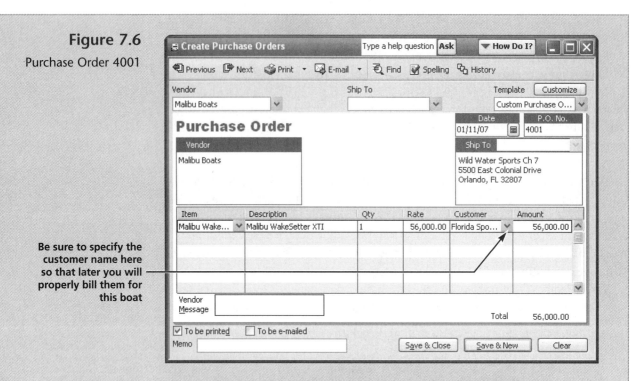

Figure 7.7

Spell Check

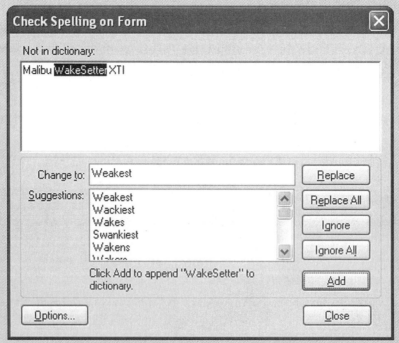

12   Select **Add New** from the drop-down Item list to display the New Item window.

13   Select **Inventory Part** from the drop-down Type list.

14   Type **Tige 22v** as the Item Number and Description for both purchase and sales transactions.

15 Type **63000** as the Cost.

16 Leave 5000 – Cost of Good Sold as the COGS account.

17 Select **Tige Boats** as the Preferred Vendor.

18 Type **78750** as the Sales Price.

19 Leave Tax as the Tax Code.

20 Select **4010** and the Income Account.

21 Leave 1120 – Inventory Asset as the Asset Account. The New Item window should look like Figure 7.8.

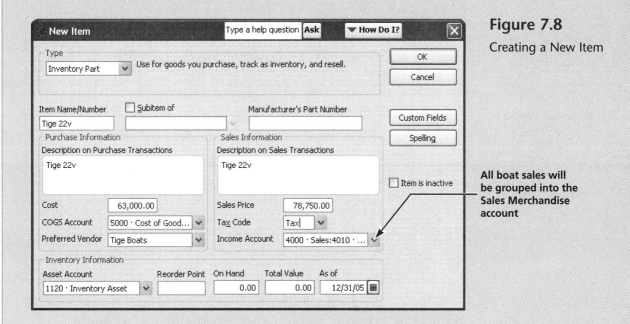

Figure 7.8

Creating a New Item

All boat sales will be grouped into the Sales Merchandise account

22 Click **OK** to accept this new item and add Tige to the dictionary if necessary.

23 Type **1** as the Qty.

24 Select **Add New** from the drop-down Customer' list to display the New Customer window.

25 Type **Performance Rentals** as the Customer Name and Company Name.

26 Type **15 Hwy 22, Orlando, FL 32807** as the customers' address.

27 Click **Copy >>** to copy the bill to address to the ship to address section. Click **OK** to accept. Your new customer window should look like Figure 7.9.

28 Click **OK** to add this new customer.

29 Click **Save & Close** to add this new purchase order.

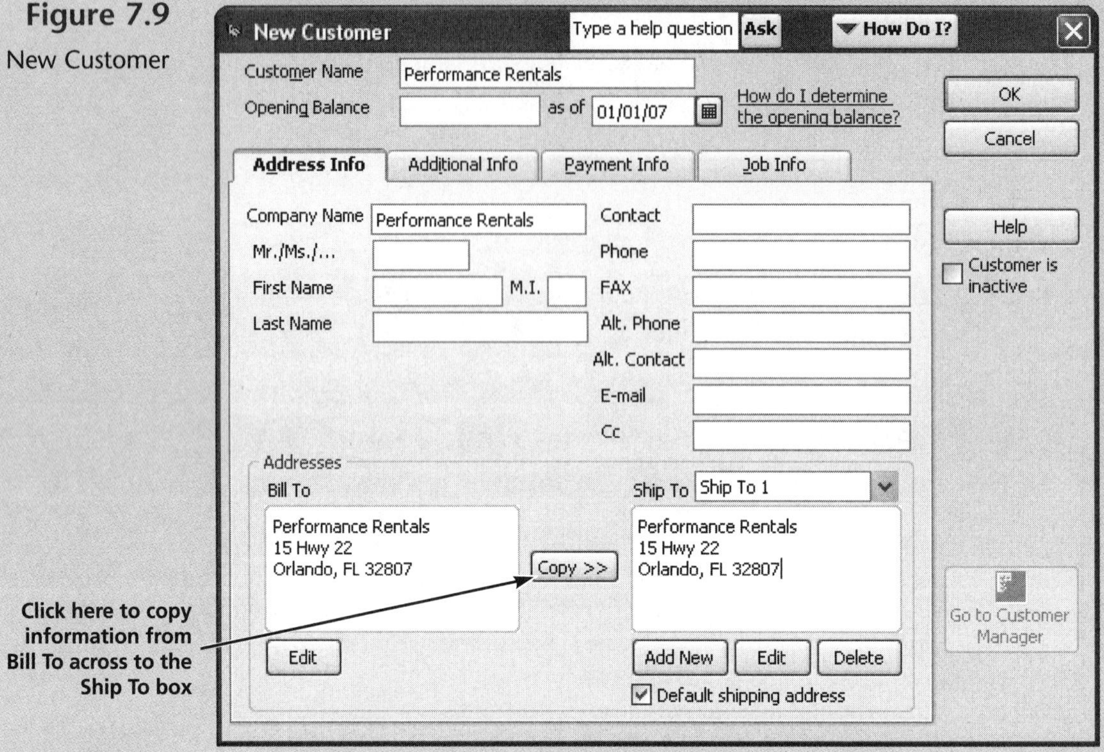

Figure 7.9

Adding a New Customer

Karen has shown you how to create purchase orders and now would like to show you how the customers' deposits should be accounted for. Remember, in both cases customers remitted cash to Wild Water, but a sale could not be recorded because the products had not been delivered and thus the earnings process was not complete.

To record the receipt of deposits on future sales:

1 Click the **Receive Payments** icon located in the Customers section of the home page.

2 Click **Yes** if asked if you accept credit card payments and No if asked if you accept on-line payments.

3 Select **Florida Sports Camp** as the customer from which the first deposit was received.

4 Type **17500** as the amount received.

5 Type the date **1/11/07.**

6 Select **Check** as the payment method.

7 Type **8755** as the check number. Your Receive Payments window should look like Figure 7.10.

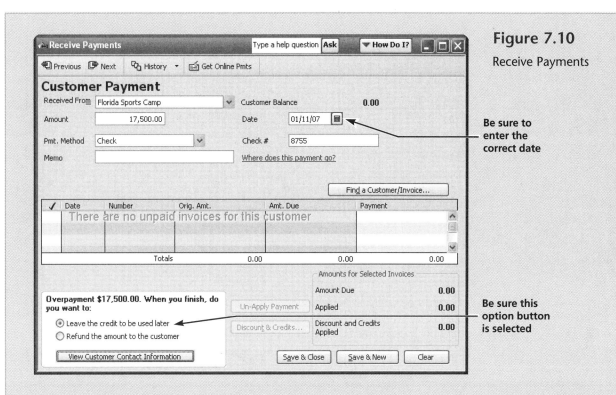

Figure 7.10

Receive Payments

8 Click **Save & New** to record another deposit.

9 Click **OK** to save the credit on the customer's account and not print a credit memo.

10 Select **Performance Rentals** as the customer from which the second deposit was received.

11 Type **19687.50** as the amount received.

12 Type the date **1/11/07**.

13 Select **MasterCard** as the payment method.

14 Type **2158-6412-9842-9855** as the credit card number and **04/08** as the expiration date. Your Receive Payments window should look like Figure 7.11.

15 Click **Save & Close** to exit, and then click **OK** once again to leave this credit balance for the customer.

"Typically we collect cash from sales on account, such as sales made to customers where we gave them credit terms like net 30," Karen comments. "If you recall when we set up our accounting system on January 1, 2007, we had some customers who owed us money from previous sales. The balances owed were reflected in accounts receivable."

"Do you record those cash collections like we just recorded deposits?" you ask.

"Yes, plus we had some cash sales during January which I'll show you as well," Karen answers. We had one cash boat sale and one cash boat service during the month, both from new customers."

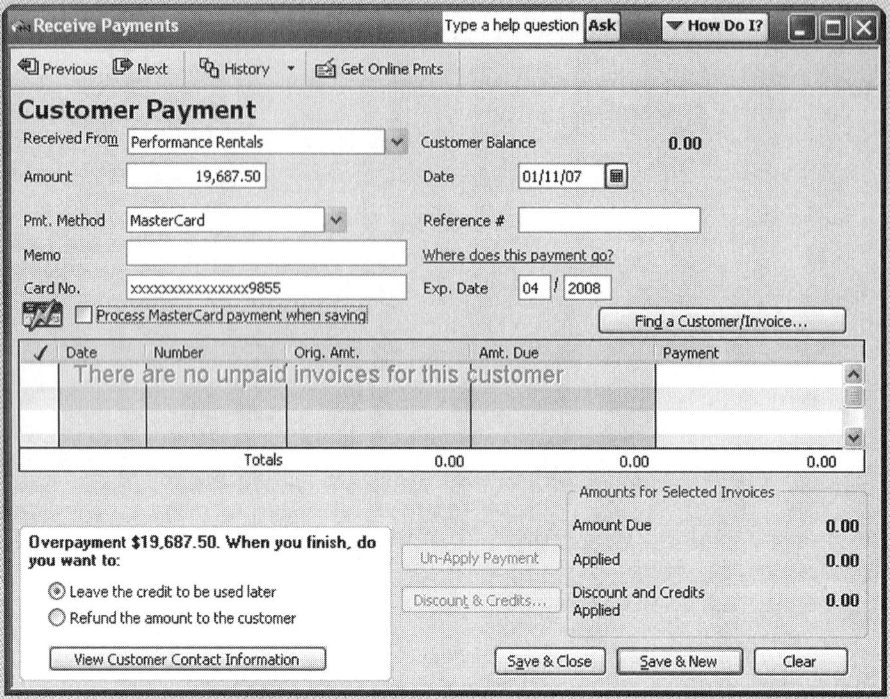

Figure 7.11

Processing a Credit Card
Received as a Deposit

To record cash collected on account:

1 Click the **Receive Payments** icon located in the Customers section of the home page.

2 Select **Buena Vista Water Sports:Boat Sales** from the Received From drop-down list.

3 Type **30000** as the amount received.

4 Type **1/15/07** as the date received.

5 Select **Check** as the payment method and type **65454** as the check number. Your screen should look like Figure 7.12.

6 Click **Save & Close** to complete this transaction.

To record cash sales:

1 Click the **Create Sales Receipts** icon located in the Customers section of the home page.

2 Select **Add New** from the Customer:Job drop-down list.

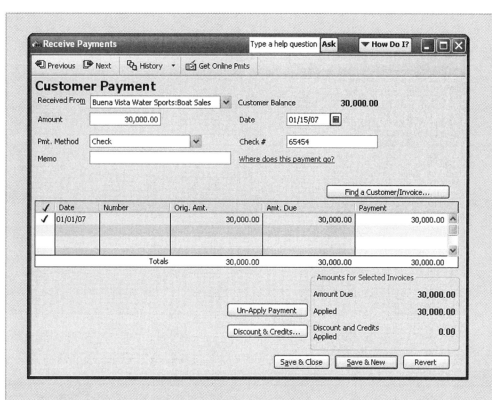

Figure 7.12

Receipt of Payments from Customers on Account

3   Type **Seth Backman** as both the Customer Name and Company Name.

4   Type this customer's bill to and ship to address as **140 Fir Ave., Miami, FL 33109.**

5   Click **OK** to accept this new customer.

6   Type **1/16/07** as the date of sale and **6001** and the Sale No.

7   Type **161** as the Check No. and select **Check** as the Payment Method.

8   Select **Malibu Sportster LX** from the drop-down list of items.

9   Type Qty (Quantity) **1.**

10 Select **Florida Sales Tax** from the Tax drop-down list.

11 Make sure the To be printed checkbox is unchecked. Your screen should look like Figure 7.13.

12 Click **Save & New** to record another sales receipt.

13 Select **Add New** from the Customer:Job drop-down list.

14 Type **Alisa Hay** as both the Customer Name and Company Name.

15 Type this customer's bill to and ship to address as **2999 Dover Blvd. Daytona Beach, FL 32114.**

Figure 7.13

Recording Cash Sales
with a Sales Receipt

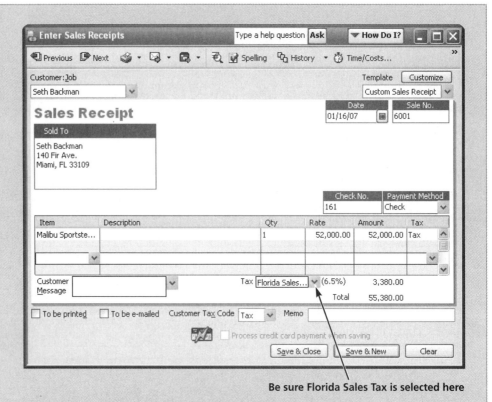

Be sure Florida Sales Tax is selected here

16 Click **OK** to accept this new customer.

17 Type **1/25/07** as the date of sale and **6002** and the Sale No.

18 Select **Cash** as the Payment Method.

19 Select **Engine Service** from the drop-down list of items.

20 Type **1** as the Qty (Quantity).

21 Select **Engine Oil** from the drop-down list of items.

22 Click **OK** in the warning window which appears. (Since you're recording these transactions after the events have already occurred, your timing may be off from the actual acquisition of inventory items like engine oil and the date you record the receipt of those items.)

23 Type **5** as the Qty (Quantity).

24 Select **Oil Filter** from the drop-down list of items.

25 Click **OK** in the warning window which appears.

26 Type **1** as the Qty (Quantity).

27 Select **Florida Sales Tax** from the Tax drop-down list.

28 Make sure the To be printed checkbox is unchecked. Your screen should look like Figure 7.14.

29 Click **Save & Close.**

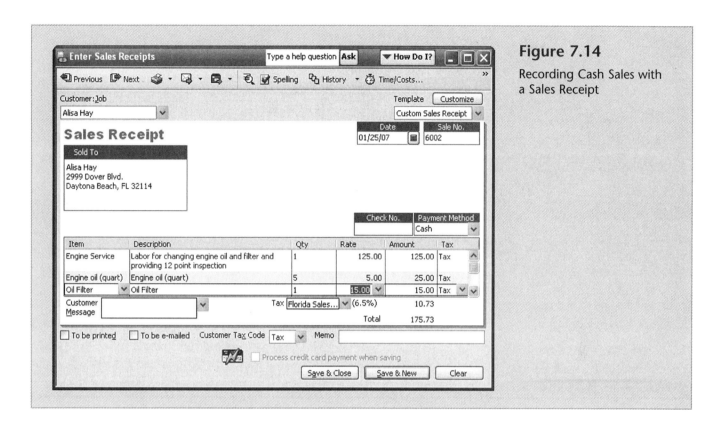

Figure 7.14

Recording Cash Sales with a Sales Receipt

"Have all of these cash receipt transactions been recorded in our checking account?" you ask.

"No, one of the preferences we specified in the company set up was that all cash receipts like payments on account, advance payments, etc., are to be recorded into an Undeposited Funds account since bank deposits are often made at a different time than cash is actually received," Karen answers. "We've made those deposits now, so let me show you how we record them in QuickBooks."

To record cash deposits made to banks:

1　Click the **Record Deposits** icon located in the Banking section of the home page. The Payments to Deposit window should appear as shown in Figure 7.15.

2　Click next to the two **1/11/07** dates to place a check next to each, and then click **OK.**

3　Type **1/12/07** as the date of deposit. Your window should look like Figure 7.16. Note the default Deposit To account should be our account 1010 Bank of Florida. Note also that the From Account is the Undeposited Funds account which is where the payments were recorded when first received and accounted for.

4　Click **Save & New.**

Figure 7.15

Payments to Deposit

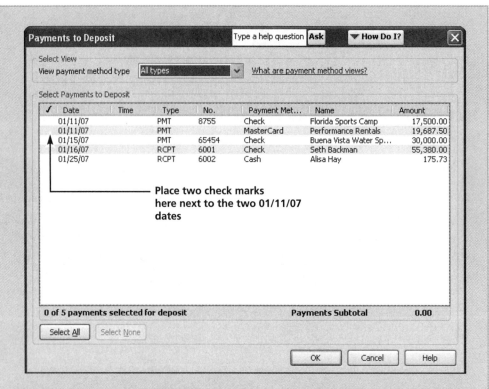

Figure 7.16

Make Deposit Window

The original sales receipt recorded the cash and credit card receipt as undeposited funds

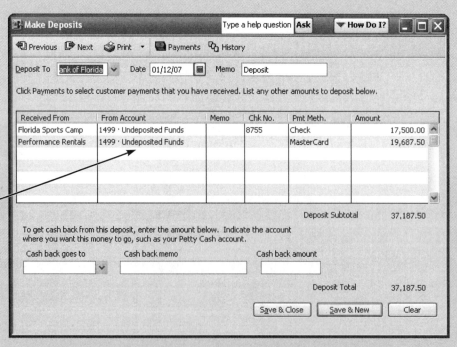

5 Click next to the **1/15/07 and 1/16/07** dates to place a check next to each and then click **OK.**

6 Type **1/16/07** as the date of deposit.

7 Click **Save & New.**

> **8** Click next to the **1/25/07** date to place a check next to that payment, and then click **OK.**
>
> **9** Type **1/26/07** as the date of deposit.
>
> **10** Click **Save & Close.**

You have now accounted for the payments received from customers and the bank deposits which reflect amounts deposited to the checking account. Karen explains that the next item on your list is to record the inventory received from Purchase Order 1001 and the related payment to the vendor.

"When inventory received is related to a purchase order, it's important to do more than just record the check which paid for the inventory," Karen points out. "We also have to close out the purchase order and properly record the receipt of inventory. In this case we received the two boats ordered under Purchase Orders 1001 and 1002. Both of these were cash only purchases in that the vendor did not extend us credit and thus payment was due on receipt. Thus we'll use the Write Checks process to record these transactions."

To record the receipt and payment of inventory:

1 Click the **Write Checks** icon located in the Banking section of the home page.

2 Select **Malibu Boats** from the Pay to the order of drop-down list. An Open PO's Exist window should appear as shown in Figure 7.17.

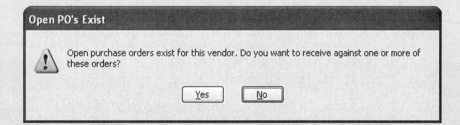

Figure 7.17

Open Purchase Order Warning

3 Click **Yes.** An Open Purchase Orders window should appear as shown in Figure 7.18.

4 Click next to the **1/11/07** date to place a check mark on the purchase order 4001 line and then click **OK.** If a Warning window appears, click **OK** and ignore the warning since, although we owe funds to Malibu Boats from a previous purchase, we are not accounting for that payment at this point.

5 Type **1004** as the check number if it is not already present.

6 Type **1/29/07** as the check date. Your window should look like Figure 7.19.

Figure 7.18

Open Purchase Orders for
Malibu Boats

Click here to select
this purchase order

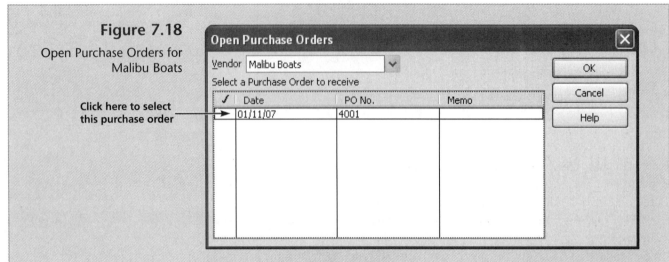

Figure 7.19

Payment on Purchase Order
4001

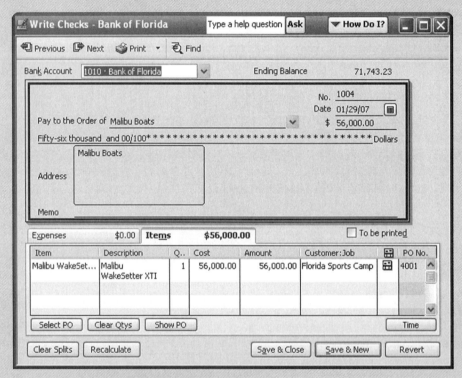

7 Note that because this transaction was treated as the payment for and receipt of inventory, the transaction is recorded using the Items tab, and the Item being received is that item ordered under purchase order 4001 for $56,000. Click **Save & New** to continue.

8 Select **Tige Boats** from the Pay to the order of drop-down list. An Open PO's Exist window should appear.

9 Click **Yes.** An Open Purchase Orders window should appear.

10 Click next to the **1/11/07** date to place a check mark on the purchase order 4002 line and then click **OK.**

11 Type **1005** as the check number if it is not already present.

12 Type **1/30/07** as the check date.

13 Click **Save & Close.**

Karen explains that, as a result of paying these vendors for boats received under purchase orders, cash has decreased and inventory has increased. Both customers, for whom these boats were ordered, were contacted, and they picked up their boats on January 30.

"I'll show you how we record the sales of these boats via the invoice process," Karen says. "Remember that both of these customers remitted their deposits when we placed the order, and thus we only need to collect the remaining 75% balance owed."

"How do we account for the deposits already received?" you ask.

"Recall that, when we received these deposits earlier in January, we credited each of these customers's accounts receivable balances," she answers. "Because of that, we need to use the invoicing process to record the sales first, apply the existing credits, and then separately record the receipt of the balance due on the sale. Let me first show you how to record these two invoices."

To record the sales of inventory, application of advanced deposits received, and receipt of payment for the balance due:

1 Click the **Invoice** icon located in the Customer section of the home page.

2 Select **Florida Sports Camp** from the Customer:Job drop-down list. A Billable Time/Costs window should appear (as shown in Figure 7.20) indicating that this customer has billable costs.

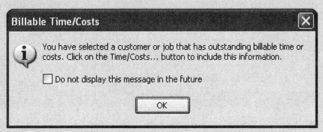

Figure 7.20

Billable Time/Costs

3 Click **OK.**

4 Click the **Time/Costs** button. A Choose Billable Time/Costs window should appear like that shown in Figure 7.21.

5 Note that this window identifies that an item has been received for Florida Sports Camp and is available for billing. Click next to the **1/29/07** date in the Use column to place a check mark there indicating you would like to bill the customer for this item.

Figure 7.21

Billable Time/Costs Window

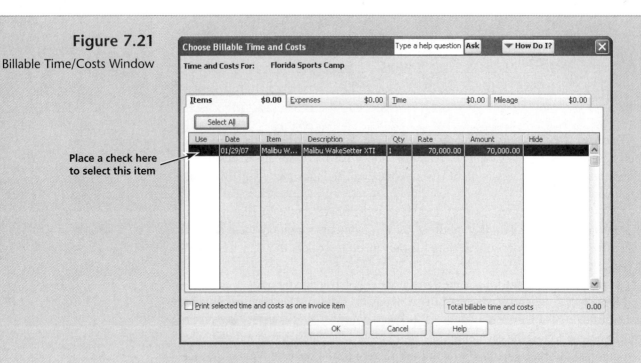

Place a check here to select this item

6   Click **OK.**

7   Type **1/30/07** as the invoice date and **10001** as the Invoice #.

8   Complete the invoice by adding a Bill To address, Ship To address, Terms, and Tax item as shown in Figure 7.22 below. Click **OK** when asked to save changes.

This is where you click initially to reveal Time/
Costs which may be billable to this customer

Figure 7.22

Invoice

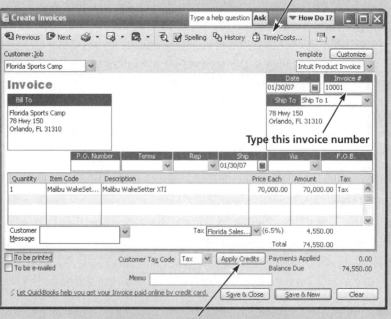

Type this invoice number

Later you will click here to apply the deposit
this customer paid with the original order

9 Click the **Apply Credits** button.

10 Click **Yes** two times to accept the changes you made to the invoice and customer. An Apply Credits window should appear like that shown in Figure 7.23.

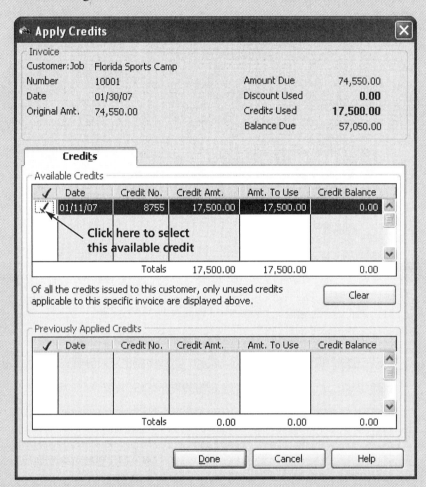

Figure 7.23

Apply Credits Window

11 Note that the credit balance shown is the deposit we recorded earlier this month and that it is prechecked for application. Click **Done** to apply this credit to the balance owed on the invoice.

12 Click **Save & New** to record this invoice.

13 Select **Performance Rentals** from the Customer:Job drop-down list and then click **OK** in the Billable Time/Costs window.

14 Click the **Time/Costs** button and then check the **Use** column next to the 1/30/07 date.

15 Click **OK.**

16 Change the tax item to **Florida Sales Tax.**

17 Click **Apply Credits** and then click **Yes** twice to save your changes.

18 Click **Done** to apply credits then click **Save & Close.**

Now that the invoices are recorded, sales and accounts receivable have been increased, cost of goods sold has been increased, and inventory has been decreased. Wild Water can now record the receipt of full payment from the customers and record the related deposit to their bank account. Florida Sports Camp remitted $57,050 as the balance due on their purchase, while Performance Rentals remitted $64,181.25.

To record the payment and deposit of funds from boat sales:

1 Click the **Receive Payments** icon located in the Customer section of the home page.

2 Select **Florida Sports Camp** from the Received From drop-down list.

3 Type **57050** as the amount received. (Note that this is the amount shown as due from them.)

4 Type **1/30/07** as the date received.

5 Type Check number **4532**. Your Receive Payments window should look like Figure 7.24.

Figure 7.24

Receive Payments window

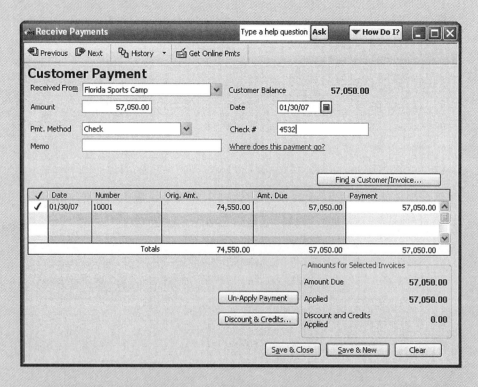

6 Click **Save & New.**

7 Select **Performance Rentals** from the Received From drop-down list.

8 Type **64181.25** as the amount received. (Note that this is the amount shown as due from them.)

9 Type **1/30/07** as the date received.

10 Type Check number **10885.**

11 Click **Save & Close.**

12 Click **Record Deposits** from the Banking section of the home page.

13 Click next to both cash receipts dated **1/30/07** to include them in this deposit, and then click **OK.**

14 Click **Save & Close** to record this deposit.

"Next," Karen comments, "I'd like to show you how Wild Water will pay for monthly expenses and bills. Currently, most of our vendors want us to pay on receipt of their bills, so we've been recording expenses only when we pay the bills. In a couple of months we will be in a position to ask for credit terms from most of our vendors. In the meantime, we write checks at the end of the month to pay for expenses."

One of their payments was for insurance for the year, which will be treated as prepaid insurance and adjusted prior to preparing financial statements. A second payment represents inventory parts received earlier in the month (oil, air filters, and oil filters used in servicing boats). Still another represents an amount due to Malibu Boats, which was established as a liability when the company was first set up. This payment requires the use of QuickBooks's bill payment process. The balance of their payments this month relate to expenses already incurred.

"Let's first look at how we pay for expenses and inventory parts," Karen suggests.

To record checks written for expenses and inventory parts:

1 Click the **Write Checks** icon in the Banking section of the home page.

2 Type **1006** as the check number if it is not already there.

3 Type **1/31/07** as the check date.

4 Type **Manchester Insurance** in the Pay to the Order of section of the check and then press **[Tab].**

5 Click **Set Up** in the Name Not Found window.

6 Select **Vendor** from the Select Name Type window, and then click **OK.**

7 Type **Manchester Insurance** in the Company Name text box.

8 Type the vendor's address as **234 Wilshire Blvd., Los Angeles, CA 91335.**

9 Click **OK** in the New Vendor window.

10 Type **22000** as the check amount and then press **[Tab].**

11 Select **Add New** from the Account drop-down list.

12 Select **Other Current Asset** from the Type drop-down list in the New Account window.

13 Type **1150** in the Number section.

14 Type **Prepaid Insurance** in the Name section, and then click **OK.**

15 Press **[Tab]** twice. Your window should look like Figure 7.25.

Figure 7.25

Payment for Prepaid Insurance

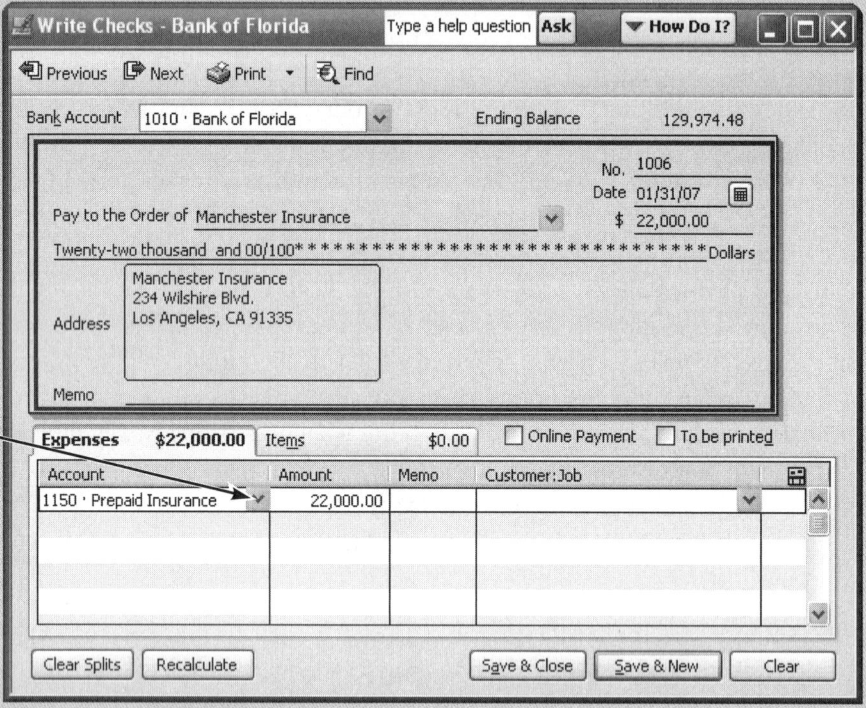

After you have created this asset account, select it from the Expense tab even though it's not an expense

16 Click **Save & New.**

17 Type **1007** as the check number if it is not already there.

18 Type **1/31/07** as the check date if it is not already there.

19 Type **Chevron/Mobil** in the Pay to the Order of section of the check, and then press **[Tab]**.

20 Click **Set Up** in the Name Not Found window.

21 Select **Vendor** from the Select Name Type window, and then click **OK.**

22 Type **Chevron/Mobil** in the Company Name text box.

23 Type the vendor's address as **2389 Peachtree Blvd., Atlanta, GA 30311.**

24 Click **OK** in the New Vendor window.

25 Type **1600** as the check amount and then press **[Tab]**.

26 Click the **Items** tab to make it active.

27 Select **Air Filter** from the Item drop-down list.

28 Type **25** as the Quantity.

29 Click in the next line below the air filter you just added.

30 Select **Engine Oil (quart)** from the Item drop-down list.

31 Type **150** as the Quantity.

32 Click in the next line below the engine oil you just added.

33 Select **Oil Filter** from the Item drop-down list.

34 Type **25** as the Quantity. Your screen should look like Figure 7.26.

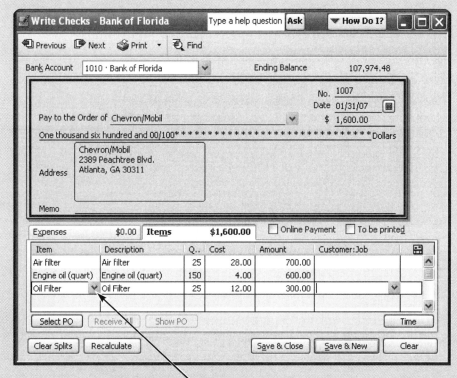

Figure 7.26

Payment for Inventory Parts

Click drop-down arrow to select item

35 Click **Save & New.**

36 Type **1008** as the check number if it is not already there.

37 Type **1/31/07** as the check date if it is not already there.

38 Type **Central Florida Gas & Electric** in the Pay to the Order of section of the check and then press **[Tab].**

39 Click **Quick Add** in the Name Not Found window.

40 Select **Vendor** from the Select Name Type window, and then click **OK.**

41 Type **890** as the amount.

42 Click the **Expenses** tab to make it active.

43 Select **6900 – Utilities** from the Account drop-down list. Your window should look like Figure 7.27.

Figure 7.27

Payment of Utilities

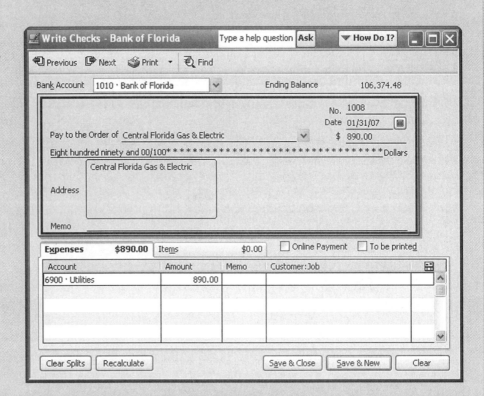

44 Click **Save & New.**

45 Type **1009** as the check number if it is not already there.

46 Type **1/31/07** as the check date if it is not already there.

47 Type **Verizon** in the Pay to the Order of section of the check, and then press **[Tab]**.

48 Click **Quick Add** in the Name Not Found window.

49 Select Vendor from the Select Name Type window, and then click **OK.**

50 Type **1700** as the amount.

51 Click the **Expenses** tab to make it active.

52 Select **6660 – Telephone** from the Account drop-down list.

53 Click **Save & Close.**

"Let's now look at how we pay for bills already established in accounts payable," Karen suggests.

To record checks written to pay bills:

1 Click the **Pay Bills** icon in the Vendor section of the home page. The Pay Bills window should appear as shown in Figure 7.28.

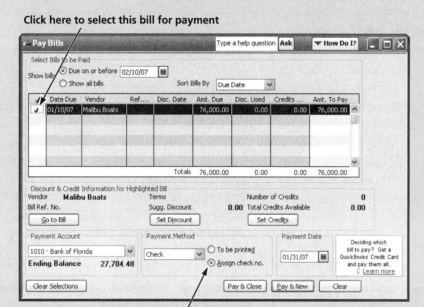

Figure 7.28

The Pay Bills Window

2 Click next to the **1/10/07** date to select this bill for payment.

3 Click in the **Assign check no.** option button.

4 Click **Pay & Close.**

5 Type **1010** as the check number assigned to this payment as shown in Figure 7.29.

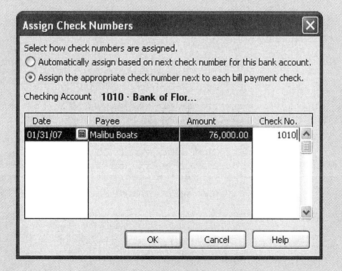

Figure 7.29

Assign Check Numbers Window

6 Click **OK.**

Now it's time to calculate payroll. Karen explains that entering information about payroll is a little tricky since Wild Water has decided not to use QuickBooks's payroll service. To participate at any level would have required a monthly or annual fee and, since Wild Water Tax has so few employees, the company has decided to manually compute payroll.

"Is that why we previously set up Wild Water to calculate payroll manually?" you ask.

"Exactly," Karen answers. "That was a part of the QuickBooks set-up process. Now we are going to enter payroll information for the month of January."

"Wouldn't it be faster to use the payroll service?" you ask.

"Well, yes," you respond, "but, as you'll see, entering payroll withholding and tax information manually isn't that difficult."

"QuickBooks has a nice timesheet capability which is how we'll track Ryder's and Pat's time," Karen explains. "It also has a job cost tracking feature so that, when either Ryder or Pat works on a specific boat, their time can be automatically charged to a customer and a specific job for that customer. Time sheets are typically used when a company is trying to keep track of hours worked on specific jobs. They are not required. Many companies who don't track job costs will only enter the hours for each employee right before processing the payroll. However, in this company's situation, time sheets are very helpful. Before we can enter the employees' time, we must make sure that a customer/job entry is set up. Later we'll do this during the month as each job is entered into, but for now we'll enter them after the fact. Two jobs were entered into in the last couple days of January, one for Florida Sports Camp and one for Freebirds. Let me show you how to create those jobs entries, both of which are for customers we've already created in QuickBooks."

To create new jobs for existing customers:

1 Click the **Customers** button on the Customers section of the home page to open the Customer Center.

2 Select **Florida Sports Camp** from the list of customers and jobs.

3 Click the **New Customer & Job** button and then select **Add Job** from the menu options provided as shown in Figure 7.30.

4 Type **50001** as the Job Name, and then click **OK.**

5 Select **Freebirds** from the list of customers and jobs.

6 Click the **New Customer & Job** button, and then select **Add Job** from the menu options provided.

7 Type **50002** as the Job Name, and then click **OK.**

8 The customer center should now reflect the two new jobs added and should look like Figure 7.31.

9 Close the Customer Center window.

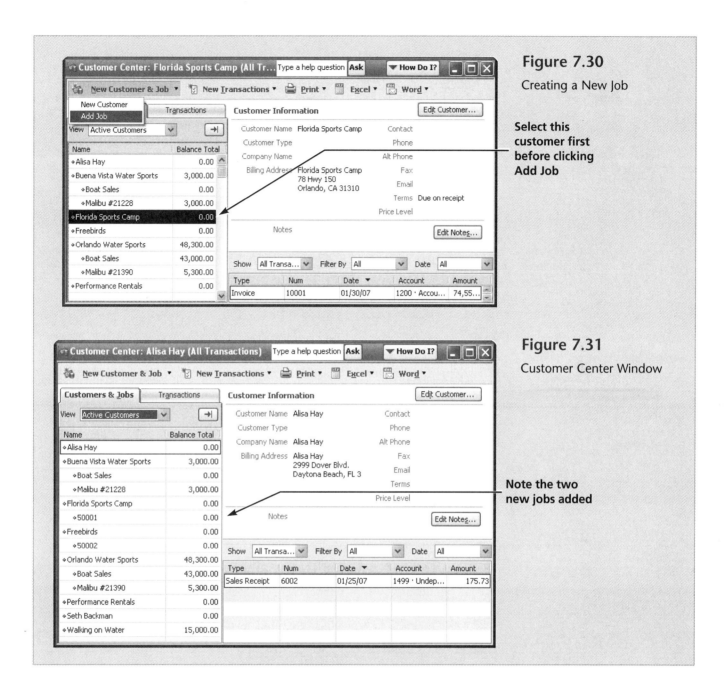

Figure 7.30

Creating a New Job

Select this customer first before clicking Add Job

Figure 7.31

Customer Center Window

Note the two new jobs added

With the two new jobs added, Karen explains that you can now enter the hours worked into QuickBooks's time sheets which are organized by week.

To complete weekly time sheets for January:

1 Click the **Enter Time** icon from the Employees section of the home page.

2 Select **Use Weekly Time Sheet** from the two menu options provided.

3 Click the **Set Date** button.

4 Enter **1/1/07** in the New Date text box, and then click **OK.**

5 Select **Ryder Zacovic** from the drop-down name list presented in the weekly time sheet.

6 Click **Yes** in the Transfer Activities to Payroll window.

7 Choose **Hourly** from Payroll Item drop-down list.

8 Type **6** and **4** as the hours worked on Th 1/4/07 and F 1/5/07, respectively.

9 Click on the **billable** icon (the far right column) to indicate this line is not billable. Your screen should look like Figure 7.32.

Figure 7.32

Timesheet for Ryder Zacovic

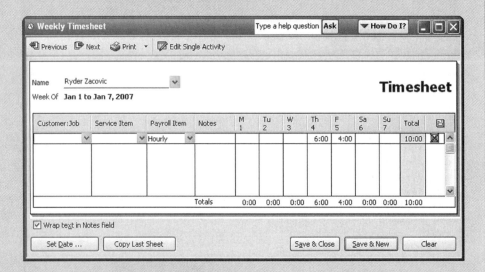

10 Click the **Next** button (Note that this creates a new time sheet for the next week for the current employee).

11 Click **Yes** if asked to save your changes.

12 Choose **Hourly** from The Payroll Item drop-down list.

13 Type **8, 6,** and **4** as the hours worked on M 1/8/07, W 1/10/07, and F 1/12/07 respectively.

14 Click on the **billable** icon (the far right column) to indicate this line is not billable.

15 Click the **Next** button**.**

16 Repeat this process for the employees and dates shown below. (Note that in all cases the payroll item is Hourly. Also note that when you add hours for different service items occurring on the same day, you just add them on the next row. For example, see Ryder's time sheet for 1/30/07 in Figure 7.33.)

Employee/ Date	Ryder Zacovic	Job/Service Item	Pat Ng	Customer
1/4/07	6 hrs.	n/a	6 hrs.	n/a
1/5/07	4 hrs.	n/a	4 hrs.	n/a
1/8/07	8 hrs.	n/a	2 hrs.	n/a
1/10/07	6 hrs.	n/a	4 hrs.	n/a
1/12/07	4 hrs.	n/a	6 hrs.	n/a
1/24/07	8 hrs.	n/a	8 hrs.	n/a
1/25/07	8 hrs.	n/a	8 hrs.	n/a
1/26/07	8 hrs.	n/a	8 hrs.	n/a
1/29/07	–	50001/Engine tune up	6 hrs.	Florida Sports Camp
1/29/07	–	50001/Cleaning	1 hrs.	Florida Sports Camp
1/29/07	–	–	1 hrs.	n/a
1/30/07	3 hrs.	50002/20 hour service check	–	Freebirds
1/30/07	4 hrs.	50002/Painting and body repairs	–	Freebirds
1/30/07	1 hr	n/a	–	n/a
Totals	60 hrs.		54 hrs.	

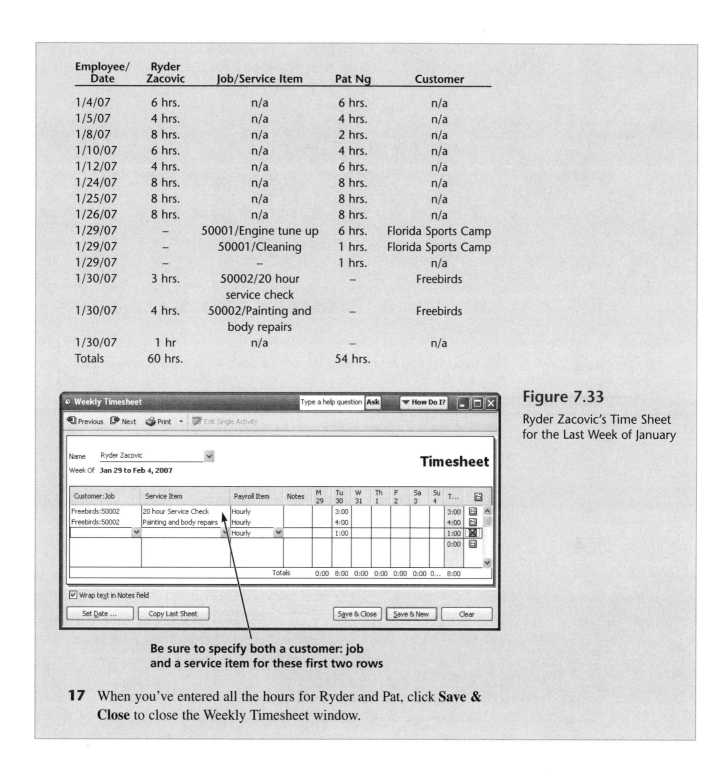

Figure 7.33

Ryder Zacovic's Time Sheet for the Last Week of January

Be sure to specify both a customer: job and a service item for these first two rows

17 When you've entered all the hours for Ryder and Pat, click **Save & Close** to close the Weekly Timesheet window.

"That takes care of January's hourly time sheets, but now we have to process payroll for those time sheets and for our two salaried employees," Karen explains. "However, since we just established our decision to manually set up payroll, QuickBooks wants to make sure we've completed all the steps."

"Didn't we do this when we set up employees and payroll items in the EasyStep Interview?" you ask.

"Well, yes and no," Karen answers. "We should go through this process to make sure all payroll items have been established and that QuickBooks is ready to receive our manually calculated payroll information."

To process payroll for January:

1 Click **Pay Employees** from the Employee section of the home page.

2 Click **No** if the QuickBooks Payroll Service window appears.

3 Click **Go to Payroll Setup** to complete the payroll setup process. The QuickBooks Payroll Setup window will appear as shown in Figure 7.34.

Figure 7.34

QuickBooks Payroll Setup Window

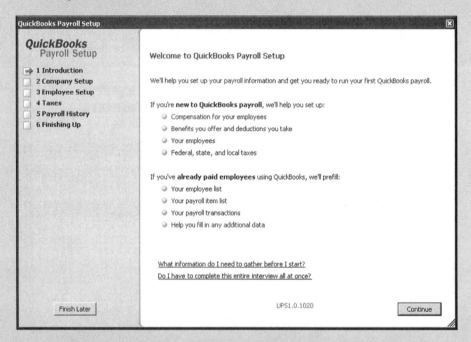

4 Click **Continue** and/or **Finish** throughout this process, just reviewing all the information you already supplied.

5 When you get to the Employee Setup section, edit each employee to make sure you've entered the correct information like their filing status, etc. Then continue to click **Continue.**

6 When you get to the State Taxes section, you should notice that no state withholding is set up, as shown in Figure 7.35. That's because Florida doesn't have a state income tax!

7 Click **Continue.**

8 When you get to the Payroll History section, select **No** since your company has not had previous payroll transactions. Then click **Continue** again until the process is finished.

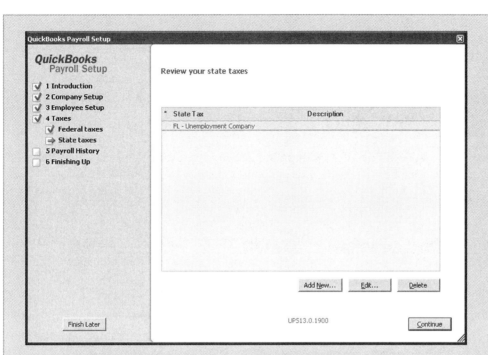

Figure 7.35

Review Your State Taxes Window

9 Close the Employee Center.

10 Click **Pay Employees** from the Employee section of the home page.

11 Click **No** if the QuickBooks Payroll Service window appears.

12 Click **Pay Employees Anyway.**

13 When the Select Employees To Pay window appears, select **To be handwritten** in the Paycheck Options section.

14 Type **1011** as the First Check Number.

15 Type **1/31/07** in the Check Date text box.

16 Type **1/31/07** in the Pay Period Ends text box.

17 Click the **Mark All** button to select all employees for payment. Your screen should look like Figure 7.36.

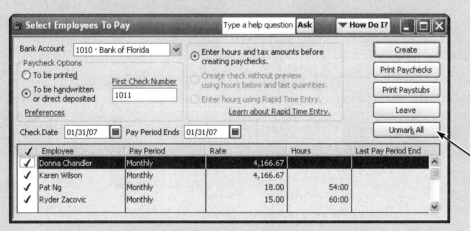

Figure 7.36

Selecting Employees to Pay

This button changed from Mark All to Unmark All after you clicked it

18 Verify the number of hours for both hourly employees to make sure you have accounted for all hours specified in the schedule provided. In this case, the Select Employees To Pay window indicates 54 hours for Pat Ng and 60 hours for Ryder Zacovic which matches the total in the detail schedule shown on page 177.

19 Click **Create.** Enter information for Donna Chandler's paycheck from Figure 7.37. Be sure to put employee amounts as negative numbers and company amounts as positive numbers.

If a company doesn't use time sheets, you would place hours worked (for hourly employees) here

Figure 7.37

Payroll Information for Donna Chandler

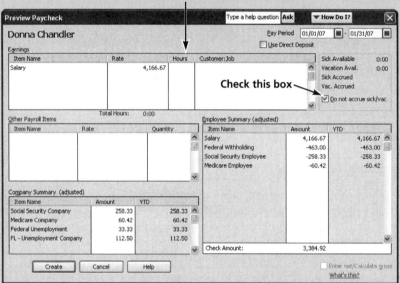

20 Verify the net check amount on your screen with the net check amount in Figure 7.37, and then click **Create.**

21 Continue the payroll process based on the payroll information below. Click **Create** after entering each of the following employee's payroll information:

Employee/Item	Karen	Pat	Ryder
Earnings	4,166.67	972.00	900.00
Federal withholding	−710.00	−133.16	−123.30
Social security employee	−258.33	−60.26	−55.80
Medicare employee	−60.42	−14.09	−13.05
Social security company	258.33	60.26	55.80
Medicare company	60.42	14.09	13.05
Federal unemployment	33.33	7.78	7.20
FL unemployment company	112.50	26.24	24.30
Check amount	3,137.92	764.49	707.85

22 Close the Select Employee's To Pay window.

"How did you determine the withholding amounts and the other tax items?" you ask.

"Withholding amounts came from the payroll tax withholding tables I downloaded from the Internal Revenue Services' web site at http://www.irs.gov," says Karen. "The others were provided by our local CPA, as follows: Social Security is 6.2% of earnings, Medicare is 1.45% of earnings, and federal unemployment is 0.8% of earnings up to $7,000, while state unemployment is 2.7% of earnings up to $7,000." (See Appendix A Payroll Accounting.)

Karen further explains that, since the hourly employees' time was recorded on time sheets, she did not have to enter hours on each employee's paycheck. If, however, our company didn't use time sheets, we would enter hours worked by hourly employees in each Preview Paycheck window.

"What about the two customer jobs we charged for Ryder's and Pat's time? "you ask. "Don't we have to bill the customers for the time charged?"

"Yes," Karen answers. "You are quite perceptive. As it turns out, both of these jobs were completed and the boats were picked up by the customers. If they were not complete, we would wait to bill them until they were complete. Let me show you the process for generating a sales receipt based on time recorded via the payroll system. This should look familiar since we have already invoiced customers for boats purchased on their behalf. In those cases, when we generated an invoice to a particular customer who had unbilled costs, QuickBooks reminded us of that fact and, as a result, we billed the customer."

"How do we know when to create an invoice and when to create a sales receipt?" you ask.

"Good question," Karen answers. "Invoices are used in two cases. If we've received advance payments (deposits) from a customer, we must create an invoice to apply his or her credit balance in accounts receivable. Invoices are also used any time we bill a customer and don't receive cash payment at the same time. Thus, sales receipts are always used when we want to bill a customer for time or costs incurred or product sales, and we collect full payment at the same time."

To bill customers for time recorded via the payroll system:

1 Click the **Create Sales Receipts** icon in the Customer section of the home page.

2 Click job **50001** located under the customer name Florida Sports Camp.

3 Click **OK** in the Billable Time/Costs window.

4 Click the **Time/Costs** button.

5 Click the **Time** tab, and then click **Select All** to place a check next to the time charged by Pat Ng to this job. Your screen should look like Figure 7.38.

Figure 7.38

Billable Time and Costs

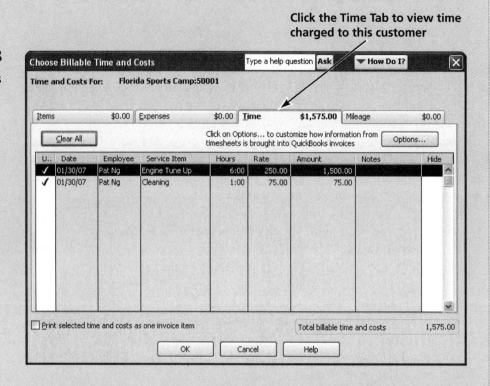

Click the Time Tab to view time charged to this customer

6   Click **OK.**

7   Type **1/31/07** as the sales receipt date.

8   Type **6003** as the sales number.

9   Click **Save & New.**

10 Click job **50002** located under the customer name Freebirds.

11 Click **OK** in the Billable Time/Costs window.

12 Click the **Time/Costs** button.

13 Click the **Time** tab, and then click **Select All** to place a check next to the time charged by Ryder Zacovic to this job.

14 Click **OK.**

15 Type **1/31/07** as the sales receipt date.

16 Type **6004** as the sales number.

17 Type **Freebirds, 1000 Boomer St. Tallahassee FL 32303** in the Sold To section of the sales receipt.

18 Select **Florida Sales Tax** from the Tax drop-down list. Your screen should look like Figure 7.39.

19 Click **Save & Close.**

20 Click **Yes** in the Name Information Changed window to preserve your changes.

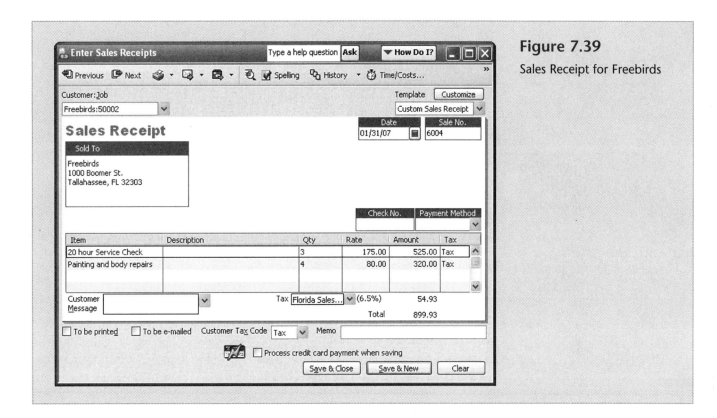

Figure 7.39

Sales Receipt for Freebirds

"Did we deposit funds collected from those two transactions?" you ask.

"No," Karen answers. "We didn't deposit them until the next month. Thus, they will stay in the undeposited funds account until we do."

You've now recorded many operating activities including cash sales, purchase orders, writing checks, and processing payroll, and you'd like to know how the business did for the month.

Evaluate a Firm's Performance and Financial Position

The best way to evaluate a firm's performance and financial position at this point is to generate an income statement and a balance sheet as of January 31, 2007. Karen suggests that you apply what you learned from past experiences with QuickBooks to create and print a standard income statement and a standard balance sheet for January.

To prepare a standard income statement and a balance sheet for January:

1 Click the **Report Center** icon from the icon toolbar.

2 Click **Standard** under the Profit & Loss section.

3 Change the From date to **1/1/07.**

4 Change the To date to **1/31/07,** and then click **Refresh.**

5 Click the **Print** button from the toolbar and then click **Print** in the Print Reports window. Your report should look like Figure 7.40.

Figure 7.40

Income Statement for January 2007

Wild Water Sports Ch 7	
Profit & Loss	
January 2007	
	Jan 07
Ordinary Income/Expense	
Income	
4000 · Sales	
4010 · Merchandise	200,750.00
4020 · Service	2,545.00
4030 · Parts	40.00
Total 4000 · Sales	203,335.00
Total Income	203,335.00
Cost of Goods Sold	
5000 · Cost of Goods Sold	160,632.00
Total COGS	160,632.00
Gross Profit	42,703.00
Expense	
6560 · Payroll Expenses	11,343.22
6660 · Telephone	1,700.00
6900 · Utilities	890.00
Total Expense	13,933.22
Net Ordinary Income	28,769.78
Net Income	**28,769.78**

6 Close the Profit & Loss report window and do not memorize this report.

7 Click **Standard** under the Balance Sheet and Net Worth section.

8 Change the As of date to **1/31/07,** and then click **Refresh.**

9 Click the **Collapse** button.

10 Click the **Print** button from the toolbar and then click **Print** in the Print Reports window. Your asset section of your report should look like Figure 7.41, while the liabilities and equity section of your report should look like Figure 7.42.

11 Close the Balance Sheet report window and do not memorize this report.

Wild Water Sports Ch 7
Balance Sheet
As of January 31, 2007

	◇ Jan 31, 07 ◇
1010 · Bank of Florida	▶ 19,789.30 ◀
1050 · Short-Term Investments	300,000.00
Total Checking/Savings	319,789.30
Accounts Receivable	
1200 · Accounts Receivable	66,300.00
Total Accounts Receivable	66,300.00
Other Current Assets	
1120 · Inventory Asset	330,400.00
1130 · Inventory Parts	1,568.00
1150 · Prepaid Insurance	22,000.00
1499 · Undeposited Funds	2,577.31
Total Other Current Assets	356,545.31
Total Current Assets	742,634.61
Fixed Assets	
1300 · Equipment	167,500.00
1400 · Furniture & Fixtures	70,000.00
Total Fixed Assets	237,500.00
TOTAL ASSETS	980,134.61

Figure 7.41

Asset Section of the Balance Sheet

Wild Water Sports Ch 7
Balance Sheet
As of January 31, 2007

	◇ Jan 31, 07 ◇
LIABILITIES & EQUITY	
Liabilities	
Current Liabilities	
Credit Cards	
2050 · MasterCard	1,000.00
Total Credit Cards	1,000.00
Other Current Liabilities	
2100 · Payroll Liabilities	3,348.04
2200 · Sales Tax Payable	13,216.79
Total Other Current Liabilities	16,564.83
Total Current Liabilities	17,564.83
Long Term Liabilities	
2500 · Loan Payable	633,800.00
Total Long Term Liabilities	633,800.00
Total Liabilities	651,364.83
Equity	
3100 · Common Stock	300,000.00
Net Income	28,769.78
Total Equity	328,769.78
TOTAL LIABILITIES & EQUITY	980,134.61

Figure 7.42

Liability and Equity Section of the Balance Sheet

"Is there a way for us to see what transactions made up these balances?" you ask.

"Yes," Karen responds. "We'll print a Transactions List by Date report which will show us every transaction recorded in chronological order. It will include the type of transaction, the date it was recorded, a number reference (like check number, invoice number, etc.), the name of the entity (vendor name, customer name, employee name, etc.), the balance sheet account affected (checking, accounts receivable, undeposited funds, etc.), other accounts affected (inventory, revenue, expenses, etc.), and the amount. Let me show you how to create this report."

To prepare a Transaction List by Date report for January:

1 Click the **Accountant and Taxes** section in the Report Center.

2 Click **Transactions List by Date** from the Account Activity section of Accountant and Taxes.

3 Type **1/1/07** in the From text box.

4 Type **1/31/07** in the To text box.

5 Click the **Refresh** button. The report shown in Figure 7.43 should appear.

Figure 7.43

Transaction List for January 2007

Wild Water Sports Ch 7
Transaction List by Date
January 2007

Type	Date	Num	Name	Memo	Account	Clr	Split	Amount
Jan 07								
General Jour...	1/1/2007	4			3000 · Opening Bal Equity		3900 · Retained Earnings	-20,300.00
General Jour...	1/1/2007	5			3000 · Opening Bal Equity		3100 · Common Stock	100,000.00
Deposit	1/3/2007			Deposit	1010 · Bank of Florida		-SPLIT-	200,000.00
Deposit	1/4/2007			Deposit	1010 · Bank of Florida		2500 · Loan Payable	250,000.00
Check	1/8/2007	1001	ETrade		1010 · Bank of Florida		1050 · Short-Term Investme...	-300,000.00
Check	1/10/2007	1002	Staples		1010 · Bank of Florida		1410 · Cost	-70,000.00
Check	1/10/2007	1003	AJ Marine Equipment		1010 · Bank of Florida		1310 · Cost	-100,000.00
Payment	1/11/2007	87558	Florida Sports Camp		1499 · Undeposited Funds	X	1200 · Accounts Receivable	17,500.00
Payment	1/11/2007		Performance Rentals		1499 · Undeposited Funds	X	1200 · Accounts Receivable	19,687.50
Deposit	1/12/2007			Deposit	1010 · Bank of Florida		-SPLIT-	37,187.50
Payment	1/15/2007	65454	Buena Vista Water Sports:Boat Sales		1499 · Undeposited Funds	X	1200 · Accounts Receivable	30,000.00
Sales Receipt	1/16/2007	6001	Seth Backman		1499 · Undeposited Funds	X	-SPLIT-	55,380.00
Deposit	1/16/2007			Deposit	1010 · Bank of Florida		-SPLIT-	85,380.00
Sales Receipt	1/25/2007	6002	Alisa Hev		1499 · Undeposited Funds	X	-SPLIT-	175.73
Deposit	1/26/2007			Deposit	1010 · Bank of Florida		1499 · Undeposited Funds	175.73
Check	1/29/2007	1004	Malibu Boats		1010 · Bank of Florida		1120 · Inventory Asset	-56,000.00
Check	1/30/2007	1005	Tige Boats		1010 · Bank of Florida		1120 · Inventory Asset	-63,000.00
Invoice	1/30/2007	10001	Florida Sports Camp		1200 · Accounts Receivable		-SPLIT-	74,550.00
Invoice	1/30/2007	10002	Performance Rentals		1200 · Accounts Receivable		-SPLIT-	83,868.75
Payment	1/30/2007	4532	Florida Sports Camp		1499 · Undeposited Funds	X	1200 · Accounts Receivable	57,050.00
Payment	1/30/2007	10885	Performance Rentals		1499 · Undeposited Funds	X	1200 · Accounts Receivable	64,181.25
Deposit	1/30/2007			Deposit	1010 · Bank of Florida		-SPLIT-	121,231.25
Check	1/31/2007	1006	Manchester Insurance		1010 · Bank of Florida		1150 · Prepaid Insurance	-22,000.00
Check	1/31/2007	1007	ChevronMobil		1010 · Bank of Florida		-SPLIT-	-1,600.00
Check	1/31/2007	1008	Central Florida Gas & Electric		1010 · Bank of Florida		6900 · Utilities	-890.00
Check	1/31/2007	1009	Verizon		1010 · Bank of Florida		6680 · Telephone	-1,700.00
Bill Pmt -Check	1/31/2007	1010	Malibu Boats	Opening bal...	1010 · Bank of Florida		2000 · Accounts Payable	-76,000.00
Paycheck	1/31/2007	1011	Donna Chandler		1010 · Bank of Florida		-SPLIT-	-3,384.92
Paycheck	1/31/2007	1012	Karen Wilson		1010 · Bank of Florida		-SPLIT-	-3,137.92
Paycheck	1/31/2007	1013	Pat Ng		1010 · Bank of Florida		-SPLIT-	-764.49
Paycheck	1/31/2007	1014	Ryder Zacovic		1010 · Bank of Florida		-SPLIT-	-707.85
Sales Receipt	1/31/2007	6003	Florida Sports Camp:50001		1499 · Undeposited Funds		-SPLIT-	1,877.38
Sales Receipt	1/31/2007	6004	Freebirds:50002		1499 · Undeposited Funds		-SPLIT-	899.93
Jan 07								

Trouble? On occasion you might accidentally enter the wrong date for a transaction (for example, accepting the default date which might be before January 2007 or after January 2007). If you're pretty sure you entered a transaction but don't see it on your transactions list, it is likely dates are your problem. To verify this, try entering 1/1/06 as the From date and 12/31/09 as the To date. If your missing transaction appears, double-click it to correct the date and you'll be good to go!

6 Close the report and Report Center windows.

"Not bad for our first month," Karen comments. "But we need to pay off some of the debt acquired with the company acquisition. Plus, we can't forget that some costs such as interest and depreciation expenses have not been accrued or paid, so this information is not complete."

End Note

The two of you decide to quit for the day because you've accomplished quite a lot. You've recorded the firm's financing, investing, and operating activities for the month of January, which included processing purchase orders, receiving inventory, paying for inventory and other bills, recognizing cash sales, and writing checks, including some for payroll. Next up are February transactions and a few noncash activities.

Chapter 7 Questions

1 Compare and contrast operating, investing, and financing activities.

2 Describe some of the financing activities you recorded for Wild Water in January.

3 Describe some of the investing activities you recorded for Wild Water in January.

4 Describe some of the operating activities you recorded for Wild Water in January.

5 Describe the process for creating new fixed asset accounts.

6 Explain the difference between the Expenses tab and the Items tab in the Write Checks window.

7 How should you account for advanced deposits received on customer orders?

8 Why are cash receipts initially recorded as undeposited funds?

9 Are time sheets required for QuickBooks to process payroll?

10 How does a business know when to create an invoice and when to create a sales receipt?

Chapter 7 Assignments

1 *Adding More Information to Wild Water Sports*

Restore the file Wild Water Sports Ch 7A.qbb found on the text CD or downloaded from the text website, and then add the following transactions in chronological order.

merchandising

job costing

Date	Transaction
2/1/07	Wrote Check No. 1015 for $1,000 to Delco (new vendor) as payment for the purchase of five sets of tune-up parts
2/1/07	Accepted a new job (50003) to tune-up a boat owned by Orlando Water Sports.
2/1/07	Paid $24,000 to Coe Marketing (new vendor) for new advertising campaign, which will last one year, with Check No. 1016. (**Hint:** You'll need to create a new current asset account titled Prepaid Advertising (#1060.)

Date	Transaction
2/1/07	Deposited funds received 1/31 of $2,577.31 into the Bank of Florida account.
2/2/07	Created Purchase Order No. 4003 to MB Sports to order an MB B52 V23 Team Edition (a new item) on behalf of our customer, Performance Rentals. Cost: $60,000 Sales Price: $75,000.
2/2/07	Collected $18,750 as an advance payment from Performance Rentals (their Check No. 2003) which was equal to the 25% down payment required on all boat orders. (Hint: use the Receive Payments function to record receipt of this payment, and do not apply this payment to any existing balances owed.)
2/2/07	Pat Ng worked four hours on Job No. 50003 tuning up a boat owned by Orlando Water Sports. (Hint: record on a time sheet now!)
2/3/07	Deposited $100,000 from a new investor, Sam Ski, in exchange for common stock representing a 25% interest in the company. Payment received was in the form of his Check No. 987.
2/3/07	Recorded Sales Receipt No. 6005 from Orlando Water Sports under job 50003 based on work performed by Pat Ng. and one set of tune-up parts. $1,331.25 was collected with Check No. 9774.
2/5/07	Deposited the advance payment received from Performance Rentals and the check received from Orlando Water Sports.
2/5/07	Received Check No. 390 for $3,000 as payment on account from Buena Vista Water Sports.
2/5/07	Deposited a $50,000 check, No. 188774, from Citi Bank (type vendor) as the proceeds from a three-year 6% loan negotiated by Sam Ski. The company plans to use these funds in the future to pay down some older, more expensive debt.
2/6/07	Wrote Check No. 1017 in the amount of $75,000 to ETrade as a short-term investment.
2/6/07	Deposited $3,000 check received on 2/4.
2/6/07	Created Purchase Order No. 4004 to Malibu Boats to order a Malibu Sunscape LSV and a Malibu Vride on behalf of a new customer, Fantasy Sports, located at 345 Sunset Rd., Orlando, FL 31312.
2/6/07	Collected $28,250 as an advance payment from Fantasy Sports (its Check No. 1005), which was equal to the 25% down payment required on all boat orders.
2/8/07	Received Check No. 1988 for $43,000 as payment on account from Orlando Water Sports.
2/8/07	Sold a Malibu WakeSetter VLX from inventory to Walking on Water for $57,000 plus tax of $3,705 and recorded the sale with Sales Receipt No. 6006. Received the customer's Check No. 232 as payment in full. Updated the customer's address as 874 Nightingale Dr., Kissimmee, FL 34743.
2/8/07	Accepted a new job (50004) to paint a boat owned by Alisa Hay.
2/9/07	Made a deposit of $131,955 from checks received on 2/6 and 2/8.
2/9/07	Ryder Zacovic worked five hours on Job No. 50004 painting a boat owned by Alisa Hay.
2/10/07	Recorded Sales Receipt No. 6007 from Alisa Hay under Job No. 50004 based on work performed by Ryder Zacovic. Check No. 741 collected $426.

Date	Transaction
2/10/07	Deposited $426 from Sales Receipt No. 6007.
2/15/07	Wrote Check No. 1018 to Sunset Auto (vendor) for $45,000 to purchase a truck for the business. Created new fixed asset accounts (1500 - Truck, 1510 - Truck:Cost, and 1590 - Truck:Accumulated Depreciation).
2/19/07	Wrote Check No. 1019 to MB Sports for $60,000 as payment for Purchase Order No. 4003 because the MB B52 V23 Team Edition ordered on behalf of Performance Rentals was received.
2/20/07	Created Invoice No. 10003 to Performance Rentals for sale of MB B51 V23 received under Purchase Order No. 4003 on 2/19. Applied the deposit received upon order.
2/20/07	Record receipt of payment from Performance Rentals of $61,125 with their Check No. 23098 on Invoice No. 10003.
2/21/07	Deposited Performance Rentals check received 2/20.
2/26/07	Wrote Check No. 1020 to Bank of Florida to pay MasterCard liability of $1,000. (**Hint:** Record this payment to the 2050 – MasterCard liability account.)
2/26/07	Wrote Check No. 1021 to Central Florida Gas & Electric for $930 for utilities expense.
2/26/07	Wrote Check No. 1022 to Verizon for $1,820 for telephone expense.
2/26/07	Wrote Check No. 1023 to Brian Szulczewski (vendor) for $2,700 for marketing and advertising expense.
2/26/07	Wrote Check No. 1024 to Staples for $4,500 for office expenses, specifically printing and reproduction.
2/28/07	Record time sheet information provided in Table 7.1 below. Note: Some of these hours are related to jobs for which time had already been recorded and should already be on your time sheet. Those hours are designated in table below with an *. All other hours not designated by an * are for nonbillable activities.
2/28/07	Process payroll per the information provided in Table 7.2, starting with Check No. 1025.

Table 7.1

Time Sheet Information

Date	Ryder Zacovic	Date	Pat Ng
2/1/07	8 hrs.	2/2	4 hrs.*
2/6/07	5 hrs.	2/5	8 hrs.
2/8/07	5 hrs.	2/7	8 hrs.
2/9/07	5 hrs.*	2/12	8 hrs.
2/13/07	8 hrs.	2/14	8 hrs.
2/15/07	8 hrs.	2/19	8 hrs.
2/20/07	8 hrs.	2/21	8 hrs.
2/22/07	8 hrs.	2/26	8 hrs.
2/28/07	8 hrs.	2/27	8 hrs.
Total	63 hrs.		68 hrs.

Employee/Item	Donna	Karen	Pat	Ryder		Table 7.2
Earnings	4,166.67	4,166.67	1,224.00	945.00		Payroll Information for
Federal withholding	−463.00	−710.00	−167.69	−129.47		Wild Water Sports
Social security employee	−258.33	−258.33	−75.89	−58.59		
Medicare employee	−60.42	−60.42	−17.75	−13.70		
Social security company	258.33	258.33	75.89	58.59		
Medicare company	60.42	60.42	17.75	13.70		
Federal unemployment	33.33	33.33	9.79	7.56		
State unemployment	112.50	112.50	33.05	25.52		
Check amount	3,384.92	3,137.92	962.67	743.24		

Print the following as of 2/28/07:

a. Customer Balance Summary

b. Vendor Balance Summary

c. Account Listing (account, type, and balance total only)

d. Item Listing (list only item, description, type, cost, quantity on hand, and price.)

e. Standard Balance Sheet

f. Standard Income Statement for the month of February

g. Transaction List by Date for the month of February

2   *Adding More Information to Central Coast Cellular*

merchandising

In Chapter 6, you created a new QuickBooks file for Central Coast Cellular (CCC), a cellular phone sales, phone rental, and consulting company. Make a copy of that file in Windows Explorer, name the file CCC3, and use that file to enter the following transactions. (Be sure to keep this QuickBooks file in a safe place as it is used as a starting file for this case in the next chapter.)

- On January 3, 2003, Mr. Van Morrison deposited $200,000 of his personal funds into the company checking account and received 25,000 shares of stock in CCC. *Hint:* You will need to create a new *equity* account named Common Stock.

- On the same date, he signed a lease with Central Coast Leasing (2830 Mcmillan Ave #7, San Luis Obispo, CA 93401, 805-544-2875) to rent retail space at $3,000 a month for five years. Payment is due on the 13th of the month.

- On January 6, 2003, the company temporarily invested $75,000 by writing Check No. 3001 to Schwab Investments (1194 Pacific Street, San Luis Obispo, CA 93401, 805-788-0502). *Hint:* You will need to create another current assets account named Short-Term Investment.

- On January 7, 2003, the company borrowed and then deposited $125,000 from Wells Fargo Bank (665 Marsh St., San Luis Obispo, CA 93401, 805-541-0143) due in five years with annual interest of 8% and payments made monthly. *Hint:* You will need to create a long-term liability account named Notes Payable.

- On January 8, 2003, the company purchased office furniture by writing Check No. 3002 for $20,000 to Russco (3046 S. Higuera St. #A, San Luis Obispo, CA 93401, 805-547-8440). *Hint:* You will need to create a fixed assets account for office furniture with two related subaccounts, cost and accumulated depreciation.

- On January 9, 2003, the company ordered inventory from the following vendors:

Purchase Order #	Vendor	Product	Quantity
101	Ericsson	LX588	40
		T19LX	60
102	Nokia	3285	25
		8290	50
		8890	15

- On January 10, 2003, the company purchased supplies from Russco for $3,000 using Check No. 3003. These supplies are expected to last over the next year. *Hint:* You will need to create another current asset account named Store Supplies.

- On January 13, 2003, the company wrote Check No. 3004 to Central Coast Leasing for $6,000 ($3,000 for January's rent, and $3,000 as a security deposit). *Hint:* You will need to create another asset account named Security Deposit.

- On January 14, 2003, the company received and deposited an advance payment of $10,000 from the City of San Luis Obispo (a customer) as part of a consulting contract to be started in February.

- On January 15, 2003, the company received a shipment of phones from Ericsson on Purchase Order No. 101. Items were received and a bill recorded due in 30 days.

- On January 16, 2003, the company created sales receipt 501 to record 50 hours of consulting services and the sale of 25 Ericsson LX588 phones to Sterling Hotels Corporation. A check was received and deposited for $7,425.

- On January 17, 2003, the company paid semi-monthly payroll starting with Check No. 3005 for the period January 1 to January 15, 2003. Megan Paulson worked 80 hours during the period. Payroll tax information is shown in Table 7.3.

Tax or Withholding/Employee	Rodriguez	Bruner	Paulson	**Table 7.3**
Gross Pay	$ 2,000.00	$ 1,500.00	$ 960.00	Payroll Information for
California Employee Training Tax	2.00	1.50	0.96	Central Coast Cellular
Social Security Company	124.00	93.00	59.52	
Medicare Company	29.00	21.75	13.92	
Federal Unemployment	6.40	4.80	3.07	
CA—Unemployment	24.00	18.00	11.52	
Federal Withholding	−300.00	−225.00	−144.00	
Social Security Employee	−124.00	−93.00	−59.52	
Medicare Employee	−29.00	−21.75	−13.92	
CA—Withholding	−100.00	−75.00	−48.00	
CA—Disability Employee	−10.00	−7.50	−4.80	
Check Amount	1,437.00	1,077.75	689.76	

Print the following:

a. Profit & Loss Standard report for the month of January 2003

b. Balance Sheet Standard as of January 17, 2003

c. Transaction List by Date for the period January 1 through January 17, 2003

3 *Using the South-Western Home Page for More Assignments or Cases*

Go to the home page for this textbook at **www.thomsonedu.com/ accounting/owen.** Click **Additional Problem Sets,** and then select the **Chapter 7** section, and complete the problem(s) that your instructor assigns.

Chapter 7 Case Problem 1:
ALOHA PROPERTY MANAGEMENT

In Chapter 6, you created a new QuickBooks file for Aloha Property Management. Make a copy of that file, and use that copy to enter the following transactions.

service

Date	Transaction
1/3/08	Adventure Travel purchased capital stock from Aloha in exchange for $50,000 cash which was deposited to the company's Bank of Hawaii checking account.
1/4/08	Received payment on account from General Motors in the amount of $75,000 on their Check No. 6874.
1/4/08	Deposited the check from General Motors into the Bank of Hawaii.
1/7/08	Wrote Check No. 984 for $40,000 to World Investments (a new other name) as a short-term investment (**Hint:** create new current asset account called Short-Term Investments—Account Number 1300).

Date	Transaction
1/8/08	Wrote Check No. 985 for $24,000 to GEICO Insurance (a new vendor) as payment for a one-year insurance policy with coverage provided from January 1, 2008 through December 31, 2008, and recorded this transaction as Prepaid Insurance—Account Number 1350.
1/9/08	Collected a $24,000 deposit from a new customer Pixar Studios.
1/9/08	Deposited the check received from Pixar into the Bank of Hawaii.
1/11/08	Recorded Sales Receipt No. 5115 for rent of Villa Unit #1 for one week. Collected MasterCard payment in full of $3,120 from a new customer, Coast Union Bank.
1/11/08	Recorded Invoice No. 7508 for rental of Moana Unit #4 for one week to Sara Rice. Applied her previously received advance payment of $6,000 to this invoice, noted terms due on receipt, and recorded receipt of balance owed of $6,480 with Check No. 654.
1/11/08	Recorded Sales Receipt No. 5116 for rent of Villa Unit #2 for one week. Collected MasterCard payment in full of $4,680 from a new customer, Berkshire Hathaway.
1/12/08	Deposited checks and MasterCard payments of $14,280 to Bank of Hawaii.
1/14/08	Set up three new accounts: 1800—Furniture, 1810—Cost (subaccount of Furniture), and 1820—Accumulated Depreciation (sub account of Furniture).
1/14/08	Wrote Check No. 986 for $23,000 to Furniture King (a new vendor) as payment for new furniture. Recorded this to account 1810.
1/15/08	Wrote Check No. 987 as payment on account to Reilly Custodial (**Hint:** use Pay Bills).
1/18/08	Recorded Sales Receipt No. 5117 for rent of Moana Unit #3 and Villa Unit #3 for one week each. Collected American Express payment in full of $8,528 from a new customer, Bridgette Hacker.
1/18/08	Recorded Sales Receipt No. 5118 for rent of Moana Unit #4 for one week. Collected Check No. 909 as payment in full of $12,480 from a new customer, Lockheed Martin.
1/18/08	Recorded Invoice No. 7509 for rental of Villa Unit #1 and #2 for one week to Boeing terms net 30.
1/21/08	Deposited $21,008 of undeposited funds to Bank of Hawaii.
1/23/08	Paid Reilly Custodial $3,000 on Check No. 988 for Cleaning (a new expense account #6145).
1/24/08	Collected a $5,125 deposit from a new customer, Exxon Mobil.
1/25/08	Recorded Invoice No. 7510 for rental of Villa Unit #4 for one week to Brice Montoya. Applied his advance payment to this invoice, noted terms due on receipt, and recorded receipt of balance owed of $3,240 with Check No. 1874.
1/28/08	Deposited $8,365 of undeposited funds to Bank of Hawaii.
1/30/08	Wrote Check No. 989 for $12,000 to Pacific Electric (a new vendor) to account 6390 Utilities expenses.
1/30/08	Wrote Check No. 990 for $3,700 to AT&T (a new vendor) to account 6340 Telephone expenses.
1/30/08	Wrote Check No. 991 for $15,000 to Sunset Media (a new vendor) to account 6105 Advertising (a new account).
1/31/08	Process payroll per the information provided in Table 7.4 starting with Check No. 992.

Pay/Tax/Withholding	Aki	Castillo	Table 7.4
Hours	n/a	150	Earnings Information for
Rate	$ 75,000	$ 20.00	Aloha Property Management
Gross pay	6,250.00	3,000.00	
Federal withholding	−856.25	−411.00	
Social Security employee	−387.50	−186.00	
Medicare employee	−90.63	−43.50	
HI withholding	−442.33	−195.33	
HI disability	−1.25	−0.60	
HI E&T	0.63	0.30	
Social Security employer	387.50	186.00	
Medicare company	90.63	43.50	
Federal unemployment	50.00	24.00	
HI unemployment	187.50	90.00	
Check amount	4,472.04	2,163.57	

Requirements

Record business transactions in chronological order (remember, dates are in the month of January 2008). After recording the transactions, create and print the following for January 2008. (Be sure to keep this QuickBooks file in a safe place as it is used as a starting file for this case in the next chapter.)

    a.   Standard balance sheet

    b.   Standard income statement

    c.   Statement of cash flows

    d.   Transaction list by date

Chapter 7 Case Problem 2:
OCEAN VIEW FLOWERS

merchandising

In Chapter 6, you created a new QuickBooks file for Ocean View Flowers, a wholesale flower distributor. Make a copy of that file and use that copy to enter the following transactions.

- On January 4, 2008, the company sold common stock to Scott Coe, an investor, for $100,000 cash. The company deposited the check into the Union checking account.

- On January 6, 2008, the company borrowed $50,000 from Santa Barbara Bank & Trust. The long-term note payable is due in three years with interest due annually at 10%. The company deposited the check into the Union checking account.

- On January 8, 2008, the company temporarily invested $25,000 in a certificate of deposit due in three months, which will earn 7% per annum. Check No. 101, drawn on the Union checking account, was made payable to Prudent Investments, 100 Main Street, San Francisco, CA 95154. (**Hint:** Create a short-term investments account to record this transaction.)

- On January 11, 2008, the company purchased office equipment from Stateside Office Supplies, 324 G St., Lompoc, CA 93436, for $20,000 with Check No. 102. (**Hint:** Be sure to create a main office equipment account as well as separate fixed asset cost and accumulated depreciation subaccounts.)

- On January 12, 2008, the company purchased computer equipment from Gateway Computers, 100 Cowabunga Blvd., Sioux City, IA 23442, for $15,000 with Check No. 103. (**Hint:** Be sure to create a main computer equipment account as well as separate fixed asset cost and accumulated depreciation subaccounts.)

- On January 13, 2008, the company ordered the following new items from Brophy Bros. Farms, who specializes in daylilies. All daylilies are recorded as sales in a subaccount of Sales called Daylilies, which you will have to create.

Daylily	Quantity Ordered	Cost	Sales Price
Almond Puff	1,000	$12.00	$24.00
Calistoga Sun	2,000	$8.00	$16.00
Caribbean Pink Sands	500	$13.00	$26.00

- On January 15, 2008, the company paid payroll. All employees worked the entire period. Kelly Gusland worked 60 hours and Margie Coe, 75 hours. Checks were written using the Union Bank account starting with Check No. 104. (Do not print these checks.) Payroll taxes and withholding for employees during the period 1/1/08 through 1/15/08 are shown in Table 7.5.

Table 7.5 Earnings Information 1/1/08 through 1/15/08	Tax or Withholding/Employee	Thomas	Gusland	Coe	McAninch	Comstock
	California Employee Training Tax	$ 2.92	$ 0.90	$ 0.90	$ 2.50	$ 2.08
	Social Security Company	180.83	55.80	55.80	155.00	129.17
	Medicare Company	42.29	13.05	13.05	36.25	30.21
	Federal Unemployment	23.33	7.20	7.20	20.00	16.67
	CA—Unemployment	1.46	0.45	0.45	1.25	1.04
	Federal Withholding	−667.00	−118.00	−118.00	−402.00	−286.00
	Social Security Employee	−180.83	−55.80	−55.80	−155.00	−129.17
	Medicare Employee	−42.29	−13.05	−13.05	−36.25	−30.21
	CA—Withholding	−192.30	−19.32	−9.32	−153.55	−61.86
	CA—Disability Employee	−14.58	−4.50	−4.50	−12.50	−10.42
	Check Amount	1,819.67	689.33	699.33	1,740.70	1,565.67

- On January 18, 2008, the company received its order in full from Brophy Bros. Farms and paid the bill with a Union Bank Check No. 109 in the amount of $34,500.

- On January 20, 2008, the company paid Stateside Office Supplies for supplies expected to last over the next six months using Union Bank Check No. 110 for $1,500.

- On January 22, 2008 the company recorded its first cash sale to Valley Florists in which they sold 100 Almond Puffs, 100 Calistoga Suns, and 100 Caribbean Pink Sands. The $6,600 sale was deposited directly to Union Bank.

- On January 25, 2008, the company recorded its second cash sale to Eastern Scents in which they sold 600 Almond Puffs and 300 Caribbean Pink Sands. The $22,200 sale was deposited directly to Union Bank.

- On January 28, 2008, the company received an advance payment on account from FTD in the amount of $5,000, which was deposited directly to Union Bank account.

- On January 29, 2008, the company wrote the following three checks:

Check #	Payee	Amount	Category
111	Hawaiian Farms	$3,000	Rent Expense
112	Edison Inc.	$500	Utilities Expense
113	GTE	$400	Telephone Expense

- On January 29, 2008, the company paid payroll for the period ended January 31, 2008. All employees worked the entire period. Kelly Gusland worked 65 hours and Margie Coe worked 70 hours. Checks were written using the Union Bank account starting with Check No. 114. (Do not print these checks.) Payroll taxes and withholding for employees during the period 1/16/08 through 1/31/08 are shown in Table 7.6.

Tax or Withholding/Employee	Thomas	Gusland	Coe	McAninch	Comstock
California Employee Training Tax	$ 2.91	$ 0.98	$ 0.84	$ 2.50	$ 2.09
Social Security Company	180.84	60.45	52.08	155.00	129.16
Medicare Company	42.29	14.14	12.18	36.25	30.21
Federal Unemployment	23.34	7.80	6.72	20.00	16.66
CA—Unemployment	1.46	0.49	0.42	1.25	1.04
Federal Withholding	−667.00	−130.00	−109.00	−402.00	−286.00
Social Security Employee	−180.84	−60.45	−52.08	−155.00	−129.16
Medicare Employee	−42.29	−14.14	−12.18	−36.25	−30.21
CA—Withholding	−192.30	−23.63	−8.12	−153.55	−61.86
CA—Disability Employee	−14.59	−4.88	−4.20	−12.50	−10.41
Check Amount	1,819.65	741.90	654.42	1,740.70	1,565.69

Table 7.6

Earnings Information
1/16/08 through 1/31/08

Requirements

Record business transactions in chronological order (remember, dates are in the month of January 2008). After recording the transactions, create and print the following for January 2008. (Be sure to keep this QuickBooks file in a safe place as it is used as a starting file for this case in the next chapter.)

    a.   Standard Balance Sheet

    b.   Standard Income Statement

    c.   Statement of Cash Flows

    d.   Transaction List by Date

Comprehensive Problems

Comprehensive Problem 1: SARAH DUNCAN, CPA

Use the following information to create a new company in QuickBooks using the EasyStep Interview. Then create and print the reports as requested below.

Sarah Duncan, CPA, is starting her new practice at One Constellation Road, Vandenberg Village, CA 93436. She'll start effective 9/1/09 and use a calendar year for fiscal and tax purposes. She'll be using QuickBooks' manual payroll calculations feature to account for herself and her one employee, and her federal tax ID number, EIN, and California EDD number is 574-85-4125. (Be sure to set payroll to manual calculations and perform payroll setup before entering transactions below.) Sarah lives at 259 St. Andrews Way, Vandenberg Village, CA 93436. Her Social Security number is 574-85-4125. She's married (one income) and earns $72,000 per year. Bob Humphrey, her other employee, lives at 453 Sirius, Vandenberg Village, CA 93436. His Social Security number is 632-78-1245. He's single and earns $20 per hour. Sarah's California unemployment tax rate is 3.4%. Her business, of course, is in the Accounting Services area as a Certified Public Accountant. She does not collect sales tax for her services, nor does she use sales receipts because she invoices her clients for services provided and gives them 15-day credit terms. She does accept credit card payments and tracks time spent on each client's services for billing purposes. She will have two payroll items: salary and hourly. She will perform audit, tax, and compilation services for $150, $150, and $100 per hour respectively. (*Hint:* Create service items for each of these and assign the appropriate income accounts and descriptions to each). Employees are paid monthly, but file weekly time sheets on Friday of each week. Clients are also invoiced on Fridays of each week once time sheets have been processed. Add the following transactions (*Note:* Be sure to enter these transactions in the proper date period):

Chronological List of Business Transactions

Date	Transaction
9/01/09	Opened a business checking account at Union Bank with a $50,000 deposit as her investment in the business in exchange for common stock.
9/01/09	Purchased a $15,000 copier from Xerox Corporation, completely financed for three years with monthly payments of $463.16 due starting

Date	Transaction
	10/1/09. Record the equipment purchase as a noncash transaction financed with a long-term loan. (Remember to created an equipment fixed asset account and related subaccounts of cost and accumulated depreciation as well as a loan payable account.)
9/01/09	Signed an engagement letter to perform tax services for Valley Medical Group, a new client located at 234 Third St., Lompoc, CA 93436. Created a new job: 2009 Tax Services for Valley Medical.
9/04/09	Purchased furniture and fixtures from Sam Snead, a prior tenant in her rented office space, for $4,000 using Check No. 1001 from Union Bank. (Be sure to create a Furniture & Fixtures account and the related subaccounts of cost and accumulated depreciation).
9/04/09	Sarah worked four hours each day on 9/2, 9/3, and 9/4 on the Valley Medical job and four hours more on each of those days that were not billable. Bob worked six hours each day on 9/3 and 9/4 on the Valley Medical job and two more hours on each of those days that were not billable.
9/04/09	Created Invoice No. 5001 to Valley Medical based on time costs incurred using terms Net 15. When you choose the hours worked for the week to be billed, be sure to click the Option button and then select the option "Combine activities with the same services" in the Options for Transferring Billable Time window.
9/07/09	Wrote Check No. 1002 for $15,000 to Dean Witter for a short-term investment.
9/07/09	Wrote Check No. 1003 to Wiser Realty as payment for the first and last months' rent and security deposit for $9,000 (one third for rent, one third for last month's rent recorded as prepaid rent, and one third for the security deposit.) (Note: Both the prepaid rent and security deposit are considered other noncurrent assets.)
9/08/09	Signed an engagement letter to perform audit services for Pactuco, a new client. Created a new job: 2009 Audit Services for Pactuco located at 345 Central Ave., Lompoc, CA 93436.
9/09/09	Signed an engagement letter to perform compilation services for Celite Corporation, a new client. Created a new job: Second Quarter Compilation Services for Celite, located at.
9/09/09	Received a payment in the amount of $5,000 from Celite Corporation as an advance on services to be rendered. Sarah anticipates completing services for this client by the end of the month. She then deposited the check into the Union Checking account.
9/11/09	Sarah worked five hours each day on 9/7, 9/8, and 9/9 on the Valley Medical job, and three more hours on each of those days which were not billable. She also worked eight hours on 9/10 on the Pactuco job, and eight hours on 9/11 on the Celite job. Bob worked three hours each day on 9/7, 9/8 and 9/9 on the Valley Medical job and four more hours on each of those days which were not billable. He also worked eight hours on 9/10 on the Pactuco job, and eight hours on 9/11 on the Celite job.
9/11/09	Created Invoice Nos. 5002, 5003, and 5004 to Valley Medical, Pactuco, and Celite based on time costs incurred using terms Net 15. Apply credits available for Celite.
9/14/09	Signed an engagement letter to perform compilation services for Lompoc Hospital, a new client. Created a new job: Second Quarter Compilation Services for Lompoc Hospital, located at 233 D St., Lompoc, CA 93436.

Date	Transaction
9/15/09	Sold the short-term investment for a gain of $1,500.
9/16/09	Received a payment of $7,200 from Valley Medical as payment on account.
9/17/09	Deposited Valley Medical's check into the Union Savings account.
9/18/09	Sarah worked four hours each day from 9/14 to 9/20 on the Pactuco job, and two hours on 9/14 and 9/15 on the Celite job. She also worked five hours each on 9/17 and 9/18 on the Lompoc Hospital job. Bob worked eight hours 9/14 on the Valley Medical job, eight hours on 9/15 on the Pactuco job, and eight hours each day on 9/16 and 9/17 on the Celite job. On 9/18 he attended eight hours of training at a local university.
9/18/09	Created Invoice Nos. 5005, 5006, 5007 and 5008 to Valley Medical, Pactuco, Celite, and Lompoc Hospital based on time costs incurred using terms Net 15. Apply credits available for Celite.
9/25/09	Sarah worked six hours each day from 9/21 through 9/24 on the Pactuco audit and two hours each of those days as nonbillable hours. Bob worked six hours each day from 9/21 through 9/25 on the Lompoc Hospital job.
9/25/09	Created Invoice Nos. 5009 and 50010 to Pactuco and Lompoc Hospital based on time costs incurred using terms Net 15.
9/29/09	Wrote Check No. 1004 to Pacific Gas & Electric for $400 in utilities expenses.
9/29/09	Wrote Check No. 1005 to Mark Jackson Insurance for $8,000 in liability insurance for the year 9/1/09 through 8/31/10. (Record to prepaid insurance!)
9/29/09	Wrote Check No. 1006 to Allan Hancock College for $300 in professional development fees for Bob's training.
9/29/09	Received a bill from Verizon Wireless in the amount of $525 for telephone expenses for September. Terms are net 30.
9/29/09	Received a bill from Staples in the amount of $1,500 for supplies (a current asset). Terms are net 30.
9/30/09	Paid herself her $6,000 monthly salary and her assistant Bob Humphrey for 123 hours of work at $20 per hour, as shown in Table 7.7. Sarah and Bob are subject to the state's employment training tax.

Table 7.7 Earnings Information	Pay/Tax/Withholding	Duncan	Humphrey
	Hours	n/a	123
	Rate	$ 72,000	$ 20.00
	Gross pay	6,000.00	2,460.00
	Federal withholding	−770.50	−305.05
	Social security employee	−372.00	−152.52
	Medicare employee	−87.00	−35.67
	CA withholding	−231.40	−77.98
	CA disability	−4.80	−1.97
	CA training tax	6.00	2.46
	Social security employer	372.00	152.52
	Medicare company	87.00	35.67
	Federal unemployment	48.00	19.68
	CA unemployment	204.00	83.64
	Check amount	4,534.30	1,886.81

Requirements

Create a QuickBooks file for Sarah Duncan, CPA. Add vendors, inventory items, customers, and employees first. Record business transactions in chronological order (remember, dates are in the month of September 2009). After recording the transactions, create and print the following for September 2009:

a.   Customer Contact List (customer, bill to, and balance total only)

b.   Vendor Contact List (vendor, address, and balance total only)

c.   Employee Contact List (employee, SS No., and address only)

d.   Standard Income Statement

e.   Standard Balance Sheet

f.   Statement of Cash Flows

g.   Transaction List by Date

Comprehensive Problem 2: PACIFIC BREW

merchandising

EasyStep

Pacific Brew Inc. was incorporated January 1, 2006, upon the issuance of 50,000 shares of $1 par value common stock for $50,000. Located at 500 West Ocean, Arcata, California, 95521, Michael Patrick, president, oversees this beer distributor's operations. The company will have a calendar fiscal year, has a federal employer ID number of 77-1357465, and plans to use QuickBooks' inventory, purchase orders, and payroll features. The items the company intends to carry in inventory, the suppliers it purchases from, and the customers lined up whose billing and shipping addresses are the same are listed below.

In addition to distributing beer, Pacific Brew provides consulting services to customers on bar operations, menu plans, and beverage selection. These services are billed to customers at the rate of $85 per hour and are recorded in an income account called consulting revenue. (*Hint:* You'll need to create a service type item called *consulting as item 100* and a consulting revenue account.)

Pacific has two other employees, as shown below. The company's unemployment rate is 3% and it uses only two payroll items for wages: salary—regular, and wages—regular. Federal withholding, unemployment, social security, and medicare are paid to the U.S. Treasury, while California withholding, unemployment, employee disability, and employee training tax are paid to the EDD (Employment Development Department). Payroll is paid semimonthly.

Vendors

Name	Mad River	Lost Coast	JD Salinger	Humboldt
Address	195 Taylor Way	123 West Third St.	101 Market St.	865 10th St.
City	Blue Lake	Eureka	San Francisco	Arcata
State	CA	CA	CA	CA
Zip	95525	95501	94102	95521
Phone	707-555-4151	707-555-4484	415-555-6141	707-555-2739

Inventory Items

Name/#	Description	Cost	Price
302	Mad River Pale Ale	5.00	6.00
303	Mad River Stout	6.00	7.00
304	Mad River Amber Ale	4.00	5.00
305	Mad River Porter	5.50	6.50
402	Lost Coast Pale Ale	5.25	6.25
403	Lost Coast Stout	6.25	7.25
404	Lost Coast Amber Ale	4.25	5.25
502	Humboldt Pale Ale	5.50	6.50
506	Humboldt IPA	6.50	7.50
507	Humboldt Red Nectar	7.00	8.00

Customers

Name	Avalon Bistro	Hole in the Wall	Ocean Grove
Address	1080 3rd St	590 G St.	570 Ewing St.
City	Arcata	Arcata	Trinidad
State	CA	CA	CA
Zip	95521	95521	95570
Phone	707-555-0500	707-555-7407	707-555-5431

Name	River House	Michael's Brew House	Bon Jovi's
Address	222 Weller St.	2198 Union St.	4257 Petaluma Hill
City	Petaluma	San Francisco	Santa Rosa
State	CA	CA	CA
Zip	95404	94123	95404
Phone	707-555-0123	415-555-9874	707-555-5634

Employees

Name	Michael Patrick	Shawn Lopez	Emilio Duarte
Address	333 Spring Rd.	234 University Dr.	23 Palm Dr. #23
City	Arcata	Arcata	Arcata
State	CA	CA	CA
Zip	95521	95521	95521
Phone	707-555-9847	707-555-1297	707-555-6655
SS#	655-85-1253	702-54-8746	012-58-4654
Earnings	Salary—$50,000	Wages—$12/hour	Wages—$11/hour
Filing Status	Married	Single	Single

Chronological List of Business Transactions

Date	Transaction
1/03/06	Sold 50,000 shares of $1 par value common stock for $50,000 cash to various shareholders. Deposited these funds into a Wells Fargo checking account.
1/04/06	Using Purchase Order No. 1001, ordered 500 each of Item 302, 303, 304, and 305 for immediate delivery. Terms: due on receipt, from Mad River. (**Note:** Use QuickBooks Help to customize the purchase order so that the terms of the sale are specified on both the screen and print versions of the purchase order. Always save the terms for the vendor.)

Date	Transaction
1/04/06	Using Purchase Order No. 1002, ordered 400 each of Item 502, 506, and 507 for immediate delivery. Terms: due on receipt, from Humboldt.
1/05/06	Using Purchase Order No. 1003, ordered 300 each of Item 402, 403, and 404 for immediate delivery on 30-day terms, from Lost Coast.
1/05/06	Rented a warehouse from JD Salinger, landlord, for $2,500 per month by paying first and last month's rent with Wells Fargo Check No. 101 for $5,000.
1/06/06	Purchased shelving, desks, and office equipment from JD Salinger for $8,000 with Wells Fargo Check No. 102. (Shelving and desks of $5,000 should be classified as Furniture/Fixtures:Cost, while the office equipment of $3,000 should be classified as Equipment:Cost.)
1/09/06	Invested $30,000 in a short-term investment with Schwab Investments with Wells Fargo Check No. 103.
1/10/06	Borrowed $40,000 from Wells Fargo Bank as a long-term note payable due in three years. The money was deposited into the company's Wells Fargo account.
1/10/06	Purchased several computer systems and printers (classified as Equipment:Cost). Check No. 104 was written for $10,200 to West Coast Computer Supply to purchase the systems.
1/11/06	Received and paid for items on Purchase Order No. 1001 to Mad River with Check No. 105 for $10,250.
1/11/06	Provided 50 hours of consulting services on Order No. 5001 to Michael's Brew House. Payment of $4,250 was deposited into Wells Fargo Bank that same day.
1/12/06	Received and paid for items on Purchase Order No. 1002 to Humboldt with Check No. 106 for $7,600.
1/13/06	Received and shipped an order (5002) to Bon Jovi's for 25 units of Item 305, 30 units of Item No. 506, and 50 units of Item 507. Payment of $787.50 was deposited into Wells Fargo Bank that same day.
1/13/06	Provided 60 hours of consulting services on Order No. 5003 to River House. Payment of $5,100 was deposited into Wells Fargo Bank that same day.
1/16/06	Received and shipped an order (5004) to Ocean Grove for 30 units of Item No. 304, 40 units of Item No. 302, and 50 units of Item No. 502. Payment of $715 was deposited into Wells Fargo Bank that same day.
1/16/06	Paid employees. Duarte worked 80 hours and Lopez worked 75 hours during the period. See tax information in Table 7.8.
1/16/06	Received and shipped an order (5005) to Avalon Bistro for 40 units of Item No. 302, 50 units of Item No. 507, and 35 units of Item No. 506. Payment of $902.50 was deposited into Wells Fargo Bank that same day.
1/16/06	Received and shipped an order (5006) to Michael's Brew House for 100 each of Item Nos. 302, 305, and 506. Payment of $2,000 was deposited into Wells Fargo Bank that same day.

Table 7.8	Pay/Tax/Withholding	Duarte	Lopez	Partick
Earnings Information for Pacific Brew Inc.	Gross Pay	$880.00	$900.00	$2,083.33
	Federal Withholding	–120.56	–123.30	–285.42
	Social security employee	–54.56	–55.80	–129.17
	Medicare employee	–12.76	–13.05	–30.21
	CA—withholding	–48.40	–49.50	–114.58
	CA—disability	–4.40	–4.50	–10.42
	CA—employment training tax	0.88	0.90	2.08
	Social security company	54.56	55.80	129.17
	Medicare company	12.76	13.05	30.21
	Federal unemployment	7.04	7.20	16.67
	CA—unemployment company	26.40	27.00	62.50
	Check amount	639.32	653.85	1,513.53

Requirements

Create a QuickBooks file for Pacific Brew, and save the file as Brew.qbw. Add vendors, inventory items, customers, and employees first. Record business transactions in chronological order (remember, dates are in the month of January 2006). After recording the transactions, create and print the following for January 2006. (Be sure to keep this QuickBooks file in a safe place as it is used as a starting file for this case in Chapter 11.)

 a. Customer Contact List (customer, bill to, phone, and balance total only)

 b. Vendor Contact List (vendor, address, phone, and balance total only)

 c. Employee Contact List

 d. Item Listing (item, description, type, cost, price, and quantity on hand only)

 e. Standard Balance Sheet

 f. Standard Income Statement

 g. Statement of Cash Flows

 h. Transaction List by Date

EasyStep   *merchandising*

Comprehensive Problem 3: SUNSET SPAS

Sunset Spas, Inc., incorporated January 1, 2007, upon the issuance of 10,000 shares of $2 par value common stock for $100,000. Located at 300 West Street, Del Mar, California, 92014, Bryan Christopher, president, oversees this spa retailers operation (use Retail:General Chart of Accounts). The company will have a calendar fiscal year, a federal employer ID number, of 77-9851247, and a California EDD number of 012-3435-8. They plan to use QuickBooks's inventory, purchase orders, and payroll features. The following tables list the suppliers they purchase from, the items they intend to carry in inventory, and the customers they have lined up. The customers' billing and shipping addresses are the same. The company collects 7.75% sales tax on all spa sales and remits amounts collected quarterly to the California State Board of Equalization. No sales tax is collected on installation services.

In addition to selling spas, Sunset Spas also provides installation services to customers. These services are billed to customers at the rate of $75 per hour and are recorded in an income account called Sales:Services (***Hint:*** You'll need to create a service type item called Installation as Item No. 100). Spa sales are recorded in an income account titled Sales: Merchandise. All customers currently have credit terms of "due on receipt."

Sunset also employs two other people, as shown below. The company's unemployment insurance rate is 3.4%. They use only two payroll items for wages: salary—regular and hourly wage—regular. Federal withholding, unemployment, social security, and medicare are paid to the U.S. Treasury, while California withholding, unemployment, employee disability, and employee training tax are paid to the EDD (Employment Development Department). Payroll is paid semi-monthly.

Vendors

Name	Sundance Spas	Cal Spas
Address	14525 Monte Vista Ave.	1462 East Ninth Street
City	Chino	Pomona
State	CA	CA
Zip	91710	91766
Phone	(909) 614-0679	(909) 623-8781

Inventory Items

Name/#	Description	Vendor	Cost	Price
201	Maxus	Sundance	$5,000	$7,000
202	Optima	Sundance	$6,000	$8,000
203	Cameo	Sundance	$7,000	$9,000
301	Galaxy	Cal Spas	$4,500	$6,500
302	Ultimate	Cal Spas	$5,500	$7,500
303	Aqua	Cal Spas	$7,500	$9,500

Customers

Name	J's Landscaping	Marriott Hotels	Pam's Designs
Address	12 Bones Way	97444 Miramar	5144 Union
City	San Diego	San Diego	San Diego
State	CA	CA	CA
Zip	92354	92145	92129
Phone	858-555-1348	858-555-7407	707-555-5748

Employees

Name	Bryan Christopher	Loriel Sanchez	Sharon Lee
Address	12 Mesa Way	2342 Court	323 Ridgefield Pl.
City	Del Mar	Del Mar	Del Mar
State	CA	CA	CA
Zip	92014	92014	92014
Phone	858-555-1264	858-555-3365	858-555-9874
SS#	556-95-4789	475-54-8746	125-58-8452
Earnings	Salary – $60,000	Wages – $13/hr.	Wages – $12/hr.
Filing Status	Married (one income)	Married (one income)	Single

Chronological List of Business Transactions

Date	Transaction
1/03/07	Sold 10,000 shares of no-par common stock for $100,000 cash to various shareholders. Deposited these funds into an account called "Checking" (type: banking). (**Hint:** You'll need to create a common stock equity account.)
1/04/07	Borrowed $200,000 from Hacienda Bank as a long-term note payable due in three years. The money was deposited into the company's bank account and a "note payable" long-term liability type account was recorded.
1/05/07	Using Purchase Order No. 5001, ordered 10 each of Item Nos. 201, 202, and 203 for immediate delivery. Terms: due on receipt, from Sundance. (Note: Use QuickBooks Help to customize the purchase order so that the terms of the sale are specified on both the screen and print versions of the purchase order. Always save the terms for the vendor.)
1/05/07	Using Purchase Order No. 5002, ordered five each of Item Nos. 301, 302, and 303 for immediate delivery. Terms: due on receipt, from Cal Spas.
1/05/07	Rented a retail store front from K Realty, landlord, for $3,000 per month by paying first and last months rent with Check No. 101 for $6,000. This is a long-term lease for five years.
1/08/07	Purchased shelving, desks, and office equipment from Office Max for $8,000 with Check No. 102. (Shelving and desks of $4,500 should be classified as Furniture/Fixtures:Cost, while the office equipment of $3,500 should be classified as Equipment:Cost.
1/09/07	Invested $30,000 in a short-term investment with Poole Investments with Check No. 103.
1/10/07	Purchased several computer systems and printers (classified as Equipment:Cost). Check No. 104 was written for $8,900 to Coast Computer Supply to purchase the systems.
1/11/07	Received and paid for items on Purchase Order No. 5001 to Sundance with Check No. 105.
1/11/07	Provided 10 hours of consulting services to J's Landscape on Sales Receipt No. 7001. Consulting services are taxable. Payment of $862 was deposited into the bank that same day. (**Hint:** Set up consulting services as a new service item (101) that is billed at $80 per hour, is taxable, and is recorded into an income account called Sales:Service.)
1/12/07	Received and paid for items on Purchase Order No. 5002 to Cal Spas with Check No. 106.
1/15/07	Received an order and delivered three Item 301, one Item 202, and one Item 303 to Pam's Design on Sales Receipt No. 7002. Payment of $39,867.50 was deposited into the checking account that same day.
1/15/07	Provided eight hours of consulting services on Sales Receipt No. 7003 to Marriott. Payment of $689.60 was deposited into the checking account that same day.
1/16/07	Received an order and delivered three Item 201, and two Item No. 203 to J's Landscape on Sales Receipt No. 7004. Payment of $42,022.50 was deposited into the checking account that same day.
1/16/07	Paid employees. Sanchez worked 75 hours and Lee worked 83 hours during the period. Checks are to be handwritten starting with Check No. 107. See tax information in Table 7.9.
1/16/07	Received a deposit from Marriott Hotels for future consulting services of $5,000, which was deposited into the checking account that same day.

Pay/Tax/Withholding	Christopher	Sanchez	Lee	Table 7.9
Hours	n/a	75	83	Earnings Information
Rate	$60,000.00	$ 13.00	$ 12.00	for Sunset Spas
Gross pay	2,500.00	975.00	996.00	
Federal withholding	–342.50	–133.58	–136.45	
Social security employee	–155.00	–60.45	–61.75	
Medicare employee	–36.25	–14.14	–14.44	
CA—withholding	–137.50	–53.63	–54.78	
CA—disability	–12.50	–4.88	–4.98	
CA—employment training tax	2.50	0.98	1.00	
Social security employer	155.00	60.45	61.75	
Medicare company	36.25	14.14	14.44	
Federal unemployment	20.00	7.80	7.97	
CA—unemployment	6.25	2.44	2.49	
Check amount	1,816.25	708.32	723.60	

Requirements

Create a QuickBooks file for Sunset Spas and save the file as Sunset_1.qbw. Add vendors, inventory items, customers, and employees first. Record business transactions in chronological order. (Remember, dates are in the month of January 2007.) After recording the transactions, create and print the following for January 2007. (Be sure to keep this QuickBooks file in a safe place as it is used as a starting file for this case in chapter 11.)

a.   Customer Contact List (customer, bill to, phone, and balance total only)

b.   Vendor Contact List (vendor, address, phone, and balance total only)

c.   Employee Contact List

d.   Item Listing (item, description, type, cost, price, and quantity on hand only)

e.   Standard Balance Sheet

f.   Standard Income Statement

g.   Statement of Cash Flows

h.   Transactions List by Date

Additional Business Activities

Learning Objectives

In this chapter, you will:

- Record additional business transactions classified as financing activities, such as repayment of loans
- Record additional business transactions classified as investing activities, such as selling short-term investments for a gain or loss
- Record additional business transactions classified as operating activities, such as purchasing and selling inventory on account
- Record business transactions classified as non-cash investing and financing activities, such as the purchase of equipment with long-term debt

Case: Wild Water Sports, Inc.

You and Karen have completed entering business events which took place during the months of January and February and are ready to begin recording transactions for March. Karen explains that so far the transactions entered involved cash related financing activities such as owner contributions; cash related investing activities such as equipment purchases; and cash related operating activities such as creating purchase orders, receipt of customer payments, cash sales, making deposits, receiving inventory, payment of purchases, invoicing time and costs, payment of expenses, accounting for employees' time, and payment of payroll.

In March and April, the company had similar business events to record in addition to some new ones. During these months, the company entered into some additional cash related financing activities such as the payment of loans, additional cash related investing activities such as the sale of short-term investments, and additional cash related operating activities such as the purchase and sale of inventory on account and the related payment and receipt of those transactions. Further, the company entered into some non-cash investing and financing activities when it purchased some equipment with long-term debt.

Karen suggests that you work through these transactions for March, paying particular attention to those you haven't experienced yet.

Recording Additional Financing Activities

You recall that as of December 31, 2006, the company had a long-term liability of $383,800. Then in January, the company borrowed an additional $250,000 from the Bank of Florida which was due in five years and carried a 5% interest cost.

"When do we make payments on those loans?" you ask.

"Our agreement on the $250,000 loan with the Bank of Florida called for monthly payments of $4,717.81 beginning February 4th," Karen answers. "I was so busy with QuickBooks and the business that I completely forgot! I wrote two checks yesterday to cover our first two payments, and the bank has been kind enough to waive the late payment fee."

The company also borrowed an additional $50,000 from Citibank on February 5th. Payments on that loan are due annually. The loan payable of $383,800 has payments due July 1 of every year.

To record the checks written to make payment on the Bank of Florida loan:

1 Restore the Wild Water Sports Ch 8.qbb file from your Data Files CD or downloaded from the Internet. See "Data Files CD" in Chapter 1 if you need more information.

2 Start the QuickBooks program.

3 Open the newly restored Wild Water Sports Ch 8.qbw file.

4 Click the **Write Checks** icon from the Banking section of the home page. The Write Checks window appears with your current system date and check 1029 ready for entry. The bank had provided a loan amortization schedule as shown in Figure 8.1.

Figure 8.1
Loan Amortization Schedule

Month	Payment	Interest	Principle	Balance
				$250,000.00
1	$4,717.81	$ 1,041.67	$3,676.14	$246,323.86
2	$4,717.81	$1,026.35	$3,691.46	$242,632.40
3	$4,717.81	$ 1,010.97	$3,706.84	$238,925.56
4	$4,717.81	$ 995.52	$3,722.29	$235,203.27
5	$4,717.81	$ 980.01	$3,737.79	$ 231,465.48
6	$4,717.81	$ 964.44	$3,753.37	$ 227,712.11
7	$4,717.81	$ 948.80	$3,769.01	$ 223,943.10
8	$4,717.81	$ 933.10	$3,784.71	$ 220,158.39
9	$4,717.81	$ 917.33	$3,800.48	$ 216,357.91
10	$4,717.81	$ 901.49	$3,816.32	$ 212,541.59
11	$4,717.81	$ 885.59	$3,832.22	$208,709.37
12	$4,717.81	$ 869.62	$3,848.19	$ 204,861.19

5 Enter the information for the check as shown in Figure 8.2. Be sure to enter the correct date.

6 Click **Save & New** to record the check.

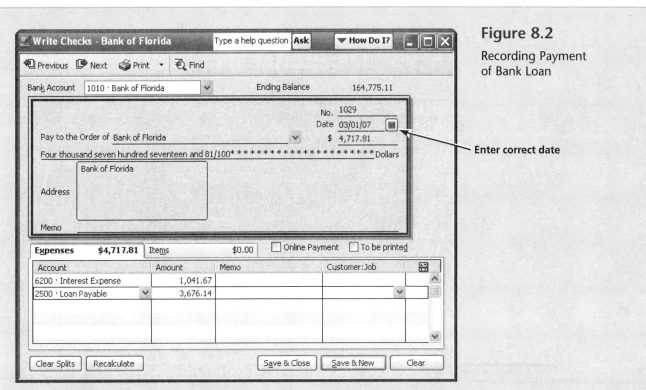

Figure 8.2

Recording Payment of Bank Loan

7 Using the amortization schedule above, enter information for check 1030, on the same date, to record the second payment using interest expense and principle information provided. Your screen should look like Figure 8.3.

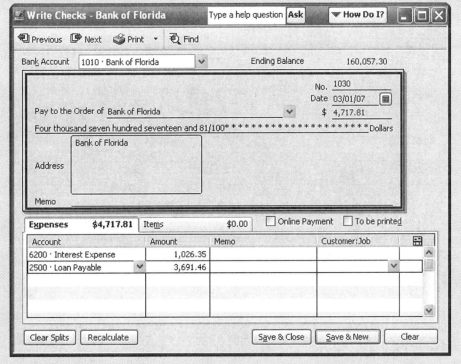

Figure 8.3

Recording the Second Payment on the Bank Loan

8 Click **Save & Close** to record the check.

With the addition of a new owner, and the related funds received from their investment, the company decided to pay down the older higher interest 10% debt with the Bank of Orlando. It made a payment of $387,690.58, which accounted for interest at 10% for 37 days ($3,890.58), and paid the principle balance due of $383,800. Before the company made this payment, it decided to electronically transfer $300,000 from its short-term investment account with ETrade to its Bank of Florida checking account. Karen suggests you try recording this transfer and loan payment that was made on 3/6 with check 1031.

To record the electronic transfer of funds and record payment on a loan:

1 Click the **Chart of Accounts** icon in the Company section of the home page.

2 Double-click account **1050 – Short-Term Investments** to open the Short-Term Investments account register.

3 Type **3/6/07** in the Date section of the account register.

4 Type **Bank of Florida** in the Payee section of the account register.

5 Type **300000** in the Deposit section of the account register.

6 Select **1010 – Bank of Florida** in the Account section of the account register.

7 Click **Record** to record this transaction. Your screen should look like Figure 8.4.

Figure 8.4

Transfer of Funds from ETrade to Bank of Florida

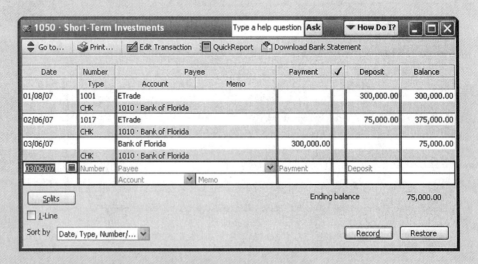

8 Close the Short-Term Investments window.

9 Close the Chart of Accounts window.

10 Click the **Write Checks** icon from the Banking section of the home page. The Write Checks window appears with your current system date and check 1031 ready for entry.

11 Enter the information for the check as shown in Figure 8.5. Be sure to enter the correct date.

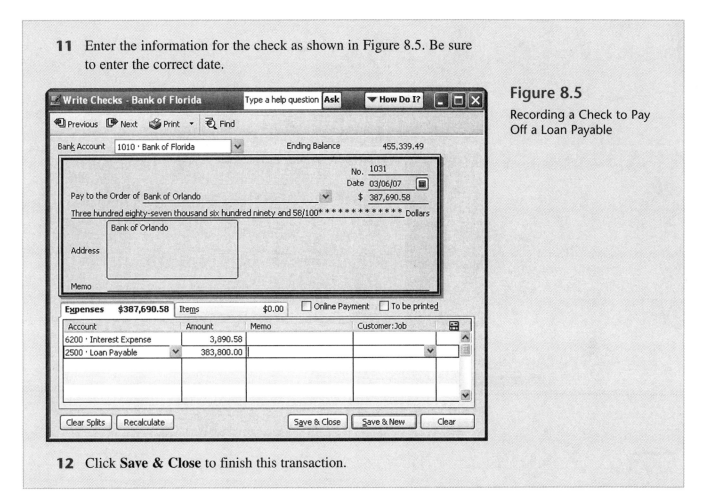

Figure 8.5

Recording a Check to Pay Off a Loan Payable

12 Click **Save & Close** to finish this transaction.

You have now recorded payments of long-term debt. Now it's time to look at some additional investing activities.

Recording Additional Investing Activities

You may recall from your accounting courses that investing activities generally result in the acquisition of noncurrent assets from buying or selling investment securities or productive equipment. Wild Water Sports engaged in several investing activities that you and Karen need to record in March. The company made some additional short-term investments, and it sold previously purchased investment securities for a profit.

In February, Wild Water Sports made an investment with ETrade for $75,000. On March 7, it sold that investment for a profit of $3,000. All funds were retained with ETrade. In addition, it used $35,000 of those money market funds to purchase stock in Apple Computer, again as a short-term investment.

To record short-term investment activity:

1 Click the **Chart of Accounts** icon in the Company section of the home page.

2 Double-click account **1050 – Short-Term Investments** to open the Short-Term Investments account register.

3 Type **3/7/07** in the Date section of the account register.

4 Type **ETrade** in the Payee section of the account register.

5 Type **3000** in the Deposit section of the account register.

6 Select **7030 – Other Income** in the Account section of the account register.

7 Click **Record** to record this transaction. Your screen should look like Figure 8.6.

Figure 8.6

Recording Profit on a Short-Term Investment

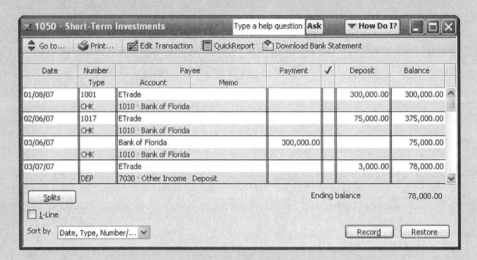

8 Close the Short-Term Investments window.

9 Close the Chart of Accounts window.

"Why didn't we record the Apple Computer stock purchase in our records?" you ask.

"Well, remember that the funds used to purchase this stock were already in our short-term investment account," Karen answers. "Thus this is just a reallocation of our short-term investment from a money market category to a stock category. We, as shareholders, consider both the money market funds and the stock investment to be short-term investments; thus, we don't differentiate them in the accounting records."

Recording Additional Operating Activities

Donna has been working hard establishing credit with the company's suppliers. Recently she's convinced both Malibu, MB Sports, and Tige to give Wild Water 15-day credit terms. Several purchase orders have been created to acquire more inventory for the company's showroom and to purchase inventory ordered by some new customers.

"Now that we have some credit with our suppliers, we'll be able to offer credit to some of our better customers," Donna points out. She suggests that you input the purchase orders created in March and the related bills received from suppliers.

To record purchase orders for the month of March:

1 Click the **Purchase Order** icon from the Vendors section of the home page.

2 Enter purchase order information from Figure 8.7. Be sure to provide address information for Malibu, which isn't currently a part of our information for this vendor.

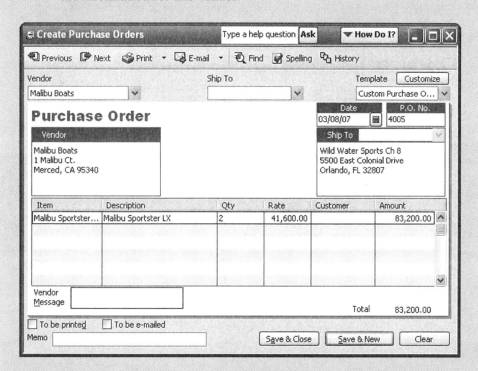

Figure 8.7
Purchase Order 4005

3 Click **Save & New.**

4 Click **Yes** to save the updated address information for Malibu Boats.

5 Create purchase order **4006** to Tige Boats on 3/12/07 ordering 1 Tige 22v and 1 Tige 24v (a new item with a cost of $70,000 and a sales price of $87,500 using the same cost of goods sold and income accounts as all other boats).

6 Create purchase order **4007** to MB Sports on 3/16/07 ordering 1 MB 220V (a new item with a cost of $50,000 and a sales price of $65,000 using the same cost of goods sold and income accounts as all other boats) for a new customer (Spirit Adventures, 500 Butterfly Lake Rd., Fort Lauderdale, FL 33308. Terms: Net 30).

7 Click **Save & Close.**

Now that the company has secured a 15-day credit line with Malibu, MB, and Tige, vendor information in QuickBooks needs to be updated. Karen demonstrates the process of modifying vendor information for terms.

To update vendor records for changes in terms:

1 Click the **Vendors** button in the Vendors section of the home page.

2 Double-click **Malibu Boats** to open the Edit Vendor window.

3 Click the **Additional Information** tab.

4 Select **Net 15** from the drop-down list of terms as shown in Figure 8.8.

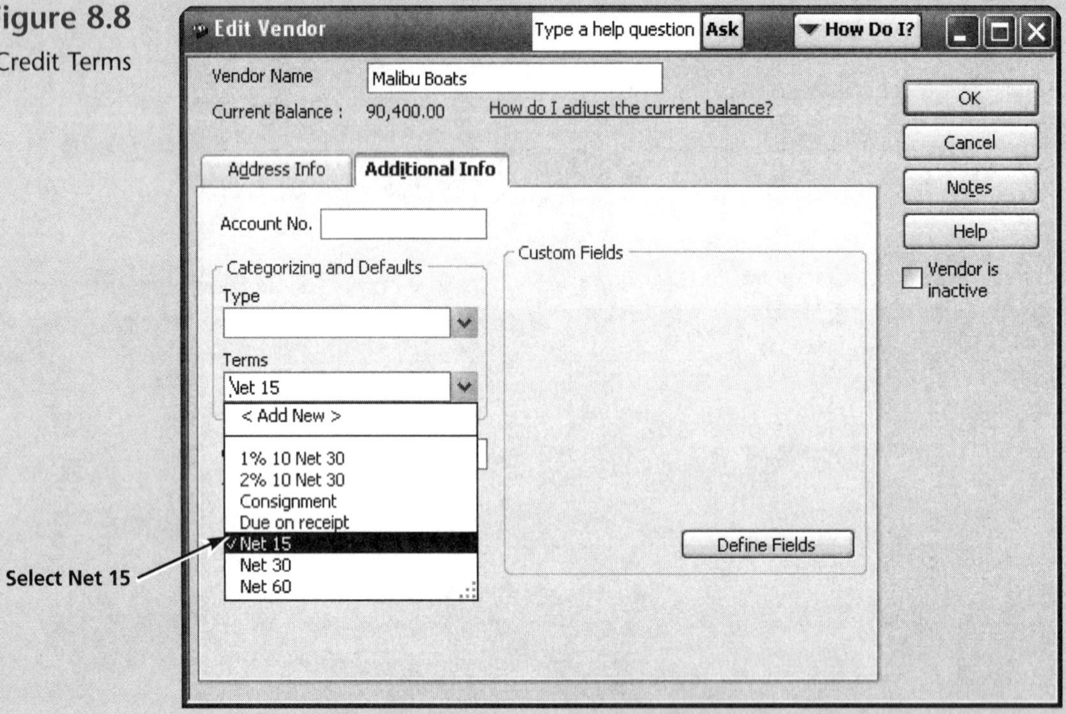

Figure 8.8

Changing Credit Terms

Select Net 15

5 Click **OK** to save this change.

6 Perform this same process for MB Sports and Tige.

Some of the boats ordered on the purchase orders entered above were received in the month of March. Since these were all ordered on account, QuickBooks requires that you record the receipt of inventory at the same time you record the receipt of the bill invoicing the company for payment. In addition, boats ordered with purchase order 4004 issued in February were received in March.

To record receipt of inventory and bill:

1 Click the **Receive Inventory** icon from the Vendors section of the company's home page.

2 Select **Receive Inventory with Bill.**

3 Select **Malibu Boats** from the Vendor list.

4 Click **Yes** when asked if you want to receive against one or more of the open purchase orders for this vendor.

5 Select purchase order **2004** as shown in Figure 8.9.

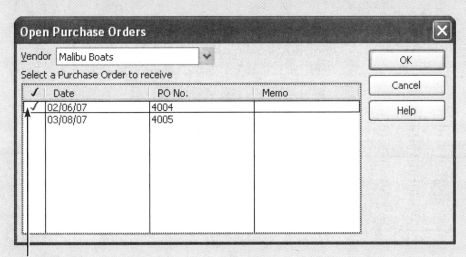

Check PO 4004

Figure 8.9

Selecting Purchase Orders
When Receiving Inventory

6 Click **OK.**

7 Type **3/6/07** as the bill date.

8 Your screen should look like Figure 8.10.

9 Note the Bill Due date of 3/21/07 (15 days from the date of receipt.) Click **Save & New.**

10 Select **Malibu Boats** from the Vendor list.

11 Click **Yes** when asked if you want to receive against one or more of the open purchase orders for this vendor.

12 Select purchase order **2005.**

13 Click **OK.**

14 Type **3/15/07** as the bill date.

15 Note the Bill Due date of 3/30/07 (15 days from the date of receipt). Click **Save & New.**

16 Select **Tige Boats** from the Vendor list.

Figure 8.10

Malibu Bill

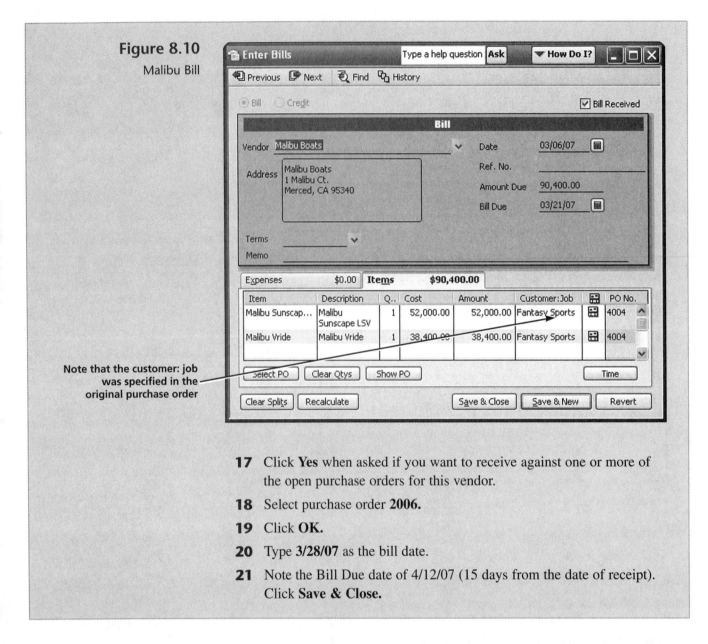

Note that the customer: job was specified in the original purchase order

17 Click **Yes** when asked if you want to receive against one or more of the open purchase orders for this vendor.

18 Select purchase order **2006.**

19 Click **OK.**

20 Type **3/28/07** as the bill date.

21 Note the Bill Due date of 4/12/07 (15 days from the date of receipt). Click **Save & Close.**

job costing

Two service-related jobs (50005 and 50006) were started and completed in the month of March. Both were to customers who were invoiced for the work and given 15-day credit terms. Karen explains that in both of these cases, jobs need to be created, time recorded, and invoices need to be recorded.

To record service related activity on account:

1 Click the **Customers** button from the Customer section of the home page.

2 Double-click **Buena Vista Water Sports.**

3 Click the **Additional Info** tab.

4 Change the Terms to **Net 15,** and then click **OK** to close the window.

5 Click **New Customer & Job** (while Buena Vista Water Sports is still selected).

6 Click **Add Job** from the drop-down menu presented.

7 Type **50005** as the Job Name and then click **OK.**

8 Double-click **Performance Rentals.**

9 Click the **Additional Info** tab.

10 Change the Terms to **Net 15,** and then click **OK** to close the window.

11 Click **New Customer & Job** (while Performance Rentals is still selected).

12 Click **Add Job** from the drop-down menu presented.

13 Type **50006** as the Job Name and then click **OK.**

14 Close the **Customer Center** window.

15 Click **Enter Time** from the Employees section of the home page.

16 Select **Ryder Zacovic** as the employee name.

17 Click **Set Date,** and then type the date **3/12/07** and then click **OK.**

18 Enter the information shown in Figure 8.11.

job costing

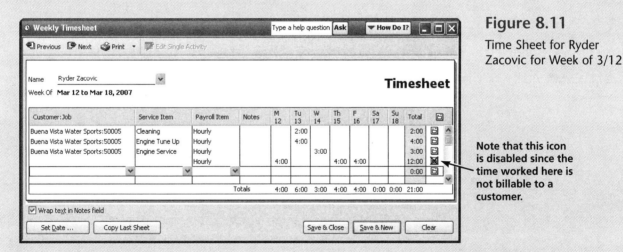

Figure 8.11

Time Sheet for Ryder Zacovic for Week of 3/12

Note that this icon is disabled since the time worked here is not billable to a customer.

19 Click **Next.**

20 Enter the information shown in Figure 8.12.

21 Click **Save & Close.**

22 Click **Invoices** from the Customers section of the home page.

23 Select **Buena Vista Water Sports 50005** from the Customer:Job list.

24 Click **OK** in the Billable Time/Costs window.

Figure 8.12

Time Sheet for Ryder Zacovic for Week of 3/19

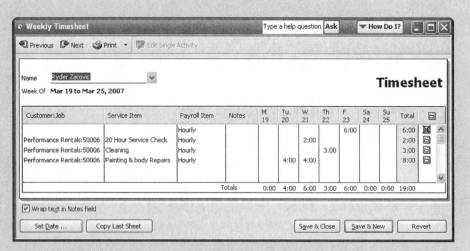

25   Type **3/16/07** as the invoice date.

26   Type **10005** as the invoice number.

27   Click the **Time/Costs** button.

28   Click the **Time** tab.

29   Click the **Select All** button to select all hours charged by Ryder to this customer, and then click **OK** to close the window.

30   Add the tune-up parts, engine oil, air filter, and oil filter to the invoice as shown in Figure 8.13. Also add the address information provided.

Figure 8.13

Invoice for Buena Vista Water Sports

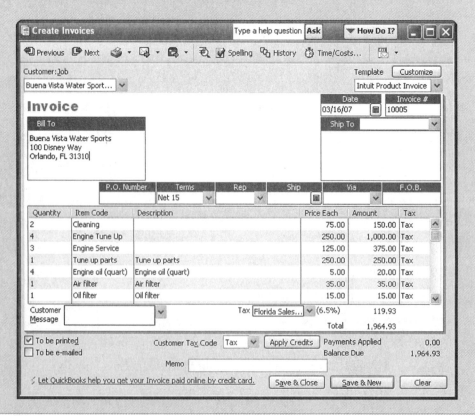

31 Click **Save & New.**

32 Click **Yes** to save the new address information for this customer.

33 Select **Performance Rentals 50006** from the Customer:Job list.

34 Click **OK** in the Billable Time/Costs window.

35 Type **3/23/07** as the invoice date.

36 Type **10006** as the invoice number.

37 Click the **Time/Costs** button.

38 Click the **Time** tab.

39 Click the **Select All** button to select all hours charged by Ryder to this customer, and then click **OK** to close the window.

40 Your screen should look like Figure 8.14.

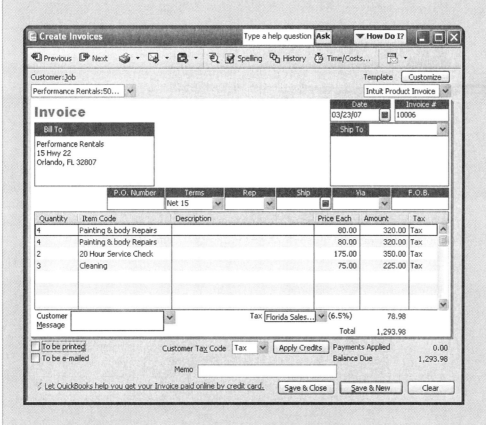

Figure 8.14

Invoice for Performance Rentals

41 Click **Save & Close.**

There was one cash boat purchase during the month to a new customer, Sonia Garcia. She purchased a Malibu Vride off the showroom floor on March 12 for $51,120 using check 8593 including sales tax.

To record a cash sale and deposit cash received:

1 Click **Create Sales Receipts** from the Customers section of the home page.

2 Type **Sonia Garcia** in the Customer:Job text edit box.

3 Click **Quick Add.**

4 Type **3/12/07** as the date of sale and **6008** as the sale number.

5 Type **8593** as the check number, and select **Check** as the Payment Method.

6 Select **Malibu Vride** as the Item.

7 Type **1** as the Qty.

8 Make sure **Florida Sales Tax** is shown as the Tax item, and then click **Save & Close** to enter this sales receipt.

9 Click **Record Deposits** from the Banking section of the home page.

10 Select the deposit shown and click **OK.**

11 Type **3/12/07** as the deposit date.

12 Click **Save & Close** to record the deposit.

Three invoices were generated in the month of March for boat sales. One, to Fantasy Sports on invoice 10004, represented an order received during the month for which Fantasy had already paid a deposit. Upon Fantasy's request, Donna approved Net 15 credit terms on the balance owed. The other two were sales from the showroom floor: on account on invoices 10007 and 10008, respectively.

To record invoices from the sale of boats on account:

1 Click **Invoices** from the Customers section of the home page.

2 Select **Fantasy Sports** from the Customer:Job list.

3 Click **OK** in the Billable Time/Costs window.

4 Type **3/7/07** as the invoice date.

5 Type **10004** as the invoice number.

6 Click the **Time/Costs** button.

7 Click the **Select All** button to select both boats received from Malibu, and then click **OK** to close the window.

8 Click the **Apply Credits** button, and then click **OK** to save this invoice.

9 Click **Done** to apply the credit of $28,250.

10 Select terms of **Net 15** from the Terms list and type **3/7/07** as the ship date. The completed invoice should look like Figure 8.15.

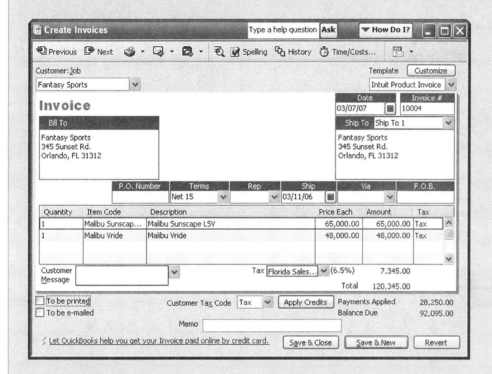

Figure 8.15

Invoice to Fantasy Sports

11 Click **Save & New.**

12 Click **Yes** to save the changed terms for this customer.

13 Select **Freebirds** from the Customer:Job list.

14 Type **3/23/07** as the invoice date.

15 Type **10007** as the invoice number.

16 Select terms of **Net 15** from the Terms list and type **3/23/07** as the ship date. Type the Bill To information provided on the invoice. The completed invoice should look like Figure 8.16.

17 Click **Save & New.**

18 Click **Yes** to save the new billing address and terms.

19 Select **Florida Sports Camp** from the Customer:Job list.

20 Type **3/29/07** as the invoice date.

21 Type **10008** as the invoice number.

22 Select terms of **Net 15** from the Terms list, and type **3/29/07** as the ship date.

23 Enter Quantity **1**, Item Code **Tige 22v**, and Tax **Florida Sales Tax.**

Figure 8.16

Invoice to Freebirds

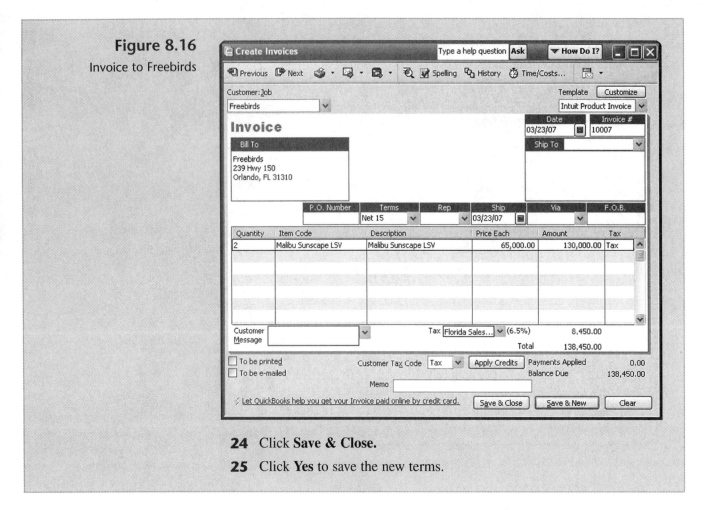

24 Click **Save & Close.**

25 Click **Yes** to save the new terms.

At the end of the month, Wild Water Sports received a check from Performance Rentals for $10,000 as a deposit toward the purchase of a boat on its showroom floor.

To record receipt of deposit from Performance Rentals:

1 Click **Receive Payments** from the Customers section of the home page.

2 Select **Performance Rentals** from the Received From drop-down list.

3 Type **10000** as the amount.

4 Type **3/31/07** as the date.

5 Click the **Un-Apply Payment** button since this is a deposit on another transaction and not a payment on invoice 10006 as suggested.

6 Click the **Leave credit to be used later** option button.

7 Click **Save & Close.**

8 Click **OK** in the Payment Credit window.

By agreement, Wild Water Sports agreed to hold this check and not deposit it in its bank account.

"When do we get around to paying the bills and collecting cash from these invoices?" you ask.

"It's important to pay bills on a timely basis to keep your suppliers happy and keep our good credit," Karen answers. "First off, we can view what bills are outstanding and when they are due and then choose which to pay and when."

To choose which bills to pay and pay bills:

1 Click **Pay Bills** from the Vendors section of the home page.

2 Click the option button to **Show all bills.**

3 Click next to the due date **3/21/07.**

4 Click the option button to **Assign check no.**

5 Type **3/21/07** as the payment date. Your screen should look like Figure 8.17.

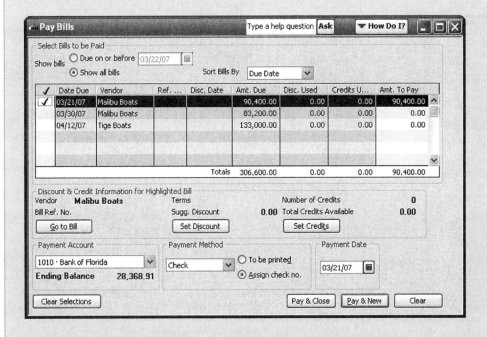

Figure 8.17

Pay Bills Window

6 Click **Pay & Close.**

7 Type **1032** as the check number in the Assign Check No. window, and then click **OK.**

"We collected two payments from customers on account in March," Karen says. "Orlando Water Sports paid us $5,300 on 3/21, and Buena Vista paid us $1,964.93 on 3/29."

To record cash collections on account and related deposit:

1 Click **Receive Payments** from the Customer section of the home page.

2 Select **Orlando Water Sports** as the customer received from.

3 Type **5300** as the Amount received.

4 Type **3/21/07** as the Date received.

5 Type **9152** as the check number of the check received as payment. Your screen should look like Figure 8.18.

Figure 8.18

Receive Payments Window

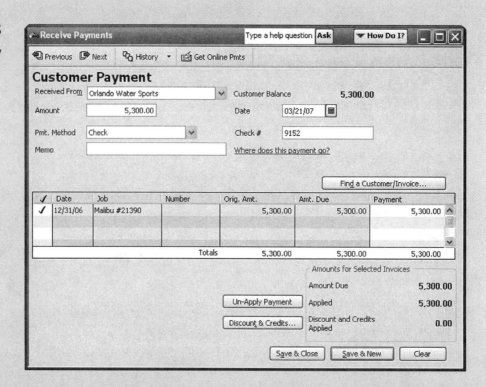

6 Click **Save & New.**

7 Select **Buena Vista Water Sports** as the customer received from.

8 Type **1964.93** as the Amount received.

9 Type **3/29/07** as the Date received.

10 Type **741** as the check number of the check received as payment.

11 Click **Save & Close.**

12 Click **Record Deposits** from the Banking section of the home page.

13 Select the two deposits shown and click **OK.**

14 Type **3/29/07** as the deposit date.

15 Click **Save & Close** to record the deposit.

"In addition to paying bills from vendors for merchandise purchased, the company also has to pay its sales tax and payroll tax obligations," Karen reminds you. "Before we can do that and pay the rest of our end of the month bills and payroll, we'll need to transfer some funds from our short-term investment account at ETrade to our checking account."

Donna offers to make the electronic transfer of $40,000 from ETrade to Bank of Florida, and you agree to record the accounting effect of that transfer and prepare checks to pay the sales tax and payroll tax obligations.

To transfer funds and pay sales tax and payroll tax obligations:

1. Click the **Chart of Accounts** icon in the Company section of the home page.

2. Double-click the **Short-Term Investments** account.

3. Type **3/29/07** as the date.

4. Type **Bank of Florida** as the payee.

5. Type **40000** as the payment.

6. Select **1010 – Bank of Florida** as the Account.

7. Click **Record** and then close the Short-Term Investments and the Chart of Accounts windows.

8. Click the **Pay Sales Tax** icon from the Vendor section of the home page.

9. Type **3/29/07** as the check date.

10. Type **2/28/07** as the Show sales tax due through date.

11. Press the **[Tab]** key to refresh the screen.

12. Type **1033** as the Starting Check No.

13. Click in the **Pay** column next to Florida Sales Tax. Your screen should look like Figure 8.19.

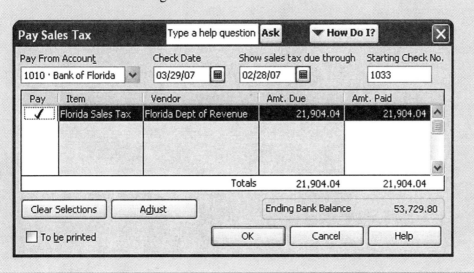

Figure 8.19

Pay Sales Tax Window

14 Click **OK.**

15 Click the **Pay Liabilities** icon from the Employees section of the home page.

16 Type **1/1/07** as the From date.

17 Type **2/28/07** as the Through date, and then click **OK.**

18 Uncheck the **To be printed** checkbox.

19 Select all of the Payroll Items.

20 Select the **Review liability check** option button.

21 Type **3/29/07** as the Check Date. Your screen should look like Figure 8.20.

Figure 8.20

Pay Liabilities Window

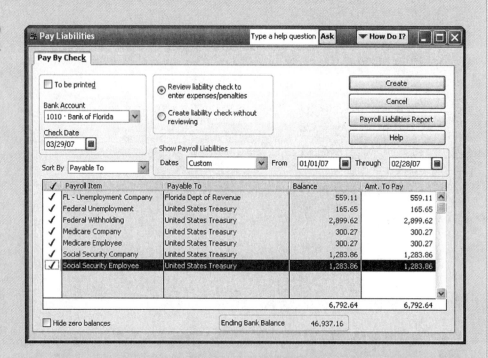

22 Click **Create.**

23 A Liability Check – Bank of Florida window should appear like Figure 8.21.

24 Click **Next** to view the United States Treasury check, which should look like Figure 8.22.

25 Close the check window.

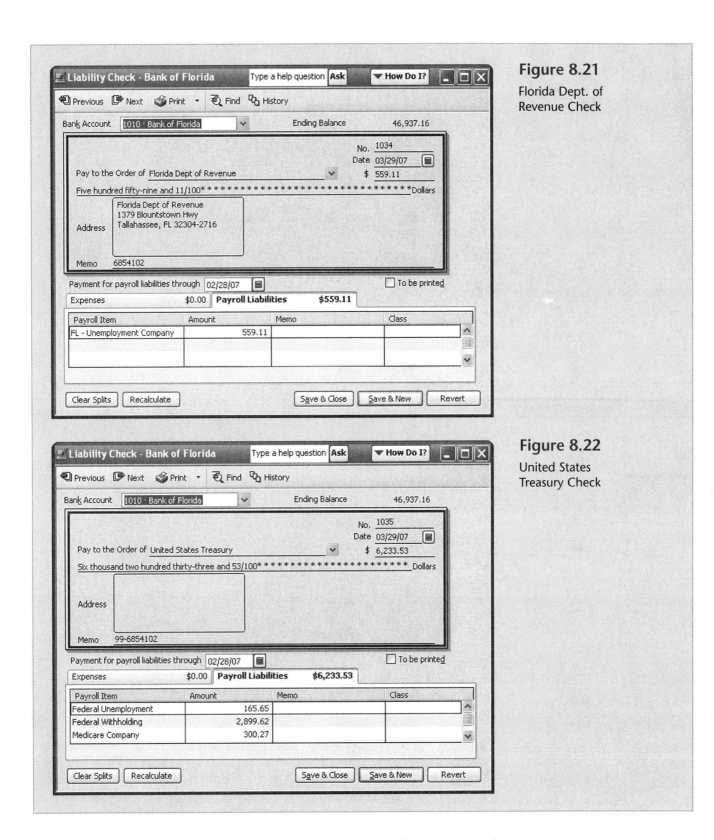

Figure 8.21

Florida Dept. of Revenue Check

Figure 8.22

United States Treasury Check

"All that is left for March is for us to record checks written for expenses and record payroll," Karen states. "Our expenses are about the same each month, so you shouldn't see too much variation in what you did the last two months. We didn't have much in the way of service this month, and so Pat didn't work and Ryder just worked the hours we recorded earlier."

To record end of the month expenses:

1   Click the **Write Checks** icon in the Banking section of the home page.

2   Type **1036** as the check number if it is not already there.

3   Type **3/30/07** as the Check Date.

4   Select **Central Florida Gas & Electric** from the Pay to the Order of section of the check.

5   Type **1050** as the amount.

6   Note that account **6900 – Utilities** should already be selected from the Account drop-down list. If it is not, select it now.

7   Click **Save & New.**

8   Type **1037** as the check number if it is not already there.

9   Type **3/30/07** as the Check Date if it is not already there.

10 Select **Verizon** in the Pay to the Order of section of the check.

11 Type **1500** as the amount.

12 Note that account **6660 – Telephone** should already be selected from the Account drop-down list. If it is not, select it now.

13 Click **Save & Close.**

To record end of the month payroll:

1   Click the **Pay Employees** icon in the Employee section of the home page.

2   Type **3/30/07** as the Check Date and **3/31/07** as the Pay Period Ends date. Your screen should look like Figure 8.23.

Figure 8.23

Select Employees To Pay

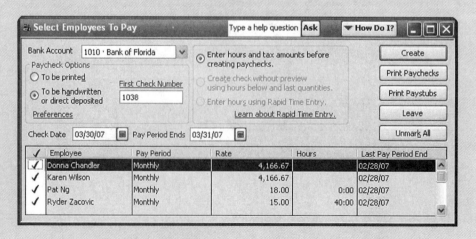

3 Click **Create.**

4 Use the information below to create payroll for Donna, Karen, and Ryder.

Employee/Item	Donna	Karen	Ryder
Earnings	4,166.67	4,166.67	600.00
Federal withholding	−463.00	−710.00	−82.20
Social Security employee	−258.33	−258.33	−37.20
Medicare employee	−60.42	−60.42	−8.70
Social Security company	258.33	258.33	37.20
Medicare company	60.42	60.42	8.70
Federal unemployment	33.33	33.33	4.80
FL unemployment company	112.50	112.50	16.20
Check amount	3,384.92	3,137.92	471.90

5 Close the Select Employees To Pay window once you've created paychecks for Donna, Karen, and Ryder for March.

Recording Noncash Investing and Financing Activities

Although noncash investing and financing activities do not affect the cash position of a company, they do have an impact on a firm's financial position. One example of such an activity was Wild Water Sports's purchase of computer equipment in March that was completely financed with long-term debt (a note payable to Staples with no interest and no payment due until 10/1/08). Karen explains the nature of this transaction to you and demonstrates how it should be recorded.

To record the purchase of equipment with long-term debt:

1 Click the **Chart of Accounts** icon from the Company section of the home page.

2 Double-click account **1310 – Cost.**

3 Type **3/30/07** as the Date.

4 Type **Staples** as the Payee.

5 Type **5000** as the amount in the Increase column.

6 Select **2500 – Loan Payable** as the Account.

7 Click **Record.** Your screen should look like Figure 8.24.

8 Close the 1310 – Cost window and the Chart of Accounts window.

Figure 8.24

Entering an Equipment
Purchase in Exchange
for a Loan

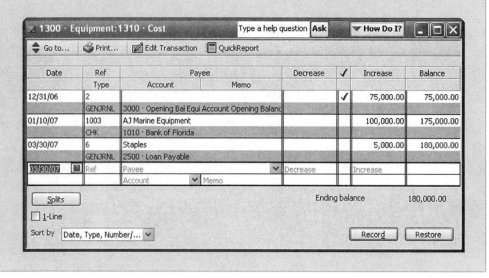

Evaluate a Firm's Performance and Financial Position

Once again, the best way to evaluate a firm's performance and financial position at this point is to generate an income statement and balance sheet. Karen suggests you do this for the entire three months ended March 31, 2007 (the first quarter of 2007) and prepare a Transaction by Date report like you did last month.

To prepare a comparative income statement, balance sheet, and transaction by date report for the first quarter of 2007:

1 Click the **Report Center** icon from the icon toolbar.

2 Click **Standard** under the Profit & Loss section.

3 Change the From date to **1/1/07.**

4 Change the To date to **3/31/07,** and then click **Refresh.**

5 Select **Month** from the Columns list.

6 Click the **Collapse** button.

7 Click the **Print** button from the toolbar, and then click **Print** in the Print Reports window. Your report should look like Figure 8.25.

8 Close the Profit & Loss report window, and do not memorize this report.

9 Click **Standard** under the Balance Sheet and Net Worth section.

10 Change the As of date to **3/31/07,** and then click **Refresh.**

11 Click the **Collapse** button.

Wild Water Sports Ch 8
Profit & Loss
January through March 2007

	Jan 07	Feb 07	Mar 07	TOTAL
Ordinary Income/Expense				
Income				
4000 · Sales	203,335.00	133,650.00	372,810.00	709,795.00
Total Income	203,335.00	133,650.00	372,810.00	709,795.00
Cost of Goods Sold				
5000 · Cost of Goods Sold	160,632.00	105,800.00	296,056.00	562,488.00
Total COGS	160,632.00	105,800.00	296,056.00	562,488.00
Gross Profit	42,703.00	27,850.00	76,754.00	147,307.00
Expense				
6200 · Interest Expense	0.00	0.00	5,958.60	5,958.60
6235 · Marketing & Advertising	0.00	2,700.00	0.00	2,700.00
6300 · Office Expenses	0.00	4,500.00	0.00	4,500.00
6560 · Payroll Expenses	11,343.22	11,673.35	9,929.40	32,945.97
6660 · Telephone	1,700.00	1,820.00	1,500.00	5,020.00
6900 · Utilities	890.00	930.00	1,050.00	2,870.00
Total Expense	13,933.22	21,623.35	18,438.00	53,994.57
Net Ordinary Income	28,769.78	6,226.65	58,316.00	93,312.43
Other Income/Expense				
Other Income				
7030 · Other Income	0.00	0.00	3,000.00	3,000.00
Total Other Income	0.00	0.00	3,000.00	3,000.00
Net Other Income	0.00	0.00	3,000.00	3,000.00
Net Income	**28,769.78**	**6,226.65**	**61,316.00**	**96,312.43**

Figure 8.25

Income Statement for the Three Months through March 2007

12 Click the **Print** button from the toolbar and then click **Print** in the Print Reports window. Your assets section of your report should look like Figure 8.26, while the liabilities and equity section of your report should look like Figure 8.27.

13 Close the Balance Sheet report window and do not memorize this report.

14 Click **Transactions List by Date** from the Account Activity section of Accountant and Taxes.

15 Type **3/1/07** in the From text box.

16 Type **3/31/07** in the To text box.

17 Click the **Refresh** button. The report shown in Figure 8.28 should appear.

18 Close the report and Report Center windows.

Figure 8.26

Assets Section of the
Balance Sheet

Wild Water Sports Ch 8
Balance Sheet
As of March 31, 2007

	Mar 31, 07
ASSETS	
Current Assets	
Checking/Savings	
1010 · Bank of Florida	37,392.42
1050 · Short-Term Investments	38,000.00
Total Checking/Savings	75,392.42
Accounts Receivable	
1200 · Accounts Receivable	330,707.73
Total Accounts Receivable	330,707.73
Other Current Assets	
1060 · Prepaid Advertising	24,000.00
1120 · Inventory Asset	295,600.00
1130 · Inventory Parts	2,112.00
1150 · Prepaid Insurance	22,000.00
Total Other Current Assets	343,712.00
Total Current Assets	749,812.15
Fixed Assets	
1300 · Equipment	172,500.00
1400 · Furniture & Fixtures	70,000.00
1500 · Truck	45,000.00
Total Fixed Assets	287,500.00
TOTAL ASSETS	**1,037,312.15**

Figure 8.27

Liabilities and Equity
Section of the Balance Sheet

LIABILITIES & EQUITY	
Liabilities	
Current Liabilities	
Accounts Payable	
2000 · Accounts Payable	216,200.00
Total Accounts Payable	216,200.00
Other Current Liabilities	
2100 · Payroll Liabilities	2,934.66
2200 · Sales Tax Payable	24,232.66
Total Other Current Liabilities	27,167.32
Total Current Liabilities	243,367.32
Long Term Liabilities	
2500 · Loan Payable	297,632.40
Total Long Term Liabilities	297,632.40
Total Liabilities	540,999.72
Equity	
3100 · Common Stock	400,000.00
Net Income	96,312.43
Total Equity	496,312.43
TOTAL LIABILITIES & EQUITY	**1,037,312.15**

Wild Water Sports Ch 8
Transaction List by Date
March 2007

Type	Date	Num	Name	Memo	Account	Clr	Split	Amount
Mar 07								
Check	3/1/2007	1029	Bank of Florida		1010 · Bank of Florida		-SPLIT-	-4,717.81
Check	3/1/2007	1030	Bank of Florida		1010 · Bank of Florida		-SPLIT-	-4,717.81
Check	3/6/2007		Bank of Florida		1050 · Short-Term I...		1010 · Bank of...	-300,000.00
Check	3/6/2007	1031	Bank of Orlando		1010 · Bank of Florida		-SPLIT-	-387,690.58
Bill	3/6/2007		Malibu Boats		2000 · Accounts Pa...		-SPLIT-	-90,400.00
Deposit	3/7/2007		ETrade	Deposit	1050 · Short-Term I...		7030 · Other I...	3,000.00
Invoice	3/7/2007	10004	Fantasy Sports		1200 · Accounts Re...		-SPLIT-	120,345.00
Sales Receipt	3/12/2007	6008	Sonia Garcia		1499 · Undeposited ...	X	-SPLIT-	51,120.00
Deposit	3/12/2007			Deposit	1010 · Bank of Florida		1499 · Undepo...	51,120.00
Bill	3/15/2007		Malibu Boats		2000 · Accounts Pa...		1120 · Invento...	-83,200.00
Invoice	3/16/2007	10005	Buena Vista Water ...		1200 · Accounts Re...		-SPLIT-	1,964.93
Bill Pmt -Check	3/21/2007	1032	Malibu Boats		1010 · Bank of Florida		2000 · Accoun...	-90,400.00
Payment	3/21/2007	9152	Orlando Water Sports		1499 · Undeposited ...	X	1200 · Accoun...	5,300.00
Invoice	3/23/2007	10006	Performance Rental...		1200 · Accounts Re...		-SPLIT-	1,293.98
Invoice	3/23/2007	10007	Freebirds		1200 · Accounts Re...		-SPLIT-	138,450.00
Bill	3/28/2007		Tige Boats		2000 · Accounts Pa...		-SPLIT-	-133,000.00
Invoice	3/29/2007	10008	Florida Sports Camp		1200 · Accounts Re...		-SPLIT-	83,868.75
Payment	3/29/2007	741	Buena Vista Water ...		1499 · Undeposited ...	X	1200 · Accoun...	1,964.93
Deposit	3/29/2007			Deposit	1010 · Bank of Florida		-SPLIT-	7,264.93
Check	3/29/2007		Bank of Florida		1050 · Short-Term I...		1010 · Bank of...	-40,000.00
Sales Tax Payment	3/29/2007	1033	Florida Dept of Rev...		1010 · Bank of Florida		2200 · Sales T...	-21,904.04
Liability Check	3/29/2007	1034	Florida Dept of Rev...	6854102	1010 · Bank of Florida		2100 · Payroll ...	-559.11
Liability Check	3/29/2007	1035	United States Treas...	99-6854102	1010 · Bank of Florida		-SPLIT-	-6,233.53
Check	3/30/2007	1036	Central Florida Gas ...		1010 · Bank of Florida		6900 · Utilities	-1,050.00
Check	3/30/2007	1037	Verizon		1010 · Bank of Florida		6660 · Teleph...	-1,500.00
Paycheck	3/30/2007	1038	Donna Chandler		1010 · Bank of Florida		-SPLIT-	-3,384.92
Paycheck	3/30/2007	1039	Karen Wilson		1010 · Bank of Florida		-SPLIT-	-3,137.92
Paycheck	3/30/2007	1040	Ryder Zacovic		1010 · Bank of Florida		-SPLIT-	-471.90
General Journal	3/30/2007	6	Staples		1310 · Cost		2500 · Loan P...	5,000.00
Mar 07								

Figure 8.28

Transaction List for March 2007

"Not bad for our first three months," Karen comments. "But we still need to accrue some revenues and expenses, adjust some prepaid assets and unearned revenue, and record depreciation."

End Note

You've now helped Karen understand even more of QuickBooks's features, including how to record the repayment of loans, sale of investments, receipt of inventory items and related bills, credit sales, and the receipt of payments on account.

Chapter 8 Questions

1 What information, contained in a loan amortization schedule, is part of the payment information recorded in QuickBooks?

2 How does a firm account for transfer of funds from one bank to another bank in QuickBooks?

3 How do you update vendor records for changes in terms from the home page?

4 What payment terms are available in QuickBooks for vendors?

5 Consider this statement: "QuickBooks records revenue when an invoice is generated even though cash has not been received." Is this practice acceptable? Why or why not?

6 What icon is clicked in the Vendors section to record the receipt of inventory and the related bill?

7 What are the steps necessary to record services performed on account for Wild Water Sports?

8 How does the QuickBooks software respond if a bill is entered with a vendor name not included on the vendor list?

9 What are the steps for paying sales tax?

10 What are noncash investing and financing activities, and how are they recorded in QuickBooks?

Chapter 8 Assignments

1 *Adding More Information to Wild Water Sports*

Restore the file Wild Water Sports Ch 8A.qbb found on the text CD or downloaded from the text website, and then add the following transactions in chronological order.

Date	Transaction
4/2	Wrote Check No. 1041 for $4,717.81 as payment 3 on loan to Bank of Florida. See loan amortization schedule in Figure 8.1 for interest and principle breakdown.
4/3	Received $92,095 as payment on account from Fantasy Sports on their Check No. 234.
4/4	Deposited payment received from Fantasy Sports.
4/4	Paid Malibu Boats bill by writing check 1042 for $83,200.
4/5	Created purchase order 4008 to Tige to purchase one Tige 22v and one Tige 24v for showroom floor inventory.

Date	Transaction
4/6	Received items ordered and bill on purchase order 4007 from MB Sports.
4/9	Received $1,293.98 as payment on account from Performance Rentals on their Check No. 987.
4/9	Accepted a new job (50007) to service a boat owned by Seth Blackman.
4/9	Pat Ng worked four hours on each day: April 9, 11, 12, and 13, which were nonbillable hours. He worked two hours performing an engine service and three hours cleaning on job 50007 on April 10.
4/10	Sold the investment in Apple Computer stock, originally purchased for $25,000 for a loss of $2,000.
4/11	Deposited payment received from Performance Rentals.
4/11	Created invoice 10009 to Sprit Adventures to record sale of an MB 220v terms Net 30.
4/11	Created invoice 10010 to Seth Backman for service under job 50007 and five quarts of oil, one air filter, and one oil filter. Terms Net 15.
4/11	Created purchase order 4009 to MB Sports to purchase one MB 220v and one MB B52 V23 for showroom floor inventory.
4/12	Received $83,868.75 as payment on account from Florida Sports Camp on their Check No. 8741.
4/12	Deposited payment received from Florida Sports Camp.
4/12	Transferred $20,000 from short-term investments to checking.
4/13	Paid Tige Boats bill by writing Check No. 1043 for $133,000.
4/16	Accepted a new job (50008) to paint a boat owned by Fantasy Sports.
4/16	Ryder Zacovic worked six hours on each day: April 17 thru April 20, which were nonbillable hours. He worked eight hours painting and repairing on job 50008 on April 16.
4/17	Created invoice 10011 to High Flying Fun (a new customer) to record sale of one Tige 24v and one Malibu WakeSetter XTI terms Net 15.
4/18	Created sales receipt 6009 to Orlando Water Sports to record the sale of one Malibu Sunsetter LXi in exchange for their Check No. 10005.
4/18	Deposited payment received from Orlando Water Sports.
4/20	Created invoice 10012 to Fantasy Sports for service under job 50008.
4/23	Created purchase order 4010 to Malibu Boats to purchase one Malibu Sportster for Freebirds, one Malibu Sunscape for Buena Vista Water Sports, one Malibu WakeSetter, and one Malibu Vride for showroom floor inventory.
4/24	Received items ordered and bill on purchase order 4009 from MB Sports.
4/24	Received items ordered and bill on purchase order 4008 from Tige Boats.
4/25	Created invoice 10013 to Half Moon Sports (a new customer) to record sale of one MB 220v terms Net 15.
4/26	Purchased another computer, printer, and other electronic equipment from Staples for $12,000, again completely financed with a note payable with no interest and no payment due until 11/1/08.
4/27	Paid payroll tax liabilities accrued as of 3/31/07 of $2,934.66 using Check No. 1044 to the Florida Dept. of Revenue and Check No. 1045 to the United States Treasury.
4/27	Paid sales tax liability as of 3/31/07 of $24,232.66 to the Florida Dept. of Revenue using Check No. 1046.
4/27	Wrote Check No. 1047 to Central Florida Gas & Electric for $1,250 for utilities expense.
4/27	Wrote Check No. 1048 to Verizon for $1,800 for telephone expense.
4/27	Wrote Check No. 1049 to Brian Szulczewski for $3,000 for marketing and advertising expense.

Date	Transaction
	Pat Ng worked four hours of unbillable time a day (Monday–Friday) for the weeks of 4/2, 4/16, and 4/23 in addition to the hours already recorded for the week of 4/9.
	Ryder Zacovic worked four hours of unbillable time a day (Monday–Friday) for the weeks of 4/2, 4/9, and 4/23 in addition to the hours already recorded for the week of 4/16.
4/30	Received $681.60 as payment on account from Fantasy Sports on their Check No. 1874.
4/30	Received $585.75 as payment on account from Seth Blackman on his Check No. 1547.
4/30	Received $13,000 as a deposit from Freebirds on their check 2514 towards the purchase of a Malibu Sportster LX ordered 4/23. Note: Do not apply this amount to their existing balance.
4/30	Received $16,250 as a deposit from Buena Vista Water Sports on their Check No. 8742 towards the purchase of a Malibu Sunscape LSV ordered 4/23.
4/30	Deposited $30,517.35 of checks received 4/30 into checking account.
4/30	Process payroll per the information provided below starting with Check No. 1050.

Table 8.1

Earnings Information

Employee/Item	Donna	Karen	Pat	Ryder
Earnings	4,166.67	4,166.67	1,458.00	1,380.00
Federal withholding	−463.00	−710.00	−199.75	−189.06
Social Security employee	−258.33	−258.33	−90.40	−85.56
Medicare employee	−60.42	−60.42	−21.14	−20.01
Social Security company	258.33	258.33	90.40	85.56
Medicare company	60.42	60.42	21.14	20.01
Federal unemployment	0	0	11.66	11.04
State unemployment	0	0	39.37	37.26
Check amount	3,384.92	3,137.92	1,146.71	1,085.37

Print the following as of 4/30/07:

a. Customer Balance Summary

b. Vendor Balance Summary

c. Account Listing (account, type, and balance total only)

d. Item Listing (List only item, description, type, cost, quantity on hand, and price.)

e. Standard Balance Sheet (collapsed version)

f. Standard Income Statement by month for January through April (collapsed version)

g. Transaction List by Date for the month of April

2 *Adding More Information: Central Coast Cellular*

In Chapter 7, you added some business transactions to your QuickBooks file for Central Coast Cellular (CCC), a cellular phone sales, rental, and consulting company. Make a copy of that file in Windows Explorer, name the file CCC8, and use that file to enter the following transactions.

- On January 20, 2003, the company received a shipment of phones from Nokia on purchase order 102. Items were received and a bill recorded due in 30 days.

- On January 21, 2003, the company invoiced the City of San Luis Obispo, using product invoice 10001 for 20 Nokia 8290 phones, 15 Nokia 8890 phones, 30 hours of consulting time, and 35 commissions earned on cell phone contracts (cell phone contracts are a new service item called Commissions, valued at $50 per contract, and recorded to a revenue account titled Commissions).

- On January 22, 2003, the company purchased equipment in the amount of $95,000 cash from Kyle Equipment, Inc. using Check No. 3008.

- On January 24, 2003, the company paid the Ericsson bill of $6,500 with Check No. 3009.

- On January 31, 2003, the company paid semi-monthly payroll starting with check 3010 for the period of January 16 to January 31, 2003. Megan Paulson worked 85 hours during the period. Payroll tax information is shown in Table 8.2.

Tax or Withholding/Employee	Rodriguez	Bruner	Paulson
Gross pay	$2,000.00	$1,500.00	$1,020.00
California employee training tax	2.00	1.50	1.02
Social Security company	124.00	93.00	63.24
Medicare company	29.00	21.75	14.79
Federal unemployment	6.40	4.80	3.26
CA—unemployment	24.00	18.00	12.24
Federal withholding	−300.00	−225.00	−153.00
Social Security employee	−124.00	−93.00	−63.24
Medicare employee	−29.00	−21.75	−14.79
CA—withholding	−100.00	−75.00	−51.00
CA—disability employee	−10.00	−7.50	−5.10
Check amount	1,437.00	1,077.75	732.87

Table 8.2

Payroll Information for Central Coast Cellular

Print the following:

a. Profit & Loss Standard report for the month of January 2003

b. Balance Sheet Standard as of January 31, 2003

c. Transaction List by Date for the period January 1 through January 31, 2003

3   *Using the South-Western Home Page for More Assignments or Cases*

Go to the home page for this textbook at **www.thomsonedu.com/ accounting/owen.** Click **Additional Problem Sets,** and then select the **Chapter 8** section, and complete the problem(s) that your instructor assigns.

Chapter 8 Case Problem 1:
ALOHA PROPERTY MANAGEMENT

In Chapter 7, you created a new QuickBooks file for Aloha Property Management. Make a copy of that file and use that copy to enter the following transactions.

Date	Transaction
2/1/08	Wrote Check No. 994 for $31,000 to GMAC Mortgage (a new vendor) as an installment payment on a 7% loan payable. (Interest expense, $22,604; loan payable, $8,396.)
2/1/08	Recorded invoice 7511 for rental of Moana Units #1, #3, #4, and Villa Units #1 and #4 for one week to Pixar. Applied $14,000 of their advance payment to this invoice, noted terms due on receipt, and recorded receipt of balance owed of $14,080. (When you apply credits, type 14000 in the column Amt. To Use and then click Done.)
2/1/08	Deposited Pixar check for $14,080 into checking account.
2/4/08	Received payment on account from Apple Computer of $25,000 on their Check No. 987426.
2/4/08	Received a bill from Reilly Custodial for cleaning expenses of $3,500.
2/5/08	Collected a $15,000 deposit from new customer American Airlines.
2/6/08	Deposited payment on account into the Bank of Hawaii checking account.
2/7/08	Received a bill from Blue Sky Pools for pool maintenance expenses of $1,800. (Set up a new account 6245 for this expense.)
2/8/08	Recorded invoice 7512 for rental of Moana Unit #4 and Villa Units #1 and #4 for one week to Pixar. Applied $10,000 of their advance payment to this invoice, noted terms due on receipt, and recorded receipt of balance owed of $11,840.
2/8/08	Deposited Pixar check for $11,840 into checking account.
2/8/08	Recorded sales receipt 5119 for rent of Moana Units #1, #2, and #3 for one week each. Collected American Express payment in full of $8,840 from new customer Accenture.
2/8/08	Deposited Accenture's American Express credit card payment of $8,840 into the checking account.
2/11/08	Received a bill from Pacific Electric for gas and electric expenses of $2,600 with terms of Net 15.
2/15/08	Recorded invoice 7513 for rental of Moana Unit #3 and Villa Unit #4 for one week to Exxon. Applied their advance payment to this invoice, noted terms due on receipt, and recorded receipt of balance owed of $5,275 from Exxon's Check No. 943098.
2/15/08	Deposited Exxon's check for $5,275 into checking account.

Date	Transaction
2/18/08	Received a bill from Service Connection (a new vendor) for repairs of $5,200. Terms are Net 15.
2/20/08	Received a bill from Sunset media for advertising of $1.450. Terms are Net 30.
2/22/08	Recorded invoice 7514 for rental of all units for one week to Boeing terms Net 30. Invoice total $39,728.
2/25/08	Collected a $3,250 deposit from new customer UCLA.
2/26/08	Collected a $7,500 deposit from new customer UCB.
2/26/08	Deposited both checks into checking account.
2/27/08	Paid all bills due on or before 2/28/08 for a total of $9,700 using Check Nos. 995–997. Note that even though there are four bills which require payment, two are to the same vendor (Blue Sky Pools) and thus only three checks are required.
2/28/08	Paid sales tax due as of 1/31/08 of $2,128 with Check No. 998.
2/28/08	Paid payroll tax liabilities due as of 1/31/08. Federal taxes are paid to the U.S. Treasury. The federal unemployment rate is 0.8%. State taxes are all paid to the State of Hawaii Department of Taxation using ID 874525. The E&T assessment rate is 0.01%. Use Check Nos. 998 through 1001.
2/29/08	Process payroll per the information provided below starting with Check No. 1002.

Pay/Tax/Withholding	Aki	Castillo
Hours	n/a	160
Rate	75,000	20.00
Gross pay	$6,250.00	$3,200.00
Federal withholding	–856.25	–438.40
Social Security employee	–387.50	–198.40
Medicare employee	–90.63	–46.40
HI withholding	–442.33	–210.53
HI disability	–1.25	–0.64
HI E&T	0.63	0.32
Social Security employer	387.50	198.40
Medicare company	90.63	46.40
Federal unemployment	50.00	25.60
HI unemployment	187.50	96.00
Check amount	4,472.04	2,305.63

Table 8.3

Earnings Information

Requirements

Record business transactions in chronological order (remember dates are in the month of February 2008). After recording the transactions, create and print the following for February 2008:

    a.   Standard Balance Sheet

    b.   Standard Income Statement

    c.   Statement of Cash Flows

    d.   Transaction List by Date

Chapter 8 Case Problem 2:
OCEAN VIEW FLOWERS

In Chapter 7, you created a new QuickBooks file for Ocean View Flowers, a wholesale flower distributor. Make a copy of that file and use that copy to enter the following transactions.

- On February 1, 2008, the company repaid a portion of the long-term debt it borrowed from Santa Barbara Bank & Trust with Union Bank Check No. 119 in the amount of $1,000. (All of this payment was principal, and none was interest.)

- On February 3, 2008, the company prepaid a one-year liability insurance policy to State Farm Insurance with Union Bank Check No. 120 in the amount of $2,500. (The transaction was properly recorded to Prepaid Insurance, another current asset account.)

- On February 5, 2008, the company created purchase order 2 to Vordale Flowers for the following items to be purchased on terms Net 30. All anthuriums are recorded as sales in a subaccount of Sales called Anthuriums, which you will have to create.

Anthuriums	Quantity Ordered	Cost	Sales Price
Bright Red	700	$20.00	$35.00
Peach	800	$22.00	$40.00
White	600	$27.00	$50.00

- On February 9, 2008, the company cashed in $5,000 of their $25,000 short-term investment early and received $5,200, which was deposited into the Union Bank account. The $200 difference represents interest revenue. (Be sure to change the company's interest income account title to interest revenue before entering this transaction.)

- On February 12, 2008, the company received the following bills. (Accept any terms changes and add any new vendors necessary.)

Vendor	Amount	Terms	Expense
GTE	$250	Net 15	Telephone
Edison	$300	Net 15	Utilities
FlowerMart	$60	Net 30	Subscriptions

- On February 15, 2008, the company paid payroll. All employees worked the entire period. Kelly Gusland worked 62 hours. Margie Coe worked 72 hours. Checks were written using the Union Bank account starting with Check No. 121. (Do not print these checks.) Payroll taxes and withholding for employees is shown in Table 8.4.

- On February 18, 2008, the company received items and entered the bill from purchase order 2 to Vordale Flowers on terms Net 30.

Tax or Withholding/Employee	Thomas	Gusland	Coe	McAninch	Comstock
California employee training tax	$ 1.17	$ 0.93	$ 0.86	$ 2.00	$ 2.08
Social Security company	180.83	57.66	53.57	155.00	129.17
Medicare company	42.30	13.48	12.53	36.25	30.20
Federal unemployment	9.33	7.44	6.91	16.00	16.67
CA—unemployment	0.58	0.46	0.43	1.00	1.05
Federal withholding	−667.00	−123.00	−113.00	−402.00	−286.00
Social Security employee	−180.83	−57.66	−53.57	−155.00	−129.17
Medicare employee	−42.30	−13.48	−12.53	−36.25	−30.20
CA—withholding	−192.30	−20.93	−8.60	−153.55	−61.86
CA—disability employee	−14.58	−4.65	−4.32	−12.50	−10.42
Check amount	1,819.66	710.28	671.98	1,740.70	1,565.68

Table 8.4

Payroll Taxes and Withholding for Employees from February 1, 2008, through February 15, 2008

- On February 22, 2008, the company created invoices to customers as follows: (If terms change, accept them as permanent.)

Customer	Invoice #	Item Sold	Total Quantity	Terms	Invoice
Latin Ladies	10001	Calistoga Sun Daylilies	400	Net 15	$ 9,000
		Caribbean Pink Sands	100		
California Beauties	10002	Anthuriums–White	500	2/10 Net 30	$25,000
FTD	10003	Anthuriums–Bright Red	300	Net 30	$10,500

- On February 24, 2008, the company paid the GTE and Edison bills using Union Bank Checks Nos. 126 and 127.

- On February 25, 2008, the company received $9,000 as payment on account from Latin Ladies. The amount was held for deposit at a later time.

- On February 26, 2008, the company purchased a warehouse and land for $300,000 ($50,000 of the purchase price is attributable to the land). A cash payment using Check No. 128 for $30,000 was made to Hawaiian Farms. The remaining balance of $270,000 was satisfied by signing a long-term note payable to the Bank of California. (Be sure to create a land and building fixed asset account along with a related subaccount of cost and accumulated depreciation for the building. Also make sure the land account appears in the chart of accounts before all other fixed assets and that cost precedes accumulated depreciation under the building account.)

- On February 26, 2008, the company paid payroll for the period ended February 29, 2008. All employees worked the entire period. Kelly Gusland worked 50 hours. Margie Coe worked 45 hours. Checks were written using the Union Bank account starting with Check No. 129. (Do not print these checks.) Payroll taxes and withholding for employees is shown in Table 8.5.

Table 8.5	Tax or Withholding/Employee	Thomas	Gusland	Coe	McAninch	Comstock
	California employee training tax	$ 0.00	$ 0.75	$ 0.54	$ 0.00	$ 0.75
Payroll Taxes and	Social Security company	180.83	46.50	33.48	155.00	129.17
Withholding for Employees	Medicare company	42.29	10.88	7.83	36.25	30.21
from February 16, 2008,	Federal unemployment	0.00	6.00	4.32	0.00	6.00
through February 29, 2008	CA—unemployment	0.00	0.38	0.27	0.00	0.37
	Federal withholding	−667.00	−96.00	−64.00	−402.00	−286.00
	Social Security employee	−180.83	−46.50	−33.48	−155.00	−129.17
	Medicare employee	−42.29	−10.88	−7.83	−36.25	−30.21
	CA—withholding	−192.30	−13.32	0.00	−153.55	−61.86
	CA—disability employee	−14.58	−3.75	−2.70	−12.50	−10.42
	Check amount	1,819.67	579.55	431.99	1,740.70	1,565.67

Requirements

Record business transactions in chronological order (remember dates are in the month of February 2008). After recording the transactions, create and print the following for February 2008:

    a.   Standard Balance Sheet

    b.   Standard Income Statement

    c.   Statement of Cash Flows

    d.   Transaction List by Date

Adjusting Entries

Case: **Wild Water Sports, Inc.**

Karen has recorded the majority of Wild Water's financing, investing, and operating activities for January through April 2007. To help her prepare financial statements for the first quarter, she asks you to prepare any necessary adjusting entries for the period January 1 through March 31, 2007.

"Some people have trouble with adjusting entries," you remark, "but I'm not one of them. I was always helping my classmates understand these types of journal entries. Why don't I give them a try?"

"Okay with me," Karen responds. "Traditional journal entries are available in QuickBooks, but you don't have to use them." Karen explains that in QuickBooks the most common adjusting entries—accruing expenses, accruing revenue, recording asset expirations, and recording liability reductions—can be made by using the Make Journal Entry menu item in the Company menu or by using account registers. You decide to use the traditional journal entry process.

Accruing Expenses

Wild Water Sports had a long-term liability of $383,800 when Karen and Donna made their initial investment. That loan was paid off along with accrued interest on March 6, 2007. The remaining balance in the loan payable account represents three different loans. The first, a $250,000, five-year, 5% loan from the Bank of Florida, was made on January 4, 2007. The second was a $50,000, three-year, 6% loan from Citibank was made on February 5, 2007. The third was just recently acquired when the company purchased a computer from Staples for $5,000. Since then the company has made two payments on the Bank of Florida loan.

According to the loan amortization schedule (see Figure 8.1), a payment of $4,717.81 is due to be made at the beginning of April on the $250,000 loan of which $1,010.97 represents interest owed. As of March 31, 2007, that interest should be included in interest expense for March. Payments are due annually on the $50,000 loan. Thus as of March 31, 2007, the company owes $750 of interest ($50,000 \times 6\% \times 3/12$). The Staples loan bears no interest.

"QuickBooks automatically assigns journal entry numbers for reference," Karen points out. "Thus the journal numbers we'll use for March 31 adjustments may follow journal entries used for April business events. What's important is the date specified in the journal."

"Okay," you respond. "I'll take the information provided above and create the adjustment necessary for interest expense as of March 31st."

To accrue interest expense:

1 Restore the Wild Water Sports Ch 9.qbb file from your Data Files CD or downloaded from the Internet.

2 Start the QuickBooks program.

3 Open the newly restored Wild Water Sports Ch 9.qbw file.

4 Click **Company,** and then click **Make General Journal Entries.**

5 An Assigning Numbers to Journal Entries window should appear explaining that QuickBooks automatically assigns numbers to journal entries. Accept this process by clicking in the **Do not display this message in the future** checkbox and then clicking **OK.**

6 Type **3/31/07** as the journal entry date.

7 Type **8** as the Entry No.

8 Select **6200 – Interest Expense** as the first account.

9 Type **1010.97** as the amount in the Debit column. This will increase interest expense (an expense account).

10 Type **Accrued Interest Payable** as the second account and then press **[Tab].**

11 Click **Set Up** in the Account Not Found window and create a new account called Accrued Interest Payable, a current liability account, and type **2025** as the account number.

12 Type **1010.97** as the amount in the Credit column. This will increase Accrued Interest Payable. The resulting journal entry should look like Figure 9.1.

13 Click **Save & New.**

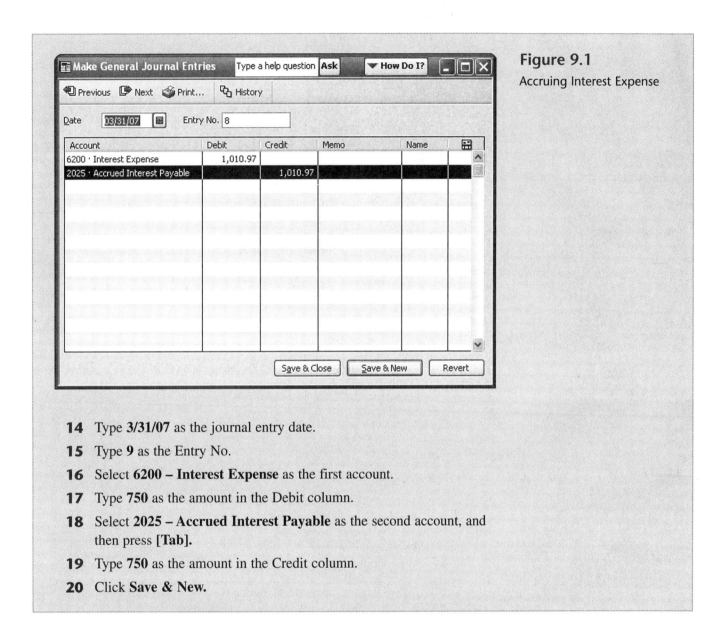

Figure 9.1

Accruing Interest Expense

14 Type **3/31/07** as the journal entry date.

15 Type **9** as the Entry No.

16 Select **6200 – Interest Expense** as the first account.

17 Type **750** as the amount in the Debit column.

18 Select **2025 – Accrued Interest Payable** as the second account, and then press **[Tab]**.

19 Type **750** as the amount in the Credit column.

20 Click **Save & New.**

Karen explains that this process properly reflects interest expenses in the correct accounting period (first quarter of 2007) and establishes the liability as of March 31, 2007. However, in April, when the company pays the next installment on the $250,000 loan, they will have to remember that the interest has already been accrued.

"Either that, or we can reverse the adjustment as of April 1 and then just record the next payment as we've done in the past with a portion of the payment going to interest expense and a portion going to reduce the loan principle," you suggest.

"I like that idea," Karen answers. "Do we do the same for the $50,000 loan?"

"No," you respond. "The $50,000 loan is on an annual payment plan and if we reversed the journal entry as of April 1, we'd have to reestablish it again as of March 31 and accrue more interest for the second quarter. I suggest we reverse the first accrual only."

To reverse an accrual entry:

1 Type **4/1/07** as the journal entry date.

2 Type **10** as the Entry No.

3 Select **2025 – Accrued Interest Payable** as the first account.

4 Type **1010.97** as the amount in the Debit column.

5 Select **6200 – Interest Expense** as the second account.

6 Type **1010.97** as the amount in the Credit column. Your journal entry should look like Figure 9.2.

Figure 9.2

Reversing Entry

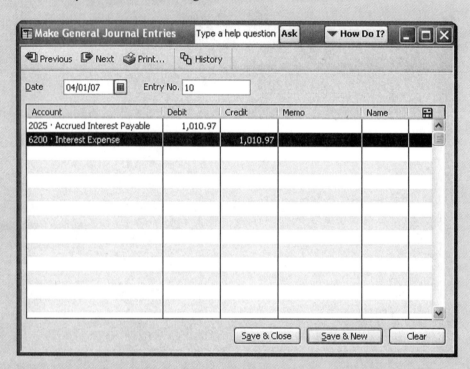

7 Click **Save & Close**.

"After this entry was recorded on April 1, the accrued interest payable balance was 0 and interest expense for April has a credit balance of $1,010.97. Now," you explain, "when we record the next payment on this loan, we can use the amortization schedule to record the interest paid and reduction of principle. The payment will reduce cash and increase interest expense by $1,010.97 creating a balance of 0 in interest expense for April. If we need to provide GAAP-based financial statements in April, we'll need to accrue interest owed at April 30."

Accruing Revenue

Karen tells you that she can also use journal entries to record revenue earned on investments. She points out that during the quarter the company had some short-investments with ETrade that earned money market interest if they were not invested in stock. The interest is paid quarterly. Since no interest was paid during the quarter, no interest revenue has been recorded. After checking with their investment advisor, Karen learns that $1,890.41 of interest revenue was earned but unpaid as of March 31, 2007.

To accrue interest income:

1 Click **Company,** and then click **Make General Journal Entries.**

2 Type **3/31/07** as the journal entry date.

3 Type **11** as the Entry No.

4 Select **1050 – Short-Term Investments** as the first account.

5 Type **1890.41** as the amount in the Debit column.

6 Select **7010 – Interest Income** as the second account.

7 Type **1890.41** as the amount in the Credit column.

8 Click **Save & New.**

"I thought we were going to record more interest revenue?" you ask. "Why did we choose to record this as interest income?"

"QuickBooks doesn't follow the accounting convention of recording interest revenue," you point out. "QuickBooks was originally created as a tool for businesses preparing tax returns, and the Internal Revenue Service (IRS) uses the income reference for interest instead of revenue. Rather than changing the account title, we'll just use interest income."

"Another issue we have to address is whether any products were delivered to customers but not recorded as sales at the end of the month," Karen comments. "For example, our records show that we delivered a boat to Spirit Adventures on March 31 but we didn't invoice them until April 2. Thus, as of March 31, 2007, we need to accrue that additional revenue, sales tax, and cost of goods sold."

"Don't you also have to reduce inventory since our records show that boat in inventory March 31?" you ask.

"Exactly," Karen answers, "plus, since this transaction is recorded as an invoice in April, we'll need to reverse this accrual entry on April 1."

To adjust for sales occurring in March but not invoiced until April:

1 Type **3/31/07** as the journal entry date.

2 Type **12** as the Entry No.

3 Select **1200 – Accounts Receivable** as the first account.

4 Type **69225** as the amount in the Debit column.

5 Select **Spirit Adventures** as the Name in this row.

6 Select **4010 – Merchandise** as the second account.

7 Type **65000** as the amount in the Credit column.

8 Select **Spirit Adventures** as the Name in this row.

9 Select **2210 – Accrued Sales Tax Payable** as the third account (a new account).

10 Type **4225** as the amount in the Credit column.

11 Select **Spirit Adventures** as the Name in this row.

12 Select **5000 – Cost of Goods Sold** as the fourth account.

13 Type **52000** as the amount in the Debit column.

14 Select **Spirit Adventures** as the Name in this row

15 Select **1120 – Inventory Asset** as the fifth account.

16 Type **52000** as the amount in the Credit column.

17 Select **Spirit Adventures** as the Name in this row

18 Mark this item as unbillable by clicking the bill icon so a red X appears. Your journal entry should look like Figure 9.3.

Red X

Figure 9.3
Accruing Sales Revenue

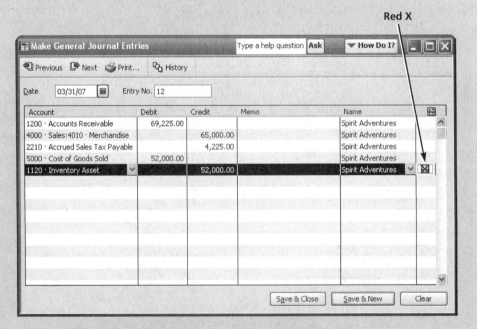

19 Click **Save & New.**

"Where did you get the Cost of Good Sold and Inventory Asset information?" you ask.

"I got it from our list of items which provides both the sales price, income account, and cost," Karen answers. "When we accrue the sales revenue, we must also accrue the related cost of good sold."

"How about the sales tax payable?" you ask. "Why didn't we just use our normal sales tax payable account?"

"I didn't use the normal sales tax payable account because that account is tied to the payment of sales tax and this accrual is for our records only. When the invoice is recorded in April, the normal sales tax account will be increased."

Karen explains that this is another case where it is best to reverse this accrual the first of the next month so that when the actual invoice is recorded in April, it will be offset by the previous accrual.

To reverse the sales accrual:

1 Type **4/1/07** as the journal entry date.

2 Type **13** as the Entry No.

3 Select **1200 – Accounts Receivable** as the first account.

4 Type **69225** as the amount in the Credit column.

5 Select **Spirit Adventures** as the Name in this row.

6 Select **4010 – Merchandise** as the second account.

7 Type **65000** as the amount in the Debit column.

8 Select **Spirit Adventures** as the Name in this row.

9 Select **2210 – Accrued Sales Tax Payable** as the third account (a new account).

10 Type **4225** as the amount in the Debit column.

11 Select **Spirit Adventures** as the Name in this row.

12 Select **5000 – Cost of Goods Sold** as the fourth account.

13 Type **52000** as the amount in the Credit column.

14 Select **Spirit Adventures** as the Name in this row

15 Select **1120 – Inventory Asset** as the fifth account.

16 Type **52000** as the amount in the Debit column.

17 Select **Spirit Adventures** as the Name in this row

18 Mark this item as unbillable by clicking the bill icon so a red X appears. Your journal entry should look like Figure 9.4.

19 Click **Save & Close.**

Figure 9.4

Reversing the Sales
Accrual April 1

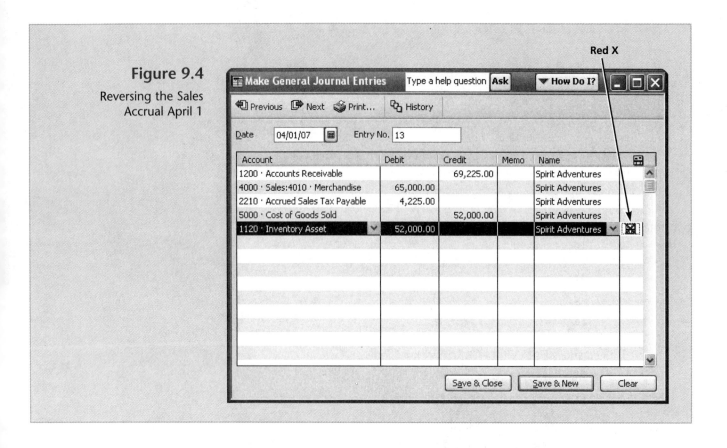

"This accrual accounting process is a lot of work!" you comment.

"Yes," Karen agrees. "But at least we get a picture of our performance and financial position based on when events occur, not just when we get around to recording them."

Recording Expenses Incurred but Previously Deferred

The adjustments that you and Karen recorded above accounted for previously unrecorded transactions. Now Karen wants to show you how to record adjustments that affect previously recorded business activity, such as the prepayment of expenses and the purchase of fixed assets.

On February 7, 2007, Wild Water Sports paid $24,000 to Coe Marketing for a one-year advertising campaign. Since this payment represented an expenditure that benefited more than the one accounting period, it was correctly recorded to prepaid advertising, an asset account.

On March 31, 2007, two months of the time period covered by the ad campaign had expired. Thus, two-twelfths of the cost ($4,000) should be recorded as advertising expense, and the prepaid advertising account reduced accordingly. Each month thereafter, one-twelfth of the cost ($2,000) should be recorded as advertising expense, and the prepaid advertising account reduced accordingly.

To adjust prepaid advertising:

1 Click **Company,** and then click **Make General Journal Entries.**

2 Type **3/31/07** as the journal entry date.

3 Type **14** as the Entry No.

4 Select **6235 – Marketing and Advertising** as the first account.

5 Type **4000** as the amount in the Debit column.

6 Select **1060 – Prepaid Advertising** as the second account.

7 Type **4000** as the amount in the Credit column.

8 Click **Save & New.**

On January 31, 2007, Wild Water Sports paid $22,000 to Manchester Insurance for a one-year liability insurance policy covering it for the calendar year 2007. Once again, since this payment represented an expenditure that benefited more than one accounting period, it was correctly recorded to prepaid insurance, an asset account.

On March 31, 2007, three months of the time period covered by the insurance policy had expired. Thus, three-twelfths of the cost ($5,500) should be recorded as insurance expense, and the prepaid insurance account reduced accordingly. Each month thereafter, one-twelfth of the cost ($1,833.33) should be recorded as insurance expense, and the prepaid insurance account reduced accordingly.

To adjust prepaid insurance:

1 Type **3/31/07** as the journal entry date.

2 Type **15** as the Entry No.

3 Select **6187 – Liability Insurance** as the first account.

4 Type **5500** as the amount in the Debit column.

5 Select **1150 – Prepaid Insurance** as the second account.

6 Type **5500** as the amount in the Credit column.

7 Click **Save & New.**

A similar adjustment called depreciation is needed to allocate the cost of previously recorded depreciable fixed assets. Wild Water Sports has three separate classifications of fixed assets: equipment, furniture & fixtures, and truck. Depreciation on fixed assets is usually accumulated in a separate contra-asset account on the balance sheet for control purposes.

While QuickBooks does have a separate module available to track fixed assets and calculate depreciation, Karen has chosen not to purchase this feature. Instead, she maintains a separate spreadsheet to track when fixed assets were purchased, how much depreciation should be recorded, and when fixed assets are sold. Her analysis indicates that $10,333 of depreciation should be recorded as of March 31, 2007, to reflect depreciation for the first quarter of 2007. Of that balance, $5,584 is related to equipment, $2,500 is related to furniture & fixtures, and $2,250 is related to truck.

To record depreciation expense:

1 Type **3/31/07** as the journal entry date.

2 Type **16** as the Entry No.

3 Select **6150 – Depreciation Expense** as the first account.

4 Type **10333** as the amount in the Debit column.

5 Select **1390 – Accumulated Depreciation** as the second account.

6 Type **5584** as the amount in the Credit column.

7 Select **1490 – Accumulated Depreciation** as the third account.

8 Type **2499** as the amount in the Credit column.

9 Select **1590 – Accumulated Depreciation** as the fourth account.

10 Type **2250** as the amount in the Credit column and then press **[Tab]**. Your journal entry should look like Figure 9.5.

Figure 9.5

Depreciation Adjustment

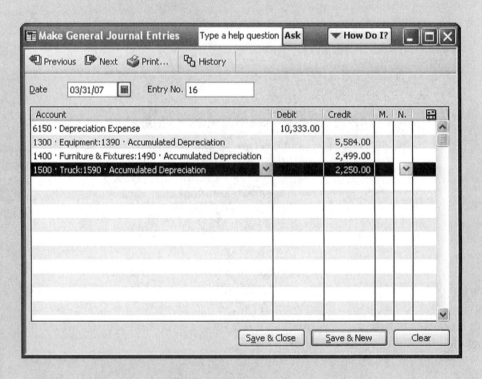

11 Click **Save & Close.**

12 If the Tracking Fixed Assets on Journal Entries window appears, check the box **Do not display this message in the future** and then click **OK.**

You find the above procedures very straightforward but are curious about the financial statement impact of these adjusting entries so far. You wonder if QuickBooks provides a way to view financial statements so you can see what effect these adjustments have had. Karen tells you that QuickBooks does have such a feature—you can view financial statements at any time without having to post entries. She suggests that you look at the balance sheet as of March 31, 2007, to see the effect of this adjustment on the balance sheet.

To view the fixed assets portion of the balance sheet as of March 31, 2007:

1 Click **Reports, Company & Financial** and then click **Balance Sheet Standard.**

2 Enter the dates From **01/01/07** to **03/31/07** in the Modify Report window, and then click **OK.**

3 Scroll down the balance sheet to the accounts receivable, other current assets, and fixed assets section as shown in Figure 9.6.

4 Close all windows.

Karen notes that the ending balance in prepaid advertising as of March 31, 2007, makes sense since they have 10 months left of the ad campaign (10 months × $2,000 per month = $20,000). She also notes that the ending balance in prepaid insurance as of March 31, 2007 also makes sense since they have 9 months left of insurance coverage (9 months × $1,833.33 per month = $16,500). She also notes the new balances in the accumulated depreciation accounts.

Having tackled prepaid asset and depreciable asset adjustments, you and Karen are now ready to move on to the last adjustment category—adjusting unearned revenue.

Figure 9.6

Balance Sheet After
Adjusting Entries So Far

Wild Water Sports Ch 9
Balance Sheet
As of March 31, 2007

	Mar 31, 07
Accounts Receivable	
1200 · Accounts Receivable	389,932.73
Total Accounts Receivable	389,932.73
Other Current Assets	
1060 · Prepaid Advertising	20,000.00
1120 · Inventory Asset	243,600.00
1130 · Inventory Parts	2,112.00
1150 · Prepaid Insurance	16,500.00
1499 · Undeposited Funds	10,000.00
Total Other Current Assets	292,212.00
Total Current Assets	759,427.56
Fixed Assets	
1300 · Equipment	
1310 · Cost	180,000.00
1390 · Accumulated Depreciation	−13,084.00
Total 1300 · Equipment	166,916.00
1400 · Furniture & Fixtures	
1410 · Cost	70,000.00
1490 · Accumulated Depreciation	−2,499.00
Total 1400 · Furniture & Fixtures	67,501.00
1500 · Truck	
1510 · Cost	45,000.00
1590 · Accumulated Depreciation	−2,250.00
Total 1500 · Truck	42,750.00
Total Fixed Assets	277,167.00

Adjusting for Unearned Revenues

On March 31, 2007, Wild Water Sports received $10,000 from its customer Performance Rentals as a deposit on a boat in stock. On this date, Performance Rentals had an existing balance outstanding, but you and Karen chose to account for this as a separate transaction and not apply this payment to the amount due. As described in Chapter 8, Karen recorded this transaction by increasing the Undeposited Funds account (since it wasn't deposited into the company's bank account) and decreasing Performance Rental's Accounts Receivable. Karen has decided to reclassify it as unearned revenue, a liability, on March 31, 2007. Here's why. Cash has been received, but the boat has not been delivered. Thus, on March 31, you need to reclassify the

$10,000 to an unearned revenue account (a liability). When the company actually sells the boat to Performance Rentals in a future period, Wild Water will create an invoice, decrease the liability, and increase sales revenue.

The effect of this adjusting journal entry is to increase accounts receivable and increase unearned revenue reflecting the fact that Wild Water still has a balance owed by Performance Rentals of $1,293.98 and owes Performance Rentals $10,000 if it doesn't deliver the boat Performance placed the deposit on.

To reclassify the $10,000 as unearned revenue at 3/31/07:

1 Click **Company,** and then click **Make General Journal Entries.**

2 Type **3/31/07** as the journal entry date.

3 Type **17** as the Entry No.

4 Select **1200 – Accounts Receivable** as the first account.

5 Type **10000** as the amount in the Debit column.

6 Select **Performance Rentals** as the Name of the customer to which this journal entry applies.

7 Type **2300** as the second account, and then press **[Tab].**

8 Click **Set Up** to create a new account.

9 Select **Other Current Liability** as the Type.

10 Type **Unearned Revenue** as the Name.

11 Click **OK** to create this new account.

12 Type **10000** as the amount in the Credit column.

13 Select **Performance Rentals** as the Name of the customer to which this journal entry applies. Your screen should look like Figure 9.7.

14 Click **Save & Close.**

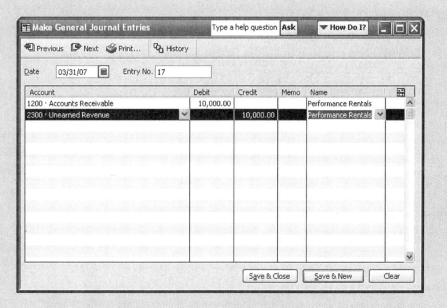

Figure 9.7

Adjusting for Unearned Revenue

"I always like to print out a copy of my adjustments to make sure everything was recorded correct," Karen comments. "QuickBooks has a journal feature that we can use to print just those transactions occurring on March 31 and April 1 so we can see the effects of our adjustments."

To print the journal for March 31 and April 1:

1 Click **Reports** from the menu bar, click **Accountant & Taxes,** and then click **Journal.**

2 Type **3/31/07** as the From date.

3 Type **4/1/07** as the To date.

4 Click **Refresh.** Your screen should look like Figure 9.8.

5 Close the Journal window.

Figure 9.8   Journal Listing

Wild Water Sports Ch 9
Journal
March 31 through April 1, 2007

Trans #	Type	Date	Num	Name	Memo	Account	Debit	Credit
159	Payment	3/31/2007		Performance Rentals		1499 · Undeposited Funds	10,000.00	
				Performance Rentals		1200 · Accounts Receivable		10,000.00
							10,000.00	10,000.00
160	General Journal	3/31/2007	8			6200 · Interest Expense	1,010.97	
						2025 · Accrued Interest Payable		1,010.97
							1,010.97	1,010.97
161	General Journal	3/31/2007	9			6200 · Interest Expense	750.00	
						2025 · Accrued Interest Payable		750.00
							750.00	750.00
162	General Journal	4/1/2007	10			2025 · Accrued Interest Payable	1,010.97	
						6200 · Interest Expense		1,010.97
							1,010.97	1,010.97
163	General Journal	3/31/2007	11			1050 · Short-Term Investments	1,890.41	
						7010 · Interest Income		1,890.41
							1,890.41	1,890.41
164	General Journal	3/31/2007	12	Spirit Adventures		1200 · Accounts Receivable	69,225.00	
				Spirit Adventures		4010 · Merchandise		65,000.00
				Spirit Adventures		2210 · Accrued Sales Tax Payable		4,225.00
				Spirit Adventures		5000 · Cost of Goods Sold	52,000.00	
				Spirit Adventures		1120 · Inventory Asset		52,000.00
							121,225.00	121,225.00
165	General Journal	4/1/2007	13	Spirit Adventures		1200 · Accounts Receivable		69,225.00
				Spirit Adventures		4010 · Merchandise	65,000.00	
				Spirit Adventures		2210 · Accrued Sales Tax Payable	4,225.00	
				Spirit Adventures		5000 · Cost of Goods Sold		52,000.00
				Spirit Adventures		1120 · Inventory Asset	52,000.00	
							121,225.00	121,225.00
166	General Journal	3/31/2007	14			6235 · Marketing & Advertising	4,000.00	
						1060 · Prepaid Advertising		4,000.00
							4,000.00	4,000.00
167	General Journal	3/31/2007	15			6187 · Liability Insurance	5,500.00	
						1150 · Prepaid Insurance		5,500.00
							5,500.00	5,500.00
168	General Journal	3/31/2007	16			6150 · Depreciation Expense	10,333.00	
						1390 · Accumulated Depreciation		5,584.00
						1490 · Accumulated Depreciation		2,499.00
						1590 · Accumulated Depreciation		2,250.00
							10,333.00	10,333.00
169	General Journal	3/31/2007	17	Performance Rentals		1200 · Accounts Receivable	10,000.00	
				Performance Rentals		2300 · Unearned Revenue		10,000.00
							10,000.00	10,000.00
TOTAL							**286,945.35**	**286,945.35**

Karen explains that most of these journals represent the adjustments you just made and seem to be in order. She points out that each transaction has a transaction number, a type, a date, journal number (if applicable), names, accounts, debits, and credits.

Preparing a Bank Reconciliation and Recording Related Adjustments

Every month, the Bank of Florida sends Wild Water Sports a bank account statement that lists all deposits received by the bank and all checks and payments that have cleared the bank as of the date of the statement. You and Karen examine the bank statements for the months of January, February, and March, which indicate an ending balance of $37,172.23 as of March 31, 2007. Normally you would reconcile your statement each month, but you've been a little busy these last couple of months. You now turn your attention toward reconciling that balance with the balance reported by QuickBooks. You note that QuickBooks indicates an ending checking account balance of $37,392.42 at that same date. You believe that most of the difference between these two amounts is probably attributable to "outstanding checks" that Wild Water Sports has written but that the bank hasn't yet paid, deposits it has recorded but have not been received by the bank, bank service charges, and interest income.

A review of all three statements shows that all checks recorded by Wild Water Sports have been paid by the bank except payroll checks written on March 30, 2007, totaling $6,994.74. All deposits recorded by the company have been received by the bank except one dated 3/29/07 for $7,264.93. Bank charges per the bank statement total $75, which has not yet been recorded by the company. Interest income credited to the company's bank account in the amount of $125 also has not yet been recorded by the company.

To reconcile the bank statement as of 3/31/07:

1 Click **Reconcile** in the Banking section of the home page.

2 Select **1010 – Bank of Florida** as the account to be reconciled.

3 Type **3/31/07** as the Statement Date.

4 Type **37172.23** as the Ending Balance.

5 Type **75** as the Service Charge, **3/31/07** as the Date, and **6130** as the Account.

6 Type **125** as the Interest Earned, **3/31/07** as the Date, and **7010** as the Account. Your screen should look like Figure 9.9.

7 Click **Continue.**

8 When the Reconcile – Bank of Florida window appears click in the checkbox at the top of the page that says **Show only transactions on or before the statement ending date.**

Figure 9.9

Beginning a Bank
Reconciliation

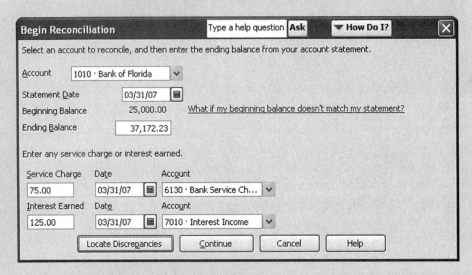

9 Place a check mark next to all of the checks, payments, and service charges except checks 1038, 1039, and 1040. (These are the payroll checks issued 3/30/07 which have not yet cleared the bank.)

10 Place a check mark next to all of the Deposits, Interest, and Other Credits except the deposit of $7,264.93 dated 3/29/07. Your screen should look like Figure 9.10.

Figure 9.10

Bank Reconciliation Process

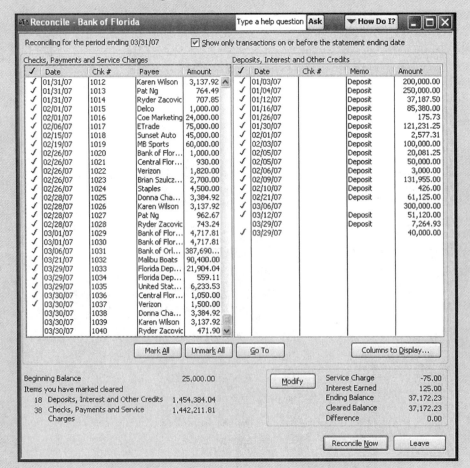

11 Note the difference of 0.00 in the lower right corner of the window.

12 Click **Reconcile Now.**

13 Click the **Summary** button. Your screen should look like Figure 9.11.

Figure 9.11

Select Reconciliation Report

14 Click the **Display** button. Your screen should look like Figure 9.12. Click **OK** in the Reconciliation Report window.

15 Close the Reconciliation Summary window.

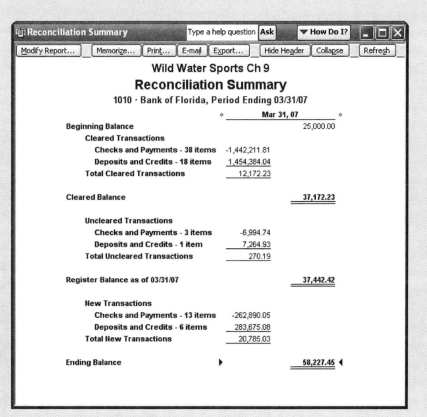

Figure 9.12

Summary Bank Reconciliation Report

The only adjustments created in this bank reconciliation were the recognition of bank service fees and interest income. QuickBooks automatically records these in the checking account. Once reconciled, QuickBooks also inserts a check mark next to each transaction that has cleared the bank in the check register.

End Note

You've now helped Karen record various adjustments including accrued expenses, accrued revenues, expiration of prepaid and depreciable assets, creation of unearned revenue, and one which reflected the completion of bank reconciliation. You're almost ready to create Wild Water Sports's financial statements.

Chapter 9 Questions

1 Explain the journal entry method of recording period end adjustments.

2 Give an example of accrued revenue other than the examples given in this chapter. Explain how this example of accrued revenue would be adjusted using journal entries.

3 Give an example of an accrued expense other than the example given in this chapter. Explain how this example of accrued expense would be adjusted using journal entries.

4 Give an example of asset expiration other than the example given in this chapter. Explain how this example would be adjusted using journal entries.

5 Give an example of unearned revenue, and explain the process for period-end adjustments involving unearned revenue.

6 Explain how to access general journal entries.

7 What menu item do you use to start bank reconciliations?

8 What account is typically used to record service charges?

9 When you've finished reconciling a bank account, what should be the difference between the ending balance and the cleared balance?

10 What information is included in the reconciliation summary report?

Chapter 9 Assignments

1 *Adding More Information to Wild Water Sports*

Restore the file Wild Water Sports Ch 9A.qbb found on the text CD or downloaded from the text website, and then add the following adjustments and perform bank reconciliation on the Bank of Florida account as of April 30, 2007.

Date	Adjustment
5/1	Invoice 10014 was recorded on this date for the sale of a Malibu Sportster LX to Alisa Hay for $52,000 plus tax. (Even though this isn't an adjusting entry, record it in QuickBooks to illustrate how the accrual and reversal works.)
4/30	Accrue interest expense of $995.52 on the $250,000 loan as per the amortization schedule in Figure 8.1.
5/1	Prepare reversing entry of interest accrual above.
4/30	Accrue interest expense of $250 on the $50,000 loan.
4/30	Accrue interest income of $100 on short-term investments.

Date	Adjustment
4/30	Records show that the company delivered a Malibu Sportster LX to Alisa Hay on April 30 but the company didn't invoice her until May 1. The boat was sold for $52,000 and cost $41,600. Sales tax in the amount of $3,380 was collected on 5/1 from the sale.
5/1	Reverse sales revenue accrual above.
4/30	Adjust prepaid advertising for April.
4/30	Adjust prepaid insurance for April.
4/30	Record depreciation expense of $3,870 for the month of April: $2,287 for Equipment, $833 for Furniture, and $750 for the Truck.
4/30	Reclassify the deposit received from Buena Vista Water Sports on 4/30/07 of $16,250 to unearned revenue.
4/30	The Bank of Florida bank statement as of 4/30 has an ending balance of $36,475.02. All checks cleared the bank account except checks 1050 to 1053. All deposits cleared the bank account except the $30,517.35 deposit made 4/30. The bank statement shows interest income of $35 and bank charges of $25.

a.   Print a collapsed standard income statement for the month of April 2007.

b.   Print an expanded standard balance sheet ended April 30, 2007.

c.   Print summary bank reconciliation as of April 30, 2007.

d.   Print journal entries recorded from April 30 to May 1, 2007.

e.   Print a collapsed standard income statement for the month of May 2007.

2   *Adding More Information to Central Coast Cellular*

In Chapter 8, you added some business transactions to your QuickBooks file for Central Coast Cellular, a cellular phone sales, phone rental, and consulting company. Make a copy of that file in Windows Explorer, name the file CCC9, and use that file to enter the following adjusting journal entries and perform bank reconciliation.

Date	Adjustment
1/31	Record depreciation expense of $1,000 for equipment and $500 for office furniture.
1/31	Accrue interest expense of $950.
1/31	Reclassify the credit balance of $10,000 in the City of San Luis Obispo account to unearned revenue.
1/31	The bank statement dated January 31, 2003 indicated a bank balance of $133,640.49, with all checks clearing except numbers 3010, 3011, and 3012. All deposits cleared. A bank service charge of $80 was reported.

a.   Print a collapsed standard income statement for the month of January 2003.

b.   Print a collapsed standard balance sheet ended January 31, 2003.

c.   Print summary bank reconciliation as of January 31, 2003.

3 *Using the South-Western Home Page for More Assignments or Cases*

Go to the home page for this textbook at **www.thomsonedu.com/ accounting/owen.** Click **Additional Problem Sets,** and then select the **Chapter 9** section, and complete the problem(s) that your instructor assigns.

Chapter 9 Case Problem 1:
ALOHA PROPERTY MANAGEMENT

In Chapter 8, you modified your QuickBooks file for Aloha Property Management. Make a copy of that file and use that copy to enter the following adjustments and bank reconciliation.

Date	Adjustment
2/29	Accrue interest expense of $22,555 on the $3,875,000 loan to a new account: Accrued Interest Payable with an account number of 2050.
3/1	Prepare reversing entry of interest accrual above.
2/29	Accrue interest income of $210 on short-term investments.
2/29	Adjust prepaid insurance for January and February 2008 to insurance expense.
2/29	Record depreciation expense of $34,612 for the months of January and February 2008: $13,334 for the Moana, $20,000 for the Villa, and $1,278 for the Furniture.
2/29	Reclassify the deposits received from American Airlines, UCLA, and UCB on 2/5/08, 2/25/08, and 2/26/08, respectively to unearned revenue (a new current liability account with a number 2300).
2/29	The Bank of Hawaii bank statement as of 2/29 has an ending balance of $115,292.39. All checks cleared the bank account except checks 998 through 1003. All deposits cleared the bank account except the $10,750 deposit made 2/26. The bank statement shows interest income of $175 and bank charges of $35.

    a.   Print a standard income statement for the month of February 2008.

    b.   Print a standard balance sheet ended February 29, 2008.

    c.   Print summary bank reconciliation as of February 29, 2008.

    d.   Print journal entries recorded February 29 through March 1, 2008.

Chapter 9 Case Problem 2:
OCEAN VIEW FLOWERS

In Chapter 8, you modified your QuickBooks file for Ocean View Flowers. Make a copy of that file, and use that copy to enter the following adjustments and bank reconciliation.

Date	Adjustment
1/31	The January bank statement reported an ending balance of $76,340.30, bank service charges of $45, and interest revenue of $100 as of January 31, 2008. Deposits for $100,000, $50,000, $6,600, and $22,200 were received by the bank. Checks 101–110 were paid by the bank. Don't forget to print summary bank reconciliation for this month.
2/29	Accrue loan interest expense of $3,190 on the $319,000 loan for two months interest to a new account: Accrued Interest Payable.
3/1	Prepare reversing entry of interest accrual above.
2/29	Accrue interest revenue of $800 on short-term investments.
2/29	Prepaid insurance of $100 expired for each month: January and February 2008.
2/29	Record depreciation expense of $3,100: $2,000 for the building, $600 for the computer equipment, and $500 for the office equipment.
2/29	Reclassify the deposit received from FTD on 1/28/08 to unearned revenue (a new current liability account).
2/29	A review of the shipping records indicates that a shipment that occurred on 2/28 was not invoiced until 3/3. Invoice 10004, recorded in the next accounting period, billed California Beauties $16,000 for 800 Calistoga Sun Daylilies, $7,200 for 300 Almond Puff Daylilies, and $20,000 for 500 Peach Anthuriums (cost: $22,600).
3/1	Prepare reversing entry for invoice 10004 above.
2/29	The February bank statement reported an ending balance of $65,579.64, bank service charges of $55, and interest revenue of $75 as of February 29, 2008. Deposits for $5,000 and $5,200 were received by the bank. Checks 111–127 were paid by the bank.

a. Print a standard income statement for the two months ended February 29, 2008.

b. Print a standard balance sheet ended February 29, 2008.

c. Print summary bank reconciliation as of January 31, 2008.

d. Print summary bank reconciliation as of February 29, 2008.

e. Print journal entries recorded from February 29 to March 1, 2008.

Budgeting

Learning Objectives

In this chapter, you will:

- Create budgets for revenues
- Create budgets for expenses
- Create a budget for assets, liabilities, and equities
- Create a budgeted income statement
- Create a budgeted balance sheet

Case: Wild Water Sports, Inc.

Today Donna asks you and Karen to prepare financial statements for the first quarter of the year. She reminds you that you have already recorded all of the transactions for January through April, so you're ready to prepare the statements as of the end of the first quarter, March 31.

"But just preparing the statements is half the job," Karen points out. "We have to be able to interpret these statements. How will we know if the company is doing well?"

Donna is quick to respond, "At the beginning of the year, I used a spreadsheet program to establish budgets for the year. I can compare the actual results shown in the statements you prepare with these budgets."

"Doesn't QuickBooks have a budgeting feature?" you ask.

"You're right!" exclaims Donna, "I didn't use that feature, but now that you mention it, I should have. Would the two of you mind entering my budget estimates into QuickBooks as well?"

"Not at all," you respond.

After Donna leaves, Karen explains to you that QuickBooks allows you to set up a budget for an account or for a customer within an account. To do this, you enter budget amounts for the income statement accounts or balance sheet accounts you wish to track.

"Are you able to track actual versus budgeted amounts?" you ask.

"Yes," Karen replies. "I'll show you how to use QuickBooks's budget reports to examine the budget by itself, as well as how to compare Wild Water Sports's actual results to its budgeted amounts."

You have another question. "Can we create different budgets based on different assumptions in QuickBooks?"

"No," Karen answers. "QuickBooks allows you to have a different budget for different fiscal years, but you may have only one budget per fiscal year."

Karen explains that QuickBooks allows you to set up budgets for specific accounts within financial statements or for all specific financial statements. While it is easier to budget for specific accounts, it might be more useful to prepare a budgeted income statement or budgeted balance sheet.

To begin, Karen suggests that you print Donna's spreadsheet budget and then the two of you can establish the monthly budget for revenues.

Budgeting Revenues

QuickBooks provides a set-up window to enter budget information. In this window, you specify fiscal year, account, customer and/or class, and the corresponding amounts for each month. As you fill in this information, you are setting up a budget for a single account, such as a balance sheet or an income statement account. If you also choose a customer:job or a class, you can set up a budget for that account and for that customer:job or class.

"I remember entering customer:job information in QuickBooks, but what are classes?" you ask.

"Classes are categories QuickBooks provides to help you group data into departments, product lines, locations, and the like," Karen responds.

"Do we need to set up budgets for customers or classes?" you ask.

"Donna's budget isn't that detailed," Karen responds. "We'll enter information for accounts only."

You also ask about QuickBooks's use of the term *income* instead of *revenues* for products and services. Karen reminds you that although revenues are the traditional accounting term for these items, QuickBooks has chosen to classify them as "income" in the type section of the chart of accounts.

Donna's budget predicts merchandise revenue of $200,000 in January 2007 and increasing by $50,000 each month throughout the year. Service and ports revenue is expected to remain constant, at $3,000 and $500 per month throughout the year.

To create a budget for specific revenues:

1 Restore the Wild Water Sports Ch 10.qbb file from your Data Files CD or downloaded from the Internet site. See "Data Files CD" in Chapter 1 if you need more information.

2 Click **Company,** then **Planning & Budgeting,** and then click **Set Up Budgets.**

3 Select **2007** as the budget year and **Profit and Loss** as the budget type in the Create New Budgets window, and then click **Next** twice.

4 Select the **Create budget from scratch** option, and click **Finish.**

5 The resulting Set Up Budgets window is shown in Figure 10.1.

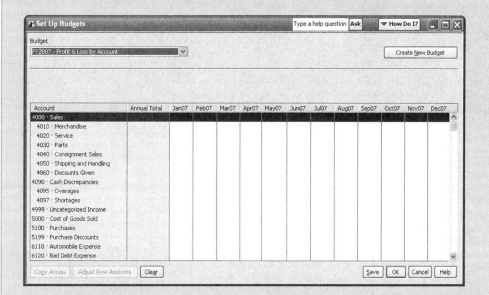

Figure 10.1
Setting Up Budgets

Trouble? Your screen may show the budget split into two 6-month periods based on your screen size. If that occurs, in order to enter information in the second 6-month period, you will need to press the Show Next 6 Months or Show Prev 6 Months button. Screen shots displayed in this chapter presume that your screen size will accommodate all 12 months.

6 Click in the cell at the intersection of the Jan07 column and the 4010 – Merchandise row. Type **200000.**

7 Click the **Adjust Row Amounts** button.

8 Select **Currently selected month** from the Start at drop-down list.

9 Select the first option button and type **50000** as the amount you want to increase each remaining month.

10 Select the **Enable compounding** checkbox. Your screen should look like Figure 10.2.

11 Click **OK.**

12 Click in between the Annual Total column title and the Jan07 title. Hold the mouse button down and increase the column width so that the amounts are completely visible.

13 Use the same method to increase the column width of the Jan07, Feb07, Mar07, and Apr07 columns.

Figure 10.2

Adjusting Row Amounts

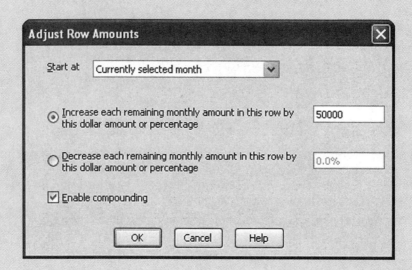

14 Click on the **4020 – Service** title of the next row so you can see the
    4010 – Merchandise row amounts more clearly. Your screen should
    look like Figure 10.3.

Figure 10.3

Increased Column Widths

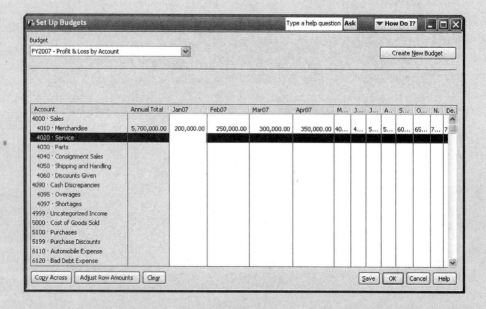

15 Click in the cell at the intersection of the Jan07 column and the
    4020 – Service row. Type **3000.**

16 Click the **Copy Across** button.

17 Click in the cell at the intersection of the Jan07 column and the
    4030 – Parts row. Type **500.**

18 Click the **Copy Across** button. The income portion of your budget
    for January through April 2007 should look like Figure 10.4.

Account	Annual Total	Jan07	Feb07	Mar07	Apr07
4000 · Sales					
4010 · Merchandise	5,700,000.00	200,000.00	250,000.00	300,000.00	350,000.00
4020 · Service	36,000.00	3,000.00	3,000.00	3,000.00	3,000.00
4030 · Parts	6,000.00	500.00	500.00	500.00	500.00

Figure 10.4

Budgeted Revenue

Now you're ready to set up budget revenue amounts for expenses.

Budgeting Expenses

The budget for Wild Water Sports cost of goods sold depends on product sales. Donna estimated that product cost should amount to approximately 80% of sales since they mark up the cost of boats 25% above their cost. Thus, as budgeted sales increase, so should budgeted cost of sales. Karen recalls that in January you set up the budget to include sales merchandise of $200,000. Thus, expected cost of sales should be 80% of the total January sales of $200,000, or $160,000. Each month thereafter, Donna expects sales of merchandise to increase by $50,000. Accordingly, the related costs of good sold should increase monthly by 80% of $50,000, or $40,000.

Karen expects payroll expenses, the largest budgeted expense item for Wild Water Sports, to remain constant at $12,000 per month throughout the year. Depreciation expenses are expected to be $3,500 per month, insurance expenses $2,000 per month, printing and reproduction office expenses $1,000 per month, marketing and advertising expense $2,500 per month, interest expense $2,800 per month, telephone expenses $2,100 per month, and utilities $900 per month.

To create a budget for specific expenses:

1 Click in the cell at the intersection of the Jan07 column and the 5000 – Cost of Goods Sold row. Type **200000*.80** then press the [**Enter**] key. This illustrates how to use the calculator function of the Budget process. The result should be 160,000.00.

2 Click the **Adjust Row Amounts** button.

3 Select **Currently selected month** from the Start at drop-down list.

4 Select the first option button, and type **40000** as the amount you want to increase each remaining month.

5 Select the **Enable compounding** checkbox.

6 Click **OK**.

7 Click in the cell at the intersection of the Jan07 column and the 6150 – Depreciation Expense row. Type **3500.**

8 Click the **Copy Across** button.

9   Click in the cell at the intersection of the Jan07 column and the 6187 – Liability Insurance row. Type **2000.**

10 Click the **Copy Across** button.

11 Click in the cell at the intersection of the Jan07 column and the 6200 – Interest Expense row. Type **2800.**

12 Click the **Copy Across** button.

13 Click in the cell at the intersection of the Jan07 column and the 6235 – Marketing & Advertising row. Type **2500.**

14 Click the **Copy Across** button.

15 Click in the cell at the intersection of the Jan07 column and the 6360 – Printing and Reproduction row. Type **1000.**

16 Click the **Copy Across** button.

17 Click in the cell at the intersection of the Jan07 column and the 6560 – Payroll Expenses row. Type **12000.**

18 Click the **Copy Across** button.

19 Click in the cell at the intersection of the Jan07 column and the 6660 – Telephone row. Type **2100.**

20 Click the **Copy Across** button.

21 Click in the cell at the intersection of the Jan07 column and the 6900 – Utilities row. Type **900.**

22 Click the **Copy Across** button.

23 Click **Save** to save your newly created budget, and then click **OK** to close the window.

Now that all of the detail income and expense amounts have been created for our budget, you can create a budgeted income statement.

Budgeted Income Statement

Now that Karen has entered budgetary information for several specific income statement accounts, she is curious to see a complete budget. Thus, she will create and print a budgeted income statement for the first quarter of 2007.

To create and print a budget overview report:

1   Click **Reports,** select **Budgets,** then select **Budget Overview.**

2   Select **FY2007—Profit & Loss by Account,** and then click **Next.**

3   Select **Account by Month,** and then click **Next.**

4   Click **Finish.**

5 Enter **1/1/07** and **3/31/07** as the from and to dates, respectively, in the Profit & Loss Budget Overview window. (Alternatively, you could use the calendar icons and choose specific dates.)

6 Click the **Refresh** button, and then click the **Collapse** button.

7 Click the **Print** button in the Report window.

8 Click **Portrait**, click the **Fit Report to One Page Wide** checkbox, and then click **Print** to print the report. Your report should look like Figure 10.5.

Wild Water Sports Ch 10
Profit & Loss Budget Overview
January through March 2007

	Jan 07	Feb 07	Mar 07	TOTAL Jan - Mar 07
Ordinary Income/Expense				
Income				
4000 · Sales	203,500.00	253,500.00	303,500.00	760,500.00
Total Income	203,500.00	253,500.00	303,500.00	760,500.00
Cost of Goods Sold				
5000 · Cost of Goods Sold	160,000.00	200,000.00	240,000.00	600,000.00
Total COGS	160,000.00	200,000.00	240,000.00	600,000.00
Gross Profit	43,500.00	53,500.00	63,500.00	160,500.00
Expense				
6150 · Depreciation Expense	3,500.00	3,500.00	3,500.00	10,500.00
6180 · Insurance	2,000.00	2,000.00	2,000.00	6,000.00
6200 · Interest Expense	2,800.00	2,800.00	2,800.00	8,400.00
6235 · Marketing & Advertising	2,500.00	2,500.00	2,500.00	7,500.00
6300 · Office Expenses	1,000.00	1,000.00	1,000.00	3,000.00
6560 · Payroll Expenses	12,000.00	12,000.00	12,000.00	36,000.00
6660 · Telephone	2,100.00	2,100.00	2,100.00	6,300.00
6900 · Utilities	900.00	900.00	900.00	2,700.00
Total Expense	26,800.00	26,800.00	26,800.00	80,400.00
Net Ordinary Income	16,700.00	26,700.00	36,700.00	80,100.00
Net Income	**16,700.00**	**26,700.00**	**36,700.00**	**80,100.00**

Figure 10.5
Budget Overview Report

9 Review the revised report, and then close its window.

Karen explains that the above report just describes the current budget but does not compare that budget with actual results from the quarter ended March 31, 2007. She suggests that you create a budget versus actual report for the quarter ended March 31, 2007, showing only quarterly amounts.

"Why not monthly?" you ask.

"Remember we only made our adjusting entries at the end of March," Karen reminds you. We didn't make adjusting entries at the end of January and February. As a result, our budget versus actual analysis on a monthly basis would reveal all sorts of discrepancies. Take insurance, for example. We budgeted insurance expense of $2,000 per month for January, February, and March. Our actual insurance expense will only be recorded in March when we made an adjusting entry for prepaid insurance. Thus, we'll be under budget in January and February and over budget in March just because of when we recorded our adjustments."

"Then why don't we make adjusting entries every month?" you ask.

"Good question," you answer. "We could, but it would take lots of time. Instead, we'll just produce financial statements every quarter, since that's when the bank wants to see how we're doing."

To create and print a budget versus actual report for the first quarter of 2007:

1 Click **Reports**, select **Budgets,** and then select **Budget vs. Actual.**

2 Select **FY2007—Profit & Loss by Account** then click **Next.**

3 Select **Account by Month,** and then click **Next.**

4 Click **Finish.**

5 Enter **1/1/07** and **3/31/07** as the from and to dates, respectively, in the Profit & Loss Budget vs. Actual window.

6 Select **Quarter** from the drop-down list of Columns.

7 Click the **Refresh** button, and then click the **Collapse** button.

8 Click the **Print** button in the report window.

9 Click **Portrait,** click the **Fit Report to One Page Wide** checkbox, and then click **Print** to print the report. Your report should look like Figure 10.6.

Figure 10.6

Budget vs. Actual Report

Wild Water Sports Ch 10
Profit & Loss Budget vs. Actual
January through March 2007

	Jan - Mar 07	Budget	$ Over Budget	% of Budget
Ordinary Income/Expense				
Income				
4000 · Sales	774,795.00	760,500.00	14,295.00	101.9%
Total Income	774,795.00	760,500.00	14,295.00	101.9%
Cost of Goods Sold				
5000 · Cost of Goods Sold	614,488.00	600,000.00	14,488.00	102.4%
Total COGS	614,488.00	600,000.00	14,488.00	102.4%
Gross Profit	160,307.00	160,500.00	-193.00	99.9%
Expense				
6130 · Bank Service Charges	75.00			
6150 · Depreciation Expense	10,333.00	10,500.00	-167.00	98.4%
6180 · Insurance	5,500.00	6,000.00	-500.00	91.7%
6200 · Interest Expense	7,719.57	8,400.00	-680.43	91.9%
6235 · Marketing & Advertising	6,700.00	7,500.00	-800.00	89.3%
6300 · Office Expenses	4,500.00	3,000.00	1,500.00	150.0%
6560 · Payroll Expenses	32,945.97	36,000.00	-3,054.03	91.5%
6660 · Telephone	5,020.00	6,300.00	-1,280.00	79.7%
6900 · Utilities	2,870.00	2,700.00	170.00	106.3%
Total Expense	75,663.54	80,400.00	-4,736.46	94.1%
Net Ordinary Income	84,643.46	80,100.00	4,543.46	105.7%
Other Income/Expense				
Other Income				
7010 · Interest Income	2,015.41			
7030 · Other Income	3,000.00			
Total Other Income	5,015.41			
Net Other Income	5,015.41			
Net Income	**89,658.87**	**80,100.00**	**9,558.87**	**111.9%**

Karen points out that, based on the budget vs. actual report, the company is doing pretty good. She'll ask Donna about budgeting for bank service charges and other income since neither was included in the budget. She also wants to investigate the actual office expenses, which, according to the report, were 50% over budget.

Budgeting Assets, Liabilities, and Equities

Karen explains to you that creating specific budgets for assets, liabilities, and stockholders' equity accounts is not a simple task. First, you cannot complete this task until the budget for revenues and expenses has been established. This is due to the relationship that exists between net income and retained earnings. Budgeted retained earnings are dependent on net income/net loss. That is, budgeted retained earnings must be increased by monthly net income and decreased by monthly net losses, if any.

Second, budgets for accounts receivable are dependent on sales, while budgets for inventory and accounts payable are dependent on cost of sales and projected sales. Budgeted accumulated depreciation accounts are increased by monthly depreciation expenses. Fortunately for you and Karen, Donna has already created this budget in her spreadsheet program.

Donna's budget for assets had forecast for the cash financing activities of issuing more stock, offering credit terms to their customers, buying more inventory for the showroom, temporarily investing some cash, and then eventually paying down some debt. She also planned to increase accounts payable by getting suppliers to offer credit terms as well.

Karen suggests that you complete this task one step at a time—first entering the budget for assets, then the budget for liabilities and for stockholders' equity. You agree with her suggestion and remind her that the budget amounts for these accounts are the ending balance expected for each quarter. For now, you'll just be creating budgeted balances for assets at the end of March 2007.

To create a budget for assets:

1 Click **Company,** then **Planning & Budgeting,** and then click **Set Up Budgets.**

2 Click the **Create New Budget** button.

3 Select **2007** as the budget year and **Balance Sheet** as the budget type in the Create New Budgets window, click **Next,** and then click **Finish.**

4 Click in the cell at the intersection of the Mar07 column and the 1010 – Bank of Florida row. Type **34250.**

5 Click in the cell at the intersection of the Mar07 column and the 1050 – Short-Term Investments row. Type **50000.**

6 Click in the cell at the intersection of the Mar07 column and the 1200 – Accounts Receivable row. Type **400000.**

7 Click in the cell at the intersection of the Mar07 column and the 1060 – Prepaid Advertising row. Type **20000.**

8 Click in the cell at the intersection of the Mar07 column and the 1120 – Inventory Asset row. Type **200000.**

9 Click in the cell at the intersection of the Mar07 column and the 1130 – Inventory Parts row. Type **2000.**

10 Click in the cell at the intersection of the Mar07 column and the 1150 – Prepaid Insurance row. Type **16500.**

11 Click in the cell at the intersection of the Mar07 column and the 1310 – Equipment Cost row. Type **180000.**

12 Click in the cell at the intersection of the Mar07 column and the 1390 – Equipment Accumulated Depreciation row. Type **–13000.**

13 Click in the cell at the intersection of the Mar07 column and the 1410 – Furniture & Fixtures Cost row. Type **70000.**

14 Click in the cell at the intersection of the Mar07 column and the 1490 – Furniture & Fixtures Accumulated Depreciation row. Type **–2500.**

15 Click in the cell at the intersection of the Mar07 column and the 1510 – Truck Cost row. Type **45000.**

16 Click in the cell at the intersection of the Mar07 column and the 1590 – Truck Accumulated Depreciation row. Type **–2250.**

17 Click **Save.** Your screen should look like Figure 10-7.

Figure 10-7

Entering Asset Information into the Budget

Account	Annual Total	Jan07	Feb07	Mar07
1010 · Bank of Florida	34,250.00			34,250.00
1050 · Short-Term Investments	50,000.00			50,000.00
1200 · Accounts Receivable	400,000.00			400,000.00
1060 · Prepaid Advertising	20,000.00			20,000.00
1120 · Inventory Asset	200,000.00			200,000.00
1130 · Inventory Parts	2,000.00			2,000.00
1150 · Prepaid Insurance	16,500.00			16,500.00
1499 · Undeposited Funds				
1300 · Equipment				
1310 · Cost	180,000.00			180,000.00
1390 · Accumulated Depreciation	-13,000.00			-13,000.00
1400 · Furniture & Fixtures				
1410 · Cost	70,000.00			70,000.00
1490 · Accumulated Depreciation	-2,500.00			-2,500.00
1500 · Truck				
1510 · Cost	45,000.00			45,000.00
1590 · Accumulated Depreciation	-2,250.00			-2,250.00

The liabilities and stockholders' equity items are less numerous and include accounts payable, loans payable, common stock, and retained earnings, to name a few. Loans payable was relatively easy to predict as they planned initially to borrow funds when they first opened up and then to pay down some of that debt when they took on another investor and sold some inventory. Common stock was also easy since Donna and Karen knew what they were going to invest and had already planned on a fourth investor. Retained earnings were linked to Donna's estimate for net income, and since they started the year with no retained earnings, ending retained earnings as of March 31 had to equal their budgeted net income since they hadn't planned to distribute any earnings via dividends.

To create a budget for liabilities and stockholders' equity:

1 Click in the cell at the intersection of the Mar07 column and the 2000 – Accounts Payable row. Type **200000**.

2 Click in the cell at the intersection of the Mar07 column and the 2025 – Accrued Interest Payable row. Type **1500**.

3 Click in the cell at the intersection of the Mar07 column and the 2100 – Payroll Liabilities row. Type **3000**.

4 Click in the cell at the intersection of the Mar07 column and the 2200 – Sales Tax Payable row. Type **15400**.

5 Click in the cell at the intersection of the Mar07 column and the 2500 – Loan Payable row. Type **300000**.

6 Click in the cell at the intersection of the Mar07 column and the 3100 – Common Stock row. Type **400000**.

7 Click in the cell at the intersection of the Mar07 column and the 3900 – Retained Earnings row. Type **80100**.

8 Click **Save**. The lower portion of your screen should look like Figure 10.8.

2000 · Accounts Payable	200,000.00			200,000.00
2050 · MasterCard				
2025 · Accrued Interest Payable	1,500.00			1,500.00
2100 · Payroll Liabilities	3,000.00			3,000.00
2200 · Sales Tax Payable	15,400.00			15,400.00
2210 · Accrued Sales Tax Payable				
2300 · Unearned Revenue				
2500 · Loan Payable	300,000.00			300,000.00
3000 · Opening Bal Equity				
3100 · Common Stock	400,000.00			400,000.00
3900 · Retained Earnings	80,100.00			80,100.00

Figure 10.8

Entering Liability and Equity Information into the Budget

9 Click **OK** to close the budget window.

Now that all of the detail asset, liability, and stockholders' equity amounts have been created for our budget you can create a budgeted balance sheet.

Budgeted Balance Sheet

Now that Karen has entered budgetary information for several specific balance sheet accounts, she is curious to see a complete budget. Thus, she will create and print a budgeted balance sheet for the quarter ended March 31, 2007.

To create and print a budget overview report:

1 Click **Reports,** select **Budgets,** and then select **Budget Overview.**

2 Select **FY2007—Balance Sheet by Account,** and then click **Next.**

3 Click **Finish.**

4 Enter **1/1/07** and **3/31/07** as the from and to dates, respectively, in the Balance Sheet Budget Overview window. Click the **Refresh** button.

5 Select **Quarter** from the Columns drop-down list.

6 Click the **Print** button in the Report window.

7 Click **Portrait,** click the **Fit Report to One Page Wide** checkbox, and then click **Print** to print the report. Your report should look like Figure 10.9.

Figure 10.9

Balance Sheet Budget Overview

Wild Water Sports Ch 10
Balance Sheet Budget Overview
As of March 31, 2007

	Mar 31, 07
ASSETS	
Current Assets	
Checking/Savings	
1010 · Bank of Florida	34,250.00
1050 · Short-Term Investments	50,000.00
Total Checking/Savings	84,250.00
Accounts Receivable	
1200 · Accounts Receivable	400,000.00
Total Accounts Receivable	400,000.00
Other Current Assets	
1060 · Prepaid Advertising	20,000.00
1120 · Inventory Asset	200,000.00
1130 · Inventory Parts	2,000.00
1150 · Prepaid Insurance	16,500.00
Total Other Current Assets	238,500.00
Total Current Assets	722,750.00
Fixed Assets	
1300 · Equipment	
1310 · Cost	180,000.00
1390 · Accumulated Depreciation	-13,000.00
Total 1300 · Equipment	167,000.00
1400 · Furniture & Fixtures	
1410 · Cost	70,000.00
1490 · Accumulated Depreciation	-2,500.00
Total 1400 · Furniture & Fixtures	67,500.00
1500 · Truck	
1510 · Cost	45,000.00
1590 · Accumulated Depreciation	-2,250.00
Total 1500 · Truck	42,750.00
Total Fixed Assets	277,250.00
TOTAL ASSETS	1,000,000.00

Figure 10.9

continued

```
LIABILITIES & EQUITY
  Liabilities
    Current Liabilities
      Accounts Payable
        2000 · Accounts Payable                    200,000.00

      Total Accounts Payable                       200,000.00

      Other Current Liabilities
        2025 · Accrued Interest Payable              1,500.00
        2100 · Payroll Liabilities                   3,000.00
        2200 · Sales Tax Payable                    15,400.00

      Total Other Current Liabilities               19,900.00

    Total Current Liabilities                       219,900.00

    Long Term Liabilities
      2500 · Loan Payable                           300,000.00

    Total Long Term Liabilities                     300,000.00

  Total Liabilities                                 519,900.00

  Equity
    3100 · Common Stock                             400,000.00
    3900 · Retained Earnings                         80,100.00

  Total Equity                                      480,100.00

TOTAL LIABILITIES & EQUITY                        1,000,000.00
```

Karen explains that once again the above report just describes the current budget but does not compare that budget with actual results from the quarter ended March 31, 2007. She suggests that you create a budget versus actual report as of the quarter ended March 31, 2007.

To create and print a budget versus actual report as of first quarter of 2007:

1 Click **Reports,** select **Budgets,** and then select **Budget vs. Actual.**

2 Select **FY2007—Balance Sheet by Account,** and then click **Next.**

3 Click **Finish.**

4 Enter **1/1/07** and **3/31/07** as the from and to dates, respectively, in the Balance Sheet Budget vs. Actual window.

5 Select **Quarter** from the drop-down list of Columns.

6 Click the **Refresh** button, and then click the **Collapse** button.

7 Click the **Print** button in the Report window.

8 Click **Portrait,** click the **Fit Report to One Page Wide** checkbox, and then click **Print** to print the report. Your report should look like Figure 10.10.

9 Close the Balance Sheet Budget vs. Actual window.

Figure 10.10

Budget vs. Actual Report

Wild Water Sports Ch 10
Balance Sheet Budget vs. Actual
As of March 31, 2007

	Mar 31, 07	Budget	$ Over Budget	% of Budget
ASSETS				
Current Assets				
Checking/Savings				
1010 · Bank of Florida	37,442.42	34,250.00	3,192.42	109.3%
1050 · Short-Term Investments	39,890.41	50,000.00	-10,109.59	79.8%
Total Checking/Savings	77,332.83	84,250.00	-6,917.17	91.8%
Accounts Receivable				
1200 · Accounts Receivable	399,932.73	400,000.00	-67.27	100.0%
Total Accounts Receivable	399,932.73	400,000.00	-67.27	100.0%
Other Current Assets				
1060 · Prepaid Advertising	20,000.00	20,000.00	0.00	100.0%
1120 · Inventory Asset	243,600.00	200,000.00	43,600.00	121.8%
1130 · Inventory Parts	2,112.00	2,000.00	112.00	105.6%
1150 · Prepaid Insurance	16,500.00	16,500.00	0.00	100.0%
1499 · Undeposited Funds	10,000.00			
Total Other Current Assets	292,212.00	238,500.00	53,712.00	122.5%
Total Current Assets	769,477.56	722,750.00	46,727.56	106.5%
Fixed Assets				
1300 · Equipment	166,916.00	167,000.00	-84.00	99.9%
1400 · Furniture & Fixtures	67,501.00	67,500.00	1.00	100.0%
1500 · Truck	42,750.00	42,750.00	0.00	100.0%
Total Fixed Assets	277,167.00	277,250.00	-83.00	100.0%
TOTAL ASSETS	**1,046,644.56**	**1,000,000.00**	**46,644.56**	**104.7%**
LIABILITIES & EQUITY				
Liabilities				
Current Liabilities				
Accounts Payable				
2000 · Accounts Payable	216,200.00	200,000.00	16,200.00	108.1%
Total Accounts Payable	216,200.00	200,000.00	16,200.00	108.1%
Credit Cards				
2050 · MasterCard	0.00			
Total Credit Cards	0.00			
Other Current Liabilities				
2025 · Accrued Interest Payable	1,760.97	1,500.00	260.97	117.4%
2100 · Payroll Liabilities	2,934.66	3,000.00	-65.34	97.8%
2200 · Sales Tax Payable	24,232.66	15,400.00	8,832.66	157.4%
2210 · Accrued Sales Tax Payable	4,225.00			
2300 · Unearned Revenue	10,000.00			
Total Other Current Liabilities	43,153.29	19,900.00	23,253.29	216.9%
Total Current Liabilities	259,353.29	219,900.00	39,453.29	117.9%
Long-Term Liabilities				
2500 · Loan Payable	297,632.40	300,000.00	-2,367.60	99.2%
Total Long-Term Liabilities	297,632.40	300,000.00	-2,367.60	99.2%
Total Liabilities	556,985.69	519,900.00	37,085.69	107.1%
Equity				
3000 · Opening Bal Equity	0.00			
3100 · Common Stock	400,000.00	400,000.00	0.00	100.0%
3900 · Retained Earnings	0.00	80,100.00	-80,100.00	0.0%
Net Income	89,658.87	0.00	89,658.87	100.0%
Total Equity	489,658.87	480,100.00	9,558.87	102.0%
TOTAL LIABILITIES & EQUITY	**1,046,644.56**	**1,000,000.00**	**46,644.56**	**104.7%**

Karen points out that, based on the budget vs. actual report, the company is right on target. She'll ask Donna about budgeting for the MasterCard and unearned revenue accounts since neither was included in the budget. She does want to investigate the inventory asset account, which was 21% over budget, and sales tax payable, which when you consider the accrued sales tax ($4,225) and sales tax payable ($24,233), actual balances exceed the budgeted sales tax payable ($15,400) by 84%.

End Note

You and Karen have now entered all budgetary information for the first quarter of 2007. Donna can make changes to the budget at any time if additional information becomes available, and QuickBooks will automatically update any related budget report.

chapter

10

Chapter 10 Questions

1 Explain how the budgeting process is accomplished in QuickBooks.

2 Can multiple budgets be created in QuickBooks? Explain.

3 Explain how the Copy Across feature helps in creating QuickBooks budgets.

4 Explain how the Adjust Row Amounts feature helps in creating QuickBooks budgets.

5 Explain the typical relationship between cost of goods sold and sales in the budgeting process and how this information is included in the QuickBooks budgeting process.

6 Compare the process of budgeting revenues and expenses with the process of budgeting assets, liabilities, and owners' equity and how this information is included in the QuickBooks budgeting process.

7 Explain the typical relationship between accumulated depreciation and depreciation expense in the budgeting process and how this information is included in the QuickBooks budgeting process.

8 Which menus are used to create budget reports in QuickBooks?

9 Describe how you use the calculator feature that is built into QuickBooks for the budgeting process.

10 Explain the typical relationship between retained earnings and net income/loss in the budgeting process and how this information is included in the QuickBooks budgeting process.

Chapter 10 Assignments

1 *Adding More Information to Wild Water Sports*

Restore the file Wild Water Sports Ch 10A.qbb found on the text CD or downloaded from the text website, and then modify the existing budget as follows:

Merchandise revenues for April are expected to be 10% higher than in March. Cost of goods sold for April is still estimated at 80% of merchandise sales. Payroll expenses for April are expected to be $15,000.
Assets, liabilities, and equities are as follows:

merchandising

Checking	60,000	Accounts payable	345,200
Short-term investments	30,000	Acc. interest payable	2,000
Accounts receivable	500,000	Payroll liabilities	3,000
Prepaid advertising	18,000	Sales tax payable	30,000
Inventory asset	290,000	Loan payable	300,000
Inventory parts	2,000	Common stock	400,000
Prepaid insurance	14,250	Retained earnings	?
Equipment: cost	192,000		
Equipment: acc. depreciation	−15,000		
Furniture & Fixtures: cost	70,000		
Furniture & Fixtures: acc. depreciation	−3,500		
Truck: cost	45,000		
Truck: acc. depreciation	−2,750		

You'll need to compute ending retained earnings based on the previous month's budget and your budget of April net income.

a. Print a collapsed Profit & Loss Budget Overview report for the month of April 2007.

b. Print a collapsed Profit & Loss Budget vs. Actual report for the month of April 2007.

c. Print a collapsed Balance Sheet Budget Overview report as of 4/30/07.

d. Print a collapsed Balance Sheet Budget vs. Actual report as of 4/30/07.

2 *Adding More Information to Central Coast Cellular*

In Chapter 9, you added some business transactions to your QuickBooks file for Central Coast Cellular, a cellular phone sales, phone rental, and consulting company. Make a copy of that file in Windows Explorer, name the file CCC10, and use that file to enter the following budget information for the first quarter of 2003 only.

Commission revenues of $2,000 are expected each month for the first quarter. Consulting revenues of $8,000 are expected in January, increasing 10% each month thereafter. Phone sales of $10,000 are expected in January, increasing by $5,000 each month thereafter. Cost of goods sold is estimated at 50% of phone sales. Bank service charges and depreciation of $80 and $1,500, respectively, are expected each month. Loan interest expense and rent of $1,000 and $3,000, respectively, are expected each month. Payroll expenses of $10,000 are expected in January, increasing by $2,000 each month thereafter. Telephone expenses of $500 are expected in January, increasing $100 each month thereafter. Gas & Electric expenses of $300 are expected in January, increasing 5% each month thereafter. Assets, liabilities, and equities as of January 31, 2003, are as follows:

merchandising

Checking	130,000	Accounts payable	24,380
Accounts receivable	14,000	Interest payable	1,000
Store supplies	3,000	Payroll liabilities	4,000
Inventory asset	18,000	Sales tax payable	2,000
Short-term investments	68,500	Common stock	200,000
Equipment: cost	95,000	Retained earnings	?
Equipment: acc. depreciation	–1,000		
Office Furniture: cost	20,000		
Office Furniture: acc. depreciation	–500		
Security deposit	3,000		

You'll need to compute ending retained earnings to make the balance sheet balance.

a. Print a Profit & Loss Budget Overview report by month for the quarter ended in March 2003.

b. Print a Profit & Loss Budget vs. Actual report for the month of January 2003.

c. Print a Balance Sheet Budget Overview report as of January 31, 2003.

d. Print a Balance Sheet Budget vs. Actual report as of January 31, 2003.

3 *Using the South-Western Home Page for More Assignments or Cases*

Go to the home page for this textbook at **www.thomsonedu.com/ accounting/owen.** Click **Additional Problem Sets,** and then select the **Chapter 10** section, and complete the problem(s) that your instructor assigns.

Chapter 10 Case Problem 1:
ALOHA PROPERTY MANAGEMENT

service

In Chapter 9, you modified your QuickBooks file for Aloha Property Management. Make a copy of that file, and use that copy to enter the following budget information.

Rental income is expected to be $60,000 in January and $100,000 in February and increase 18% per month thereafter through 2008. Advertising is expected to be $12,500 in January (for an initial advertising campaign) and then $1,500 per month thereafter. Cleaning costs vary with the number of units rented (they should average about 5% of rental income). Depreciation should be about $17,000 per month. Insurance, interest, pool maintenance, repairs, telephone, utilities, and payroll expenses are expected to be $2,000, $23,000, $900, $2,500, $4,000, $3,000, and $10,000, respectively, each month throughout the year. Expected assets, liabilities, and equities as of February 29, 2008, are as follows:

Bank of Hawaii	101,000	Accounts payable	10,000
Accounts receivable	50,000	Interest payable	23,000
Short-term investments	40,000	Payroll liabilities	4,000
Prepaid insurance	20,000	Sales tax payable	5,000
Moana: cost	2,000,000	Loan payable	3,859,600
Moana: acc. depreciation	–513,000	Common stock	60,000
Villa: cost	3,000,000	Retained earnings	38,400
Villa: acc. depreciation	–720,000		
Furniture: cost	23,000		
Furniture: acc. depreciation	–1,000		

You'll need to compute ending retained earnings to make the balance sheet balance.

a. Print a Profit & Loss Budget Overview report in total for the two months ended in February 2008.

b. Print a Profit & Loss Budget vs. Actual report for the two months ended in February 2008.

c. Print a collapsed Balance Sheet Budget Overview in total report as of February 29, 2008.

d. Print a collapsed Balance Sheet Budget vs. Actual report in total as of February 29, 2008.

Chapter 10 Case Problem 2:
OCEAN VIEW FLOWERS

In Chapter 9, you modified your QuickBooks file for Ocean View Flowers, a wholesale flower distributor. Make a copy of that file, and use that copy to enter the following transactions. Budgeted revenues and expenses follow:

merchandising

Account	January	February
Sales Anthuriums	$ 5,000	$50,000
Sales Daylilies	30,000	30,000
Cost of sales	16,000	42,000
Depreciation	1,500	1,500
Insurance	100	100
Interest expense	1,600	1,600
Payroll expenses	20,000	20,000
Legal fees	500	500
Rent	1,400	1.400
Telephone	400	400
Utilities	300	300
Interest revenue	500	1,000

Budgeted balances as of 2/29/08 for assets, liabilities, and equity accounts follow:

Bank of Hawaii	46,300		Accounts payable	52,800
Accounts receivable	62,200		Payroll liabilities	14,000
Short-term investments	25,000		Long-term note	320,000
Prepaid insurance	1,000			
Office supplies	1,500			
Inventory	30,000			
Land	50,000			
Building: cost	250,000			
Building: acc. depreciation	−2,000		Common stock	100,000
Computer equip: cost	16,000		Retained earnings	13,200
Computer equip: acc. depr.	−500			
Office equip: cost	21,000			
Office equip: acc. depr.	−500			

a. Print a collapsed Profit & Loss Budget Overview report by month for the two months ended February 2008.

b. Print a Profit & Loss Budget vs. Actual report in total for the two months ended February 2008.

c. Print a collapsed Balance Sheet Budget Overview report in total as of February 29, 2008.

d. Print a Balance Sheet Budget vs. Actual report in total as of February 29, 2008.

Reporting Business Activities

Learning Objectives

In this chapter, you will:

- Create and memorize a customized income statement
- Create and memorize a customized balance sheet
- Create graphs to illustrate financial information
- Create additional detail reports
- Export reports to Excel

Case: **Wild Water Sports, Inc.**

Now that you have entered the budget information for Wild Water Sports's first year and have entered in the first four months of operating, investing, and financing transactions as well as adjustments, you are ready to prepare financial statements to send to the bank for Wild Water Sports's first three months. Donna has asked you and Karen to prepare these statements and to provide any additional information that will help her better understand Wild Water's financial performance. You and Karen decide that you'll create more customized financial statements than you've printed so far and give Donna the related supporting schedules and graphs that QuickBooks can so easily create.

You decide to prepare a customized income statement, a customized balance sheet, an accounts receivable and accounts payable schedule, and an inventory status report. To further enhance Donna's financial analysis of the business, you also decide to prepare a graph showing income and expenses and another showing the aging of accounts receivable and payable.

"The report and graph features of QuickBooks are quite extensive," Karen explains. "You can customize each report by adding percentages, hiding cents, changing report titles, and modifying the page layout."

"Can we graphically compare the current quarter's results with the budget we just created?" you ask.

"Absolutely!" Karen confirms. "Now that we have created the budget in QuickBooks, we can take the report information we created comparing our budgeted activity with our actual results and produce a graphic illustration.

This will help Donna or other users of this information to visually evaluate the financial results."

"Sounds like QuickBooks saves hours of work," you remark. "Let's get started."

Creating and Memorizing a Customized Income Statement

Karen decides to create one customized income statement for the three-month period ended March 31 without examining each month separately, because adjustments were made only as of March 31.

Karen explains that QuickBooks enables you to create reports for any period you desire. It also lets you create separate columns for a time segment—such as a day, a week, four weeks, a month, a quarter, and so on—within each period. At the end of the fiscal year, Karen will create an income statement report for the year with separate columns for each quarter.

Karen decides to print two customized versions of the income statement. One will be a left page layout alignment, without cents, include a % of income column, and be titled Income Statement for the three months ended March 31, 2007, in an expanded format. The other will be a collapsed version of the same report but sorted by total from largest to smallest amounts.

"Do we have to go through this customization effort every time?" Karen asks.

"No," you reply. "QuickBooks has a Memorize feature that can "memorize" or retain the customization—what columns we want, what period, what layout, and so on. That way the next time we want a similar report, it will be available from a memorized report list."

To create and memorize a customized income statement:

1 Restore the Wild Water Sports Ch 11.qbb file from your Data Files CD or downloaded from the Internet site. See "Data Files CD" in Chapter 1 if you need more information.

2 Click **Reports, Company & Financial,** and then **Profit & Loss Standard.**

3 Click the **Modify Report** button, and then click the **Display** tab.

4 Change the report dates to read from **01/01/07** to **3/31/07** in the Modify Report window, and then click the **% of Income** checkbox.

5 Click the **Fonts & Numbers** tab, and then click the **Without Cents** checkbox.

6 Click the **Header/Footer** tab. Change the Report Title to **Income Statement.** Select **Left** from the Page Layout alignment drop-down edit box, and alter the Subtitle to read **for the three months ended March 31, 2007.** Then click **OK.**

7 Click the **Print** button.

8 Click **Portrait** in the Orientation box. (If the Print Features window appears, click **OK.**) Then click **Print** in the Print Reports window to print the report shown in Figure 11.1.

Figure 11.1
Customized Income Statement

Wild Water Sports Ch 11
Income Statement
for the three months ended March 31, 2007

	Jan - Mar 07	% of Income
Ordinary Income/Expense		
Income		
4000 · Sales		
4010 · Merchandise	767,500	99%
4020 · Service	6,685	1%
4030 · Parts	610	0%
Total 4000 · Sales	774,795	100%
Total Income	774,795	100%
Cost of Goods Sold		
5000 · Cost of Goods Sold	614,488	79%
Total COGS	614,488	79%
Gross Profit	160,307	21%
Expense		
6130 · Bank Service Charges	75	0%
6150 · Depreciation Expense	10,333	1%
6180 · Insurance		
6187 · Liability Insurance	5,500	1%
Total 6180 · Insurance	5,500	1%
6200 · Interest Expense	7,720	1%
6235 · Marketing & Advertising	6,700	1%
6300 · Office Expenses		
6360 · Printing and Reproduction	4,500	1%
Total 6300 · Office Expenses	4,500	1%
6560 · Payroll Expenses	32,946	4%
6660 · Telephone	5,020	1%
6900 · Utilities	2,870	0%
Total Expense	75,664	10%
Net Ordinary Income	84,643	11%
Other Income/Expense		
Other Income		
7010 · Interest Income	2,015	0%
7030 · Other Income	3,000	0%
Total Other Income	5,015	1%
Net Other Income	5,015	1%
Net Income	**89,659**	**12%**

9 Further customize this income statement by clicking the **Collapse** button.

10 Change the sorting by selecting **Total** from the Sort By drop-down list and clicking the **Sort** button next to the Sort By drop-down list so that it reads Z to A (meaning largest to smallest).

11 Click the **Print** button.

12 Click **Portrait** in the Orientation box. (If the Print Features window appears, click **OK.**) Then click **Print** in the Print Reports window to print the report shown in Figure 11.2.

Figure 11.2

A Variation on the Customized Income Statement

Wild Water Sports Ch 11
Income Statement
for the three months ended March 31, 2007

	Jan - Mar 07	% of Income
Ordinary Income/Expense		
Income		
4000 · Sales	774,795	100%
Total Income	774,795	100%
Cost of Goods Sold		
5000 · Cost of Goods Sold	614,488	79%
Total COGS	614,488	79%
Gross Profit	160,307	21%
Expense		
6560 · Payroll Expenses	32,946	4%
6150 · Depreciation Expense	10,333	1%
6200 · Interest Expense	7,720	1%
6235 · Marketing & Advertising	6,700	1%
6180 · Insurance	5,500	1%
6660 · Telephone	5,020	1%
6300 · Office Expenses	4,500	1%
6900 · Utilities	2,870	0%
6130 · Bank Service Charges	75	0%
Total Expense	75,664	10%
Net Ordinary Income	84,643	11%
Other Income/Expense		
Other Income		
7030 · Other Income	3,000	0%
7010 · Interest Income	2,015	0%
Total Other Income	5,015	1%
Net Other Income	5,015	1%
Net Income	89,659	12%

13 Click the **Memorize** button.

14 Type **Customized Income Statement** in the name text box as shown in Figure 11.3.

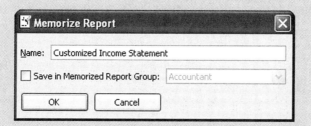

Figure 11.3

Memorizing Reports

15 Click **OK** to retain this customized report as Customized Income Statement.

16 Close the Customized Income Statement window.

17 Click **Reports** from the menu bar, then click **Memorized Reports,** and then select **Customized Income Statement** as shown in Figure 11.4.

Figure 11.4

Retrieving a Memorized Report

18 Note how this report is identical to what you created before.

19 Close all windows.

Karen suggests that you take note of the % of income column. She explains how this column reports each item's percentage of total revenue (what QuickBooks calls total income). Cost of goods sold at 79% and payroll expenses at 4% are the company's largest costs as a percentage of total revenue. Notice also that Wild Water's profit margin ratio (net income divided by total revenue) is 12%. You suggest a cup of coffee before you come back to customize a balance sheet.

Creating and Memorizing a Customized Balance Sheet

You return to your office to create the balance sheet Donna needs as of 3/31/07. Karen explains to you that QuickBooks can prepare balance sheets for any accounting period you specify. Since Donna needs balance results as of 3/31/07, the two of you start by preparing a standard balance sheet. You want to keep the report simple—you'll include the main accounts from the chart of accounts and collapse the subaccounts into their main accounts. You decide to customize the balance sheet to include a percentage column,

To create and memorize a customized balance sheet:

1 Click **Reports, Company & Financial,** and then **Balance Sheet Standard.**

2 Click the **Modify Report** button.

3 Change the report dates to read from **01/01/07** to **03/31/07,** and then click in the **% of Column** checkbox.

4 Click the **Fonts & Numbers** tab, and then click the **Without Cents** checkbox.

5 Click the **Header/Footer** tab. Select **Left** from the Page Layout alignment drop-down edit box, and then click **OK.**

6 Click the **Collapse** button.

7 Click the **Print** button.

8 Click **Portrait** in the Orientation box, and then click **Print** in the Print Reports window to print the report shown in Figure 11.5.

9 Click the **Memorize** button.

10 Type **Customized Balance Sheet** in the name text box.

Figure 11.5

Customized Balance Sheet

Wild Water Sports Ch 11
Balance Sheet
As of March 31, 2007

	Mar 31, 07	% of Column
ASSETS		
Current Assets		
Checking/Savings		
1010 · Bank of Florida	37,442	4%
1050 · Short-Term Investments	39,890	4%
Total Checking/Savings	77,333	7%
Accounts Receivable		
1200 · Accounts Receivable	399,933	38%
Total Accounts Receivable	399,933	38%
Other Current Assets		
1060 · Prepaid Advertising	20,000	2%
1120 · Inventory Asset	243,600	23%
1130 · Inventory Parts	2,112	0%
1150 · Prepaid Insurance	16,500	2%
1499 · Undeposited Funds	10,000	1%
Total Other Current Assets	292,212	28%
Total Current Assets	769,478	74%
Fixed Assets		
1300 · Equipment	166,916	16%
1400 · Furniture & Fixtures	67,501	6%
1500 · Truck	42,750	4%
Total Fixed Assets	277,167	26%
TOTAL ASSETS	**1,046,645**	**100%**
LIABILITIES & EQUITY		
Liabilities		
Current Liabilities		
Accounts Payable		
2000 · Accounts Payable	216,200	21%
Total Accounts Payable	216,200	21%
Other Current Liabilities		
2025 · Accrued Interest Payable	1,761	0%
2100 · Payroll Liabilities	2,935	0%
2200 · Sales Tax Payable	24,233	2%
2210 · Accrued Sales Tax Payable	4,225	0%
2300 · Unearned Revenue	10,000	1%
Total Other Current Liabilities	43,153	4%
Total Current Liabilities	259,353	25%
Long Term Liabilities		
2500 · Loan Payable	297,632	28%
Total Long Term Liabilities	297,632	28%
Total Liabilities	556,986	53%
Equity		
3100 · Common Stock	400,000	38%
Net Income	89,659	9%
Total Equity	489,659	47%
TOTAL LIABILITIES & EQUITY	**1,046,645**	**100%**

11   Click **OK** to retain this customized report.

12   Close the Customized Balance Sheet window.

Trouble? Notice that QuickBooks includes a line item called "Net Income" in the (Owners') Equity section. Standard accounting practice does not allow inclusion of such an income statement category in a balance sheet. Usually this net income is included in the Retained Earnings account.

Karen comments that at first she thought the percentage column was the same as the one shown in the income statement: the percentage each item is to the total revenue (what QuickBooks calls "income"). But now she sees that this column shows the percentage of total assets. For example, total cash (that is, the total amount in checking and savings) is 7% of Wild Water Sports's total assets, and accounts receivable is 38% of total assets. She comments that it looks like a large portion of those assets came from accounts payable (21%) and loans payable (28%) and most of the balance is from equity (47%).

Creating Graphs to Illustrate Financial Information

"This is very helpful information," Donna comments as she quickly skims the customized income statement, balance sheet, and budget versus actual reports you previously created. "I can see Wild Water's financial position, and how we stand in relation to where I thought we'd be. Can I see this information expressed in graphical form?" she asks. "I'm afraid I might miss something when I look at this detailed report. A graph would help me see things I might miss when I look at just numbers."

Both you and Karen agree that some graphs would be helpful. In particular, Donna is anxious to know more about product sales and expenses. It is clear that graphic representations of sales, revenue, and expenses will be helpful.

To create a sales graph:

1   Click **Reports,** click **Sales,** and then click **Sales Graph.**

2   Click the **Dates** button and change the dates to read from **01/01/07** to **03/31/07** in the Change Graph Dates window. Then click **OK.**

3   Click the **By Item** button in the QuickInsight: Sales Graph window, if it is not already selected. Selecting this button causes QuickBooks to display sales in the graph by item, in this case by the hardware and the services that Wild Water sells.

4   QuickBooks generates two graphs—a bar chart and a pie chart.

5 Click **Print** from the button bar, and then click **Print** from the
Print Graphs window. Your printed graph should look like
Figure 11.6.

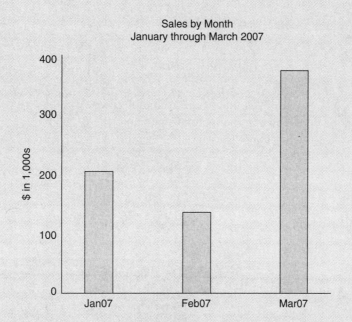

Sales by Month
January through March 2007

Figure 11.6

Sales Graph by Item

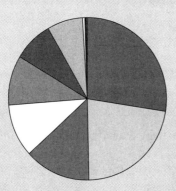

Sales Summary
January through March 2007

Malibu Sunscape LSV	%27.47
Tige 22v	22.19
Malibu Vride	13.53
MB B52 V23 Team Edition	10.57
Malibu WakeSetter XT1	9.86
Malibu WakeSetter VLX	8.03
Malibu Sportster LX	7.33
Engine Tune Up	0.49
Painting & body Repairs	0.19
20 Hour Service Check	0.12
Other	0.22
Total	$709,795.00

6 Click the **By Customer** button in the QuickInsight: Sales Graph
window to create a graph that illustrates sales for the quarter by
customer.

7 Click **Print** from the button bar, and then click **Print** from the Print
Graphs window. Your printed graph should look like Figure 11.7.

8 Close the Sales Graph window.

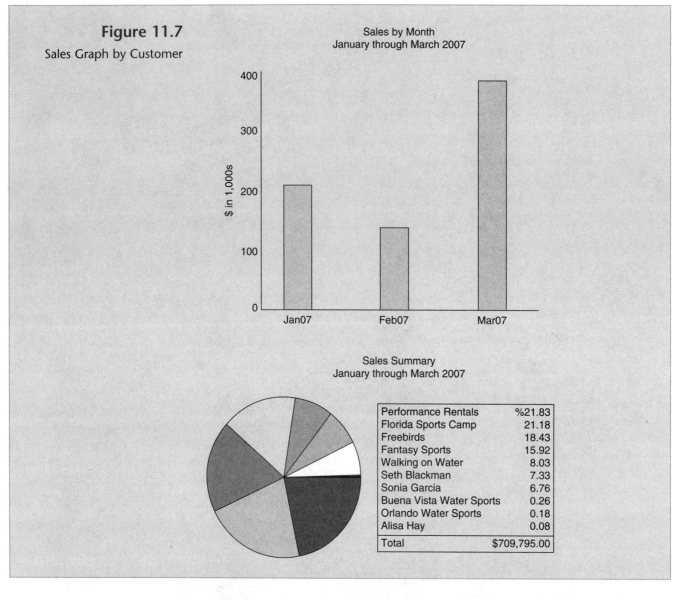

Figure 11.7

Sales Graph by Customer

Sales by Month
January through March 2007

Sales Summary
January through March 2007

Performance Rentals	%21.83
Florida Sports Camp	21.18
Freebirds	18.43
Fantasy Sports	15.92
Walking on Water	8.03
Seth Blackman	7.33
Sonia Garcia	6.76
Buena Vista Water Sports	0.26
Orlando Water Sports	0.18
Alisa Hay	0.08
Total	$709,795.00

Graphs such as these help managers interpret financial information, because they often reveal important relationships not obvious from the financial statements. For example, in Figure 11.7, sales growth by month is illustrated and the source of sales by customer is revealed. In this case, customer Performance Rentals represents almost 22% of sales for the three months.

Next you decide to produce a graph that illustrates Wild Water Sports's revenues (or "income," as QuickBooks calls it) and expenses.

To create an income and expense graph:

1　Click **Reports,** click **Company & Financial,** and then click **Income & Expense Graph.**

2 Click the **Dates** button and change the dates to read from **01/01/07** to **03/31/07** in the Change Graph Dates window. Then click **OK.**

3 Click the **By Account** button at the top of the screen and the **Expense** button at the bottom of the QuickInsight: Income and Expense Graph window, if they are not already selected.

4 Click **Print** from the button bar, and then click **Print** from the Print Graphs window. Your printed graph should look like Figure 11.8.

Trouble? Your vertical axis scale might be different, depending on the size of the figure you choose to view.

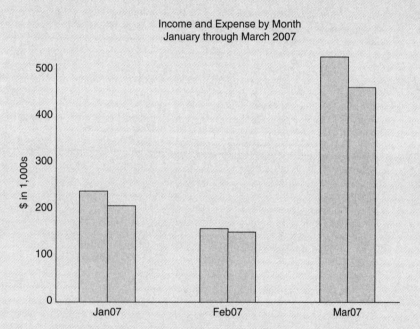

Figure 11.8

Income and Expense Graph

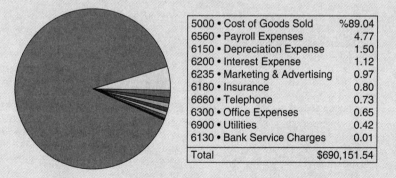

5 Close all windows.

These two graphs help to explain revenues and expenses, but they do not provide insight into the financial position of the company as of March 31.

"Does QuickBooks have similar graphing capabilities for items such as accounts receivable and accounts payable?" you ask.

"Yes," Karen responds. "In fact, we should probably create a graph for both accounts to demonstrate how current or noncurrent our receivables and payables are. QuickBooks can create a bar chart that illustrates aging for accounts receivable and then another for accounts payable, and simultaneously identify who owes us or who we owe, respectively, at any single time, such as March 31, 2007."

To create accounts receivable and accounts payable graphs:

1 Click **Reports,** click **Customers & Receivables,** and then click **Accounts Receivable Graph.**

2 Click the **Dates** button, and change the date to **03/31/07** in the Change Graph Dates window. Then click **OK.**

3 Click **Print** from the button bar, and then click **Print** from the Print Graphs window. Your printed graph should look like Figure 11.9.

Figure 11.9

Accounts Receivable Graph

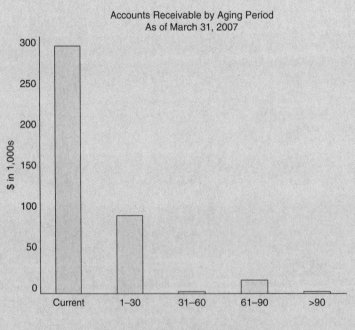

4 Click **Reports,** click **Vendors & Payables,** and then click **Accounts Payable Graph.**

5 Click the **Dates** button, and change the date to **03/31/07** in the Change Graph Dates window. Then click **OK.**

6 Click **Print** from the button bar, and then click **Print** from the Print Graphs window. Your printed graph should look like Figure 11.10.

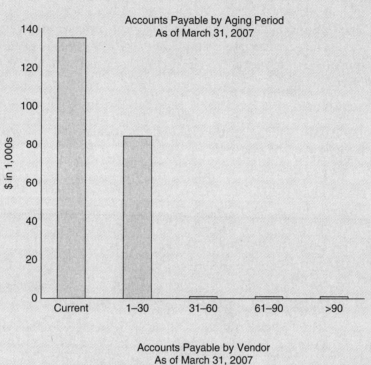

Figure 11.10

Accounts Payable Graph

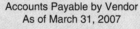

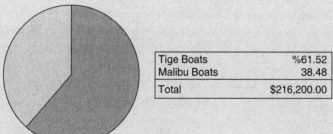

7 Close all windows.

When you show Donna these graphs, she comments that they will be very helpful. But she wants to see even more information derived from the financial statements—specifically, she wants to see detailed reports on sales, purchases, accounts receivable, accounts payable, and inventory.

Create Additional Detail Reports

With QuickBooks you can generate many supporting reports for the financial statements—what accountants consider traditional support in the form of schedules. Karen reads through QuickBooks Help and discovers two reports that QuickBooks generates that will help Donna—the Sales by Customer Summary and the Summary Sales by Item. Together you decide that the Sales by Customer Summary should identify sales for each month of the quarter so you can see to which customers you sold product or services. The Summary Sales by Item reports on the number of items sold, the average price of each item sold, and each item's related average cost. This report also identifies the gross margin (sales revenue minus cost of goods sold) amount for each item and summarizes the gross margin for all items sold during the period. Karen suggests that you produce this report on a monthly basis.

To create the Sales by Customer Summary and the Summary Sales by Item reports:

1 Click **Reports,** click **Sales,** and then click **Sales by Customer Summary.**

2 Change the report dates to read from **01/01/07** to **03/31/07.**

3 Click the **Collapse** button.

4 Select **Total** in the Sort By drop-down list, and then click the sort button to read Z – A so the report lists sales to customers from largest to smallest.

5 Select **Month** from the Columns drop-down edit box and then click **OK.**

6 Click **Print** from the button bar, and then click **Print** from the Print Reports window. Your printed report should look like Figure 11.11.

Figure 11.11

Sales by Customer

Wild Water Sports Ch 11
Sales by Customer Summary
January through March 2007

	Jan 07	Feb 07	Mar 07	TOTAL
Performance Rentals	78,750.00	75,000.00	1,215.00	154,965.00
Florida Sports Camp	71,575.00	0.00	78,750.00	150,325.00
Freebirds	845.00	0.00	130,000.00	130,845.00
Fantasy Sports	0.00	0.00	113,000.00	113,000.00
Walking on Water	0.00	57,000.00	0.00	57,000.00
Seth Blackman	52,000.00	0.00	0.00	52,000.00
Sonia Garcia	0.00	0.00	48,000.00	48,000.00
Buena Vista Water Sports	0.00	0.00	1,845.00	1,845.00
Orlando Water Sports	0.00	1,250.00	0.00	1,250.00
Alisa Hay	165.00	400.00	0.00	565.00
TOTAL	203,335.00	133,650.00	372,810.00	709,795.00

7 Click **Memorize.**

8 Type **Customized Sales by Customer Summary** in the Name text box, and then click **OK.**

9 Close the Sales by Customer Summary window.

10 Click **Reports, Sales,** and then click **Sales by Item Summary.**

11 Change the report dates to read from **01/01/07** to **03/31/07.**

12 Select **Total Only** from the Columns drop-down edit box.

13 Adjust the column width to view more of the report on your screen. You may need to scroll down the report to view items sold and total sales.

14 Click **Print** from the button bar, and then click **Print** from the Print Reports window. Your printed report should look like Figure 11.12.

Figure 11.12

Sales by Item

Wild Water Sports Ch 11
Sales by Item Summary
January through March 2007

	Qty	Amount	% of Sales	Avg Price	COGS	Avg COGS	Gross Margin	Gross Margin %
				Jan - Mar 07				
Inventory								
Air filter	1	35.00	0.0%	35.00	28.00	28.00	7.00	20.0%
Engine oil (quart)	9	45.00	0.0%	5.00	36.00	4.00	9.00	20.0%
Malibu Sportster LX	1	52,000.00	7.3%	52,000.00	41,600.00	41,600.00	10,400.00	20.0%
Malibu Sunscape LSV	3	195,000.00	27.5%	65,000.00	156,000.00	52,000.00	39,000.00	20.0%
Malibu Vride	2	96,000.00	13.5%	48,000.00	76,800.00	38,400.00	19,200.00	20.0%
Malibu WakeSetter VLX	1	57,000.00	8.0%	57,000.00	45,600.00	45,600.00	11,400.00	20.0%
Malibu WakeSetter XTI	1	70,000.00	9.9%	70,000.00	56,000.00	56,000.00	14,000.00	20.0%
MB B52 V23 Team Edition	1	75,000.00	10.6%	75,000.00	60,000.00	60,000.00	15,000.00	20.0%
Oil filter	2	30.00	0.0%	15.00	24.00	12.00	6.00	20.0%
Tige 22v	2	157,500.00	22.2%	78,750.00	126,000.00	63,000.00	31,500.00	20.0%
Tune up parts	2	500.00	0.1%	250.00	400.00	200.00	100.00	20.0%
Total Inventory		703,110.00	99.1%		562,488.00		140,622.00	20.0%
Service								
20 Hour Service Check	5	875.00	0.1%	175.00				
Cleaning	6	450.00	0.1%	75.00				
Engine Service	4	500.00	0.1%	125.00				
Engine Tune Up	14	3,500.00	0.5%	250.00				
Painting & body Repairs	17	1,360.00	0.2%	80.00				
Total Service		6,685.00	0.9%					
TOTAL		709,795.00	100.0%					

15 Click **Memorize.**

16 Type **Customized Sales by Item Summary** in the Name text box and then click **OK.**

17 Close the Sales by Item Summary window.

Karen tells you that two additional reports are commonly prepared to support the balance sheet: an accounts receivable aging and an accounts payable aging. QuickBooks can easily generate these reports.

To create Accounts Receivable and an Accounts Payable Aging reports:

1 Click **Reports,** click **Customers & Receivables,** and then click **A/R Aging Summary.**

2 Change the report date to read **03/31/07,** and then click **Refresh.**

3 Click the **Collapse** button.

4 Click the **Print** button in the button bar, and then click **Print** in the Print Reports window.

5 Choose a **Portrait** orientation.

6 The report shown in Figure 11.13 appears. Examine this report.

Figure 11.13

A/R Aging Summary

Wild Water Sports Ch 11
A/R Aging Summary
As of March 31, 2007

	Current	1 - 30	31 - 60	61 - 90	> 90	TOTAL
Fantasy Sports	0.00	92,095.00	0.00	0.00	0.00	92,095.00
Florida Sports Camp	83,868.75	0.00	0.00	0.00	0.00	83,868.75
Freebirds	138,450.00	0.00	0.00	0.00	0.00	138,450.00
Performance Rentals	1,293.98	0.00	0.00	0.00	0.00	1,293.98
Spirit Adventures	69,225.00	0.00	0.00	0.00	0.00	69,225.00
Walking on Water	0.00	0.00	0.00	15,000.00	0.00	15,000.00
TOTAL	292,837.73	92,095.00	0.00	15,000.00	0.00	399,932.73

7 Click **Memorize.**

8 Type **Customized A/R Aging Summary** in the Name text box, and then click **OK.**

9 Close the A/R Aging Summary window.

10 Click **Reports,** click **Vendors & Payables,** and then click **A/P Aging Summary.**

11 Change the report date to read **03/31/07,** and then click **Refresh.**

12 Click the **Collapse** button.

13 Click the **Print** button in the button bar, and then click **Print** in the Print Reports window.

14 Choose a **Portrait** orientation.

15 The report shown in Figure 11.14 appears. Examine this report.

Figure 11.14

A/P Aging Summary

Wild Water Sports Ch 11
A/P Aging Summary
As of March 31, 2007

	Current	1 - 30	31 - 60	61 - 90	> 90	TOTAL
Malibu Boats	0.00	83,200.00	0.00	0.00	0.00	83,200.00
Tige Boats	133,000.00	0.00	0.00	0.00	0.00	133,000.00
TOTAL	133,000.00	83,200.00	0.00	0.00	0.00	216,200.00

16 Click **Memorize.**

17 Type **Customized A/P Aging Summary** in the Name text box, and then click **OK.**

18 Close the A/P Aging Summary window.

Karen forwards these detail reports to Donna who can now follow up on the Walking on Water outstanding accounts receivable of $15,000 which she believes is left over from when they bought the company January 1. She also plans to follow up on the Fantasy Sports receivable and make sure she pays the Malibu Boats accounts payable soon.

Exporting Reports to Excel

Karen explains that in QuickBooks you can export any reports you create to Microsoft's Excel spreadsheet program.

"Why export to Microsoft Excel when QuickBooks gives us so many report options?" you ask.

Karen explains that, occasionally, she may need to change a report's appearance or contents in ways that are not available within QuickBooks. Since the changes you make in Excel do not affect your QuickBooks data, you are free to customize a report as needed or even change report data to run "what if" scenarios.

Karen reads through QuickBooks Help and discovers that exporting a report to Excel is as simple as clicking a new button on the report's button bar. She suggests the two of you experiment with this feature by exporting an income statement you have already memorized.

To export a previously memorized report:

1 Open the Customized Income Statement that you previously memorized.

2 Click the **Export** button on the Report button bar to display the Export Report window shown in Figure 11.15.

3 Uncheck the box that adds a new worksheet with Excel tips.

4 Click the **Advanced** tab in the Export Report window to view advanced options such as formatting and printing, as shown in Figure 11.16.

5 Make sure the options checked in the Advanced Options window are the same as those shown in Figure 11.16.

6 Now click **Export** in the Export Report window. Your Excel program will now be opened and the report exported into Excel.

Figure 11.15

Exporting a Report

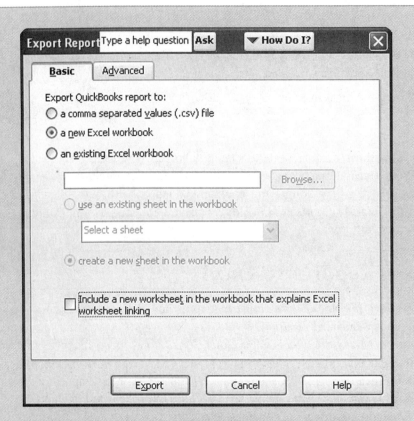

Figure 11.16

Advanced Options for
Exporting a Report to Excel

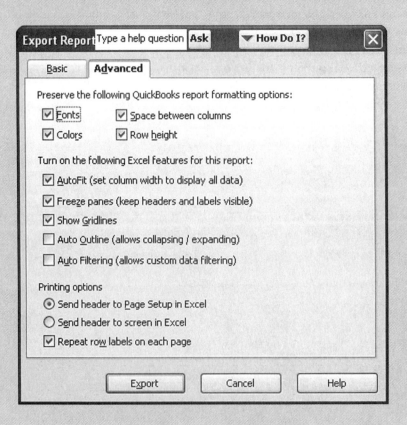

Trouble? To export reports to Excel you must have Microsoft Excel '97 or higher installed on your computer.

7 Select cell **F10** in the report just exported. Note that the export process has created not only a spreadsheet with values, but also one with formulas, as shown in Figure 11.17.

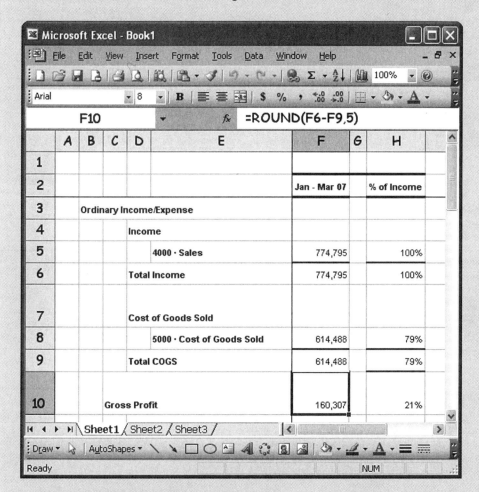

Figure 11.17
Exported Excel Report

8 Click **File** in Excel, and then click **Print Preview.** Note the header information is that which you modified in QuickBooks previously.

9 Click **Setup** and then click the **Sheet** tab in the Page Setup window. Place a check mark in the **Gridlines** and **Row and column headings** checkboxes. (This will enable the printing of gridlines and row and column headings.)

10 Click the **Page** tab, click the **Fit to:** option button to scale printing to one page wide and one page tall, and then click **OK.**

11 Click **Print** in the Excel Print Preview window, and then click **OK** in the Print window to print the Excel document you just created. Your spreadsheet should look like Figure 11.18.

Figure 11.18

Printed Excel Report

Wild Water Sports Ch 11
Income Statement
for the three months ended March 31, 2007

	A	B	C	D	E	F	G	H
1								
2						Jan - Mar 07		% of Income
3			Ordinary Income/Expense					
4				Income				
5					4000 · Sales	774,795		100%
6				Total Income		774,795		100%
7				Cost of Goods Sold				
8					5000 · Cost of Goods Sold	614,488		79%
9				Total COGS		614,488		79%
10			Gross Profit			160,307		21%
11				Expense				
12					6560 · Payroll Expenses	32,946		4%
13					6150 · Depreciation Expense	10,333		1%
14					6200 · Interest Expense	7,720		1%
15					6235 · Marketing & Advertising	6,700		1%
16					6180 · Insurance	5,500		1%
17					6660 · Telephone	5,020		1%
18					6300 · Office Expenses	4,500		1%
19					6900 · Utilities	2,870		0%
20					6130 · Bank Service Charges	75		0%
21				Total Expense		75,664		10%
22			Net Ordinary Income			84,643		11%
23			Other Income/Expense					
24				Other Income				
25					7030 · Other Income	3,000		0%
26					7010 · Interest Income	2,015		0%
27				Total Other Income		5,015		1%
28			Net Other Income			5,015		1%
29	Net Income					89,658		12%

12 Click **File** in Excel, and then **Exit** to quit the Excel program.

13 Click **No** to not save the spreadsheet since it will no longer be used.

14 Close all windows in QuickBooks.

End Note

You've completed the reports for Donna and decide to deliver them to her office. After quickly skimming each report, she compliments you both on your fine work and you turn to walk back to your office.

As you walk back to your office, you comment, "That's the first time I've ever created financial statements without using debits and credits. How is that possible?"

"All the debits and credits are done for you," Karen explains. "Tomorrow I'll show you that QuickBooks, in fact, still keeps data in a debit and credit format and can provide the traditional general ledger, journal entries, and trial balance procedures you are more familiar with."

Chapter 11 Questions

1 Explain how you can use QuickBooks to modify any report.

2 What are the optional columns available in the Modify Report window when you create a balance sheet?

3 What time periods are available for the columns of a balance sheet?

4 What options are available in the Fonts & Numbers tab for a balance sheet?

5 How do you resize a report that would normally print on two pages to one page?

6 When you create a balance sheet, what result does clicking the Collapse button have?

7 What different graphs are available in QuickBooks?

8 Discuss why percentage changes identified in the budgeted vs. actual reports need to be interpreted carefully.

9 Describe the information available in the accounts receivable and accounts payable aging reports.

10 Describe the information available in the inventory stocks status report by item.

Chapter 11 Assignments

1 *Adding More Information to Wild Water Sports*

merchandising

Restore the file Wild Water Sports Ch 11A.qbb found on the text CD or downloaded from the text website, and then create and print the following reports, graphs, or spreadsheets. (***Hint:*** Be sure to use the memorized reports you created before where applicable and just change the dates as appropriate.)

a. Collapsed Income Statement for the four months ended 4/30/07 including a % of income column, without cents, titled "Income Statement," with a left page layout, a subtitle "for the four months ended April 30, 2007," and sorted by total from largest to smallest amount.

b. Collapsed Balance Sheet as of 4/30/07 with a % of column, without cents, and with a left page layout.

c. Sales Graph by Item for the four-month period ended 4/30/07.

d. Sales Graph by Customer for the four-month period ended 4/30/07.

e. Income and Expense Graph for the four-month period ended 4/30/07.

f. Accounts Receivable Graph as of 4/30/07.

g. Accounts Payable Graph as of 4/30/07.

h. Collapsed Sales by Customer Summary Report for the four-month period ended 4/30/07 sorted by total from largest to smallest amount with month columns.

i. Sales by Item Summary Report for the four-month period ended 4/30/07 where columns display total only.

j. Collapsed Accounts Receivable Aging Summary Report as of 4/30/07.

k. Collapsed Accounts Payable Aging Summary Report as of 4/30/07.

l. Export item (a) above to Excel, and then print the Excel worksheet with gridlines and row and column headers showing.

2 *Adding More Information to Central Coast Cellular*

In Chapter 10, you added some budget information to your QuickBooks file for Central Coast Cellular (CCC), a cellular phone sales, phone rental, and consulting company. Make a copy of that file in Windows Explorer and use that file to create the following. (**Hint:** Be sure to use the memorized reports as appropriate.)

merchandising

a. Collapsed Income Statement for the month ended 1/31/03 including a % of income column, without cents, titled "Income Statement," with a left page layout, a sub title "January 2003," and sorted by total from largest to smallest amount.

b. Collapsed Balance Sheet as of 1/31/03 with a % of column, without cents, and with a left page layout.

c. Sales Graph by Item for the month ended 1/31/03.

d. Sales Graph by Customer for the month ended 1/31/03.

e. Income and Expense Graph for the month ended 1/31/03.

f. Accounts Receivable Graph as of 1/31/03.

g. Accounts Payable Graph as of 1/31/03.

h. Collapsed Sales by Customer Summary Report for the month ended 1/31/03 sorted by total from largest to smallest amount with month columns.

i. Sales by Item Summary Report for the month ended 1/31/03 where columns display total only.

j. Collapsed Accounts Receivable Aging Summary Report as of 1/31/03.

    k. Collapsed Accounts Payable Aging Summary Report as of 1/31/03.

    l. Export item (a) above to Excel, and then print the Excel worksheet with gridlines and row and column headers showing.

3   *Using the South-Western Home Page for More Assignments or Cases*

Go to the home page for this textbook at **www.thomsonedu.com/accounting/owen.** Click **Additional Problem Sets,** and then select the **Chapter 11** section, and complete the problem(s) that your instructor assigns.

Chapter 11 Case Problem 1:
ALOHA PROPERTY MANAGEMENT

service

In Chapter 10, you modified your QuickBooks file for Aloha Property Management. Make a copy of that file in Windows Explorer, and use that file to create the following. (*Hint:* Be sure to use the memorized reports as appropriate.)

    a. Collapsed Income Statement for the two months ended 2/29/08 including a % of income column, without cents, titled "Income Statement," with a left page layout, a subtitle "for the two months ended February 29, 2008," and sorted by total from largest to smallest amount.

    b. Collapsed Balance Sheet as of 2/29/08 with a % of column, without cents, and with a left page layout.

    c. Sales Graph by Item for the two-month period ended 2/29/08.

    d. Sales Graph by Customer for the two-month period ended 2/29/08.

    e. Income and Expense Graph for the two-month period ended 2/29/08.

    f. Accounts Receivable Graph as of 2/29/08.

    g. Accounts Payable Graph as of 2/29/08.

    h. Collapsed Sales by Customer Summary Report for the two-month period ended 2/29/08 sorted by total from largest to smallest amount with month columns.

    i. Sales by Item Summary Report for the two-month period ended 2/29/08 where columns display total only.

    j. Collapsed Accounts Receivable Aging Summary Report as of 2/29/08.

    k. Collapsed Accounts Payable Aging Summary Report as of 2/29/08.

    l. Export item (a) above to Excel, and then print the Excel worksheet with gridlines and row and column headers showing.

Chapter 11 Case Problem 2:
OCEAN VIEW FLOWERS

merchandising

In Chapter 10, you modified your QuickBooks file for Ocean View Flowers, a wholesale flower distributor. Make a copy of that file in Windows Explorer, and use that file to create the following. (***Hint:*** Be sure to use the memorized reports as appropriate.)

a. Collapsed Income Statement for the two months ended 2/29/08 including a % of income column, without cents, titled "Income Statement," with a left page layout, a subtitle "for the two months ended February 29, 2008," and sorted by total from largest to smallest amount.

b. Collapsed Balance Sheet as of 2/29/08 with a % of column, without cents, and with a left page layout.

c. Sales Graph by Item for the two-month period ended 2/29/08.

d. Sales Graph by Customer for the two-month period ended 2/29/08.

e. Income and Expense Graph for the two-month period ended 2/29/08.

f. Accounts Receivable Graph as of 2/29/08.

g. Accounts Payable Graph as of 2/29/08.

h. Collapsed Sales by Customer Summary Report for the two-month period ended 2/29/08 sorted by total from largest to smallest amount with month columns.

i. Sales by Item Summary Report for the two month period ended 2/29/08 where columns display total only.

j. Collapsed Accounts Receivable Aging Summary Report as of 2/29/08.

k. Collapsed Accounts Payable Aging Summary Report as of 2/29/08.

l. Export item (a) above to Excel, and then print the Excel worksheet with gridlines and row and column headers showing.

Comprehensive Problems

Comprehensive Problem 1: SPORTS CITY

Restore the file Sports City.qbb found on the text CD or downloaded from the text website, and then create and print the following reports, graphs, or spreadsheets. (***Hint:*** Be sure to use the memorized reports you created before where applicable and just change the dates as appropriate.)

Chronological List of Business Transactions

Date	Transaction
4/16	Received a bill from Office Max for $250 for office supplies purchased on account (record as Supplies: Office, an expense, terms: due on receipt).
4/17	Received items and entered a bill from Nike for a previously recorded purchase order 1 (terms: due on receipt).
4/18	Received items and entered a bill from Wilson Sporting Goods for a previously recorded purchase order 2 (terms: due on receipt).
4/19	Hired a new employee, Anne Franks, 112 East Fir #3, Lompoc, CA 93436, a single woman, Social Security number 233-89-4232. She will earn an hourly wage of $8.00, be paid semi-monthly like all employees, and is subject to all payroll taxes including the training tax.
4/20	Received a $400 payment on account from Cabrillo High School, which is grouped with other undeposited funds.
4/21	Invoiced Buena Vista Elementary for 100 shirts and 5 footballs.
4/22	Received a $600 payment on account from Lompoc High School, which is also grouped with other undeposited funds.
4/24	Borrowed $10,000 from Mid-State Bank with a short-term note payable.
4/25	Paid all bills due by 4/30/04.
4/29	Deposited by mail all previously received but undeposited payments, totaling $1,000, to Mid-State Bank.
4/30	Paid all employees for the pay period 4/16 – 4/30. Ms. Franks worked 75 hours during this period. (See tax information table below.)

	Sam Snead	Kelly Flowers	Anne Franks
Gross pay	$1,458.33	$1,250.00	$600.00
Federal withholding	−244.00	−147.00	−73.00
Social Security employee	−90.41	−77.50	−37.20
Social Security employer	90.41	77.50	37.20
Medicare employee	−21.14	−18.12	−8.70
Medicare employer	21.14	18.12	8.70
CA—withholding	−57.39	−40.72	−7.66
CA—disability employee	−7.29	−6.25	−3.00
CA—training tax	1.46	1.25	0.60
Federal unemployment	11.66	10.00	4.80
CA—unemployment	0.73	0.62	0.30
Check amount	1,038.11	960.41	470.44

Date	Transaction
4/30	Recorded depreciation of $2,000 on furniture & fixtures.
4/30	Recorded the expiration of $3,000 in prepaid rent.
4/30	Reclassified the advance payment made by Arroyo Grande High School to unearned revenue.
4/30	Reconciled the bank account. The ending bank balance per the statement is $5,333.52. The bank charged a $40 service charge. Checks for the April 30 payroll do not appear on the statement, nor does the $1,000 deposited by mail on April 30.

Budget information for April through June 2004 is as follows:

Account	April 04	Following
Sales	$10,000	15% increase each month thereafter
Cost of sales	$6,000	60% of sales
Depreciation	$2,000	Constant each month thereafter
Payroll	$6,500	$500 increase each month thereafter
Rent	$3,000	Constant each month thereafter
Telephone	$100	5% increase each month thereafter
Utilities	$200	5% increase each month thereafter

Create, memorize and print the following reports:

a. Transactions List by Date for April 2004 in landscape orientation.

b. Collapsed Profit and Loss Statement for April 2004 with a % of income column.

c. Collapsed Balance Sheet as of 4/30/04 with a % of column.

d. Statement of Cash Flows for April 2004.

e. Collapsed Profit and Loss Budget vs. Actual for April 2004.

f. Collapsed Profit and Loss Budget Overview for April 2004 through June 2004.

g. Sales by Customer Summary Report for the month ended 4/30/04 sorted by total from largest to smallest amount with month columns.

h. Sales by Item Summary Report for the month ended 4/30/04 sorted by total from largest to smallest amount with total only columns in landscape orientation.

i. Accounts Receivable Aging Summary Report as of 4/30/04.

j. Accounts Payable Aging Summary Report as of 4/30/04.

k. Export the Balance Sheet created above to Excel, and then print the Excel worksheet with gridlines and row and column headers.

Comprehensive Problem 2: PACIFIC BREW

This is a continuation of the Pacific Brew, Inc., comprehensive problem from Chapter 7. Make a copy of the QuickBooks file you created for Pacific Brew in Chapter 7. Record the following business transactions in chronological order (remember, dates are in the month of January 2006). Then create, memorize, and print the reports specified below.

merchandising

Chronological List of Business Transactions

Date	Transaction
1/17	Received items and entered a bill from purchase order 1003 to Lost Coast.
1/17	Received a bill from Staples for $2,500 of office supplies purchased on account terms net 15. These supplies will be used over the next six months; thus, you will need to create an Office Supplies (Current Asset) account.

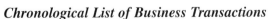

Date	Transaction
1/17	Using purchase order 1004, ordered 1,000 of item 402, 1,500 of item 403, and 2,000 of item 404 for immediate delivery, terms: net 15 from Lost Coast.
1/17	Using purchase order 1005, ordered 750 each of items 302, 303, 304, and 305 for immediate delivery, terms: net 30 from Mad River.
1/18	The manager believes the company charges too little for its products and increases all product prices 50%. (Use QuickBooks Help to find out how to increase sales prices of items by a percentage.)
1/19	Using purchase order 1006, ordered 500 of each items 502, 506, and 507 for immediate delivery, terms: net 15 from Humboldt.
1/20	Received and shipped an order to Bon Jovi's for 200 units of item 302, 150 units of item 303, and 100 units of item 507. Invoice number 7001 was generated to bill the customer on net 15 terms. (Be sure to use the Intiut product invoice form to record this transaction.)
1/20	Received and shipped an order to Ocean Grove for 100 units each of items 302, 304, and 305. Invoice number 7002 was generated to bill the customer on net 15 terms.
1/23	Received and shipped an order to Avalon Bistro for 150 units each of items 505, 506, and 507. Invoice number 7003 was generated to bill the customer on net 30 terms.
1/24	Received items and entered a bill from purchase order 1004 to Lost Coast.
1/24	Received a bill from Verizon for telephone services for the month of January in the amount of $500, terms: due on receipt.
1/24	Received a bill from the City of Arcata for electrical services for the month of January in the amount of $1,500, terms: due on receipt.
1/25	Received payment on account from Bon Jovi's of $4,575 on invoice 7001, which will be deposited later in the week.
1/26	Received an advance on future orders from River House in the amount of $1,200, which will be deposited later in the week.
1/27	Deposit checks received earlier in the week to Wells Fargo.
1/30	Received items and entered a bill from purchase order 1005 to Mad River.
1/30	Paid bills from Verizon, City of Arcata, and Staples for a total of $4,500, assigning check numbers 110, 111, and 112, respectively.
1/30	Received and shipped an order (5007) to Hole in the Wall for 250 units each of items 303, 305, and 404. Payment of $7,032.50 was deposited and mailed to Wells Fargo Bank that same day.
1/30	Paid employees. Duarte worked 83 hours, and Lopez worked 79 hours during the period. See tax information in the table below.

Tax/Withholding	Duarte	Lopez	Patrick
Gross pay	$913.00	$948.00	$2,083.33
Federal withholding	−125.08	−129.88	−285.42
Social Security employee	−56.61	−58.78	−129.17
Medicare employee	−13.24	−13.75	−30.21
CA—withholding	−50.22	−52.14	−114.58
CA—disability	−4.57	−4.74	−10.42
CA—employment training tax	0.91	0.95	2.08
Social Security employer	56.61	58.78	129.17
Medicare company	13.24	13.75	30.21
Federal unemployment	7.30	7.58	16.67
CA—company unemployment	27.39	28.44	62.50
Check amount	663.28	688.74	1,513.53

Date	Transaction
1/31	Recorded depreciation of $500 on equipment and $300 on furniture and fixtures for the month with journal entry 1.
1/31	Recorded the use of office supplies of $400 with journal entry 2.
1/31	Reclassified payment from River House to unearned revenue with journal entry 3.
1/31	Accrued interest expense on short-term investments of $2,000 with journal entry 4.
1/31	Accrued interest expense on long-term note payable of $2,600 with journal entry 5.
1/31	Reconciled the Wells Fargo bank account.
1/31	Budget information for January through March is as follows. Consulting revenue is expected to remain constant at $15,000 per month. Sales of $20,000 are expected in January, increasing $5,000 each month thereafter. Cost of goods sold of $15,000 is expected in January, increasing $2,500 each month thereafter. Depreciation, interest, rent, and office supplies expenses are expected to remain constant at $1,000, $2,000, $2,500, and $500, respectively. Telephone expenses of $450 are budgeted for January and are expected to increase $50 each month thereafter. Payroll expenses are budgeted at $8,500 for January and February and then $10,000 for March. Electric expenses are budgeted at $1,200 for January and are expected to increase by 5% each month thereafter. Interest income of $1,500 is expected each month.

Create, memorize, and print the following reports:

a. Transactions List by Date for January 2006 in landscape orientation.

b. Collapsed Profit and Loss Statement for January 2006 with a % of income column with a right layout and no cents.

c. Collapsed Balance Sheet as of 1/30/06 with a % of column with a right layout and no cents.

d. Statement of Cash Flows for January 2006 with a right layout and no cents.

e. Collapsed Profit and Loss Budget vs. Actual for January 2006 with no cents.

f. Collapsed Profit and Loss Budget Overview for January 2006 through March 2006 with no cents.

g. Sales by Customer Summary Report for the month ended 1/30/06 sorted by total from largest to smallest amount with month columns.

h. Sales by Item Summary Report for the month ended 1/30/06 sorted by total from largest to smallest amount with total only columns in landscape orientation.

i. Accounts Receivable Aging Summary Report as of 1/30/06.

j. Accounts Payable Aging Summary Report as of 1/30/06.

k. Export the income statement created above to Excel, and then print the Excel worksheet with gridlines and row and column headers.

merchandising

Comprehensive Problem 3: SUNSET SPAS

This is a continuation of the Sunset Spas, Inc., comprehensive problem from Chapter 7. Make a copy of the QuickBooks file you created for Sunset in Chapter 7. Record the following business transactions in chronological order (remember dates are in the month of January 2007). Then create, memorize, and print the reports specified on page 317.

Chronological List of Business Transactions

Date	Transaction
1/17	Paid $18,000 in liability insurance for the year to Hartford Insurance using check 110. (**Hint:** Record this in a new account called Prepaid Insurance and Other Current Assets.)
1/17	Received a bill from Staples (an office supply store) for $500 in office supplies purchased on account. Terms are net 30. (Quick Add this vendor.)
1/17	Using purchase order 5003, ordered one each of items 301, 302, and 303 for immediate delivery, terms: net 30, from Cal Spas.
1/18	Sold two of item 302 to a new customer Landmark Landscaping (Attn: Loriel Angel 8500 Ridgefield Place, San Diego, CA 92129) with six hours of installation (item 100) on sales invoice 10001 payment terms net 15.
1/19	Sold four of item 202 and one of item 302 to Marriott Hotels with 15 hours of installation on sales invoice 10002 payment terms net 15. Marriott Hotels had paid an advance towards future sales on 1/16/07. Apply any remaining credit to this invoice when prompted.
1/20	Hired a new employee, Walton Perez, 530 Miramar Rd. Apt 230, San Diego, CA 92145, a single man, Social Security number 323-99-2394. He will earn an hourly wage of $9.00, be paid semi-monthly, and is subject to all payroll taxes. He will start work 2/1/07.
1/21	Purchased tools and equipment for installation and support of spa services from Outlet Tool Supply for $25,000 on account with 30-day terms. (Record as equipment.)
1/22	Deposited a $3,500 check from a new customer, Kristen's Spa Resort, for work to be performed next month. (Instead of recording this as a customer payment, record this as a deposit directly into the checking account coming from a new other current liability account: Unearned Revenue.)
1/23	Received a $23,000 bill from the City of San Diego for permits, licenses, and fees payable with terms net 15.
1/24	Sold six of item 203 to Pam's Designs with 18 hours of installation on sales invoice 10003, payment terms net 15.
1/25	Received a $1,400 bill from Verizon for telephone installation and services terms net 15. (Record as telephone expense.)
1/26	Took delivery of a shipment from Cal Spas (our PO 5003). All items were received. (Terms are net 30.)
1/27	Received $5,000 payment on account from Landmark Landscaping, which was deposited into the checking account.
1/30	Paid two bills in full: City of San Diego and Verizon using Check Nos. 111 and 112, respectively.
1/31	Paid employees. Sanchez worked 84 hours, and Lee worked 67 hours during the period. Checks are to be handwritten starting with Check No. 113. See tax information in the table on the next page.

Date	Transaction
1/31	Recorded the expiration of one month's prepaid insurance costs to the liability insurance expense account on journal entry 1.
1/31	Recorded depreciation expense of $1,750 on journal entry 2 ($1,500 on equipment, $250 on furniture). (***Hint:*** You will need to establish two new accumulated depreciation accounts. Set them up so they display below cost on the balance sheet.)
1/31	Accrued interest expense on note payable for $1,000 on journal entry 3. (***Hint:*** Create a new other current liability account titled "Accrued Interest Payable.")
1/31	Accrued interest income on short-term investments for $75 on journal entry 4.
1/31	Reconciled the bank account. There were no bank service charges. The bank statement balance was $34,793.43 at 1/31/07. Check Nos. 104, 113, 114, and 115 had not been paid according to the bank statement. One deposit, made on 1/27/07 for $5,000, was not reflected on the bank statement.
1/31	Budget information for January through March is as follows: Merchandise Sales of $170,000 are expected in January, increasing $10,000 per month thereafter. Service sales of $10,000 are expected in January, increasing $1,000 per month thereafter. Cost of goods sold are expected to be 75% of merchandise sales. Depreciation, insurance, interest, supplies, rent, and telephone are expected to remain constant at $1,800, $1,500, $1,000, $500, $3,000, and $1,500, respectively. A one-time license and permit fee of $20,000 was expected for January. Payroll expenses are estimated at $10,000 per month.

Pay/Tax/Withholding	Christopher	Sanchez	Lee
Hours	n/a	84	67
Rate	$ 60,000.00	$ 13.00	$ 12.00
Gross pay	2,500.00	1,092.00	804.00
Federal withholding	−342.50	−149.60	−110.15
Social Security employee	−155.00	−67.70	−49.85
Medicare employee	−36.25	−15.83	−11.66
CA—withholding	−137.50	−60.06	−44.22
CA—disability	−12.50	−5.46	−4.02
CA—employment training tax	2.50	1.09	0.80
Social Security employer	155.00	67.70	49.85
Medicare company	36.25	15.83	11.66
Federal unemployment	20.00	8.74	6.43
CA—unemployment	6.25	2.73	2.01
Check amount	1,816.25	793.35	584.10

Create, memorize and print the following reports:

a. Transactions List by Date for January 2007 in landscape orientation.

b. Collapsed Profit and Loss Statement for January 2007 with a % of income column, without cents, and centered.

c. Collapsed Balance Sheet as of 1/30/07 with a % of column, without cents, and centered.

d. Statement of Cash Flows for January 2007 without cents and centered.

e. Bank Reconciliation Summary for January 2007 without cents and centered.

f. Collapsed Profit and Loss Budget vs. Actual for January 2007 without cents and centered.

g. Collapsed Profit and Loss Budget Overview for January 2007 through March 2007 without cents and centered.

h. Sales by Customer Summary Report for the month ended 1/30/07 sorted by total from largest to smallest amount with total only columns centered and without cents.

i. Sales by Item Summary Report for the month ended 1/30/07 sorted by total from largest to smallest amount with total only columns in landscape orientation centered and without cents.

j. Accounts Receivable Aging Summary Report as of 1/30/07.

k. Accounts Payable Aging Summary Report as of 1/30/07.

l. Export the Income Statement created above to Excel, and then print the Excel worksheet with gridlines and row and column headers.

Payroll Taxes

Learning Objectives

In this appendix, you will:

- Calculate federal income tax withholding
- Calculate Social Security and Medicare taxes
- Calculate federal unemployment taxes
- Learn about state income and unemployment taxes

Overview

Throughout this text, you have been provided information for employee payroll tax withholding and employer payroll tax expenses. QuickBooks has the ability to calculate each of these for you; however, they charge you an annual fee to do so. Some businesses will find this service very valuable and worth the cost, and some will not. Payroll tax computations are not straightforward. They are, in fact, quite convoluted and dependent on all sorts of exceptions and rules. For example, federal income tax withholding is dependent on an employee's income, whether they are being paid weekly, biweekly, semi-monthly, monthly, etc., the number of exemptions they claim, and their filing status: married, single, head of household, etc.

This appendix is designed to provide you a basic overview of the payroll tax conundrum and is focused on federal taxes only, as each state has their own rules for income tax withholding, unemployment, etc.

Federal Income Tax Withholding

As previously mentioned, federal income tax withholding is dependent on an employee's income, whether they are being paid weekly, biweekly, semi-monthly, monthly, etc., the number of exemptions they claim, and their filing status: married, single, head of household, etc. Guiding employers in this regard is Circular E (Employer's Tax Guide), which can be found online at the Internal Revenue Service website: **http://www.irs.gov/pub/irs-pdf/p15.pdf.**

The IRS provides tables in this document to compute the specific amount to be withheld from each employee. It also provides a percentage method, which is much easier to produce for our purposes. Employees must supply employers with payroll tax information each year such as their filing status: married, single, head of household, and the number of exemptions they are claiming.

The steps necessary for computation of an employee's federal income tax withholding are as follows:

1 Determine the frequency of wage payments: weekly, biweekly, semi-monthly, monthly, etc.

2 Determine the employee's filing status.

3 Based on the above, choose the appropriate table for Percentage Method of Withholding found in Figure A1.1.

Figure A1.1

Tables for Percentage Method of Withholding

Tables for Percentage Method of Withholding
(For Wages Paid in 2006)

TABLE 1—WEEKLY Payroll Period

(a) SINGLE person (including head of household)—

If the amount of wages (after subtracting withholding allowances) is: The amount of income tax to withhold is:

Not over $51 . . . . . $0

Over—	But not over—		of excess over—
$51	—$192 . .	10%	—$51
$192	—$620 . .	$14.10 plus 15%	—$192
$620	—$1,409 . .	$78.30 plus 25%	—$620
$1,409	—$3,013 . .	$275.55 plus 28%	—$1,409
$3,013	—$6,508 . .	$724.67 plus 33%	—$3,013
$6,508	. . . . . .	$1,878.02 plus 35%	—$6,508

(b) MARRIED person—

If the amount of wages (after subtracting withholding allowances) is: The amount of income tax to withhold is:

Not over $154 . . . . . $0

Over—	But not over—		of excess over—
$154	—$440 . .	10%	—$154
$440	—$1,308 . .	$28.60 plus 15%	—$440
$1,308	—$2,440 . .	$158.80 plus 25%	—$1,308
$2,440	—$3,759 . .	$441.80 plus 28%	—$2,440
$3,759	—$6,607 . .	$811.12 plus 33%	—$3,759
$6,607	. . . . . .	$1,750.96 plus 35%	—$6,607

TABLE 2—BIWEEKLY Payroll Period

(a) SINGLE person (including head of household)—

If the amount of wages (after subtracting withholding allowances) is: The amount of income tax to withhold is:

Not over $102 . . . . . $0

Over—	But not over—		of excess over—
$102	—$385 . .	10%	—$102
$385	—$1,240 . .	$28.30 plus 15%	—$385
$1,240	—$2,817 . .	$156.55 plus 25%	—$1,240
$2,817	—$6,025 . .	$550.80 plus 28%	—$2,817
$6,025	—$13,015 . .	$1,449.04 plus 33%	—$6,025
$13,015	. . . . . .	$3,755.74 plus 35%	—$13,015

(b) MARRIED person—

If the amount of wages (after subtracting withholding allowances) is: The amount of income tax to withhold is:

Not over $308 . . . . . $0

Over—	But not over—		of excess over—
$308	—$881 . .	10%	—$308
$881	—$2,617 . .	$57.30 plus 15%	—$881
$2,617	—$4,881 . .	$317.70 plus 25%	—$2,617
$4,881	—$7,517 . .	$883.70 plus 28%	—$4,881
$7,517	—$13,213 . .	$1,621.78 plus 33%	—$7,517
$13,213	. . . . . .	$3,501.46 plus 35%	—$13,213

Figure A1.1

(*Continued*)

TABLE 3—SEMIMONTHLY Payroll Period

(a) SINGLE person (including head of household)—

If the amount of wages (after subtracting withholding allowances) is: The amount of income tax to withhold is:

Not over $110 . . . . $0

Over—	But not over—		of excess over—
$110	—$417 . .	10%	—$110
$417	—$1,343 . .	$30.70 plus 15%	—$417
$1,343	—$3,052 . .	$169.60 plus 25%	—$1,343
$3,052	—$6,527 . .	$596.85 plus 28%	—$3,052
$6,527	—$14,100 . .	$1,569.85 plus 33%	—$6,527
$14,100	. . . . . .	$4,068.94 plus 35%	—$14,100

(b) MARRIED person—

If the amount of wages (after subtracting withholding allowances) is: The amount of income tax to withhold is:

Not over $333 . . . . $0

Over—	But not over—		of excess over—
$333	—$954 . .	10%	—$333
$954	—$2,835 . .	$62.10 plus 15%	—$954
$2,835	—$5,288 . .	$344.25 plus 25%	—$2,835
$5,288	—$8,144 . .	$957.50 plus 28%	—$5,288
$8,144	—$14,315 . .	$1,757.18 plus 33%	—$8,144
$14,315	. . . . . .	$3,793.61 plus 35%	—$14,315

TABLE 4—MONTHLY Payroll Period

(a) SINGLE person (including head of household)—

If the amount of wages (after subtracting withholding allowances) is: The amount of income tax to withhold is:

Not over $221 . . . . $0

Over—	But not over—		of excess over—
$221	—$833 . .	10%	—$221
$833	—$2,687 . .	$61.20 plus 15%	—$833
$2,687	—$6,104 . .	$339.30 plus 25%	—$2,687
$6,104	—$13,054 . .	$1,193.55 plus 28%	—$6,104
$13,054	—$28,200 . .	$3,139.55 plus 33%	—$13,054
$28,200	. . . . . .	$8,137.73 plus 35%	—$28,200

(b) MARRIED person—

If the amount of wages (after subtracting withholding allowances) is: The amount of income tax to withhold is:

Not over $667 . . . . $0

Over—	But not over—		of excess over—
$667	—$1,908 . .	10%	—$667
$1,908	—$5,670 . .	$124.10 plus 15%	—$1,908
$5,670	—$10,575 . .	$688.40 plus 25%	—$5,670
$10,575	—$16,288 . .	$1,914.65 plus 28%	—$10,575
$16,288	—$28,629 . .	$3,514.29 plus 33%	—$16,288
$28,629	. . . . . .	$7,586.82 plus 35%	—$28,629

4   Determine the amount of wage payment.

5   Determine the number of employee withholding allowances.

6   Use Figure A1.2 to calculate the value of one withholding allowance.

Table 5. Percentage Method—2006 Amount for One Withholding Allowance

Payroll Period	One Withholding Allowance
Weekly.	$ 63.46
Biweekly.	126.92
Semimonthly	137.50
Monthly	275.00
Quarterly	825.00
Semiannually	1,650.00
Annually	3,300.00
Daily or miscellaneous (each day of the payroll period)	12.69

Figure A1.2

One Withholding Allowance

7 Compute the employee's withholding amount by multiplying the employee's withholding allowances by the value of one withholding allowance determined above.

8 Calculate the net wages by subtracting the employee's withholding amount determined above from his or her wage payment.

9 Using net wages determined above, calculate the required federal income tax withholding using the table you selected above found in Figure A1.1.

For example, a single employee, claiming two withholding allowances, is paid $600 weekly.

To calculate the federal income tax withholding:

1 Frequency of wage payments: **weekly.**

2 Employee's filing status: **single.**

3 Appropriate table for Percentage Method of Withholding: **Table 1(a).**

4 Amount of wage payment: **600.**

5 Number of employee withholding allowances: **2.**

6 Value of one withholding allowance: **63.46.**

7 Employee's withholding amount: $2 \times 63.46 =$ **126.92.**

8 Net wages: $600.00 - 126.92 =$ **473.08.**

9 Required federal income tax withholding:
$14.10 + [15\% \times (473.08 - 192.00)] =$ **56.26.**

A second example, a married employee, claiming three withholding allowances, is paid $1,500 semi-monthly.

To calculate the federal income tax withholding:

1 Frequency of wage payments: **semimonthly.**

2 Employee's filing status: **married.**

3 Appropriate table for Percentage Method of Withholding: **Table 3(b).**

4 Amount of wage payment: **1500.**

5 Number of employee withholding allowances: **3.**

6 Value of one withholding allowance: **137.50.**

7 Employee's withholding amount: $3 \times 137.50 =$ **412.50.**

8 Net wages: $1,500.00 - 412.50 =$ **1,087.50.**

9 Required federal income tax withholding:
$62.10 + [15\% \times (1.087.50 - 954.00)] =$ **82.13.**

A third example, a married employee, claiming five withholding allowances, is paid $8,000 monthly.

To calculate the federal income tax withholding:

1 Frequency of wage payments: **monthly.**

2 Employee's filing status: **married.**

3 Appropriate table for Percentage Method of Withholding: **Table 4(b).**

4 Amount of wage payment: **8,000.**

5 Number of employee withholding allowances: **5.**

6 Value of one withholding allowance: **275.**

7 Employee's withholding amount: $5 \times 275 = $ **1,375.**

8 Net wages: $8,000 - 1,375 = $ **6,625.**

9 Required federal income tax withholding:
$688.40 + [25\% \times (6,625 - 5,670)] = $ **927.15.**

Social Security and Medicare Taxes

The Federal Insurance Contributions Act (FICA) provides for a federal system of old-age, survivors, disability, and hospital insurance. The old-age, survivors, and disability insurance part is financed by the Social Security tax. The hospital insurance part is financed by the Medicare tax. Each of these taxes is reported separately. Generally, you are required to withhold Social Security and Medicare taxes from your employees' wages and you must also pay a matching amount of these taxes. Certain types of wages and compensation are not subject to Social Security taxes. Generally, employee wages are subject to Social Security and Medicare taxes regardless of the employee's age or whether he or she is receiving Social Security benefits.

Social Security and Medicare taxes have different rates, and only the Social Security tax has a wage base limit. The wage base limit is the maximum wage that is subject to the tax for the year. Determine the amount of withholding for Social Security and Medicare taxes by multiplying each payment by the employee tax rate. There are no withholding allowances for Social Security and Medicare taxes. The current employee tax rate for Social Security is 6.2% (amount withheld). The employer tax rate for Social Security is also 6.2% (12.4% total). The 2005 wage base limit was $90,000. For 2006, the wage base limit is $94,200. The current employee tax rate for Medicare is 1.45% (amount withheld). The employer tax rate for Medicare tax is also 1.45% (2.9% total). There is no wage base limit for Medicare tax; all covered wages are subject to Medicare tax. Guiding employers in this regard is Circular E (Employer's Tax Guide), which can be found online at the Internal Revenue Service website: **http://www.irs.gov/pub/irs-pdf/p15.pdf.**

The steps necessary for computation of an employee's withholding and employer's computation of Social Security and Medicare taxes are as follows:

1 Determine the employee's cumulative earnings year-to-date prior to this paycheck.

2 Determine the amount of wage payment for the current period.

3 Determine if the employee's cumulative earnings exceed or are close to the Social Security wage base limit.

4 Calculate the Social Security tax by multiplying the appropriate wage payment by 6.2%.

5 Calculate the appropriate Medicare tax by multiplying the wage payment by 1.45%.

For example, in 2006, a single employee, claiming two withholding allowances, is paid $600 in the current week. Cumulative earnings to date are $3,000.

To calculate the Social Security and Medicare tax:

1 Cumulative earnings year-to-date: **3,000.**

2 Wage payment: **600.**

3 Cumulative earnings compared to the Social Security wage base limit: **3,000 is less than 94,200.**

4 Social Security tax: $600 \times 6.2\% =$ **37.20.**

5 Medicare tax: $600 \times 1.45\% =$ **8.70.**

A second example, in 2006, a married employee, claiming three withholding allowances, is paid $1,500 semi-monthly. Cumulative earnings to date are $6,000.

To calculate the Social Security and Medicare tax:

1 Cumulative earnings year-to-date: **6,000.**

2 Wage payment: **1,500.**

3 Cumulative earnings compared to the Social Security wage base limit: **6,000 is less than 94,200.**

4 Social Security tax: $1,500 \times 6.2\% =$ **93.00.**

5 Medicare tax: $1,500 \times 1.45\% =$ **21.75.**

A third example, in 2006, a married employee, claiming five withholding allowances, is paid $8,000 monthly. Cumulative earnings to date are $88,000.

> ### To calculate the Social Security and Medicare tax:
>
> **1** Cumulative earnings year-to-date: **88,000.**
>
> **2** Wage payment: **8,000.**
>
> **3** Cumulative earnings compared to the Social Security wage base limit: **88,000 is less than 94,200 but close. Difference is 6,200.**
>
> **4** Social Security tax: $6,200 \times 6.2\% = $ **384.40** (since this will bring the employee up to the wage limit).
>
> **5** Medicare tax: $8,000 \times 1.45\% = $ **116.00.**

Federal Unemployment Taxes

Use Form 940 (or Form 940-EZ) to report your annual Federal Unemployment Tax Act (FUTA) tax. FUTA tax, together with state unemployment systems, provides for payments of unemployment compensation to workers who have lost their jobs. Most employers pay both federal and state unemployment taxes. Only the employer pays FUTA tax. Do not collect or deduct it from your employees' wages. The tax, currently at 0.8%, applies to the first $7,000 you pay each employee in a year after subtracting any exempt payments. The $7,000 amount is the federal wage base. Your state wage base may be different. Instructions can currently be found at **http://www.irs.gov/pub/irs-pdf/i940.pdf.**

The steps necessary for computation of an employee's federal income tax withholding are as follows:

1 Determine the employee's cumulative earnings year-to-date prior to this paycheck.

2 Determine the amount of wage payment for the current period.

3 Determine if the employee's cumulative earnings exceed or are close to the FUTA wage base limit.

4 Calculate the FUTA tax by multiplying the appropriate wage payment by 0.8%.

For example, in 2006, a single employee, claiming two withholding allowances, is paid $600 in the current week. Cumulative earnings to date are $3,000.

> ### To calculate the FUTA tax:
>
> **1** Cumulative earnings year-to-date: **3,000.**
>
> **2** Wage payment: **600.**
>
> **3** Cumulative earnings compared to the FUTA wage base limit: **3,000 is less than 7,000.**
>
> **4** FUTA tax: $600 \times 0.8\% = $ **4.80.**

A second example, in 2006, a married employee, claiming three withholding allowances, is paid $1,500 semi-monthly. Cumulative earnings to date are $6,000.

To calculate the FUTA tax:

1 Cumulative earnings year-to-date: **6,000.**

2 Wage payment: **1,500.**

3 Cumulative earnings compared to the FUTA wage base limit: **6,000 is less than 7,000 but close. Difference is 1,000.**

4 FUTA tax: 1,000 × 0.8% = **8.00.**

A third example, in 2006, a married employee, claiming five withholding allowances, is paid $8,000 monthly. Cumulative earnings to date are $88,000.

To calculate the FUTA tax:

1 Cumulative earnings year-to-date: **88,000.**

2 Wage payment: **8,000.**

3 Cumulative earnings compared to the FUTA wage base limit: **88,000 is more than 7,000.**

4 FUTA tax: 0 × 0.8% = **0.00.**

State Income Tax Withholding and Unemployment Taxes

Each state, of course, has its own rules for withholding state income taxes and computing the employer's cost for unemployment. Some states, Florida and Nevada for instance, do not have a state income tax. Other states, such as California and Hawaii, not only have state income taxes but also have training taxes.

Most of the state income tax computations are similar to the federal computations in that they have different tables for different filing status: single, married, etc., and they have tables for exemption allowances. Rather than explain how to calculate taxes for each and every state in the union, I suggest you visit your local state tax agency to determine income tax and unemployment tax rates and requirements. Some website references follow (remember, these sites worked when this text was published. They may no longer work if the state moved them or reconfigured their website):

California   **http://www.edd.ca.gov/taxrep/taxrte9x.htm**
Florida   **http://www.myflorida.com/dor/taxes/**
Hawaii   **http://www.hawaii.gov/tax/a1_3tax_address.htm**

Appendix 1 Questions

1 What factors affect an employee's federal income tax withholding?

2 Where can employers get guidance on federal income tax withholding?

3 What do withholding allowances do to the computation of federal income tax withholding?

4 What does the Social Security tax finance?

5 What does the Medicare tax finance?

6 What is the Social Security tax rate?

7 Is there a wage base limit to the Social Security tax? If so, what is it for 2006?

8 What is the Medicare tax rate?

9 Is there a wage base limit to the Medicare tax? If so, what is it for 2006?

10 Who pays FUTA, and what is the current rate and computational structure?

Appendix 1 Assignments

1 In 2006, a married employee, claiming one withholding allowance, is paid $800 in the current week. Cumulative earnings to date are $4,000. Calculate the following:

    a.   Federal income tax withholding.

    b.   Employee Social Security taxes to be withheld.

    c.   Employee Medicare taxes to be withheld.

    d.   Employer Social Security tax.

    e.   Employer Medicare tax.

    f.   FUTA.

2 In 2006, a single employee, claiming three withholding allowances, is paid $2,000 semi-monthly. Cumulative earnings to date are $6,500. Calculate the following:

    a.   Federal income tax withholding.

    b.   Employee Social Security taxes to be withheld.

    c.   Employee Medicare taxes to be withheld.

    d.   Employer Social Security tax.

    e.   Employer Medicare tax.

    f.   FUTA.

3   In 2006, a single employee, claiming zero withholding allowances, is paid $10,000 monthly. Cumulative earnings to date are $90,000. Calculate the following:

    a.   Federal income tax withholding.

    b.   Employee Social Security taxes to be withheld.

    c.   Employee Medicare taxes to be withheld.

    d.   Employer Social Security tax.

    e.   Employer Medicare tax.

    f.   FUTA.

Traditional Accounting: Debits and Credits

Learning Objectives

In this appendix, you will:

- Examine a trial balance and view underlying source documents
- Examine a general ledger and view underlying source documents
- Examine a journal and view underlying source documents

Case: Wild Water Sports

You and Karen have been recording basic business transactions for Wild Water Sports without using journal entries or mentioning the terms *debit* and *credit* even once. This is another one of the benefits of using QuickBooks: It enables business-people who were not accounting majors to "do accounting." Moreover, accountants appreciate QuickBooks because they can use it with clients who want to have more control over their finances but who do not have formal accounting training.

As a user of QuickBooks, you should know that although you haven't actually used debits and credits in this book other than for adjusting journal entries, QuickBooks is based on a dual-entry or double-entry accounting system. Every transaction that you entered in Chapters 6 through 11 had an effect on two or more accounts in the chart of accounts. For example, every sales invoice increased Sales Revenue and Accounts Receivable. Every time you initiated a QuickBooks activity such as "receive payments," Cash was increased and Accounts Receivable was decreased.

QuickBooks actually provides three equivalent ways for you to record transactions using the double-entry system: You can record transactions by using business documents (what QuickBooks refers to as Forms), by using registers, or by making journal entries. So far in this textbook, you have used all three. Recall that using a document involves recording a transaction by completing a business document, such as a sales invoice or a check. When you correctly complete the document, the effect(s) of the transaction on the financial statements are automatically entered. For example, when Wild Water paid its yearly insurance premium of $22,000 on

1/31/07, the dual effects of this transaction on the Prepaid Insurance account (increased) and the Bank of Florida account (decreased) were processed by filling out a business document, specifically a check. In contrast, using registers involves accessing a particular account's register and inputting the effects of the transaction. For example, you could choose either the Prepaid Insurance register or the Bank of Florida (cash) register and enter the changes (increase/decrease) as needed.

You ask if it is possible, however, to still use debits and credits in QuickBooks, because your formal accounting training focused primarily on journal entries as the source of every transaction. Karen explains that, yes, it is indeed possible, and she offers to demonstrate QuickBooks's ability to prepare a trial balance, a general ledger, and a journal entry. You point out that under normal circumstances you would begin the accounting process with a journal entry. In this case, however, you will view the steps with her in reverse order, because the process has already been completed.

Trial Balance

The trial balance is a two-column listing of all asset, liability, owners' equity, revenue, and expense accounts. Accounts that have debit balances are listed in the debit column, and accounts that have credit balances are listed in the credit column. Although not foolproof, an equality between debits and credits generally indicates that the accounting process has been followed correctly.

With QuickBooks you can quickly create a trial balance. All you need is the date as of which you want the trial balance. Then you can use QuickBooks's QuickZoom feature to view supporting accounts and supporting journals or business documents.

To create the trial balance and examine supporting detail:

1 Open Wild Water Sports Ch 11 A.qbw.

2 Click **Reports, Accountant & Taxes,** and then click **Trial Balance.**

3 Change the report dates to read from **01/01/07** to **03/31/07,** and then click **Refresh** to view the trial balance you have prepared, as shown in Figure A2.1.

4 Double-click the **16,500.00** Prepaid Insurance amount to view the Prepaid Insurance account shown in Figure A2.2.

5 Double-click on the **−5,500.00** amount to view the prepaid insurance adjusting journal entry in the Make General Journal Entries window, as shown in Figure A2.3. Recall that this adjusting journal entry increases an expense and decreases an asset.

6 Close all windows.

Figure A2.1

Trial Balance

Wild Water Sports Ch 11A
Trial Balance
As of March 31, 2007

	Mar 31, 07	
	Debit	Credit
1010 · Bank of Florida	37,442.42	
1050 · Short-Term Investments	39,890.41	
1200 · Accounts Receivable	399,932.73	
1060 · Prepaid Advertising	20,000.00	
1120 · Inventory Asset	243,600.00	
1130 · Inventory Parts	2,112.00	
1150 · Prepaid Insurance	16,500.00	
1499 · Undeposited Funds	10,000.00	
1300 · Equipment:1310 · Cost	180,000.00	
1300 · Equipment:1390 · Accumulated Depreciation		13,084.00
1400 · Furniture & Fixtures:1410 · Cost	70,000.00	
1400 · Furniture & Fixtures:1490 · Accumulated Depreciation		2,499.00
1500 · Truck:1510 · Cost	45,000.00	
1500 · Truck:1590 · Accumulated Depreciation		2,250.00
2000 · Accounts Payable		216,200.00
2050 · MasterCard	0.00	
2025 · Accrued Interest Payable		1,760.97
2100 · Payroll Liabilities		2,934.66
2200 · Sales Tax Payable		24,232.66
2210 · Accrued Sales Tax Payable		4,225.00
2300 · Unearned Revenue		10,000.00
2500 · Loan Payable		297,632.40
3000 · Opening Bal Equity	0.00	
3100 · Common Stock		400,000.00
3900 · Retained Earnings	0.00	
4000 · Sales:4010 · Merchandise		767,500.00
4000 · Sales:4020 · Service		6,685.00
4000 · Sales:4030 · Parts		610.00
5000 · Cost of Goods Sold	614,488.00	
6130 · Bank Service Charges	75.00	
6150 · Depreciation Expense	10,333.00	
6180 · Insurance:6187 · Liability Insurance	5,500.00	
6200 · Interest Expense	7,719.57	
6235 · Marketing & Advertising	6,700.00	
6300 · Office Expenses:6360 · Printing and Reproduction	4,500.00	
6560 · Payroll Expenses	32,945.97	
6660 · Telephone	5,020.00	
6900 · Utilities	2,870.00	
7010 · Interest Income		2,015.41
7030 · Other Income		3,000.00
TOTAL	1,754,629.10	1,754,629.10

Figure A2.2

Prepaid Insurance

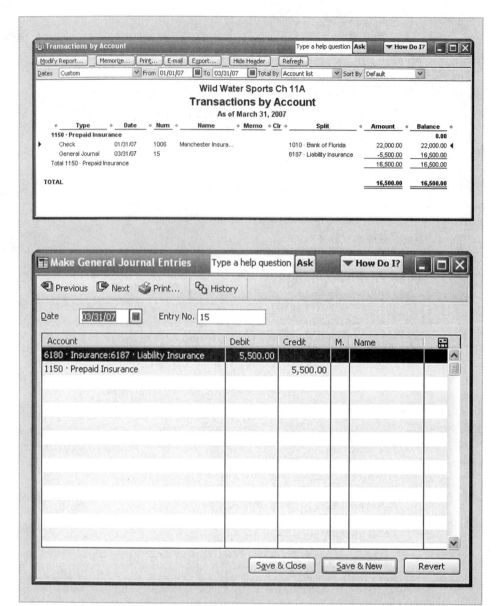

Figure A2.3

Prepaid Insurance Adjusting
Journal Entry

The journal entry shown in the Prepaid Insurance register was actually recorded by entering an adjustment via a journal entry. The adjustment itself was an adjusting entry prompted by the existence of a business source document, such as a check, an invoice, or a bill.

General Ledger

The general ledger is used in accounting information systems to store the effects of individual asset, liability, owners' equity, revenue, and expense accounts. In manual accounting systems, journals are used to record business transactions, the effects of which are then posted or transferred to a general ledger. This recording and posting is compressed into one step in QuickBooks as the transactions are recorded. Karen decides to use a sales invoice to demonstrate to you how the effects of a transaction are stored in the general ledger.

She explains to you that the invoice itself is used as a source business document. Information is entered into the invoice, and when you click OK, the invoice is stored and the consequence of that invoice is immediately recorded. In accounting jargon, once you enter the invoice, a debit is posted to the Accounts Receivable account in the general ledger, and a credit is posted to the Sales Revenue account in the general ledger.

"In my accounting classes, we usually posted all the sales for a month with one journal entry," you comment. "In this case, it looks like each sale is recorded individually. Doesn't that take a lot of time?"

"Yes," Karen agrees. "But once you enter this invoice, several steps are completed simultaneously. Accounts Receivable is debited, and Sales Revenue is credited. If we're selling inventory, the same invoice updates the perpetual inventory record, credits the Inventory account, and debits the Cost of Goods Sold account. Plus, the customer's account is adjusted accordingly so we know how much each customer owes and when amounts are due. Let's take a look at QuickBooks's general ledger and some underlying transactions."

To create the general ledger:

1 Click **Reports, Accountant & Taxes,** and then click **General Ledger.**

2 Change the report dates to read from **01/01/07** to **03/31/07,** and then click **Refresh.**

3 Scroll down the general ledger until you can view the 1200 – Accounts Receivable account, as shown in Figure A2.4.

1200 · Accounts Receivable — 96,300.00

Type	Date	Num	Name	Split	Amount	Balance
Payment	01/11/07	8755	Florida Sports Camp	1499 · Undep...	-17,500.00	78,800.00
Payment	01/11/07		Performance Rent...	1499 · Undep...	-19,687.50	59,112.50
Payment	01/15/07	65454	Buena Vista Wate...	1499 · Undep...	-30,000.00	29,112.50
Invoice	01/30/07	10001	Florida Sports Camp	-SPLIT-	74,550.00	103,662.50
Invoice	01/30/07	10002	Performance Rent...	-SPLIT-	83,868.75	187,531.25
Payment	01/30/07	4532	Florida Sports Camp	1499 · Undep...	-57,050.00	130,481.25
Payment	01/30/07	10885	Performance Rent...	1499 · Undep...	-64,181.25	66,300.00
Payment	02/02/07	2003	Performance Rent...	1499 · Undep...	-18,750.00	47,550.00
Payment	02/05/07	390	Buena Vista Wate...	1499 · Undep...	-3,000.00	44,550.00
Payment	02/06/07	1005	Fantasy Sports	1499 · Undep...	-28,250.00	16,300.00
Payment	02/08/07	1988	Orlando Water Spo...	1499 · Undep...	-43,000.00	-26,700.00
Invoice	02/20/07	10003	Performance Rent...	-SPLIT-	79,875.00	53,175.00
Payment	02/20/07	23098	Performance Rent...	1499 · Undep...	-61,125.00	-7,950.00
Invoice	03/07/07	10004	Fantasy Sports	-SPLIT-	120,345.00	112,395.00
Invoice	03/16/07	10005	Buena Vista Wate...	-SPLIT-	1,964.93	114,359.93
Payment	03/21/07	9152	Orlando Water Spo...	1499 · Undep...	-5,300.00	109,059.93
Invoice	03/23/07	10006	Performance Rent...	-SPLIT-	1,293.98	110,353.91
Invoice	03/23/07	10007	Freebirds	-SPLIT-	138,450.00	248,803.91
Invoice	03/29/07	10008	Florida Sports Camp	-SPLIT-	83,868.75	332,672.66
Payment	03/29/07	741	Buena Vista Wate...	1499 · Undep...	-1,964.93	330,707.73
Payment	03/31/07		Performance Rent...	1499 · Undep...	-10,000.00	320,707.73
General Journal	03/31/07	12	Spirit Adventures	-SPLIT-	69,225.00	389,932.73
General Journal	03/31/07	17	Performance Rent...	2300 · Unear...	10,000.00	399,932.73
Total 1200 · Accounts Receivable					303,632.73	399,932.73

Figure A2.4

Accounts Receivable Portion of the General Ledger

4 Double-click Invoice **10001** dated 1/30/07 to Florida Sports Camp to view the underlying source document: the specific sales invoice that increased accounts receivable by $74,550, as shown in Figure A2.5.

Figure A2.5

Invoice

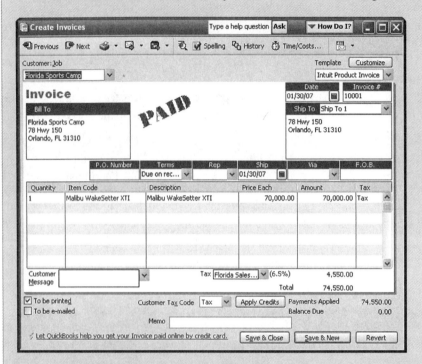

5 Close the Create Invoice window. Double-click the payment dated 1/30/07 from Florida Sports Camp on their check **4532** to view the underlying source document: the specific payment that decreased accounts receivable by $57,050, as shown in Figure A2.6.

Figure A2.6

Receive Payment

6 Print the first page of the General Ledger by clicking the **Print** button on the General Ledger window.

7 Click the **Pages** option button in the Page Range: section of the Print Reports window.

8 Type **1** in the To: text box and then click **Print.**

9 Close all windows.

After seeing how easy this is, you might wonder why QuickBooks—or some other similar program—isn't used all the time in business. The reason is that many companies often have their own accounting software that has been customized to their specifications. However, many smaller businesses, which often can't afford such a luxury as customized software, have found QuickBooks to be an inexpensive, yet powerful and easy-to-use alternative.

General Journal

"I'm still not convinced that QuickBooks follows the debit and credit convention," you comment. "Most times you drill down from the general ledger or trial balance you got to a source document, not to a journal entry."

"That's true," Karen reponds. "Remember we entered most of these transactions from source documents and not journal entries like you did in your accounting classes. However, I can still show you that, if you need it, QuickBooks can provide you the underlying debits and credits for all business transactions recorded."

To view journal entry support for business transactions:

1 Click **Reports, Accountant & Taxes,** and then click **Journal.**

2 Change the report dates to read from **02/01/07** to **02/28/07,** and then click **Refresh.**

3 The first four transactions for the month of February are shown as in Figure A2.7.

4 The first transaction shown debits the Inventory Parts account and credits the Bank of Florida account by $1,000. Double-click the transaction with **Delco** to reveal the check (source document) that was used to pay Delco for the parts purchased.

5 Close the check window. Scroll down the Journal window until you come to Sales Receipt 6005 recorded on 2/3/07, as shown in Figure A2.8.

Figure A2.7

Journal

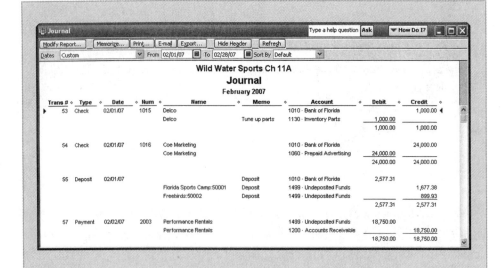

Figure A2.8

Sales Receipt of 2/3/07

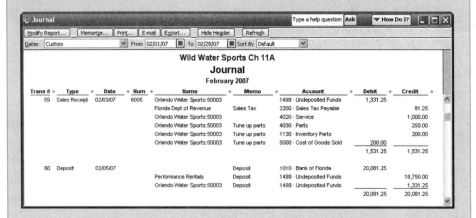

6 The sales receipt transaction shows debits to Undeposited Funds (an asset) and Cost of Goods Sold (an expense), and credits to Sales Tax Payable (a liability), Parts (an income account), and Inventory Parts (an asset).

7 Double-click **Sales Receipt 6005** to view the underlying source document that created this journal entry.

8 Close the sales receipt window.

9 The transaction below the Sales Receipt 6005 should be the deposit made on 2/5/07. This transaction shows a debit to the Bank of Florida account and two credits to the Undeposited Funds account. (Recall that the previous transaction recorded the collection of cash as an increase in Undeposited Funds since they were not immediately deposited into the company's bank account.)

10 Double-click the **Deposit** journal entry to view the underlying source document that created this journal entry.

11 Close the deposit window.

12 Print the first page of the Journal by clicking the **Print** button on the Journal window.

13 Click the **Pages** option button in the Page Range: section of the Print Reports window.

14 Type **1** in the To: text box, and then click **Print.**

15 Close all windows.

You can now see why accountants want to see the Journal information. It validates QuickBooks as a "real" accounting prorgram with underlying debits and credits like they learned in their accounting courses.

End Note

Many accountants prefer to use journal entries (that is the debit-credit format) to record business transactions. But Intuit Inc. designed QuickBooks for business-people who did not want to use journal entries. Although QuickBooks allows you to enter all transactions using the journal entry format, you then must sacrifice QuickBooks's specialized invoicing, bill payment, payroll, and other useful features. The choice is yours!

Appendix 2 Questions

1 In what order does QuickBooks list accounts in the trial balance report?

2 What QuickBooks feature allows you to access supporting accounts or journals when viewing the trial balance?

3 What happens when you double-click an amount on the trial balance?

4 Explain how a transaction recorded through an account register also creates a general journal entry.

5 Why does QuickBooks have a general ledger?

6 What advantages does QuickBooks's document-initiated recording method have over the standard journal entry method?

7 What happens when you double-click on an amount in the general ledger?

8 How do you print one page of the General Ledger?

9 What information about business transactions is shown in the Journal?

10 Why would someone want to look at a QuickBooks Journal?

Appendix 2 Assignments

1 *Creating a Trial Balance, General Ledger, and Journal for Wild Water Sports*

Use Wild Water Sports Ch 11 A.qbw to do the following:

a. Create and print a Trial Balance for the period January 1 to April 30, 2007.

b. View the General Ledger for the period April 1 to April 30, 2007. Print Page 1 in landscape view.

c. View the Journal for the period April 1 to April 30, 2007. Print Page 1 in landscape view.

2 *Creating a Trial Balance, General Ledger, and Journal for Central Coast Cellular*

Use the file you completed for the Central Coast Cellular assignment in Chapter 11 to do the following:

a. Create and print a trial balance for the period January 1 to January 31, 2005.

   b. View the General Ledger for the period January 1 to January 31, 2005. Print Page 1 in landscape view.

   c. View the Journal for the period January 1 to January 31, 2005. Print Page 1 in landscape view.

Appendix 2 Case Problems

1 *Creating a Trial Balance, General Ledger, and Journal for Aloha Property Management*

Use the file you completed for the Aloha Property Management case in Chapter 11 to do the following:

   a. Create and print a trial balance for the period January 1 to February 29, 2008.

   b. View the General Ledger for the period February 1 to February 29, 2008. Print Page 1 in landscape view.

   c. View the Journal for the period February 1 to February 29, 2008. Print Page 1 in landscape view.

2 *Creating a Trial Balance, General Ledger, and Journal for Ocean View Flowers*

Use the file you completed for the Ocean View Flowers case in Chapter 11 to do the following:

   a. Create and print a trial balance for the period January 1 to February 29, 2008.

   b. View the General Ledger for the period February 1 to February 29, 2008. Print Page 1 in landscape view.

   c. View the Journal for the period February 1 to February 29, 2008. Print Page 1 in landscape view.